The Abolitionist Sisterhood

The Abolitionist Sisterhood

Women's Political Culture in
Antebellum America

*Jean Fagan Yellin and
John C. Van Horne, editors*

Published in cooperation
with the Library Company of Philadelphia

Cornell University Press
Ithaca and London

Library of Congress Cataloging-in-Publication Data

The Abolitionist sisterhood : women's political culture in Antebellum
    America / edited by Jean Fagan Yellin and John C. Van Horne.
        p.   cm.
    Includes bibliographical references and index.
    ISBN 0-8014-2728-2. — ISBN 0-8014-8011-6
    1. Women abolitionists—United States—History—19th century.
    2. Women—United States—Political activity—History—19th century.
    3. Afro-American women—Political activity—History—19th century.
    I. Yellin, Jean Fagan.   II. Van Horne, John C.
    E449.A1555   1994
    973'.0496073'082—dc20   93-42427

First published 1994 by Cornell University Press.

Printed in the United States of America

♾ The paper in this book meets the minimum requirements of the
American National Standard for Information Sciences—Permanence of
Paper for Printed Library Materials, ANSI Z39.48-1984.

Dedicated to

Dorothy Porter Wesley
Dorothy Sterling

Foremothers

Contents

Contents

Preface

The Anti-Slavery Conventions of American Women, held in New York in 1837 and in Philadelphia in 1838 and 1839, were signal events in American history. They opened a new path for women's political concerns, offering an organized expression of those concerns a decade before the first women's rights convention at Seneca Falls, New York, in 1848. They were racially integrated, with black women and white women working together in a common cause. They drew their strength from women all across the region. And the principal participants went on to shape other nineteenth-century reform movements.

Nevertheless, 1987 and 1988, the one hundred fiftieth anniversaries of the first two conventions, passed without any recognition of their importance, though the anniversary of the third and last convention was indeed celebrated in 1989 in Philadelphia, site of two of the gatherings. That celebration—a symposium at the Library Company of Philadelphia—grew into this book.

The essays in this volume, however, move far beyond a consideration of the conventions themselves to explore women's political culture more broadly defined. Our book is organized around several broad themes, beginning with the female antislavery societies. One of the earliest, groundbreaking studies of these extraordinary organizations was Amy Swerdlow's paper on the Ladies' New York City Anti-Slavery Society, presented at the Third Berkshire Conference on the History of Women at Bryn Mawr College in 1976. That influential essay, which has been widely circulated, is published here for the first time. In it, Swerdlow recovers the world of the conservative New York abolitionist women who opposed women's rights, and she distinguishes these women from their more radical sisters in Boston and Philadelphia. She concludes that the New Yorkers' close ties to evangelical revivalism, a movement devoted to the preservation of bourgeois morality and social order, prevented them from embracing ideas or actions that might have weakened the traditional family structure. Nancy A. Hewitt, who was present at the 1976 conference, has written an analysis of Swerdlow's work which places it in its historiographical context. She extends the analysis by examining how abolition's conservative sisters fared in Rochester, New York, when face-to-face with their more radical colleagues, and by suggesting that, in their rush to link antislavery to women's rights, historians have overlooked radical black women and conservative white women.

Debra Gold Hansen traces the rise and swift decline of the Boston Female Anti-Slavery Society, analyzing the divisions of race, class, and religion which, despite the organization's significant accomplishments, prevented it from reaching its potential and led to its dissolution in 1840. Discussing the longer-lived Philadelphia Female Anti-Slavery Society, Jean R. Soderlund examines the changes in its membership and its policies from 1833, when it began as an active, expanding group of young women, to the early 1850s, when it had become a more narrow, introspective circle of antislavery veterans.

The second part of this volume presents essays that explore the growth of black women's political culture in the antebellum North. Emma Jones Lapsansky vividly describes the fast-changing urban scene in antebellum Philadelphia. She explains how the free black community adapted to the new order by advocating self-improvement, self-education, and economic autonomy and by forming organizations designed to create a cohesive black bourgeoisie. Julie Winch explores the three literary societies formed by Philadelphia's free black women, illuminating the relationship between these societies and the female antislavery movement. These elite black women wrote for the abolitionist press, and their literary organizations provided the Anti-Slavery Conventions of American Women with some of their most able officers. Anne M. Boylan's essay, portraying both the enormous resourcefulness of African American women in meeting family and community needs and their vulnerability to white racial attitudes and gender expectations, examines the benevolent and antislavery organizations they established in New York and Boston. Nell Irvin Painter discusses the former slave Isabella, who as Sojourner Truth became an important presence among antislavery and women's rights reformers from the 1850s to the 1870s. Painter argues that Truth created her own naive persona that emphasized her illiteracy, her physical strength, and her personal experience of slavery to set herself apart from her white audiences. Thus Truth raised the important issue of the black woman's role in the antislavery and women's rights movements.

The third section of the book addresses the goals of the antislavery feminists and the strategies and tactics they devised to further their cause. Carolyn Williams, looking at the intersection between African Americans' rights and women's rights in the antislavery movement, argues that these women effectively opposed both racism and sexism. Deborah Bingham Van Broekhoven explores female petitioning against slavery in the 1830s and 1840s, examining the development of petitions from humble supplications of inferiors to those in authority to overtly political demands couched in republican language. Phillip Lapsansky makes a unique contribution to our book with his heavily illustrated essay presenting images both of antislavery and of antiabolitionism. This visual propaganda—"incendiary" cuts in newspapers, periodicals, books, tracts, and broadsides, and the antislavery images reproduced on goods women made and sold at their antislavery fairs—was used significantly by both sides. One group of images shows the horrors of slavery; the other, the dangers of abolitionism and "amalgamation." Keith Melder next explores the process of personal liberation which enabled Abby Kelley to commit herself to the antislavery and feminist causes; out of personal crisis and deep soul-searching Kelley emerged as an effective orator, reformer, and agitator. Lee Chambers-Schiller studies the role of the annual Boston Anti-Slavery Fair in politicizing Boston's antislavery women. The fair's moral suasionist beginnings gradually changed, she explains, as increasing numbers of newly active abolitionists turned to the political wing of the movement. Margaret Hope Bacon demonstrates how some of the participants in the Anti-Slavery Conventions of American Women not only pioneered the relationship between antislavery and women's rights but also forged a link between antislavery and the philosophy of nonresistance—what we today call nonviolence. By using moral weapons, such as boycotting the products of slave labor, these women established the validity of economic tactics for suffragists and other successors.

The essay by Kathryn Kish Sklar provides a coda to our collection because it moves our discussion of antislavery women into the international sphere. Sklar compares the American women who participated in the World Anti-Slavery Convention in London in 1840 with their British colleagues. She begins with the familiar story of the rejection of female delegates by their fellow abolitionists at this convention and the organization by Lucretia Mott and Elizabeth Cady Stanton of the first separate women's rights convention at Seneca Falls, New York, eight years later. Sklar analyzes the 1840 convention to explain the differences between women's political culture in Great Britain and in America and then discusses how those cultures related to the larger polities of the two nations.

Political culture is a new field of historical inquiry, and our book is intended as a progress report on the subject of women's political culture in the first half of the nineteenth century. Our scholarship will, we hope, inspire further research. The antislavery women discussed here certainly deserve more study. Although they did not always agree with one another, nor were they, alas, all antiracist and antisexist, they did create a female political culture within the structures of antislavery. By asserting a public culture for themselves, they cleared a path for all American women. May our book about their trailblazing make the going easier for those who follow.

The Library Company's 1989 symposium honored two women who inspire us. Dorothy B. Porter Wesley and Dorothy Sterling were preserving, researching, and writing the history of black and white American women before most of our essayists were born. Colleagues and friends, over the decades they have helped each other—and generations of the likes of us—with a generosity rare both within the academy and outside it. Each is an extremely prolific writer. This is not the place to list all their scholarly productions, but it is appropriate to note some of those that have been most important to the authors of our book.

Dorothy Porter Wesley's work ranges from pioneering publications on African and Brazilian resources to essential bibliographical listings such as the groundbreaking "Early American Negro Writing: A Bibliographical Study," *Papers of the Bibliographical Society of America* 39 (1945): 192–268, and the useful *Index to the Journal of Negro Education, 1932–1962* (Washington, D.C., 1963), to compilations of rare materials such as *Negro Protest Pamphlets* (New York, 1969), to essays outlining future work such as "Women Activists, Wives, Intellectuals, Mothers, and Artists," in *Proceedings of a Symposium on Candidates for Rediscovery: The Boston Version* (Boston, 1977), pp. 76–84, to historical studies such as "The Remonds of Salem, Massachusetts: A Nineteenth-Century Family Revisited," *Proceedings of the American Antiquarian Society* 95 (1986): 259–95.

Principal works by Dorothy Sterling range from social commentary including *Tender Warriors,* with Donald Gross (New York, 1958), to documentary histories such as *The Trouble They Seen: Black People Tell the Story of Reconstruction* (Garden City, N.Y., 1976; rept. 1994) and *We Are Your Sisters: Black Women in the Nineteenth Century* (New York, 1984), to biographies such as the brief *Black Foremothers: Three Lives* (Old Westbury, N.Y.,

Preface

1979) and the full-length *Ahead of Her Time: Abby Kelley and the Politics of Antislavery* (New York, 1991). Through these and other publications, through the personal relationships they have built, and through their example of committed antiracist feminist scholarship, these two pioneering women historians have nurtured generations of scholars. We are pleased to honor them here.

We express our gratitude to John R. McKivigan of West Virginia University, who read the manuscript for Cornell University Press and whose incisive and detailed comments and questions improved our book. We thank Richard Newman for his bibliographical help. At the Press we benefited from the careful editing of Carol Betsch and Barbara Dinneen. Denise M. Larrabee of the Library Company of Philadelphia provided editorial assistance and compiled the index. Independence Foundation was the principal sponsor of our 1989 symposium, and the Andrew W. Mellon Foundation, through the publication fund it established at the Library Company, supported the publication of this volume.

JOHN C. VAN HORNE

Philadelphia, Pennsylvania

Abbreviations

AASS	American Anti-Slavery Society
ACS	American Colonization Society
AFASS	American and Foreign Anti-Slavery Society
AME	African Methodist Episcopal
BFASS	Boston Female Anti-Slavery Society
ICY	Institute for Colored Youth
LNYCASS	Ladies' New York City Anti-Slavery Society
MASS	Massachusetts Anti-Slavery Society
MES	Massachusetts Emancipation Society
MFES	Massachusetts Female Emancipation Society
NEASS	New England Anti-Slavery Society
NENRS	New England Non-Resistance Society
PASS	Pennsylvania Anti-Slavery Society
PFASS	Philadelphia Female Anti-Slavery Society
RFASS	Rochester Female Anti-Slavery Society
RLASS	Rochester Ladies' Anti-Slavery Society
WILPF	Women's International League for Peace and Freedom
WNYASS	Western New York Anti-Slavery Society

Chronology

Prudence Crandall establishes her school for "colored girls" in Canterbury, Connecticut

February 22, 1832: Black women of Salem, Massachusetts, establish antislavery society

July 1, 1832: Rhode Island women establish antislavery society

1833   Abolition of slavery in the British colonies

Lydia Maria Child, *An Appeal in Favor of That Class of Americans Called Africans,* published in Boston

October 14, 1833: Boston Female Anti-Slavery Society established

December 4–6, 1833: American Anti-Slavery Society convention held in Philadelphia

December 9, 1833: Philadelphia Female Anti-Slavery Society established

1834   First antislavery fair in Boston at the Anti-Slavery Office on Washington Street, led by Lydia Maria Child, raises three hundred dollars

Colored Female Anti-Slavery Society (Middletown, Connecticut) founded

1835   Ladies' New York City Anti-Slavery Society founded

Women join antislavery petitioning campaign

1836   Sarah M. Grimké, *An Epistle to the Clergy of the Southern States,* published in New York

September 1836: Angelina E. Grimké, "Appeal to the Christian Women of the South," *Anti-Slavery Examiner* 1 (September 1836)

May 26, 1836: U.S. House of Representatives adopts Gag Rule tabling antislavery petitions without reading

December 1836: Angelina E. and Sarah M. Grimké begin their speaking tour

1837   Catharine E. Beecher, *An Essay on Slavery and Abolitionism, with Reference to the Duty of American Females,* published in Philadelphia and Boston

An Appeal to the Women of the Nominally Free States Issued by an Anti-Slavery Convention of American Women, published in New York

March 1837: Angelina E. Grimké publicly addresses a "promiscuous assembly" in Poughkeepsie at a meeting called by the black community

May 9–12, 1837: First Anti-Slavery Convention of American Women (New York)

August 1837: Pastoral letter of the General Association of Massachusetts sent to orthodox Congregational churches that,
among other intents, condemned women's lecturing in public

1838 Angelina E. Grimké, *Letters to Catharine E. Beecher in Reply to an
Essay on Slavery and Abolitionism,* published in Boston (first
published in a series in the *Liberator,* 1837)

Sarah M. Grimké, *Letters on the Equality of the Sexes, and the Condition of Women,* published in Boston (first published in a series
in the *New England Spectator,* 1838)

Black women of Philadelphia organize the Female Vigilant Committee to support the Underground Railroad

February 21, 1838: Angelina E. Grimké speaks to the Massachusetts
legislature

May 15–18, 1838: Second Anti-Slavery Convention of American
Women (Philadelphia)

May 15, 1838: Abby Kelley begins her lecture career by speaking to
the first promiscuous audience at the convention

May 17, 1838: Maria Weston Chapman makes her first public
speech at the convention

May 17, 1838: Burning of Pennsylvania Hall, site of the convention

September 6, 1838: American Free Produce Association established
in Philadelphia

1839 British and Foreign Anti-Slavery Society founded in London to
promote international cooperation in combating slavery and
the slave trade

Massachusetts Female Emancipation Society (antifeminist abolitionists) established

Maria Weston Chapman, *Right and Wrong in Massachusetts,*
which interpreted the split in antislavery ranks as largely one
over women's rights, published in Boston

Liberty Bell, first successful antislavery annual, edited by Maria
Weston Chapman, published by the Boston Female Anti-
Slavery Society

May 1–3, 1839: Third Anti-Slavery Convention of American
Women (Philadelphia)

1840 American and Foreign Anti-Slavery Society (anti-Garrisonian) established by group opposed to Abby Kelley's presence on the
business committee of the American Anti-Slavery Society

Manhattan Abolition Society established by New York black
women

Chronology

National Anti-Slavery Standard started by the American Anti-Slavery Society

Abby Kelley and Lydia Maria Child elected officers of the American Anti-Slavery Society

May 12–13, 1840: American Anti-Slavery Society Convention (New York)

June 12–23, 1840: World Anti-Slavery Convention (London) hosted by the British and Foreign Anti-Slavery Society, which refuses to seat American female abolitionist delegates

1841   *May 1841:* Lydia Maria Child becomes editor of the *National Anti-Slavery Standard*

1844   *December 3, 1844:* Gag Rule repealed

1848   *July 1848:* First Woman's Rights Convention (Seneca Falls, New York)

        August 1848: Second Woman's Rights Convention (Rochester, New York)

1850   *Narrative of Sojourner Truth* published in Boston

Introduction

Ruth Bogin and Jean Fagan Yellin

In 1835, protesting the mob attack on antislavery women in Boston, the activist Maria Weston Chapman claimed that the women had merely been following accepted practices: "This is a new scene for us. When before, in this city, have gentlemen of standing and influence, been incensed against a benevolent association of ladies, for holding their annual meeting, inviting a lecturer to address them, and requesting their friends to attend, after the custom of benevolent societies?" But in 1837, Angelina Grimké, the abolitionist lecturer, signaled her awareness that she had traveled far beyond the boundaries of customary female behavior: "I feel as if it is not the cause of the slave only which we plead but the cause of Woman as a responsible & moral being.... What an untrodden path we have entered upon!" These contradictory statements suggest the complexities of the political culture of the antislavery women.[1]

---

1. Maria Weston Chapman to the editor of the [Boston] *Courier,* in *Right and Wrong in Boston. Report of the Boston Female Anti-Slavery Society . . . 1835* (Boston, 1836), p. 24; Angelina E. Grimké to Jane Smith, May 29, 1837, William L. Clements Library, University of Michigan, Ann Arbor. For Chapman, see Alma Lutz, *Crusade for Freedom: Women of the Antislavery Movement* (Boston, 1968); William H. Pease and Jane H. Pease, *Bound with Them in Chains: A Biographical History of the Antislavery Movement* (Westport, Conn., 1972), pp. 28–59; Blanche Glassman Hersh, *The Slavery of Sex: Feminist-Abolitionists in America* (Urbana, Ill., 1978); and Catherine Clinton, "Maria Weston Chapman," in G. S. Barker-Benfield and Catherine Clinton, eds., *Portraits of American Women,* 2 vols. (New York, 1990), 1:147–67. For Angelina Grimké and her sister Sarah, see Elizabeth Ann Bartlett, ed., *Sarah Grimké: Letters on the Equality of the Sexes and Other Essays* (New Haven, 1988); Gilbert H. Barnes and Dwight L.

Chapman correctly noted the similarities between the activities of the Boston Female Anti-Slavery Society and those of other women's benevolent organizations in the city. Although organized public activity by American women was a relatively new phenomenon, several organizations were energetically engaged in a wide range of public efforts—fund-raising, writing and publishing texts, even lobbying and petitioning legislatures to change the laws—actions that late twentieth-century historians would call women's political culture.[2]

The Boston mobs, too, coupled BFASS with other women's benevolent organizations. Besides attacking the abolitionist women's meeting, they also broke up a gathering of the Ladies' Moral Reform Society and harassed women holding a fair at Armory Hall.[3] This spillover violence may have been accidental, but to Boston's "gentlemen of property and standing" who composed the antiabolitionist mob, the actions of the female antislavery society may have made all women's public activity seem threatening.

Historians have identified three levels of women's antebellum political culture: first, group activity beyond the limits of the family; next, gender-conscious group activity (that is, women acting consciously *as* women); and finally, group activity intended to advance women's rights and women's interests.[4] Under this schema, most of the Boston women's organizations in 1835 can be characterized as gender conscious. In that year, the "antislavery females" were adapting this gender-conscious female political culture to abolitionism. They organized fairs to raise money for the antislavery cause, wrote and published abolitionist pamphlets and giftbooks, and circulated antislavery and antiracist petitions to state and federal governments. These women were using and transforming the conventional forms of women's organizations to construct an antislavery women's political culture that was varied, dynamic, and contradictory.

In this process, as Grimké's later statement suggests, the more radical of these women were becoming aware of the need to advance their own rights—of the need to build a new feminist ideology. Historians have

---

Dumond, eds., *Letters of Theodore Dwight Weld, Angelina Grimké Weld, and Sarah Grimké, 1822–1844*, 2 vols. (1934; rpt. New York, 1970); and the following biographies: Catherine Birney, *The Grimké Sisters: Sarah and Angelina Grimké, the First Women Advocates of Abolition and Women's Rights* (Boston, 1885); Gerda Lerner, *The Grimké Sisters from South Carolina: Rebels against Slavery* (Boston, 1967); and Katharine Du Pré Lumpkin, *The Emancipation of Angelina Grimké* (Chapel Hill, N.C., 1974).

2. For the literature on women's political culture and the antislavery movement, see Bibliographical Notes, pp. 335–40, in this volume.

3. *Right and Wrong in Boston*, p. 26.

4. See Kathryn Kish Sklar's essay, Chapter 15 in the present volume, note 6.

pointed out that this group developed and elaborated upon a self-conscious antislavery feminism that fed into the women's rights movement. But other activists did not. The culture of female antislavery involved women who rejected traditional gender patterns and women who accepted them, as well as women who at times rejected and at other times embraced emerging antislavery feminism.

Throughout this book we focus on the complex political culture of the antislavery feminists—that small circle of black and white American women who, in the 1830s and 1840s, initially banded together to remedy the public evils of slavery and racism and who ultimately struggled for equal rights for women as well as for slaves. But because the path from abolitionism to feminism was not straight, our book also treats the political culture of the antislavery feminists' more traditional abolitionist sisters. The connections among these women were real. During the evangelical thirties and forties, while some Americans were beginning to construct a new culture of party politics to effect social change, others were trying to redeem America by moving hearts and minds.[5] The antislavery women shared with many reformers a belief in the moral salvation of America. But they focused on slavery and racism, which, unlike the evils denounced by some other activists, have proved critical to American history.

Perhaps because many of the abolitionist women chose to target both slavery and racism, structures profoundly embedded in American life, and perhaps because, as a result, they were attacked both from inside and outside the abolitionist movement, these women devised new strategies and tactics. One of their most significant innovations was the female speaker who addressed public "promiscuous" audiences of men and women on political issues. By attending to these speakers—becoming aware of the nov-

5. Some historians hold that the term "feminism" should be used only in connection with the formal inauguration of the women's rights movement at Seneca Falls in 1848. However, because these antislavery women earlier created an ideology and a practice to further women's rights, here we call them "antislavery feminists." For more on this issue, see Nancy F. Cott, *The Grounding of Modern Feminism* (New Haven, 1987), pp. 3–10. For connections between abolition and antebellum feminism, see Ellen DuBois, "Women's Rights and Abolition: The Nature of the Connection," in Lewis Perry and Michael Fellman, eds., *Antislavery Reconsidered: New Perspectives on the Abolitionists* (Baton Rouge, 1979), pp. 238–51. For a structural analysis of one component of women's political culture in the antislavery movement, see Gerda Lerner, "The Political Activities of Anti-Slavery Women," chap. 8 in her book *The Majority Finds Its Past: Placing Women in History* (New York, 1987), pp. 112–28. For the development of an ideology that permitted one female grouping to become feminist, see Nancy Hewitt, "The Fragmentation of Friends: The Consequences for Quaker Women in Antebellum America," in Elizabeth Potts Brown and Susan Stuart, eds., *Witness for Change: Quaker Women over Three Centuries* (New Brunswick, 1989), pp. 93–108.

elty of their presence on the platform despite the traditional character of their phraseology—we can chart some of the characteristics of the developing political discourse of the antislavery feminists.

As early as 1831, Maria W. Stewart, a young black Bostonian, had mounted the platform. Stewart, like those who followed her, blended the rhetoric of "true womanhood" and "republican motherhood" with the public sound of protofeminist speech, proclaiming: "All the nations of the earth are crying out for Liberty and Equality. Away, away with tyranny and oppression! And shall Afric's sons be silent any longer?"[6]

While characterizing her black audiences as members of a family, Stewart reached out to whites as well, first with a pamphlet and then a series of public lectures, both given wider circulation through reprinting in the *Liberator*. Not content with inculcating only the general attributes of good citizenship, Stewart defined specific political tasks for her "sons." She summoned "every man of color throughout the United States" to join in petitioning Congress to abolish slavery in the District of Columbia, announcing that "African rights and liberty is a subject that ought to fire the breast of every free man of color."[7]

By contrast, she called on black women to develop the capacities of their sons and daughters and thereby to counter the prejudice and deprivation that oppressed "the generality of my color." In exhorting male and female to follow different paths in the struggle to better the lives of free and enslaved blacks, Stewart complied in some measure with contemporary prescriptions for a separate and essentially private sphere for women. But at the same time, Stewart thrust insistently against this barrier to fulfill her own mission. "What if I am a woman?" she argued in her final Boston lecture in 1833. She felt empowered to speak out publicly because she accepted the possibility "that God at this eventful period" had "raise[d] up . . . females to strive, by their example both in public and private, to assist" the work of race advancement.[8]

Like Stewart, other abolitionist women placed great emphasis on the religious imperatives that they believed made dedicated antislavery work a

6. Bert James Loewenberg and Ruth Bogin, eds., *Black Women in Nineteenth-Century Life: Their Words, Their Thoughts, Their Feelings* (University Park, Pa., 1976), p. 186. For Stewart, see Marilyn Richardson, ed., *Maria W. Stewart: America's First Black Woman Political Writer, Essays and Speeches* (Bloomington, Ind., 1987); Dorothy Sterling, ed., *We Are Your Sisters: Black Women in the Nineteenth Century* (New York, 1984); and William L. Andrews, introduction to *Sisters of the Spirit*, ed. Andrews (Bloomington, Ind., 1986), pp. 1–22.

7. *Liberator*, January 7, 1832, published an extract of her *Religion and the Pure Principles of Morality, the Sure Foundation on Which We Must Build* (1831); Loewenberg and Bogin, *Black Women*, p. 195.

8. Loewenberg and Bogin, *Black Women*, pp. 198, 199.

moral duty. Yet some of them began to separate themselves from their sisters in benevolent societies by interpreting these religious imperatives in new, nontraditional ways. In a resolution introduced at the 1837 Anti-Slavery Convention of American Women, Lydia Maria Child called anti-slavery work "the cause of God, who created mankind free." Angelina Grimké, at the same convention, denounced the return of fugitive slaves as "a daring infringement of the divine commands." Her sister Sarah urged women to discuss all aspects of slavery and prepare themselves "to act as women, and as Christians on this all-important subject." Rejecting arguments that women should not forsake their male-appointed domestic sphere, Maria Weston Chapman offered her own definition: "Woman's work . . . is to be a minister of Christian love."[9]

The commitment of the antislavery women was informed by the knowledge that the sexual violation of female slaves was widespread. Child and the Grimkés were particularly outspoken on the issue of sexual purity, despite a general public attitude that the very mention of sexual impurity would shock a female audience and possibly tarnish the reputation of a female author or speaker.

In addition to antislavery arguments that apparently accepted restrictive definitions of woman's concerns, female antislavery activists also developed political analyses that were at least potentially subversive of those restric-

9. *Proceedings of the Anti-Slavery Convention of American Women . . . 1837* (New York, 1837), pp. 7, 8, 9; Chapman, "Ten Years of Experience," published as *Ninth Annual Report of the Boston Female Anti-Slavery Society . . . 1841–42* (Boston, 1842), p. 26. For Child, see Milton Meltzer and Patricia G. Holland, eds., *The Collected Correspondence of Lydia Maria Child, 1817–1880* (microform, Milwood, N.Y., 1980); Meltzer and Holland, eds., *Lydia Maria Child, Selected Letters, 1817–1880* (Amherst, 1982); Meltzer, *Tongue of Flame: The Life of Lydia Maria Child* (New York, 1965); William S. Osborne, *Lydia Maria Child* (New York, 1980); John G. Whittier, ed., *Letters of Lydia Maria Child with a Biographical Introduction by John G. Whittier and an Appendix by Wendell Phillips* (Boston, 1882); Helene G. Baer, *The Heart is Like Heaven: The Life of Lydia Maria Child* (Philadelphia, 1964); Susan P. Conrad, *Perish the Thought: Intellectual Women in Romantic America, 1830–1860* (New York, 1976); Jean Fagan Yellin, *Women and Sisters: The Antislavery Feminists in American Culture* (New Haven, 1989), pp. 53–76; Carolyn Karcher, introduction to *Homobok and Other Writings on Indians by Lydia Maria Child*, ed. Karcher (New Brunswick, 1986); Karcher, "Lydia Maria Child's *A Romance of the Republic:* An Abolitionist Vision of America's Racial Destiny," in Arnold Rampersad and Deborah E. McDowell, eds., *Slavery and the Literary Imagination* (Baltimore, 1989), pp. 81–103; Karcher, "From Pacifism to Armed Struggle: Lydia Maria Child's 'The Kansas Emigrants' and Antislavery Ideology in the 1850's," *ESQ: Journal of the American Renaissance* 34 (1988): 141–58; Karcher, "Censorship, American Style: The Case of Lydia Maria Child," *Studies in the American Renaissance* (1986): 287–303; and Karcher, "Rape, Murder, and Revenge in 'Slavery's Pleasant Homes,' Lydia Maria Child's Antislavery Fiction and the Limits of Genre," *Women's Studies International Forum* 9 (1986): 323–32.

tions. Stewart, having no formal education, had confounded the two fundamental documents that define American political life, but she understood their import in the struggle for abolition. To her religious arguments she therefore added references to government. "This is the land of freedom. The press is at liberty. Every man has a right to express his opinion. . . . and, according to the Constitution of these United States, [God] hath made all men free and equal." These two lines of reasoning also appeared in the Philadelphia Female Anti-Slavery Society's constitution. "We believe that slavery and prejudice are contrary to the laws of God and the principles of our Declaration of Independence." For Angelina Grimké, the right of petition was "natural and inalienable, derived immediately from God, and guaranteed by the Constitution of the United States." The women made these statements in the context of public, not private, behavior.[10]

Such bold engagement in political action defied gender conventions of submissiveness and domesticity, and some determined antislavery activists devised elaborate and subtle arguments to show that they were not "stepping out of [their] sphere." Slavery was not "merely a political question," Sarah T. Smith asserted, but also "a question of justice, of humanity, of morality, of religion"—all realms accepted as particularly appropriate to women. In the course of the 1830s, others went further and insisted that political matters *were* appropriate concerns of women, and these individuals moved toward a new ideology of equal rights.[11]

Adherence to separate spheres within antislavery work, after all, was impeding the contributions that some of the women were determined to make. Stewart attributed her initial activism to William Lloyd Garrison's welcome to women in the early pages of the *Liberator.* His encouragement stimulated the creation of separate female antislavery societies, not as a mechanism to exclude women from already existing societies but as an effective way to harness their potential for serious work. A group of black women formed an antislavery society in Salem, Massachusetts, on February 22, 1832. In Boston later that year, a dozen women organized the Boston Female Anti-Slavery Society. In Philadelphia, women attended the founding meeting of the American Anti-Slavery Society in December 1833, and at least four of them, including Lucretia Mott, entered into the discussions, although they were not asked to sign the new "Declaration of Sentiments

10. Loewenberg and Bogin, *Black Women,* p. 186; *Fourth Annual Report of the Philadelphia Female Anti-Slavery Society, Jan. 11, 1838* (Philadelphia, 1838), p. 2, quoted in Amy Swerdlow's essay, Chapter 2 in the present volume, p. 37.

11. In Philadelphia, 1838; see Elizabeth Cady Stanton et al., eds., *History of Woman Suffrage* (New York, 1881), 1:339–40.

and Purposes." Within days, they had organized the Philadelphia Female Anti-Slavery Society. Four black women were among the eighteen charter members: Grace Douglass and the Forten sisters Margaretta, Sarah Louisa, and Harriet.[12]

Stewart's move from Boston to New York after September 1833 made no headlines, but Child's *An Appeal in Favor of that Class of Americans Called Africans,* published in Boston the same year, immediately became notorious. Child was already a highly regarded popular young author when she produced this provocative volume. The very title, insisting that slaves and free blacks in the United States were "Americans" and therefore entitled not only to freedom but to *all* the rights of Americans, was "frightening to her contemporaries."[13]

The *Appeal* tackled political issues with a firmness previously unknown for an American woman writer. "He who votes for admitting a slave-holding State into the Union," Child wrote in a clear reference to congressional debates, "fearfully augments the amount of this crime." To substantiate her assertion that "our slave laws are continually increasing in severity," she devoted many pages to specific state legislation on slavery adopted since an 1827 compendium was published. She examined the progress toward emancipation throughout South and Central America and linked the United States with "the empire of Brazil" as "the only American nations" that had not begun formal steps to eliminate slavery. Unwilling to blame only the slaveholders and their southern political allies, she also condemned the economic complicity and the "coldhearted, ignoble prejudice" of northerners. She admitted that "the *form* of slavery" did not exist in the North but insisted that its "very *spirit* . . . is here in all its strength," and showed how individual actions could work against it.[14]

12. Loewenberg and Bogin, *Black Women,* pp. 197–98; Sterling, *We Are Your Sisters; Right and Wrong in Boston,* pp. 3–6; Stanton, *History of Woman Suffrage,* 1:324–25; Darlene Clark Hine, "Lifting the Veil, Shattering the Silence: Black Women's History in Slavery and Freedom," in Hine, ed., *The State of Afro-American History* (Baton Rouge, La., 1986), p. 231; reprinted in Hine, ed., *Black Women in American History: Theory and Practice,* 2 vols. (New York, 1990), 1:235–62.

13. Margaret Farrand Thorp, *Female Persuasion* (New Haven, 1949), p. 224; Loewenberg and Bogin, *Black Women,* p. 189. Only a short time earlier, Stewart had used the term "American" to mean whites, when she wrote: "Possess the spirit of independence. The Americans do, and why should not you?"

14. Lydia Maria Child, *An Appeal in Favor of That Class of Americans Called Africans* (Boston, 1833, New York, 1836; rpt. of 1836 ed. New York, 1968), pp. 37, 66, 94, 195; George M. Stroud, *A Sketch of the Laws Relating to Slavery in the Several States of the United States of America* (Philadelphia, 1827).

Child acknowledged her boldness in alluding to the sexual exploitation of female slaves, which, she said, she could not "unveil so completely as it ought to be." "The facts are so important," she declared, "that it is a matter of conscience not to be fastidious." Writing in an era when women were expected to be innocent of sexual matters, and addressing a northern audience perhaps ignorant of the domestic relations that slavery made possible, Child informed them that a slave woman and her daughters were "allowed to have no conscientious scruples, no sense of shame ... [but] must be entirely subservient to the will of their owner." She chose her words carefully: "Those who know human nature would be able to conjecture the unavoidable result, even if it were not betrayed by the amount of mixed population."[15]

This assertiveness on the part of antislavery women provoked hostile responses and sparked a debate over women's role in the movement. Two years after writing the *Appeal,* Child provided a gendered rationale for her political activity in a letter to the 1835 meeting of the Boston Female Anti-Slavery Society: "Where women are brutalized, scourged, and sold, shall we not inquire the reason? My sisters, you have not only the right, but it is your solemn *duty.*"[16]

Committed to this antislavery duty, some women began to question the social restrictions on their public role. Chapman was echoing traditional gender ideology when she emphasized the compatibility of this obligation with a woman's position in her family: "We deem there is nothing unfeminine in aiding our husbands, brothers, and sons, to support the principles they have adopted." Similarly, in 1835 she signed a letter with the revealing phrase, "The mothers, wives, and daughters of abolitionists of New England." A short year later, she was apparently the author of an address by the Boston society which utilized the rhetoric both of citizenship and of domesticity by appealing to "Sisters and Friends" as "*immortal souls,*" as "*women,*" and also as "*wives* and *mothers ... sisters* and daughters.*"[17]

Although the Boston society intermittently replicated traditional patterns of discourse, it was innovative in its initiatives. In one instance, it backed a suit (and paid the counsel's fees) in an action that won the freedom of a slave child brought into Massachusetts by her owner.[18]

15. Child, *Appeal,* p. 23.
16. *Right and Wrong in Boston,* p. 94.
17. Ibid., pp. 84, 85. *Right and Wrong in Boston in 1836. Annual Report of the Boston Female Anti-Slavery Society* (Boston, 1836), pp. 28–29.
18. Med Sommersett's case. *Right and Wrong in Boston in 1836,* pp. 66–71.

Introduction

The developing thought of South Carolina's famous Grimké sisters, Sarah and Angelina, charted the path from traditional gender consciousness to the new advocacy of women's rights. Members of the wealthy planter elite, they had witnessed slavery at firsthand and knew from the inside what Child's *Appeal* described from an outsider's perspective. Their testimony on the sexual immorality of the slave system and its impact on white women as well as on blacks was particularly striking. Even before they left the South, the Grimkés had been learning to act boldly on their religious convictions, and they had become increasingly independent in their search for satisfactory affiliations and for personal pathways to action. After joining the Quakers, they became familiar with the idea of women speaking aloud on serious topics, even in front of men. Sarah Grimké, in fact, after her arrival in Philadelphia in the early 1820s, held membership in a Quaker meeting where Lucretia Mott was a minister. A decade later, after encountering Child and her husband at the Philadelphia Female Anti-Slavery Society, Angelina Grimké began to correspond with several antislavery women in New England. Such contacts quickened the exchange of ideas and strengthened the loose network of women activists.[19]

When during the summer of 1836 Angelina Grimké was invited to become a speaker for the American Anti-Slavery Society at women's sewing circles and parlor meetings in New York, the sisters became the earliest female agents for abolitionism in the United States. They were the only women who joined the forty males attending a training convention for new agents conducted by Theodore Weld (whom Angelina later married), and the Grimké sisters were invited by unanimous vote to participate equally in discussions. When their training was done, and their New York meetings outgrew the parlors and began to move into church facilities, the sisters quailed at the prospect of their conspicuous and unconventional role. Although they endorsed the right of women to speak in public and even to speak before mixed audiences, they were sufficiently encumbered by tradition to be reluctant pioneers. After they moved on to Boston, a more conservative antislavery worker agonized over the propriety of the Grimkés' speaking before "*gentlemen* as well as ladies." "Is it not very difficult to draw the boundary line?" she wondered. "On the one hand, we are in danger of servile submission to the opinions of the other sex, & on the other hand, in perhaps equal danger of losing that modesty, & instinctive delicacy

---

19. Early in 1836, the Grimké sisters were delighted to encounter Quakers from Providence, Rhode Island, who were confirmed abolitionists, unlike many leaders in the Philadelphia meetings. Lerner, *Grimké Sisters*, pp. 60, 130–34.

of feeling, which our Creator has given as a safeguard." By opening a path for women lecturers on antislavery and other public issues, the Grimkés decisively and irrevocably shifted that boundary line.[20]

A close look at the innovative Anti-Slavery Convention of American Women held in New York in 1837 illuminates the process by which some activist antislavery women created a new female political culture and demonstrates how that convention served as a precursor of the 1848 meeting at Seneca Falls. Challenging both slavery and racism, the women activists rejected traditional attitudes toward membership. Most women's benevolent groups were composed of people connected by family and by neighborhood, although some associations included members of different religious denominations, different ethnic backgrounds, and even different classes. In contrast to this pattern, several antislavery women's organizations offered equal membership to both black and white women. By rejecting segregation, the women in these racially mixed societies created a gender-specific organizational structure that posed an institutional challenge to American racism.[21]

In 1837 the first of the three "national" conventions of American antislavery women brought together both black and white members of the key female societies. Maria Stewart, now a New Yorker, was in attendance, as were Mott, the Grimkés, and Child. The white women, struggling for acceptance by white men as full colleagues in the antislavery cause, were often oblivious to the fact that black women had both racism and sexism to confront. While the 1837 convention was still in the planning stages, the African American Sarah Mapps Douglass, a member of the Philadelphia

20. Earlier, of course, the British woman Frances Wright had played the role of female public lecturer in America. But Wright was a notorious "infidel"; Angelina Grimké, writing to a friend, worried that her own lecture "would be called a Fanny Wright meeting" (Angelina Grimké to Jane Smith, December 17, 1838; Birney, *Grimké Sisters*, pp. 137–38, cited in Lerner, *Grimké Sisters*, p. 137). Lerner, *Grimké Sisters*, pp. 145, 152; Juliana Tappan to Anne Warren Weston, July 21, 1837, Boston Public Library, quoted in Keith E. Melder, *Beginnings of Sisterhood: The American Woman's Rights Movement, 1800–1850* (New York, 1977), p. 90.

21. For kinship and neighborhood connections among organized women in Rochester, New York, for example, see Hewitt, *Women's Activism and Social Change: Rochester, New York, 1822–1872* (Ithaca, 1984). For the racial attitudes expressed in the Ladies' NYCASS, see Amy Swerdlow's essay, Chapter 3 in the present volume. For the complex relationships among black and white women in racially mixed female antislavery societies, see Lawrence J. Friedman's *Gregarious Saints: Self and Community in American Abolitionism* (Cambridge, 1982); and Dorothy Sterling, ed., *Turning the World Upside Down: The Anti-Slavery Convention of American Women Held in New York City May 9–12, 1837* (New York, 1987). See, in addition, the essays by Debra Hansen, Jean Soderlund, and Carolyn Williams, Chapters 3, 4, and 9 in the present volume.

women's group and a daughter of one of its founding members, wrote to the Grimkés that she hesitated to commit herself to the journey after learning that blacks would not be welcomed by their New York hosts. Angelina Grimké responded quickly, not only convincing the New Yorkers to admit black delegates but arguing to Douglass that she had a responsibility to help in overcoming racism within the movement. "You, my dear Sisters, have a work to do in rooting out this wicked feeling as well as we," she wrote back, persuading both Sarah Douglass and her mother to attend as delegates.[22]

The minutes of the 1837 convention do not identify the black delegates and corresponding members, and minimal evidence of their participation and comments appears in the written record.[23] But Sarah Pugh afterward reported to a friend: "About one-tenth of our number were colored. They did not take part in the general business, but when the subject of Colonization was taken up they spoke with earnestness. They responded also upon prejudice against color."[24] The last sentence is apparently an allusion to a resolution Angelina Grimké introduced on the subject of racism, calling for association with "our oppressed brethren and sisters ... as though the color of the skin was of no more consequence than that of the hair, or the eyes." (Interestingly, Grimké's use of the first-person plural in this and other resolutions meant "we whites.")[25]

Analysis of those who enrolled their names as members of the 1837 convention shows sixty-seven white delegates and four blacks, a ratio of about 94 percent to about 6 percent. Corresponding members, attending in an unofficial capacity, were mainly from New York; of these, the division was probably eighty-nine white and fourteen black, a ratio of about 86 percent to about 14 percent. This places the overall proportion of black participants at 10 percent, matching Sarah Pugh's "about one-tenth." Both of the Grimkés served on the ten-member Committee on Arrangements, as did Sarah Douglass. Grace Douglass was one of six vice-presidents nominated by those making preliminary arrangements for the convention. The minutes do not specify the tasks of this steering committee beyond proposing

22. For the exchange between Douglass and Grimké, see Darlene Clark Hine, "Lifting the Veil," pp. 231–32. For the Grimkés' anti-racism, see Gerda Lerner, "The Grimké Sisters and the Struggle against Race Prejudice," *Journal of Negro History* 48 (1963): 277–91.

23. An annotated list (unpublished) prepared by Dorothy Sterling in 1986 has helped clarify this.

24. *Memorial of Sarah Pugh: A Tribute of Respect from Her Cousins* (Philadelphia, 1888), p. 18. An anonymous report in the *Liberator* of June 2, 1837 specified that two of the black women spoke against expatriation.

25. *Proceedings . . . 1837*, p. 13.

Ruth Bogin and Jean Fagan Yellin

the agenda, but the creation of the other committees was probably the work of this group. Several committees included at least one black member.[26]

This convention differed from meetings of other women's benevolent societies not only in its racial composition but also in the ideological orientation of its leaders: three of the vice-presidents—Sarah Grimké, Lucretia Mott, and Lydia Maria Child—were, with Angelina Grimké, particularly active in presenting resolutions and shaping the work of the convention. (Maria Weston Chapman could not attend because of a death in her family, but she sent a compelling message to the gathering.) This leadership and a dedicated cadre of antislavery women transformed the political character of the convention. Not only did they confront the issue of racism within the antislavery movement, but they also formally aired—sometimes amid controversy—almost every major theme concerning women's rights that would be explored a full decade later at the 1848 Seneca Falls Woman's Rights Convention.

A principal consideration behind the decision to hold the 1837 convention was the desire to circulate antislavery petitions more effectively. The traditional right of women to petition, inherited through the common law of England and long used in securing redress of individual grievances, was now becoming an opening wedge into the political world. Stewart's earlier injunction to her male auditors to sign petitions for the abolition of slavery in the District of Columbia heralded women's recognition of petitioning as a feasible instrument for their own participation. Petitions to state legislatures and to Congress had exerted pressure ever since the Revolution, and Garrison publicized this activity in the opening issue of the *Liberator*, providing an address where "all the friends of the cause" might add their names. In November 1831, women in the Society of Friends in Philadelphia met to consider "the propriety" of their memorializing Congress on behalf of the slaves in the District of Columbia, and in December Garrison recorded that they had garnered over two thousand signatures from other women. Praising their "noble example," he found it "proper . . . not only that their white sisters should feel, but express in the most public manner a deep sympathy in their behalf."[27]

By the mid-1830s, female petitioning was gathering force as an antislavery instrument. The passage by the United States House of Representatives of the so-called Gag Rule of May 1836, which rejected all antislavery petitions without reading them, served only to encourage the antislavery women to redouble their efforts. In July of 1836, the Boston society adopted

26. Ibid., pp. 4–6.
27. Melder, *Beginnings of Sisterhood*, pp. 74–75; *Liberator*, December 17, 1831.

an impassioned "Address . . . to the Women of Massachusetts," calling on women "as *women*" to petition Congress for abolition in the District of Columbia. The address explicated the religious duty of women to accept responsibility for influencing "the human race" to end the "sinful system of Slavery," and it provided basic information on the constitutional right of petition and the congressional jurisdiction over the District of Columbia. Fourteen women volunteered to circulate copies of the petition to at least one person in every town in Massachusetts. By midwinter Garrison commended the Boston women for obtaining over five thousand names coming from all parts of Massachusetts. "It is meet that the maids and matrons of this Commonwealth should take the lead in this matter," he editorialized, "but what are the men doing?"[28]

At the 1837 convention, Angelina Grimké presented a resolution proclaiming "the duty" of every American woman "annually to petition Congress . . . for the immediate abolition of slavery in the District of Columbia and the Territory of Florida, and the extermination of the inter-state slave-trade." After this resolution was adopted, Child presented another (also adopted) favoring petitions to repeal the laws of non-slave states that allowed masters to retain slaves within their jurisdiction for a specified period.[29] On the third day of the convention, most of the free states pledged to gather signatures "by their daughters rising to the call." At the closing session Child's additional remarks elicited pledges from key cities to send a copy of the congressional petition "to each town in their several states."[30]

The convention participants understood that by gathering women's signatures, they had produced results far beyond the female proportion of the movement. Using the only tool available to them for reaching the representatives of the people, they had helped force abolition onto the nation's political agenda. The delegates demonstrated their political sophistication in a letter to Congressman (and former president) John Quincy Adams, who had protested the Gag Rule as a violation of the First Amendment. They praised Adams for "his recent services in defending the right of pe-

---

28. *Right and Wrong in Boston in 1836*, pp. 26–32, with an ironic footnote on pp. 26–27: "It has been objected in past years, that our power to effect any change was so *little*, that it was absurd to exercise it. . . . It is *now* objected that our power is so *great*, that it is dangerous to exercise it." *Liberator*, January 2, 1837; Garrison also urged those forwarding petitions to Congress to keep "a true reckoning" of "the places from which they originate—the number of signatures—whether males or females, etc." because the congressional count would probably mask the real numbers.

29. *Proceedings . . . 1837*, p. 8.

30. *Liberator*, June 2, 1837; *Proceedings . . . 1837*, pp. 12, 15.

tition for women, and for slaves," but the women criticized his opposition to the goal of the petitions, abolition in the District of Columbia. "He did not," they wrote, "sustain the cause of freedom and of God." Very proper but utterly forthright, this letter is proof of the women's growing political maturity.[31]

At this meeting, economic concerns made an unusual appearance when Child resolved that it was "the duty of abolitionists to encourage our oppressed brethren and sisters in their different trades and callings by employing them whenever opportunities offer." This statement echoed Stewart's plea at a public lecture in Boston in 1832 for "equal opportunity" for employment of "our girls" who, regardless of qualifications, were almost completely barred from all but "mean, servile labor."[32]

More central to the concerns of the convention was the Grimkés' readiness to lead the women to confront societal restrictions. Sarah Grimké introduced a resolution affirming that American women, "as moral and responsible beings," were "solemnly" called into action against slavery "by the spirit of the age and the signs of the times." Lucretia Mott spoke in support. So did Angelina Grimké, who offered an assertive resolution of her own: "The time has come for woman to move in that sphere which Providence has assigned her, and no longer remain satisfied in the circumscribed limits with which corrupt custom and a perverted application of Scripture have encircled her." Mott endorsed this wording, but amendments were introduced that led to "an animated and interesting debate" on "the rights and duties of women." When Angelina Grimké's resolution was adopted without any changes, a dozen women wished their partial disagreement noted. The following day, Child attempted to conciliate the dissenters by moving that the convention reconsider the resolution on "the province of women," but her motion failed. Then Abby Cox, one of the dissenters, offered a resolution expressing a more traditional notion of women's political culture. Emphasizing women's role as mothers, Cox resolved that free mothers, contrasting their own joy in their children with the bitter lot of the slave mother, should "lift up their hearts to God on behalf of the captive" and guard the minds of their own children from "proslavery and prejudice." Sarah Grimké countered with a stronger interpre-

---

31. *Proceedings . . . 1837*, p. 16. The critique in this letter had been forcefully anticipated when in 1833 Child had closed her *Appeal* by writing of Adams: "He offered the petitions only to protest against them" (*Appeal*, p. 216).

32. *Proceedings . . . 1837*, p. 17; Loewenberg and Bogin, *Black Women*, pp. 192–94, quotations on 192–93.

tation of the duty of American mothers: that they "educate their children in the principles of peace, and special abhorrence of that warfare, which gives aid to the oppressor against the oppressed." Hers was the resolution that passed.[33]

One clue to the delegates' feelings about challenging traditional gender patterns is suggested by the ways they wanted their names to appear on the membership roll. A roll call revealed that more than a dozen women asked to be listed with "the appellation of Mrs. and Miss." The rest chose to omit titles revealing their marital status, although the minutes make clear that "a large proportion of the members who declined the appellation of Mrs. or Miss, were *not* members of the Society of Friends," where this was customary. These innovative women were not, however, entirely comfortable with the idea of struggling on their own behalf. Maria Weston Chapman, by referring to the abolitionist emblem of an enchained supplicant, likened the situation of the women to that of self-emancipated slaves: "Are we FREE! it is because we have burst our manacles in the effort to undo those that weigh so heavily" on the slave. But even Chapman felt the need to emphasize that, in their private roles, the women would "sedulously continue to fulfill every the most minute household duty" while keeping their minds on the public responsibilities they were assuming.[34]

The convention over, the innovations in the women's public behavior continued. When the Grimké sisters went on to Boston, where they were to address gatherings of women as they had in New York, Angelina Grimké voiced her worried awareness of her pioneering role in a letter to a friend. But—despite some opposition—she and her sister were well received. There were many meetings, and big ones, with men attending in ever-greater numbers. On June 21 over six hundred men and women overflowed a hall in Lynn, where attendance was officially open to all, and repeat appearances had to be scheduled. From then on, with all their meetings open to men and women, the sisters attracted a great deal of attention. During the same period they each began a brilliant series of public polemics—Angelina's *Letters to Catharine Beecher*, which replied to attacks on women abolitionists, and Sarah's groundbreaking *Letters on the Equality of the Sexes*.[35]

All this excitement intensified the opposition to Garrisonian "immediate" abolitionism from New England churchmen who leaned toward the colonization-and-gradualist approach, if they objected to chattel slavery at

33. *Proceedings . . . 1837*, pp. 8–12.
34. Ibid., pp. 15, 19, 20. For six of the nine women named to corresponding committees, a footnote directed that their letters be sent in care of male relatives. Ibid, p. 16.
35. Lerner, *Grimké Sisters*, pp. 169, 183.

all. Although they did not succeed in barring abolitionist meetings from all Congregational churches, the daring behavior of the Grimké sisters in addressing promiscuous audiences must have rekindled the clerics' hostile reaction to the New York convention, especially to Child's resolutions and to Angelina Grimké's insulting language ("perverted application of Scripture," indeed!).[36]

A harsh pastoral letter from the General Association of Massachusetts (Orthodox) to the Churches under Their Care renewed opposition to the Garrisonians and to their itinerant speakers and castigated women who, by assuming the "male role" of public speakers, were accused of ignoring their duties as set forth in the New Testament. This Pastoral Letter underlines another distinction between the female antislavery societies and other women's groups: few other female organizations earned such vehement clerical opposition, and no other group of women exhibited such vigorous anticlericalism as the antislavery women did. The Pastoral Letter did not deter the Grimkés from their exhausting round of lectures, with crowds now augmented by curiosity and sometimes hostility. A highlight of their subsequent work, and a milestone in the movement for women's rights, was the Grimkés' three-day appearance before a committee of the Massachusetts legislature, which held hearings on antislavery petitions in February 1838. Child and Chapman also attended.[37]

Two annual conventions of antislavery women were held in Philadelphia following the New York convention of 1837. By this time, the number of female antislavery societies had grown. At the 1838 convention, financial support was pledged by thirty-three societies located not only in large cities but also in small towns in Maine, New Hampshire, and Rhode Island, as well as in Massachusetts and Pennsylvania. The mobbing of the 1838 convention and the burning of Pennsylvania Hall marked the zenith of the violence that forever distinguished the experience of the antislavery women from that of other organized women, but neither Philadelphia convention produced a rich body of new theory or practice. The central resolutions and arguments presented at the 1837 convention in New York were essentially restated in Philadelphia, where steadfastness and dedication were the new watchwords. An 1838 resolution pledged to continue antislavery pressure "until the prayers of every woman within the sphere of our influence shall

36. Angelina E. Grimké to Jane Smith, May 29, 1837, William L. Clements Library, University of Michigan; Lerner, *Grimké Sisters*, chap. 12. See especially pp. 184–89.

37. Eleanor Flexner, *Century of Struggle: The Woman's Rights Movement in the United States* (Cambridge, 1958), p. 49; Lerner, *Grimké Sisters*, p. 222. In addition to targeting the Grimkés and other female antislavery activists, this Pastoral Letter implicitly criticized the antiprostitution campaign of the female moral reform societies.

be heard in the halls of Congress."[38] The women's antislavery societies, appealing particularly to women's humanitarian and religious concerns, made the petition campaign into a primary vehicle for educating women about slavery and moving them toward political action. At the same time, petitioning by women became a way to expand the public's conception of women's legitimate activities.

In 1839, a circular which urged weary supporters to sign yet another petition reveals how hard it was, as the years passed, to sustain the mammoth undertaking and fulfill the solemn pledges never to give up. Reiterating the significance of petitioning by women, it said: "It is our only means of direct political action. It is not ours to fill the offices of government, or to assist in the election of those who shall fill them. We do not enact or enforce the laws of the land. The only direct influence which we can exert upon our Legislatures, is by protests and petitions." Lucretia Mott was a member of the business committee that prepared the circular. In view of her subsequent role in the Seneca Falls convention, it seems likely that she had a hand in formulating this brief statement of women's political deprivations.[39]

Also in 1839 Chapman made the new culture of the antislavery women— conflicted in ideology, in language, and in activities—the subject of a humorous poem, "Lines Inscribed to the Intolerant, throughout New England and the Coast Thereof."[40] Here Chapman acknowledges the difficulty of reconciling women's traditional organized benevolence with antislavery feminism, especially within a context where some male activists supported the nontraditional women while others attacked them.

> We thought, by baskets, caps, and collars,
> We well might raise one thousand dollars,
> By which, if properly expended,
> Would right prevail, and wrong be ended.

Chapman first bemoans the disruptiveness of the women who would not participate in women's traditional fundraising activities:

---

38. *Proceedings of the Anti-Slavery Convention of American Women . . . 1838* (Philadelphia, 1838), p. 5.

39. *Proceedings of the Third Anti-Slavery Convention of American Women . . . 1839* (Philadelphia, 1839), pp. 7, 26.

40. [Friends of Freedom], *Liberty Bell* (Boston 1839), pp. 57–58. For more on the tensions within the abolitionist movement, see Friedman, *Gregarious Saints*.

> But, wo the while, a recreant few
> Refuse to stitch, or knit, or sew,
> "Because," forsooth, "such fairs as these,
> Go sore against their *consciences!*"

Next, after mimicking clichés reinforcing women's subordination, she lectures the antifeminist abolitionist:

> What man is this, who proudly sneers,
> As these strained arguments he hears
> From custom, gospel, law, and chance
> In favor of intolerance?

Chapman concludes with the hope that the antifeminist abolitionist will revise his ideas about female behavior, and with the plea that an inclusive antislavery culture will embrace male and female, antifeminist and feminist abolitionists alike:

> Oh would eternal Providence
> Enlarge his soul—increase his sense
> To see that on this mole-hill earth,
> A congress and a sewing-meeting
> May each to like events give birth . . .
> That FREEDOM is our only goal:—
> That every true and faithful soul
> Must choose its own means to effect it;
> And, be it ballot, be it fair,
> Or free produce, or monthly prayer,
> Bell, book, or candle, or what e'er,
> Grant others freedom to reject it.

A year later it was too late to plead for tolerance. When in 1840 the Garrisonians gained control of the American Anti-Slavery Society and the anti-Garrisonians left to form a separate national organization, Mott, Child, and Chapman "broke all precedents and accepted appointments to the new executive committee . . . now thoroughly committed to supporting woman's rights as reformers."[41] From this moment, it can be argued, the political culture of the antislavery feminists manifested itself most fully not in single-sex female antislavery societies but in mixed-sex organizations.

41. Melder, *Beginnings of Sisterhood*, p. 110.

Introduction

Debate over the proper role of women in the antislavery movement reached a crescendo at the World Anti-Slavery Convention held in London in June 1840, where all female delegates, from mixed-sex societies as well as from female societies, were denied recognition and forced to sit in the gallery. This experience paved the way for the pregnant encounter between Mott (who attended as a delegate) and Elizabeth Cady Stanton (who was accompanying her delegate husband on their bridal journey) and led to Seneca Falls.[42]

The setback in London failed to slow the women activists in America. Although female lecturers were still controversial and although the press was seldom kind to them, women like Abby Kelley continued to assert their right to the podium. Kelley's vast travels and magnetism inspired others not only to join the struggle but even to emulate her labors. The political culture of the antislavery women that had emerged during the 1830s, with its conflicting attitudes toward women's rights, persisted through the next few years by means of example, restatement of principles, and wider communication of practices and ideas that had already been refined through intensive debate.

The black and white antislavery women created a political culture related to, but distinct from, both "the custom of benevolent societies" that Chapman had cited in 1835 and the post-1848 feminism heralded by Grimké's sense that she was walking "an untrodden path."[43] This culture was extraordinarily complex. Black female abolitionists developed new cultural forms out of their unique heritage and in response to the pressures of institutionalized racism and sexism both outside and inside the abolitionist movement. Some activist women, black and white, continued to use the traditional rhetoric of gender and to stay within their prescribed sphere. Others appropriated the rhetoric of antislavery to women's cause and, protesting "the slavery of sex," moved toward Seneca Falls and 1848. Still others alternately rejected and accepted the developing ideas and language of antislavery feminism. The essays that follow chart this dynamic and contradictory political matrix.

42. For Stanton's description, see *History of Woman Suffrage*, 1:420–21.
43. See n. 1, above.

{ Part I }

The Female Antislavery Societies

{ 1 }

On Their Own Terms
A Historiographical Essay

Nancy A. Hewitt

*In 1976 when Amy Swerdlow presented her paper "Abolition's Conservative Sis-*ters: The Ladies' New York City Anti-Slavery Societies, 1834–1840," few studies of the abolitionist campaign focused on the contributions of women. Only one, *Crusade for Freedom* by Alma Lutz, took women's role in the movement as its central theme.[1] Less than a decade after Lutz's 1968 work, however, women abolitionists had attracted significantly greater attention. In 1976 alone, several pathbreaking studies appeared in print, including Gerda Lerner's *Grimké Sisters of South Carolina,* "The Black/White Fight against Slavery and for Women's Rights," by William Loren Katz, Carol Thompson's "Women and the Anti-Slavery Movement," and *The Anti-Slavery Appeal* by Ronald Walters. Two years later, Blanche Glassman Hersh published the first full-length scholarly study of female abolitionism, *"The Slavery of Sex": Feminist-Abolitionists in America.*[2] Over the next de-

1. Lutz, *Crusade for Freedom: Women in the Antislavery Movement* (Boston, 1968). Jane H. Pease and William H. Pease included a chapter on Maria Weston Chapman in their *Bound with Them in Chains: A Biographical History of the Antislavery Movement* (Westport, Conn., 1972); and Lewis Perry, *Radical Abolitionism: Anarchy and the Government of God in Anti-Slavery Thought* (Ithaca, 1973) presents women in a positive light in terms of their participation in the Garrisonian wing of the abolitionist movement. Aileen Kraditor, *Means and Ends in American Abolitionism: Garrison and His Critics on Tactics and Strategy, 1835–1850* (New York, 1967), focuses on the role of women's rights in fomenting divisions within the antislavery movement but is less attentive to the independent activities of women abolitionists.
2. Lerner, *The Grimké Sisters of South Carolina: Rebels against Slavery* (New York, 1967); William Loren Katz, "The Black/White Fight against Slavery and for Women's Rights in America," *Freedomways* 16:4 (1976): 230–36; Carol Thompson, "Women and the Anti-Slavery

cade, as the field of women's history flourished, studies of female antisla-very leaders, women's antislavery societies, and female and familial imagery in antislavery rhetoric and artifacts multiplied.

Yet two aspects of antislavery historiography have remained substantially unchanged. First, many general histories of the movement continue to mini-mize or ignore the myriad activities and associations documented by wom-en's historians. Male students of radical abolitionism *did* follow the early lead of Ronald Walters and Lewis Perry, incorporating questions of gender into their analyses.[3] But far more voluminous is the literature, including general histories of abolition and histories of political antislavery, that mar-ginalizes women's role in the cause. Antislavery anthologies did begin to include a token article on female abolitionists, but it often sat awkwardly amid the essays on male associations and leaders and men's political activ-ities. And the most recent "comprehensive" study of slavery and antislavery, Robert Fogel's *Without Consent or Contract,* published in 1989, wholly ignores the vast literature on women. Here even the Grimké sisters get short shrift; they are mentioned only as the wife and sister-in-law of Theodore Weld.[4]

Movement," *Current History* 70 (May 1976): 198–201; Ronald Walters, *The Anti-Slavery Appeal* (Baltimore, 1976). Walters did not focus solely on women, but his analysis incorporates wom-en's activities to a far greater extent than any previous, and most later, general histories of the antislavery movement. Also in 1976, Judith Wellman presented her important work on female petitioners, "To the Father and the Rulers of Our Country: Abolitionist Petitions and Female Abolitionists in Paris, New York, 1835–45," at the Berkshire Conference on the History of Women, Bryn Mawr College, Philadelphia; and Gerda Lerner presented her more sweeping analysis of "The Political Activities of Anti-Slavery Women" at the Southern Historical As-sociation Meeting in Atlanta (later published in her book *The Majority Finds Its Past: Placing Women in History* [New York, 1979], pp. 112–28). A year later Keith Melder published *The Beginnings of Sisterhood: The American Women's Rights Movement, 1800–1850* (New York, 1977), which gave a prominent place to women's antislavery activity. This was followed by Blanche Glassman Hersh's *"The Slavery of Sex": Feminist Abolitionists in America* (Urbana, Ill., 1978).

3. See especially Lawrence J. Friedman, *Gregarious Saints: Self and Community in American Abolitionism, 1830–1870* (New York, 1982).

4. Fogel provides an extreme example; see his *Without Consent or Contract: The Rise and Fall of American Slavery* (New York, 1989), especially p. 278. Yet other scholars who are more sympathetic to women's history in general have still found it difficult to incorporate women into their analyses. See, for example, John R. McKivigan, *The War against Proslavery Religion: Abolitionism and the Churches, 1830–1865* (Ithaca, 1984). The anthologies focus on a variety of themes, but few do more than offer a single, separate article on women. My own publication record benefitted from this approach. See Hewitt, "The Social Origins of Women's Anti-slavery Politics in Western New York," in Alan M. Kraut, ed., *Crusaders and Compromisers: Essays on the Relationship of the Antislavery Struggle to the Antebellum Party System* (Westport, Conn., 1983), pp. 205–33.

A Historiographical Essay

The second aspect of antislavery historiography that remains largely unaltered involves women's history itself. If general histories of abolition undervalue female activists, women's histories of the cause marginalize conservative women. Feminist scholars have been less interested in analyzing the antislavery movement on its own terms than in treating it as a prelude to the women's rights movement. We have thus selectively recovered the history of female antislavery activism, highlighting those individuals and organizations who made the transition from the battle against racial inequity to the struggle for sexual equality.[5] As Swerdlow cautioned us in 1976: "What is often forgotten or ignored is that there were women who opposed their own rights within the movement."[6]

The omission is now more visible than ever, for in recent years the divisions among politically active women have loomed large. The vehemence with which some women advocated a limited sphere for their sex and rejected a more emancipatory vision demands analysis, and the potency of conservative religious and domestic appeals to women requires explanation.[7] Today, it is particularly important to explore those moments when women stepped beyond prescribed boundaries only to retreat from radical demands for women's equality with men. The New York City female antislavery societies provide one such moment.

Historiographical as well as historical moments are important to consider. When I heard Amy Swerdlow present her analysis at the Berkshire Conference at Byrn Mawr in 1976, I was not yet planning to study antebellum women's activism. Two years later, when I decided on my dissertation topic, I had forgotten how much I owed to Swerdlow's study. In fact, the idea that religion and class divided women abolitionists against themselves first struck me during her presentation. Now, in rereading "Abolition's Conservative Sisters," I realize how closely my own analysis was modeled on hers. Swerdlow's approach is essential to understanding the

5. This pattern reaches back to Alma Lutz, Gerda Lerner, William Loren Katz, Keith Melder, and Blanche Glassman Hersh and forward at least to my own work on Rochester, New York. Though I was interested in differentiating women abolitionists by class, religious affiliation, and ideology, my primary interest was in tracing the more radical path that led to women's rights. (See citations in notes 1, 2, and 4). The present volume is particularly important because it breaks with this pattern and thereby offers a far more complex portrait, or perhaps more accurately a mosaic, of women's antislavery efforts.

6. Swerdlow, "Abolition's Conservative Sisters: The Ladies' New York City Anti-Slavery Societies," Chapter 2 in the present volume, p. 31.

7. Much excellent work on each of these questions in a variety of historical settings is now available. For an overview, see *Gender and History* 3 (Autumn 1991), special issue on gender and the right.

complex and contradictory meanings of women's antislavery activism and women's political activism more generally.

Swerdlow's analysis of the New York City female antislavery societies should have rid us of the notion of a linear progression from benevolence to reform to radicalism much earlier, for she clearly charts the labyrinthine detours and deadends of one important group of women activists. By comparing the more radical racial and sexual formulations of the female antislavery societies of Boston and Philadelphia with those of the more conservative New York societies, Swerdlow illuminates the divisions among women with particular clarity. By applying her analysis to another place, we can extend the significance of her initial insight.

In Rochester, New York, requests for aid from New York's Juliana Tappan, lecture tours by Boston's Abby Kelley, and the Quaker ministry of Lucretia Mott all converged. Here, then, we can see how abolition's conservative sisters fared when competing directly with their more radical counterparts.[8] In Rochester the existence of a more conservative form of female antislavery activism was critical to white women's willingness to participate in the movement during the 1830s. Though a black women's antislavery association had been founded in 1834, white women seemed reluctant to follow suit until they had secured the approval of their fathers, husbands, and ministers. Not until the petition drive of 1837 did the Rochester Female Anti-Slavery Society flourish, and then only in direct response to Juliana Tappan's request for assistance to RFASS president Susan Farley Porter.

Juliana Tappan and Susan Porter shared not only a commitment to the antislavery cause but also to evangelical religion. Porter in the early 1830s like Tappan in the mid-1830s was inspired by the preaching of Charles Grandison Finney. One of Porter's co-workers in RFASS, Elizabeth Atkinson, would become Finney's second wife. Another co-worker, Mrs. Elon Galusha, was the wife of the local Baptist minister, and Susan Porter, her husband, and three sisters-in-law, all active in RFASS, were founders of the staunchly evangelical and abolitionist congregation at Bethel Presbyterian Church.

Tappan, Porter, and their co-workers were also similarly involved in a range of benevolent ventures. Though the members of LNYASS were more affluent than their boomtown counterparts in western New York—Juliana Tappan was related to wealthy silk merchants and evangelical activists Arthur and Lewis Tappan—Porter and her co-workers were members of the upwardly mobile merchant and artisan class. As members of the new

8. For a detailed analysis of the Rochester case, see Hewitt, "The Social Origins of Women's Antislavery Politics in Western New York."

urban bourgeoisie, they felt duty bound to aid the less fortunate, including orphans, destitute women, and slaves. Finally, both groups of women were reminded that they had stepped beyond women's traditional sphere by more conservative women who denounced any public political efforts undertaken by their sex. In Rochester, Mrs. Jonathan Childs—daughter of the city's founder, wife of its first mayor, sister-in-law of the Episcopal minister, and officer of the local Female Charitable Society—voiced her disapproval. She replied to RFASS's call for assistance in 1835 by asserting that "the combined public effort or co-operation" of women "could not be exerted with propriety" on the subject of slavery.[9]

For a few years RFASS dominated women's antislavery activism, but a second and more radical coterie of less affluent and less evangelical women slowly emerged. They had been dismissed from Quaker meetings or excommunicated from Presbyterian churches in the 1830s, usually as a result of their active support of abolition. That support most often involved a simple signature on an antislavery petition. Though a minority among the female signers on the two huge petitions circulated in Rochester in 1837, Hicksite Quaker women, who broke with their Orthodox co-worshipers in 1828, became increasingly outspoken by 1840. Their efforts were encouraged by Abby Kelley, who became the living symbol of radical abolitionism and sexual equality after her election to the business committee of the American Anti-Slavery Society in 1840. This election crystallized long-standing tensions between radical and reform-minded abolitionists and led directly to the schism in the AASS and the formation of two competing national societies. Kelley's co-worker from Philadelphia, Lucretia Mott, regularly attended the Genesee Yearly Meeting of Hicksite Friends, where she made her antislavery views known to the Quakers of western New York. Kelley, having left the Society of Friends, translated Mott's principles into worldly practice.

In 1842, during a visit to Rochester, Kelley helped organize the Western New York Anti-Slavery Society, serving on the resolutions committee and encouraging such local women as Amy Post and Sarah Fish to join the executive committee. Samuel Porter, Susan's husband, presided at the founding meeting of WNYASS at the Washington Street (formerly Bethel) Presbyterian Church, but Sarah Fish was the only former RFASS member in attendance. By 1842, RFASS had dropped from sight, its members retreating to domesticity or limiting their public work to the orphan asylum or the newly established Rochester Female Moral Reform Society. The West-

9. Mrs. Jonathan Child to Mrs. Sarah D. Fish, May 14, 1835, Fish Family Papers, University of Rochester, Rochester, New York. Mrs. Fish was then secretary of RFASS.

ern New York Anti-Slavery Society, though a mixed sex society, became the main local platform for women's antislavery activism.

The women of WNYASS, led by Amy Post, followed the lead of their sisters in Boston and Philadelphia. They invited black women to join their committees, they were active in the Underground Railroad, they raised funds through antislavery fairs to support the local publication of Frederick Douglass's *North Star,* and they prided themselves on taking the boldest stand on issues of race, peace, and women. In 1848, moreover, these women added the fight for women's rights to their agenda, attending the Seneca Falls convention in July and organizing a second women's rights convention in Rochester in August. At the Rochester convention, women members of WNYASS served as officers and speakers and insisted, over the objections of Lucretia Mott and Elizabeth Cady Stanton, that one of their number preside.[10]

Yet the increasingly radical vision of WNYASS women did not go unchallenged. Indeed, the growing radicalism of local women abolitionists inspired their more conservative sisters in Rochester to reappear on the public stage. In 1851 a huge festival in honor of British antislavery orator George Thompson brought together former members of RFASS, current members of WNYASS and of the newly formed Union Anti-Slavery Sewing Society composed of African American women, and several white women who had never before appeared in public antislavery ranks. The success of the festival encouraged all of these women to continue their abolitionist efforts, but not with such cooperation. The former RFASS members, including Susan Porter and her sister-in-law Maria G. Porter, joined newly active women from Orthodox Quaker meetings, the Unitarian Society, and the Reformed Presbyterian Church to establish the Rochester Ladies' Anti-Slavery Society.

This group continued on the more conservative path to abolition first traced out by RFASS. The Rochester Ladies' Anti-Slavery Society was an all-female, all-white organization; its chief object was to raise funds for Frederick Douglass's publishing ventures and for the political abolitionist organizations Douglass now supported. Many male relatives of RLASS members had been founders of the local Liberty party, including Samuel Porter, and nearly all advocated party politics as the best means for abolishing slavery. The officers of RLASS appealed to their affluent neighbors, conformed to community codes of racial and sexual conduct, rejected de-

10. On WNYASS women's role in the women's rights movement, see Hewitt, "Feminist Friends: Agrarian Quakers and the Emergence of Women's Rights," *Feminist Studies* 12 (Spring 1986): 27–49. The rest of this section is based on Hewitt, "The Social Origins of Women's Antislavery Activism in Western New York."

mands for women's rights, and demonstrated their respectability both privately and publicly. They emphatically contrasted their own efforts with those of their counterparts in WNYASS who wore bloomers, discussed the sexual brutality of slavery in public, demanded sexual equality, and socialized in mixed racial company to the dismay of most of their neighbors.

Despite the different approaches of women in these two associations, the gulf between them was not unbridgeable. Rochester was still a small city where activist women met on numerous occasions. Moreover, many citizens disdained the activities of both associations. Some women, despite their different approaches to public action, developed long-term friendships that survived debates over tactics and style; many others developed mutual respect. Fragments of evidence indicate that a few RLASS members even recognized the necessity of more radical action by the 1850s, though they were unwilling to adopt it themselves. In 1856, for instance, Elizabeth Atkinson Finney, who had left Rochester on her marriage a few years earlier, confided to Susan B. Anthony that women's rights had "the sympathy of a large portion of the educated women. . . . In my circle I hear the movement much talked of & earnest hopes for its success expressed. But," she added, "these women dare not speak out their sympathy," for fear of being labeled "Infidels."[11]

During the crisis of the Civil War, interactions between the two groups of women increased when Amy Post and the Porters worked together to raise funds for teachers, clothing, and other items to be distributed to newly freed blacks who had reached Union lines in Virginia and Washington, D.C. After the war, women abolitionists confronted difficult decisions. Should they support the Fourteenth and Fifteenth Amendments to the Constitution, which guaranteed citizenship and suffrage to black men but simultaneously defined these rights as sex-specific by inserting the word "male" into the supreme law of the land? Disagreement on this issue resulted in the creation of two women's suffrage associations by 1869, the National (which gave woman suffrage and a federal amendment primacy) and the American (whose leaders supported black male suffrage through the Fifteenth Amendment and sought women suffrage on a state-by-state basis).[12] Despite Anthony's local prominence, Rochester's antislavery

11. Susan B. Anthony to Elizabeth Cady Stanton, May 26, 1856, Scrapbook, vol. 1, Elizabeth Cady Stanton Papers, Vassar College, Poughkeepsie, New York. Anthony is relating to Stanton her conversation with Atkinson.

12. The most significant study of the post–Civil War divisions among women abolitionists remains Ellen DuBois, *Feminism and Suffrage: The Emergence of an Independent Women's Movement in America,* 1848–1869 (Ithaca, 1978). DuBois's analysis does, however, leave the motives and makeup of the American Woman Suffrage Association in shadow.

women did not readily divide over the issue of the rights of women versus the rights of blacks. Even after Amy Post joined the National Woman Suffrage Association, for instance, she maintained ties with Boston friends active in the rival American Woman Suffrage Association and remained as committed to racial as to sexual equality. Indeed, Anthony herself was more closely tied in the postwar years to former members of RLASS, staying more closely in contact with Susan and Maria G. Porter than with their WNYASS counterparts. At least in the case of Rochester, the positions that women's historians have posed as irreconcilable appear surprisingly fluid, and at moments the advocates of more conservative and more radical positions seem even to have recognized that only by their combined efforts would change occur.

If we heed the advice of Amy Swerdlow and we recognize that some abolitionist women rejected demands for women's rights, we must reexamine the range, content, and context of women's political activism. This would entail a reconsideration of the activities and agendas of black as well as white women abolitionists. These issues speak to present as well as past choices of historians of women and of women who seek to make history. How appropriate that Amy Swerdlow's article should be published here for the first time, since this collection finally gives voice in our times to our sisters who spoke so forcefully in their own.

{ 2 }

Abolition's Conservative Sisters

The Ladies' New York City
Anti-Slavery Societies, 1834–1840

Amy Swerdlow

Historians of women and of the antebellum period generally agree that conscious feminist activity in the United States began in the late 1830s. During this decade, militant abolitionist women such as the Grimké sisters of South Carolina, Lucretia Mott of Philadelphia, and Abby Kelly Foster and Maria Weston Chapman of Boston asserted their right to speak and act in the political arena and to participate fully with men in the leadership of the American Anti-Slavery Society. Few would disagree with Aileen Kraditor's assessment that "the founders of the women's rights movement were all abolitionists, although not all abolitionists believed in equal rights for women."[1] The early history of abolitionism is replete with instances of male objections to female leadership at the top levels of the American Anti-Slavery Society. But what is often forgotten or ignored is that there were women who opposed their own rights within the movement, and that the center for this opposition was the little-known Ladies' New York City Anti-Slavery Society.[2]

1. Kraditor, *The Ideas of the Woman Suffrage Movement, 1890–1920* (New York, 1971), p. 1. Kraditor claims that some abolitionists who objected to women speaking in public did so out of fear that such actions would alienate the public from the cause. My thesis is that ideology, not expediency, prevented the New York City antislavery women from supporting women's rights.

2. Dwight L. Dumond, in *Anti-Slavery: The Crusade for Freedom in America* (Ann Arbor, 1961), p. 277, asserted that "there are no printed records of the New York Society." Ironically, if he had looked in his own work, *A Bibliography of Anti-Slavery in America* (Ann Arbor, 1961), he would have found the records of two New York City female antislavery societies—the Female Anti-Slavery Society of Chatham Street Chapel and the Ladies' New York City Anti-Slavery Society (pp. 51, 72).

Amy Swerdlow

When in May 1840 the male-led faction that opposed women's participation in the governing bodies of the American Anti-Slavery Society
walked out to form a new organization, the New York city "ladies" left with
the men, declaring, "We are opposed to the public voting and speaking of
women in meetings, to their acting on committees or as officers of the society with men."[3] Who were these women who opposed their own rights?
How did their consciousness and ideology differ from those of their sisters
in the Boston and Philadelphia female antislavery societies, who had
learned in struggling for the slave that they were themselves enchained—
and who had dared to oppose their own bondage?[4] In this essay I examine
why the New Yorkers, who shared the political commitment to the radical
and unpopular antislavery cause and who were as willing as the others to
risk social opprobrium and even bodily harm to defend the rights of the
slave, were unwilling to defend their own.

Such an investigation reveals that the New Yorkers' close ties to evangelical revivalism prevented them from embracing thoughts or actions that
might weaken the "God-given" hierarchical family structure. The church-
going Christian family, with the mother in her proper and secondary
sphere as religious and moral guardian, was deemed by the New York City
evangelicals as the best protection from the poor, the morally depraved, and
the non-Protestant immigrants. These groups posed a constant threat to
the safety and privileges of middle-class life in a growing commercial port
city that was suffering the frequent economic and social dislocations of rapidly expanding capitalism.[5]

I was able to discover family backgrounds and religious affiliations of
twenty-nine of a group of forty officers of the two female abolitionist societies of record in New York City as well as personal data on a few other

3. Resolution passed at the Fifth Annual Meeting of the Ladies' New York City Anti-
Slavery Society, May 27, 1840. Reported in a letter to James G. Birney in Dwight L. Dumond,
ed., *Letters of James Gillespie Birney, 1831–1857* (New York, 1938), pp. 579–80.

4. Abby Kelley Foster expressed her awareness of the interrelationship of the causes in
"Anti Slavery Album," undated MS in Library of Congress, quoted in Keith Melder, "The
Beginning of the Woman's Rights Movement in the United States, 1800–1840" (Ph.D. diss.,
Yale University, 1963), p. 189: "We have good cause to be grateful to the slave for the benefit
we have received to ourselves in working for him. In striving to strike his irons off, we found
most surely that we were manacled ourselves, not by *one* chain only, but by many. In every
struggle we have made for him, we find we have been also struggling for ourselves."

5. For a description and significant insights into women's role in the evangelical movement
in New York City I am indebted to Carroll Smith-Rosenberg, *Religion and the Rise of the
American City: The New York Mission Movement, 1812–1870* (Ithaca, 1971), and "Beauty, the Beast
and the Militant Woman: A Case Study in Sex Roles and Social Stress in Jacksonian America,"
American Quarterly 23 (1971): 562–83.

New York City women who played prominent roles in three national women's antislavery conventions. The information provides the following picture:[6]

The majority of these women were the wives and daughters of prosperous merchants. The next largest group were either married to or the offspring of evangelical clergymen—Presbyterian, Methodist, and Baptist—in that order. Fifteen of the women for whom I could identify religious affiliations were Presbyterian, four Methodist, two Baptist, and one Quaker. None listed themselves as Congregationalist, Unitarian, Episcopalian, or Catholic. Only two women, both widows, were employed outside the home, one as the proprietor of a day school and the other as the first woman missionary of the New York Female Moral Reform Society to receive a salary.

Many of these antislavery women were new arrivals to the city from the rural areas and small towns of New England and New York. For the most part, they began their active opposition to slavery after participating in the wave of religious revivals that swept New England and New York State in the late 1820s and the early 1830s. These revivals, marked by an innovation called "the new measures," which permitted females to pray aloud in church and repent together with males, attracted large numbers of women.[7]

In the preachings of revivalist Charles Grandison Finney, the women found not only the promise of salvation in heaven and peace and grace on earth but also a meaningful place for themselves in the public life of religion. Released from the labors of the farm and from household drudgery by their husbands' new affluence and by inexpensive immigrant labor, these middle-class women were eager to heed Finney's call for personal involvement in good works. Finney himself described their participation in the "great revival," preached in the spring of 1833 at Chatham Street Chapel.

6. *Constitution and Address of the Female Anti-Slavery Society of Chatham Street Chapel* (New York, 1834), p. 6, lists officers; *First Annual Report of the Ladies' New York City Anti-Slavery Society* (New York, 1836), p. 2, lists officers and board of managers. The information regarding the marital and organizational connections of the women was compiled from *Longworth's American Almanac, New York Register and City Directory, 1833–40*, from Flora L. Northrup, *The Record of a Century, 1834–1934* (New York, 1934), which lists the officers of the New York Moral Reform Society from 1834 on, and from *Proceedings* and *Annual Reports of the American Anti-Slavery Society* and articles in the *Emancipator,* the *Anti-Slavery Record,* and the *Colored American.*

7. For a description of the "new measures," see William G. McLaughlin, ed., *Lectures on the Revival of Religion by Charles Grandison Finney* (Cambridge, 1960); Whitney Cross in *The Burned-Over District: The Social and Intellectual History of Enthusiastic Religion in Western New York, 1800–1850* (Ithaca, 1950) suggests that this breakdown of prohibitions against women praying in church marked the beginning of the movement for women's rights.

"They would go out into the highways and the hedges, and bring people to hear preaching. . . . Our ladies were not afraid to go and gather in all classes from the neighborhood roundabout."[8] These militant women, many already actively involved in such evangelical benevolent organizations as the New York Female Moral Reform Society and the New York Female Benevolent Society, formed the first women's abolitionist group in New York City in 1834 at Chatham Street Chapel, the Second Free Presbyterian Church where Finney was pastor.

The first director of the society was Mrs. William Green, Jr., who was also the second director of the New York Female Moral Reform Society. Her husband, a wealthy merchant, was one of Finney's closest associates. Together with Lewis Tappan, the leader of the New York City evangelical movement, William Green, Jr., was a financial backer of several Presbyterian free churches and of the national and local antislavery organizations.

In addition to the Chatham Street Chapel society, a larger citywide organization calling itself the Ladies' New York City Anti-Slavery Society was organized in 1835. The structural plan of this group was to recruit one antislavery woman from every Protestant congregation in the city to sit on its board of managers. In this way, the group hoped to cover "a wider field of influence" than the two hundred members recruited in its first year.[9] Although LNYCASS claimed to be nondenominational, its officers were mainly Presbyterians—wives and daughters of merchants, clergymen, and doctors. The first director, listed as Mrs. Reverend Martyn, was the wife of a Presbyterian minister active in antislavery work. Like Mrs. Green of Chatham Street, Grace Martyn was also a manager of the New York Female Moral Reform Society and later became a director of the Women's Prison Association. Most of the husbands of the other directors and managers of this society were also active in evangelical benevolence and abolition.

I can identify no Methodists on the LNYCASS board of managers, but several New York City Methodist women, some the wives of Methodist evangelical ministers, played an active and conservative role in the deliberations of the women's antislavery conventions in 1837 and 1838.[10] It cannot be as-

8. Quoted in Susan Hayes Ward, *The History of the Broadway Tabernacle* (New York, 1901), pp. 25–26.

9. Letter to BFASS from LNYCASS, September 23, 1835, in *Right and Wrong in Boston. Report of the Boston Female Anti-Slavery Society . . . 1835* (Boston, 1836), pp. 86–90.

10. The Female Methodist Wesleyan Society was listed as a contributor to the printing of the *Proceedings* of the antislavery conventions of American women in 1838 and 1839. Margaret Dye, a Methodist woman active in the evangelical movement and wife of a Methodist clergyman, was appointed to the committee to edit the "Appeal to the Women of the Nominally Free States," *Proceedings of the Anti-Slavery Convention of American Women . . . 1838* (Philadel-

sumed, however, that these women joined antislavery societies because their men recruited them. Which member of a family was the first to "see the light" is an open question. Wendell Phillips, for instance, the radical abolitionist orator, was converted by his fiancée, Anne Terry Greene. "My wife . . . made me an out and out abolitionist," he declared in later years, "and she always preceded me in the adoption of the various causes I advocated."[11]

In the early stages of the abolition movement, antislavery organizations believed that enlightened Christian sentiment alone would be sufficient to win their cause. They published and distributed numerous constitutions, addresses, appeals, and reports "calculated to wake up a slumbering nation." The documents of the New York City female antislavery groups bear witness to their benevolent, moralist stance. The preamble to the constitution of the Chatham Street Chapel society attacked slavery as a sinful violation of female chastity and of the sanctity of the Christian family. "More than a million of our own sex . . . are subjected to a traffic in bodies and souls more dreadful than death, to the sudden and cruel sundering of the most sacred relations of domestic live . . . are deprived of the light of knowledge, and . . . of the hopes of the blessed gospel."[12]

All the constitutions of male and female New York antislavery societies dedicated their organizations to the elevation of the character and conditions of the people of color. The two New York City women's groups were no exceptions. But their statements exhibited far less racism and paternalism than the men's. The male New York City Anti-Slavery Society promised to encourage the intellectual, moral, and religious improvement of colored people and to correct the prejudices of public opinion. It warned, however, that it would "never countenance the oppressed in vindicating their rights by resorting to physical force."[13]

---

phia, 1838), p . 3. Methodist women actually opposed a resolution on separation from churches condoning slavery at the 1838 convention, following the line of male Methodist abolitionists such as Orange Scott, who opposed "coming out" of churches instead of "laboring from within" to reform them. See Donald G. Mathews, "Orange Scott: The Methodist Evangelist as Revolutionary," in Martin Duberman, ed., *The Antislavery Vanguard* (Princeton, 1965), pp. 77–78, and "Methodist Convention" in the *Emancipator,* no. 3 (May 17, 1838), p. 12.

11. Quoted in Richard Hofstadter, "Wendell Phillips, the Patrician as Agitator," in *The American Political Tradition* (New York, 1948), p. 141.

12. *Constitution and Address of the Female Anti-Slavery Society of Chatham Street Chapel,* "Preamble," pp. 3–4.

13. *Constitution and Address of the New York City Anti-Slavery Society* (New York, 1833), p. 46. The New York State society and the national society used almost identical wording.

The women, whose societies were founded later than the men's, might have copied this wording, but they chose not to do so. They never undertook to improve the minds, the character, or the morals of the free black population, nor did they presume to dictate to the slaves the acceptable tactics for winning their freedom. In their *Address to the Public*, the women of Chatham Street Chapel society declared, with rare sensitivity for their time, "We would not join hypocrisy to persecution by *dictating* to them how they are to improve their character and their prospects."[14]

The Ladies' New York City Anti-Slavery Society—the larger group—though also affirming its dedication to the religious improvement of the colored population, revealed a greater interest in benevolence and the Bible than in institutional reform. Its constitution promised to "diffuse a correct state of Christian feeling to the slave, on the principles laid down by our blessed Savior Himself, inasmuch as ye have done it unto one of the least of these my brethren, ye have done it unto me."[15]

The Boston Female Anti-Slavery Society, which was organized in October of 1833, addressed the issue of slavery from a very different perspective. Their reports and appeals reveal leaders who were influenced more by the egalitarian traditions of the American Revolution and by the principle of natural rights than by doctrines of sin and salvation. The very first paragraph of the *Address of the Boston Female Anti-Slavery Society to the Women of New England* states clearly: "The true descendants of the pilgrims cannot fail to cherish in their inmost souls, the principles of Christian freedom;—the children of the far sighted founders of New England cannot fail to perceive that while, under any pretense, one human being is held in slavery in a nation of which they form a part, their own freedom is in peril."[16]

According to a report by the contemporary British journalist Harriet Martineau, BFASS was composed of women of every Protestant sect, "as well as of all complexions." The president, Mary S. Parker, was Presbyterian; the chief secretary, Maria Weston Chapman, a Unitarian; and the membership, numbering approximately two hundred fifty in 1835, was composed of Quakers, Episcopalians, Methodists, Congregationalists, and a few Swedenborgians.[17]

14. *Constitution and Address of the Female Anti-Slavery Society of Chatham Street Chapel*, p. 4 (emphasis in original).

15. *First Annual Report of the Ladies' New York City Anti-Slavery Society*, p. 18.

16. *Address of the Boston Female Anti-Slavery Society to the Women of New England*, undated handbill in Anti-Slavery Collection, Boston Public Library.

17. Harriet Martineau, *The Martyr Age of the United States* (Boston, 1893), p. 27; *Anti-Slavery Almanac*, 1836, p. 44.

The Philadelphia Female Anti-Slavery Society, on the other hand, always linked the two issues of political inequality and sin. The Philadelphia women declared in their constitution: "We believe that slavery and prejudice are contrary to the laws of God and the principles of our Declaration of Independence."[18] The women of PFASS were almost all Quakers. Founded in December 1833, the society had about eighty members three years later.

From their very beginnings, all three female antislavery societies—New York, Philadelphia, and Boston—had to defend themselves from those who held them up to ridicule and scorn for assuming the responsibility of statesmen. To assure the public and each other that they were not straying from their traditional roles, the Presbyterian women of Chatham Street Chapel Society compared themselves with the female friends of the Savior, "who with heavy hearts followed him to Calvary, and were very probably ridiculed for meddling in politics."[19] The Philadelphia women, steeped in the Quaker tradition of active female participation in religious life, used a biblical metaphor to defend their right to work against slavery; they compared themselves not with the followers of the Savior, but with Esther, a savior herself, whose "woman's petition achieved the salvation of a million of her fellow creatures from 'the mouth of the sword.' "[20]

When Boston women laid claim to the religious sphere, they politicized it. "The cause of human freedom is our religion," they declared, "the same taught by him who died on Calvary, the great *reformer* Christ."[21]

For those who were still unsure how freely women could be allowed to move, even in the religious sphere, the Chatham Street Chapel Society *Address* made clear that its members would not wander far. "Whatever else it may be, slaveholding must be eminently a *domestic evil*," they declared. "It works its mischief among the sweet charities which naturally flourish in the family circle. . . . Can it be pretended that here is the ground in which *woman* has no interest. Why it is the ground on which she naturally moves. Here she lives."[22]

The *First Annual Report* of LNYCASS went even further in defining antislavery activity as true woman's work. "We long to see the women of our

18. "Constitution of the Philadelphia Female Anti-Slavery Society" in the *Fourth Annual Report of the Philadelphia Female Anti-Slavery Society, Jan. 11, 1838* (Philadelphia, 1838), p. 2.

19. *Constitution and Address of the Female Anti-Slavery Society of Chatham Street Chapel*, p. 8.

20. *Address of the Female Anti-Slavery Society of Philadelphia to the Women of Pennsylvania with the Form of Petition to the Congress of the United States* (Philadelphia, 1836), p. 7.

21. Martineau, *The Martyr Age*, p. 24.

22. *Constitution and Address of the Female Anti-Slavery Society of Chatham Street Chapel*, p. 7 (emphasis in original).

country rising with energy, to take their appropriate part in this mighty struggle.... We are not calling upon them for anything that would interfere with the sacredness of the feminine character, but rather for what is essential to prove its existence. The duties we urge may be performed without calling them from their own firesides, or identifying them with the scenes of political strife."[23]

The Boston antislavery women made no such apologies. They were particularly proud of their revolutionary foremothers who had left their firesides to participate actively in "political strife." In a report describing their own courageous defense of free speech and assembly against a male mob that attacked a BFASS meeting in October 1835, they declared: "We, at least, shall never forget the noble daring of those from whom we are descended. We shall devoutly cherish the memory of those who never shrunk from any duty because it was a new and painful one.... With gratitude and deep reverence we name such women; approving of their principles; ... though not of the 'warlike measures' dictated by their time. They acted according to their light; and no man spoke of them but with thanks and blessing."[24]

The petitioning of Congress was one of the most important contributions women made to the antislavery cause. As the most radical extension of women's role into the public sphere, it engendered a storm of criticism against women who asserted their right to citizenship. The female antislavery societies of New York, Boston, and Philadelphia each addressed this issue differently. The New York City women defined their right mainly through their relationships to males. "We have fathers, husbands, sons," they asserted. "Are we not something in, and something to our country? Can the nation bleed, and we be free of pain?"[25] But the Boston women, daughters of the Enlightenment, claimed citizenship in their own right. "We cannot... believe that this garment of womanhood wherewith our souls are invested debars us from the duties of immortal souls," they declared.[26]

The Philadelphia antislavery women not only claimed citizenship but also gave it peculiarly feminine responsibilities. Their *Address to the Women of Pennsylvania* published in 1836 stated, "Yes, although we are *women, we* still are citizens, and it is to us that the captive wives and mothers, sisters and daughters of the South have a peculiar right to look for help."[27]

23. *First Annual Report of the Ladies' New York City Anti-Slavery Society*, p. 9.
24. *Report of the Boston Female Anti-Slavery Society*, pp. 44–49.
25. Ibid., p. 10.
26. Ibid., p. 50.
27. *Address of the Female Anti-Slavery Society of Philadelphia to the Women of Pennsylvania*, p. 5.

Finally, although all three groups saw themselves as republican mothers responsible for the virtue and character of future generations, the Boston women wished specifically to preserve for their children the democratic ideals of their ancestors, "an inheritance pure and undefiled, and that fadeth not away,"[28] whereas the New York women emphasized the ideals of Christian charity. "We are sure it can do the Commonwealth no damage," says the LNYCASS report, "if every free mother in the land, as she gathered her children round her for their evening orisons, and felt how *priceless* were these her "jewels," should pray for the slave and instill into the minds of these children, as they advance into stations of influence, a sacred horror of oppression and a yearning to the side of the poor."[29]

During its first eighteen months, LNYCASS engaged in the usual abolitionist activities, circulating petitions to Congress and to the General Assembly of the Presbyterian Church, distributing tracts, and collecting funds for the national society. Meanwhile, a special auxiliary sewed anti-slavery articles, such as needlework book covers inscribed with the slogan "May the use of our needles prick the consciences of slaveholders." But, as the *First Annual Report* of LNYCASS reveals, the society's leaders were dissatisfied with their influence and accomplishments. In October 1836, therefore, when Angelina and Sarah Grimké arrived in the city to discuss the possibility of becoming the first women agents of the American Anti-Slavery Society, the New York women saw an opportunity to widen their audience.

The Grimkés, southern slaveowners who had embraced abolition, were ideal vehicles for the evangelical message. LNYCASS arranged to sponsor a series of parlor lectures. No middle-class parlor could hold the audiences anticipated, however, and the lectures were transferred to the session room of the Reverend Duncan Dunbar's Beriah Baptist Church. The public announcement of church lectures by women not only brought opposition from many quarters but also caused great anxiety for the Grimké sisters and the New York abolitionists. Even Gerrit Smith, president of the New York state society and a friend of women's rights, questioned the propriety of an action that might be viewed as a "Fanny Wright affair" and damage the cause. After much soul-searching and prayer, the Grimké sisters and LNYCASS decided to proceed with their plans, with the meetings restricted to women. The minister left directly after his invocation, and when a

28. *Right and Wrong in Boston*, p. 39.
29. *First Annual Report of the Ladies' New York City Anti-Slavery Society*, p. 9.

"warmhearted male abolitionist" made his way in, he was promptly escorted out.[30]

The lectures reached so many new women that the leaders of LNYCASS were full of praise for the Grimké sisters. The Grimkés, however, did not return the compliment. Angelina Grimké described the New York City women as utterly inefficient, paralyzed by their sinful prejudice, which shut women of color from leadership and discouraged them from membership.[31]

The New York City women were, however, not quite as ineffectual as Angelina Grimké asserted. In addition to organizing the winter lecture series, they were, by May 1837, sufficiently numerous and energetic to host a four-day national convention of antislavery women and to send eighteen delegates and eighty corresponding members to the meeting. (Corresponding members apparently participated in the proceedings.) Gerda Lerner, in her biography of the Grimké sisters, reports that the Grimkés made a point of encouraging black women to participate in the convention. They succeeded in some small measure at least, even in the New York contingent, for the Colored Ladies' Literary Society of New York City and the Rising Daughters of Abyssinia were listed in the *Proceedings*.[32]

Although the New York City women hosted the convention, they did not lead it, and, as a group, they played the most conservative role, opposing radical positions on both the tactics of abolition and the questions of woman's sphere. On the second day of the convention Angelina Grimké offered a resolution in effect extending woman's sphere which was opposed almost exclusively by New York City women. Grimké's resolution read in part: "The time has come for women to move in that sphere which Providence has assigned, and no longer remain satisfied in the circumscribed limits with which corrupt custom and a perverted application of Scripture

---

30. Catherine H. Birney, *The Grimké Sisters, Sarah and Angelina Grimké: The First Women Advocates of Abolition and Woman's Rights* (Boston, 1885), p. 162.

31. This charge is supported by a letter from Anne Warren Weston, sister of Maria Weston Chapman and a leading figure in Massachusetts abolitionist circles, to her sister, Deborah Weston, Oct. 22, 1836, Weston Papers, Boston Public Library: "Everybody has their own troubles, and the New York brethren have theirs. Mrs. Cox is the life and soul of the New York Society and she is in a very sinful state of wicked prejudice about colour; they do not allow any coloured women to join their society. The Tappans have none of the prejudice, therefore they and Mrs. Cox are hardly on speaking terms" (cited in Leon Litwack, *North of Slavery: The Negro in the Free States* [Chicago, 1961], p. 221). Abby Ann Cox, it is interesting to note, was the sister-in-law of the Reverend Sam Cox, an abolitionist clergyman whose church was gutted in the antiabolitionist riot of 1834 because he was said to preach amalgamation. Such was the racist climate in New York City at the time. See Gerda Lerner, *The Grimké Sisters from South Carolina: Pioneers for Woman's Rights and Abolition* (New York, 1976), chap. 10.

32. *Proceedings of the Anti-Slavery Convention of American Women . . . 1837*, p. 15.

have encircled her; therefore it is the duty of woman to do all that she can by her voice and her pen and the influence of her example to overthrow the horrible system of American slavery."[33]

The debate over this resolution was apparently heated and divisive, because on the next day Lydia Maria Child, the Boston writer and antislavery publicist, moved to reopen the question in the interest of unity. Although the motion to overturn was lost, Abby Ann Cox and Rebecca Spring of New York City offered a supplementary resolution that identified female antislavery with traditional womanhood. "Resolved: That there is no class of women to whom the anti-slavery cause makes so direct and powerful an appeal as *mothers,* and they are solemnly urged by all the blessings of their own and their children's freedom and by all the contrasted bitterness of the slave-mother's condition, to lift up their hearts to God on behalf of the captive."[34] This resolution was unanimously approved. No one could vote against motherhood.

Another issue, which arose on the last day of the convention, shows that many antislavery women were beginning to think in self-conscious feminist terms. On this issue, too, the New York City women upheld tradition. After debating whether the published roll of the convention should list the participants' own names or add the appellation of Mrs. or Miss, the convention voted that each member could designate her individual preference. Half of the New York City delegates and eighteen out of eighty corresponding members chose to use Miss or Mrs.—a sharp contrast to the decisions of the Boston and Philadelphia women, who all opted to use their own names. (A footnote to the *Proceedings* points out that not all those who used their own names were members of the Society of Friends.)[35]

After the 1837 convention, the Grimkés left New York to lecture in Massachusetts before mixed audiences. When the sisters were attacked by the council of Congregationalist ministers for daring to assume the place and tone of man as public reformer, one of the very active New York City women, Juliana Tappan, the daughter of Lewis Tappan, leader of the orthodox evangelical abolitionists, reacted to the controversy in a letter to Anne Warren Weston dated July 1837.

I perceive by the papers that they are addressing *gentlemen* as well as ladies. Someone adds, that as they are *Quakers,* there is nothing wrong with it. If it is forbidden in Scripture, as many contend, it is wrong whether Quakers or not. What do you think about it? Is it not very

33 . Ibid., p. 9.
34. Ibid., p. 11.
35 . Ibid., p. 15.

difficult to draw the boundary lines? On the one hand, we are in danger of servile submission to the opinions of the other sex, and on the other hand, in perhaps equal danger of losing that modesty and instinctive delicacy of feeling that our Creator has given as a safeguard, to protect us from danger, to which on account of our weakness we are continually exposed. How difficult it is to ascertain what duty is, when we consult the stereotyped opinion of the world.[36]

Juliana Tappan headed the petition drive in New York City and one might speculate that with further experience exercising her political rights she might learn to reject "stereotyped public opinion." But she and her colleagues never did.

When the second national convention of antislavery women met in Philadelphia in May 1838, the meeting hall was attacked by a violent racist mob that eventually burned it to the ground. An anonymous woman wrote to the New York *Emancipator,* "As we retired the colored members of the Convention were protected by their white sisters, and oh! shame to say, at both were thrown a shower of stones."[37] Although the New York City women withstood the attack as courageously as any others, Juliana Tappan's response, on the next day, was to call for fasting, humiliation, and prayer. Another New Yorker, Sarah Ingraham, editor of New York's *Advocate of Moral Reform,* urged that prayers be offered to God to protect the colored people from future dangers. Sarah Grimké, on the other hand, offered a less benevolent and more egalitarian and radical proposal. She asked abolitionists to try harder to identify themselves with their colored sisters "by sitting with them in places of worship, by appearing with them in our streets and by visiting them at their homes and encouraging them to visit us." Grimké also linked the attack with concurrent efforts to disenfranchise free blacks in Pennsylvania.[38] As Gerda Lerner points out, this was an "astute political and social analysis." Such analysis seems to have eluded the capacities of the New York City women, who, clinging to their original evangelical position, preferred prayer to political action.[39]

36. Quoted in Melder, *Beginnings of Sisterhood: The American Woman's Rights Movement, 1800–1850* (New York, 1977), p. 90.

37. *Emancipator,* May 24, 1838.

38. *Proceedings of the Anti-Slavery Convention of American Women . . . 1838,* pp. 3, 12–14.

39. Lerner, *The Grimké Sisters,* p. 250. For further information on the role of New York City women in the three antislavery conventions of American women, see Amy Swerdlow, "Remember Them That are in Bonds as Bound with Them: An Examination of the New York City Female Anti-Slavery Societies, 1834–1840," unpublished MA essay, Sarah Lawrence College, 1974.

In 1839 and 1840, during the debate within the American Anti-Slavery Society over the woman issue, it was the New York City Anti-Slavery Society, led by Lewis Tappan, that most actively opposed women's participation. Husbands and fathers of the members of the board of managers of LNYCASS led the exodus from the national organization, agreeing with Tappan that women were useful in benevolent organizations, but only in traditional subordinate roles.[40] Although Juliana Tappan reported in May 1840 that LNYCASS had become an auxiliary of the newly formed American and Foreign Anti-Slavery Society, no record exists of any further organizational activity by this group.[41] We can understand from this evidence of their conservative theological and political ideas why the middle-class ladies of New York City were unable to move from benevolent Christian action for the unfortunate slave to radical demands for a change in their own status. In Boston, as well, the women who were connected with the orthodox evangelical clergy—women such as Mary S. Parker, the Presbyterian president of BFASS—led the fight against women's rights within that group. But in Boston the religious liberals prevailed. Maria Weston Chapman, a Unitarian, Abby Kelley Foster, a Quaker, and Lydia Maria Child, a Unitarian who in later years claimed to be "swinging loose" from any religious society, stayed within the American Anti-Slavery Society and called for women's rights from abolition platforms. In Philadelphia, where the women did have a separate female society but often served jointly with men on special boards and spoke publicly in church and in meetings, women's rights never became a divisive issue. Lucretia Mott, Mary Grew, and the other leaders of PFASS remained in the American Anti-Slavery Society and promoted the causes of abolition and women's rights in their public addresses.

40. Among those who left were the husband of the first director, the Reverend J. H. Martyn; Roe Lockwood, the husband of Julia Lockwood, the treasurer; the Reverend Duncan Dunbar, the father of Jane Anna Dunbar, a manager; S. W. Benedict, the publishing agent of the American Anti-Slavery Society and the husband of Mary F. Benedict, a member of the LNYCASS board of managers; the Reverend La Roy Sunderland, the husband of Mehitable Sunderland, a Methodist woman who played an active role in the 1837 Anti-Slavery Convention of American Women. See Bertram Wyatt-Brown, *Lewis Tappan and the Evangelical War against Slavery* (Cleveland, 1969), pp. 185–97; *Emancipator,* May 23, 1839, p. 1. Lewis Tappan to Theodore Weld, May 26, 1840, quoted in Melder, "The Beginning of the Women's Rights Movement," p. 350.

41. Abby Hopper Gibbons, a Quaker woman, remained with the American Anti-Slavery Society in an auxiliary, the Manhattan Anti-Slavery Society, which was composed almost entirely of black women. In 1841, in a letter to Anne and Deborah Weston, she reported, "Here I am, the only *white* female member of the Manhattan Anti-Slavery Society and the *colour* inefficient" (Sarah H. Emerson, ed., *Life of Abby Hopper Gibbons, Told Chiefly through Her Correspondence,* 2 vols. [New York, 1897], 1:99 [emphasis in original]).

We might conclude that the New York City women's dedication to evangelism and their use of Scripture to legitimize their antislavery beliefs prevented them from transcending the biblical view of women's secondary status. But this is too simple. After all, even the most religiously orthodox abolitionists had learned to use the Bible selectively, ignoring those passages that seemed to justify slavery. Although the Bible might have reinforced the conservative view of woman's sphere, it cannot fully explain why the New York City women did not adopt a reading more in their own interests. The question is complex, but I believe the answer lies in the evangelical movement's high esteem for women as dispensers of morality, salvation, and benevolence and the evangelical woman's own identification with the needs of her men and her class. Trained for benevolence and giving, she could not justify "selfish" demands on her own behalf—especially since these demands threatened the deferential order of the whole society and could undermine her own and her children's privileged economic and social position. The New York City women, working for morality rather than equality, neither heard nor understood the Boston women's argument for natural rights. Furthermore, the New York City women had no tradition of resistance to illegitimate authority, which was part of the Quaker women's heritage, so they had no precedent for resisting their own husbands and fathers, who were the vociferous forces in the fight against women's equality.

We must remember that the antislavery women of New York City still surpassed most of their sisters in the churches and in their city in political understanding and commitment to action outside the domestic sphere. Their conservative ideological and tactical inclination, shared by most contemporary women, probably helped to create a climate favorable to antislavery in the city and made New York one of the first states to put abolition on the ballot.

{ 3 }

The Boston Female Anti-Slavery Society and the Limits of Gender Politics

Debra Gold Hansen

"It was on the whole the bloodiest battle we have fought yet!" reported Anne Warren Weston of the Boston Female Anti-Slavery Society meeting held in July 1839.[1] At this quarterly gathering, the city's women abolitionists, debating how to allocate their funds, had found that they were hopelessly divided. In meeting after meeting throughout the winter of 1839–1840, shouts of "I doubt the vote" interrupted attempts to transact official business. Weston's faction, headed by her sister Maria Weston Chapman, accused the current women officers of miscounting votes to ensure victory for their positions. In return, the Ball sisters, Martha and Lucy, claimed that the Weston contingent so disrupted the balloting that an accurate count was impossible. In April 1840, with the society still deadlocked over its election of officers for the current year, nominal vice-president Catherine Sullivan moved that upon adjournment the society be dissolved. Though this vote, too, was contested, a majority of the members left the hall, and the Boston Female Anti-Slavery Society disbanded.

Within seven short years, BFASS had risen to national prominence, only to dissolve amid confusion, acrimony, and a bitterness that lasted for decades. Yet during its brief history, the women's group had compiled an impressive list of accomplishments. It orchestrated three national women's conventions, organized a multistate petition campaign, sued southerners

I thank Jean Fagan Yellin for her discerning criticism and painstaking editing on earlier drafts of this essay.

1. Anne Warren Weston to Deborah Weston, July 11, 1839, Antislavery Collection, Boston Public Library (hereafter cited as BPL).

who brought slaves into Boston, and sponsored elaborate, profitable fund-raisers that kept male abolition organizations solvent. Ironically, when the society divided in the spring of 1840, it appeared to be at the height of power, preparing to host the fourth national Anti-Slavery Convention of American Women.

The apparent strength of BFASS was deceptive, built on shared myths of heroism and self-sacrifice rather than on common principles or an articulated political program. The Boston Female Anti-Slavery Society was actually a loose coalition of three groups: white, upper-class Unitarians and Quakers; white, middle-class Congregationalists and Baptists; and elite African Americans drawn from local black Baptist and Methodist churches. As a result of its social, religious, and racial diversity, the organization's public image and plan of action never wholly satisfied the entire membership. Upper-class women found their middle-class colleagues too restrictive and cautious in developing antislavery policy, whereas middle-class abolitionists deplored the aggressive public style adopted by the elite among them. The African Americans, meanwhile, were more interested in developing programs that provided direct assistance to the black community than in debating the policy issues that consumed their white associates. By 1839, BFASS had coalesced into two hostile camps, each determined to win control of the women's abolition movement in New England.

The disagreements within BFASS over the appropriate public role for women mirrored the discord in many female reform and benevolent groups of that time. Moreover, the character and consequences of the society's division, though often overlooked, shaped women's political action in the early nineteenth century.[2] Drawing on the history of BFASS, in this essay I explore the difficulties inherent in creating a political movement that is based on gender alone.

The Boston Female Anti-Slavery Society was formed in October 1833 by a small group of black and white Baptist and Congregational women who were "anxious to wash away the guilt of Slavery from their *consciences,* and

2. Several recent studies have focused on the differences between early nineteenth-century women's groups and have been useful in the conceptualization of this paper. See Anne M. Boylan, "Women in Groups: An Analysis of Women's Benevolent Organizations in New York and Boston, 1797–1840," *Journal of American History* 71 (December 1984): 497–523; Nancy A. Hewitt, *Women's Activism and Social Change: Rochester, New York, 1822–1872* (Ithaca, 1984); and Lori D. Ginzberg, *Women and the Work of Benevolence: Morality, Politics, and Class in the Nineteenth-Century United States* (New Haven, 1990). Mary P. Ryan's *Cradle of the Middle Class: The Family in Oneida County, New York, 1790–1865* (New York, 1981) and Paul Johnson's *A Shopkeeper's Millennium: Society and Revivals in Rochester, New York, 1815–1837* (New York, 1978) also strongly influenced this study.

if possible, from the *world*."[3] In organization and style, the women's abolition group typified church-sponsored female societies in antebellum New England. As was the custom, a minister's wife, Charlotte Phelps, served as the society's first president, though the Reverend Amos Phelps probably directed the women in writing a constitution, conducting meetings, soliciting members, and initiating correspondence with other female antislavery societies.[4] During the organization's first year, its members attended lectures, invited clergymen to address their meetings, and sewed goods to raise money for the needy. In early 1834, several members established a primary school for black girls, and others helped organize the Samaritan Asylum, a home for indigent and orphaned African American children.[5] Although the society's first annual report states that these latter projects were undertaken by private individuals, in subsequent years the organization allocated funds for their continued maintenance.[6]

However modest in origin and intent, BFASS was extraordinary in one respect: the organization was integrated from its inception and condemned other societies that exhibited "sinful" and "wicked prejudices" by excluding blacks from their membership.[7] During most of the 1830s at least one African American was included among the officers, and BFASS chose two blacks as official delegates to the first women's antislavery convention held in 1837. In addition, the African American school employed not only white teachers but also a black teacher, Julia Williams, and Eunice Davis, a black Baptist from Andover, was listed as a manager of the society's Samaritan Asylum. Susan Paul joined white women at various fund-raisers, and she and several other African Americans (whom I have been unable to identify) occasionally attended parties at white abolitionists' homes.

Paul was undoubtedly the most prominent African American woman in BFASS. Daughter of Thomas Paul, founder and first pastor of the African

---

3. *Liberator,* January 3, 1835. See also Boston Female Anti-Slavery Society, *Constitution,* April 1834, BPL.

4. See, for example, Amos Phelps to Charlotte Phelps, May 6, 1834, BPL, and Charlotte Phelps to Amos Phelps, August 29, 1835, BPL. Charlotte's association with the society was limited; she died in August 1835.

5. For more on the origins and operation of the Samaritan Asylum, see Nancy Prince, *A Narrative of the Life and Travels of Mrs. Nancy Prince* (Boston, 1850), pp. 35–36.

6. *Liberator,* January 3, 1835.

7. Anne Warren Weston to Debora Weston, October 22, 1836, BPL. Working and traveling with blacks enabled the whites to experience segregation firsthand. For interesting accounts of white and black abolitionists' journeys to the women's conventions, see William Lloyd Garrison to Helen Garrison, May 6, 1837, in Louis Ruchames et al., eds., *The Letters of William Lloyd Garrison,* 6 vols. (Cambridge, 1971–81), 2:260–62, and "Scene on Board of a Steam-Boat," in the *Liberator,* May 24, 1839.

Baptist Church, Boston's oldest and most influential black church, Susan Paul was herself a leader in the African American community, participating in benevolent and cultural organizations as well as in the antislavery movement. Tragically, in 1841 she died of consumption at the age of thirty-two, and few records remain of her life and thought. In an 1834 letter to the *Liberator*, however, Paul reflected on the "cruel prejudice" against her people "which deprives us of every privilege whereby we might elevate ourselves—and then absurdly condemns us because we are not more refined and intelligent."[8]

Of the white members, Lydia Maria Child was arguably the most prominent during the society's formative period. In 1833 the well-known novelist and author of women's and children's books had moved beyond these customary, hence acceptable, female literary pursuits to publish *An Appeal in Favor of That Class of Americans Called Africans*. This polemic quickly became an antislavery classic,[9] and in recognition of Child's contribution to the cause, BFASS president Charlotte Phelps encouraged her to join their association. Child hesitated at first, feeling, as she later explained, that female-only organizations were like "half a pair of scissors." But she soon reconsidered and with her close friend Louisa Loring, another upper-class intellectual, she joined BFASS.[10]

Not satisfied with the modest sewing-circle approach to social activism, Child and Loring launched a more aggressive program of promotion and fund-raising. In December 1834, the pair organized an antislavery fair at

8. Susan Paul to the Editor of the *Liberator*, April 1, 1834, BPL. For more information on Susan Paul, see *Liberator*, February 22, 1834 and April 23, 1841. See also J. Marcus Mitchell, "The Paul Family," *Old Time New England* 63 (Winter 1973): 73–77. African Americans in antebellum Boston also have received some scholarly attention. See Donald M. Jacobs, ed., *Courage and Conscience: Black and White Abolitionists in Boston* (Bloomington, 1993); James Horton and Lois Horton, *Black Bostonians: Family Life and Community Struggle in the Antebellum North* (New York, 1979); James O. Horton, "Generations of Protest: Black Families and Social Reform in Ante-Bellum Boston," *New England Quarterly* 49 (June 1976): 242–56; Lois Horton, "Community Organization and Social Activism: Black Boston and the Antislavery Movement," *Sociological Inquiry* 55 (Spring 1985): 182–99; George Levesque, "Black Boston: Negro Life in Garrison's Boston, 1800–1860" (Ph.D. diss., State University of New York, Binghamton, 1976); and John Radford, "Blacks in Boston," *Journal of Interdisciplinary History* 12 (Spring 1982): 677–84.

9. Lydia Maria Child, *An Appeal in Favor of That Class of Americans Called Africans* (Boston, 1833; New York, 1836). For criticism of Child's literary work, see Carolyn Karcher, ed., *Hobomok and Other Writings on Indians by Lydia Maria Child* (New Brunswick, N.J., 1986) and William S. Osborne, *Lydia Maria Child* (Boston, 1980).

10. Lydia Maria Child to Charlotte Phelps, January 2, 1834, BPL; Lydia Maria Child to Lucretia Mott, March 5, 1839, in Milton Meltzer and Patricia G. Holland, eds., *Lydia Maria Child: Selected Letters, 1817–1880* (Amherst, Mass., 1982), p. 106.

which the Boston women sold food and goods donated by local abolitionists. This sale proved so successful, both in profits and public relations, that it became an annual event. Scheduled during the Christmas season, the fair eventually offered desirable English and European wares that attracted buyers from the city's wealthiest circles, making it, to quote Harriet Beecher Stowe, "decidedly the most fashionable shopping resort of the holidays." Although antebellum women's charities often used this type of "vanity fair" to raise money, BFASS's sale was extraordinarily profitable and earned thousands of dollars for reform treasuries over the next two decades.[11]

Although documentation is sketchy, Loring and Child probably attracted other socially conscious elite Bostonians into the society, for following the fair, the names of many prominent white Unitarian and Quaker women appeared beside those of the Congregationalists and Baptists comprising the original membership. These new members set BFASS on a course that carried them far beyond the customary activities of Christian female benevolent societies. For instance, the society vigorously supported the 1835 lecture tour of British abolitionist George Thompson, whose controversial speeches were creating a stir throughout the North. Despite widespread public animosity toward Thompson, society members faithfully attended his lectures, cheering and clapping as loudly as their male colleagues. On one occasion several of Boston's women abolitionists were credited with rescuing him from an anticipated assault.[12]

Though ridiculed by the press as "petticoat politicians," BFASS also planned for Thompson to address their annual meeting on October 21, 1835. The women anticipated some form of antiabolition demonstration that day, in light of past violence directed against the Englishman. Indeed, Maria Weston Chapman wrote to a friend, "At the time you are holding your meeting at Braintree *we* shall be in session at Boston, and we are prepared to say that in the strength of God our duty *shall be done,* let the events of the day be what they may."[13] Chapman was not alone in her prediction, for no property owner in the city would rent the society a hall for its meeting.

11. *Report of the Twenty-first National Anti-Slavery Bazaar* (Boston, 1855), p. 32. For useful discussions of abolition fairs, see Ronald Walters, *The Antislavery Appeal: American Abolitionism after 1830* (New York, 1984), pp. 23–24, and Benjamin Quarles, "Sources of Abolitionist Income," *Mississippi Valley Historical Review* 32 (June 1945): 63–76. See Chapter 13 of this volume, Lee Chambers-Schiller, " 'A Good Work among the People': The Political Culture of the Boston Antislavery Fair."

12. For more information on George Thompson's lecture tour, see C. Duncan Rice, "The Anti-Slavery Mission of George Thompson to the United States, 1834–1835," *Journal of American Studies* 2 (April 1968): 13–31.

13. Maria Weston Chapman to unidentified correspondent, n.d., MS. A.9.2.4, p. 90, BPL.

On the afternoon of October 21, a crowd of angry, abusive white men gathered in the street outside the Massachusetts Anti-Slavery Society offices where the women were assembling. As the men grew more menacing, Boston's mayor, Theodore Lyman, arrived to disperse the mob and cancel the meeting. The women, however, refused to leave, insisting, as Maria Weston Chapman proclaimed, "If this is the last bulwark of freedom, we may as well die here, as any where."[14] The mayor finally persuaded them to abandon the building, which they did, reconvening at Chapman's West Street home.[15]

The mobbing of BFASS and the subsequent attack on William Lloyd Garrison, who had been in the antislavery offices, catapulted the society into the forefront of the abolition movement. Stories of the "Garrison Mob," or the "Mob of Gentlemen of Property and Standing," occupied local and reform newspapers for several weeks, and abolitionists admiringly recounted the courageous stand taken by the Boston women during the siege.[16] Building upon this reputation, some of the more ambitious members initiated new projects that increasingly brought them into the male preserve of law and politics. For example, Maria Weston Chapman, her sisters, Ann Phillips, and the women of the Southwick and Sargent families appeared at state legislative sessions, court hearings, and other political meetings to demonstrate their support for various antislavery measures. "Women at that time were not in the habit of attending political gatherings of any kind," Sarah Southwick recalled, but after these individuals broke the barrier, "anti-slavery women, certainly, always went when they wanted to."[17]

During 1836, the women's organization also initiated several lawsuits, hiring influential local lawyers to plead their cases. The most important suit involved a young slave girl brought to Boston by southerners summering in the North. The society's lawyers—including the husbands of members Louisa Loring and Louisa Sewell—successfully argued before the Massa-

14. *Right and Wrong in Boston: Report of the Boston Female Anti-Slavery Society . . . 1835* (Boston, 1836), p. 34.

15. Ibid., pp. 34–36. Two excellent histories of the mob attack are Leonard Richards, *"Gentlemen of Property and Standing": Anti-Abolition Mobs in Jacksonian America* (New York, 1970) and Theodore M. Hammett, "Two Mobs of Jacksonian Boston: Ideology and Interest," *Journal of American History* 62 (March 1976): 845–68. Margaret Munsterberg, in "The Weston Sisters and the 'Boston Mob,'" *Boston Public Library Quarterly* 9 (October 1958): 183–94, provides a useful selection of letters written by the Westons describing the events leading to the attack on their society.

16. The society's second annual report reprints a number of newspaper articles and letters concerning the mob attack on the meeting. See *Right and Wrong in Boston . . . 1835*, pp. 55–71.

17. Sarah Southwick, in *Old Anti-Slavery Days . . .* (Danvers, Mass., 1893), p. 137.

chusetts Supreme Court that since slavery was unconstitutional in Massachusetts, any slave, upon entering the state, was automatically free. "The Boston Female Anti-Slavery Society may be excused for their rejoicing at this event," wrote Henrietta Sargent to lawyer Ellis Gray Loring in a letter indicating that the organization would assume all legal expenses for the trial.[18] The society was justifiably proud, for their landmark case established not only that Bostonians could reject slavery within their environs but also that women could use the American court system to pursue political goals.

The Boston Female Anti-Slavery Society became further involved in governmental affairs in 1836 by coordinating a multistate petition campaign among female abolition societies in New England. Through careful organization and the skillful use of family connections and female reform networks, the society ran a singularly successful campaign. In fact, during the first year of petitioning, New England women collected nearly twice as many signatures as their male counterparts, and in Boston the women's society sent more names to Congress than the combined states of Maine, Rhode Island, and Connecticut.[19] Although the campaign had little legislative impact (Congress routinely tabled antislavery petitions), its effectiveness in rallying women against slavery further established the Boston society as a leader of the female abolition movement. As a result, rural women's groups increasingly viewed themselves as auxiliary to BFASS as well as to the male New England Anti-Slavery Society.[20]

Now among the most powerful women's groups within the northern reform community, BFASS was instrumental in organizing the first Anti-Slavery Convention of American Women, held in New York City during the spring of 1837. At least ten society members attended the conference, and Lydia Maria Child was vocal during the sessions. In addition, the delegates honored BFASS by electing its president, Mary Parker, to preside over the meetings. "The same voice which for a moment allayed the fury of a

---

18. *Right and Wrong in Boston in 1836: Annual Report of the Boston Female Anti-Slavery Society* (Boston, 1836), p. 69. The society also played a significant role in *Commonwealth v. Eldridge,* an 1836 case involving the detention of two black women as runaway slaves. For information about this case, see Leonard W. Levy, "The 'Abolition Riot': Boston's First Slave Rescue," *New England Quarterly* 25 (March 1952): 85–92.

19. New England males collected 16,989 signatures; New England females gathered 31,435. For this statistical report, see *Liberator,* April 28, 1837.

20. See, for example, donations to BFASS by unofficial female auxiliaries listed in the *Liberator,* December 22, 1837 and March 9, 1838. For more on antislavery petitioning, see Deborah Bingham Van Broekhoven, " 'Let Your Names Be Enrolled': Method and Ideology In Women's Antislavery Petitioning," Chapter 10 in this volume.

portion of the Boston mob," reflected one conferee, "threw a sanctity over this consecrated assembly."[21]

During the planning and execution of the first women's antislavery convention, the Boston women forged a fateful relationship with Sarah and Angelina Grimké, and soon thereafter the Grimkés embarked upon a lecture tour of Massachusetts. As firsthand witnesses to slavery in the South, the sisters attracted large crowds wherever they spoke, and soon men as well as women were attending their lectures. In Lynn, over one thousand persons attended the sisters' meetings, in Lowell fifteen hundred heard their lecture and in Salem their three talks attracted an estimated twenty-four hundred listeners. In Amesbury, Angelina's argument with two men over the biblical sanctioning of slavery was promoted as the first public debate between the sexes.[22]

Despite popular interest in the sisters' lectures, the Grimkés' public appearances drew increasingly negative comment from the local press and pulpit. To counter the criticism, the women published a series of public letters: Angelina's *Letters to Catharine Beecher* and Sarah's *Letters on the Equality of the Sexes*. These two now-historic sets of essays explicated the Grimkés' opinions of women's roles in political movements and laid the groundwork for a fledgling woman's movement. As Sarah passionately argued, God created women and men in his own image. "Dominion was given to both over every other creature, but not over each other." All women asked from men, she furthered, is that they "take their feet from off our necks, and permit us to stand upright on that ground which God designed us to occupy."[23]

As the Grimkés pursued their pathbreaking work in Massachusetts, they were "truly refreshed" by their association with the state's abolitionists. "There is some elasticity in this atmosphere," Sarah explained to Theodore Weld. "I feel as if I was helped, strengthened, invigorated." The Boston Female Anti-Slavery Society enthusiastically promoted the Grimkés' lecture tour and urged members of other female abolition societies to attend the lectures both to show support for the antislavery movement and to demonstrate women's right to voice their opinions on social issues. Ignoring

21. *Liberator,* June 2, 1837.

22. For more on the Grimkés' lecture tour, see Gerda Lerner, *The Grimké Sisters from South Carolina: Rebels against Slavery* (Boston, 1967) and Keith Melder, "Forerunners of Freedom: The Grimké Sisters in Massachusetts, 1837–38," *Essex Institute Historical Collections* 103, 3 (1967): 223–49.

23. Sarah Grimké, *Letters on the Equality of the Sexes and Other Essays* (1838; rept. New Haven, 1988), pp. 32, 35. For the significance of these essays, see Elizabeth Ann Bartlett's introduction to the above edition, Melder, "Forerunners of Freedom," and Jean Fagan Yellin, *Women and Sisters: The Antislavery Feminists in American Culture* (New Haven, 1989), pp. 38–40.

the widespread criticism of the sisters' public speaking, BFASS also sponsored a series of lectures by them and rented Boston's largest hall to accommodate the anticipated audiences. Even after the Massachusetts Association of Congregational Ministers issued a pastoral letter denouncing the Grimkés' behavior as "a scandalous offense against propriety and decency," Angelina reported that "Mary Parker sent us word that the Boston women would stand by us if *every* body else forsook us." And, indeed, Sarah's *Letters on the Equality of the Sexes* was addressed to Mary Parker, the president of BFASS.[24]

As a result of the controversies raised by the Grimkés' speeches and essays, many Boston women began to embrace feminist ideas as well. "I had a long talk with the brethren on the rights of women," Angelina wrote to a friend, "and found a very general sentiment prevailing that it is time our fetters were broken. L. M. Child and Maria Chapman strongly supported this view; indeed very many seem to think a new order of things is very desirable in this respect."[25] Accordingly, Chapman introduced feminist statements in her own antislavery writings. "Scripture has generally been presented to woman through a distorted medium," she wrote in the 1837 BFASS annual report. "She is fettered in body and in mind by commentators and translators and partial reasoners, but by revelation never. What is the sphere and duty of woman, it rests with each one for herself to determine."[26]

Although Maria Weston Chapman, Lydia Maria Child, and other prominent BFASS members were receptive to the Grimkés' feminist ideas, many New England abolitionists, both male and female, hesitated to attach women's rights and other controversial reforms, particularly nonresistance, to the antislavery cause.[27] In an "Appeal of Clerical Abolitionists on Anti-

---

24. *Liberator*, August 11, 1837; Sarah Grimké to Theodore Weld, June 11, 1837; Angelina Grimké to Theodore Weld, August 12, 1837, in Gilbert H. Barnes and Dwight L. Dumond, eds., *Letters of Theodore Dwight Weld, Angelina Grimké Weld, and Sarah Grimké, 1822–1844*, 2 vols. (New York, 1934), pp. 401, 419.

25. Quoted in Alma Lutz, *Crusade for Freedom: Women of the Antislavery Movement* (Boston, 1968), pp. 105–6.

26. *Right and Wrong in Boston. Annual Report of the Boston Female Anti-Slavery Society . . . 1837* (Boston, 1837), p. 75.

27. Nonresistance was a form of Christian anarchism which repudiated all forms of domination. Because governments were based upon coercive laws and policing agencies, nonresistants disavowed any allegiance to the state and refused to participate in political elections. See Lewis Perry, *Radical Abolitionism: Anarchy and the Government of God in Antislavery Thought* (Ithaca, 1973) and Ronald Walters, *American Reformers, 1815–1860* (New York, 1978). See Chapter 14 of this volume, Margaret Hope Bacon, "By Moral Force Alone: The Antislavery Women and Nonresistance."

Slavery Measures" and other public statements, several locally prominent ministers expressed the concern that their more radical colleagues sought by "overthrowing slavery to overthrow government, civil and domestic, the Sabbath and the church and ministry."[28]

This clerical appeal precipitated a major rift in the American antislavery movement, as abolitionist ministers and their supporters tried to oust William Lloyd Garrison and his supporters from power. Much of the controversy centered upon the "woman question," that is, the role women were to play within organized abolition. The Garrisonians urged that women be accepted as equals into male abolition societies. The clericals, led by Amos Phelps, Charles Fitch, Nathaniel Colver, and other minister-husbands of BFASS members, believed that attempts at sexual integration distracted abolitionists from the original aims of the movement. After both the Massachusetts Anti-Slavery Society and the New England Anti-Slavery Society voted to admit women as full members, Phelps and other church-based abolitionists officially broke with these organizations and, in May 1839, created the Massachusetts Abolition Society.[29]

The division among male abolitionists was extremely disruptive to BFASS. Originally organized by Phelps, who in 1836 served as the society's paid agent,[30] the women's group retained strong connections to local Congregational and Baptist churches. In 1835 many members of BFASS helped found the First Free Congregational Church; they saw Phelps installed as pastor there in July 1839. Many women in the society enjoyed close relationships with the Reverend Nathaniel Colver and other Baptist ministers who joined Phelps in establishing the Massachusetts Abolition Society. As a result of these strong denominational ties, a majority of the officers and membership of BFASS sought to align the society with the clerics in what was becoming known among abolitionists as the "Boston controversy."

By late 1837, Maria Weston Chapman was one of the few Garrison supporters still on the board. As a feminist and a disaffected Unitarian, she shared Garrison's contempt for the "spiritual domination of the Boston

28. *Liberator,* September 1, 1837.

29. For more discussion of the divisions among New England abolitionists, see Lawrence Friedman, *Gregarious Saints: Self and Community in American Abolitionism, 1830–1870* (New York, 1982) and Russel B. Nye, *William Lloyd Garrison and the Humanitarian Reformers* (Boston, 1955).

30. The Boston Female Anti-Slavery Society initially funded agents for the Massachusetts Anti-Slavery Society, though it kept the source of the funding hidden so that Phelps and others would be "more favourably received." See *Right and Wrong in Boston . . . 1837,* pp. 25–26.

ministry."[31] Indeed, when President Mary Parker quoted Chapman's minister, William Ellery Channing, to make a point, Chapman retorted, "You know I never consider Dr. Channing as authority."[32] As I noted earlier, Chapman, as corresponding secretary, was responsible for writing the society's annual reports. In her account of the events of 1837, she set forth her opinion of the pastoral letter and the clerical appeal. "We find that at almost every step we have taken towards the slave, our progress has been impeded by the same obstacle. As church members, we have been hindered by the ministry:—as women, we are hindered by the ministry:—as abolitionists, still comes a 'clerical abolitionist', to prevent, as far as in him lies, the vigorous prosecution of our efforts."[33]

In a series of meetings BFASS officers, particularly those associated with the ministers Phelps and Colver, voiced concern over Chapman's frankly anticlerical passages and insisted that such statements had no place in an antislavery document. "This course is *uncalled* for with regard to the affairs of the Church & will not be expected from us," President Parker complained. Vice-President Catherine Sullivan agreed that it did not come "within our limits to discuss the affairs of the Free Church—We were an anti-slavery society." Nevertheless, Chapman refused to alter her report. "In a case of this kind," she insisted, "the opinions of any society are as immaterial to me as the wind that blows." In the end Chapman published her 1837 BFASS annual report as originally written. "I shall never submit to any custom of any society that interferes with my righteous freedom" she steadfastly maintained.[34] The society's officers, however, appended a disclaimer to the title page: "While we give our cordial approbation to many of the sentiments of this Report—the love of freedom and justice constrain us to state that to some portions of it we cherish the most serious objections."[35] Chapman's immediate response was to resign as corresponding secretary.

For the next two years, anticlerical and proclerical blocs within BFASS struggled for control. The proclerical officers hoped to thwart the independent actions of the Chapman faction and to align the organization with the Massachusetts Abolition Society. They therefore refused to call the special meetings the anticlerical members requested and failed to recognize them at regularly scheduled sessions. According to Chapman's supporters, the

31. Boston Female Anti-Slavery Society, "Reports. A.S. Meetings," 1837, p. 14, BPL.
32. Ibid., p. 11.
33. *Right and Wrong in Boston . . . 1837,* pp. 71–72. For Chapman's full account of the events of 1837, see *Right and Wrong in Massachusetts* (Boston, 1839).
34. Quotations taken from BFASS, "Reports. A.S. Meetings," 1837, pp. 3, 7, 9, 11, BPL.
35. *Right and Wrong in Boston . . . 1837,* n.p.

officers also packed important meetings with women from local Baptist and Congregational churches and intentionally miscounted votes to pass their own motions. The Chapman faction responded to the officers' strategies by pursuing their antislavery agenda independent of the society. Thus, Chapman and her sisters, their cousin Ann Phillips, Lydia Maria Child, Thankful Southwick, and other longtime members petitioned, lectured, attended meetings, and even hosted a fair, either as private individuals or, after 1839, as the "women of the Massachusetts Anti-Slavery Society." Chapman's supporters also contacted other women's antislavery groups and urged them to protest the board's anti-Garrison stance by disassociating their organizations from current BFASS projects.

As part of this competition between proclerical and anticlerical wings, white society members struggled to secure the support of African American women in the organization. In fact, the whites deemed black support so significant that in one disputed election officer Lucy Ball was accused of miscounting seven of the twenty-two pro-Chapman African American votes and recording them in favor of the proclerical board. During other crucial debates, whites carefully monitored the positions taken by blacks. For example, Anne Weston was pleased when board member Eunice Davis "spoke up like a woman on behalf of the coloured folks in defense of the Liberator," especially since she had thought Davis "a coloured peeler"— that is, a supporter of the clerical clique. Weston also reported that Julia Williams "was the only person that voted with the peelers among the colored folks" and elsewhere suggested that Williams's affiliation with the clerics resulted in the closure of her school, since, according to Weston, Boston's African American community refused to patronize institutions sponsored by Garrison's opponents.[36]

The society's officers also sought African American support for their positions. For example, treasurer Lucy Ball publicly charged that one of the more prominent Chapmanites had initially fought the admission of blacks into the society "because it would make the anti-slavery cause unpopular," and added that she "hoped the colored friends would notice this."[37] On

36. These quotations and accusations were taken from Maria Weston Chapman, "Names on Miss L. M. Ball's List," 1839, BPL; Anne Weston to Aunt Mary, January 13, 1839, BPL; Anne Weston to Deborah Weston April 8, 1839, BPL; and Anne Weston to Deborah Weston, December 15, 1839, BPL.

37. Lucy Ball's accusations are contained in a *Liberator* report of the society's meeting, November 1, 1839, and were directed at Lydia Maria Child. There is some question as to the race of Lucy Ball and her sister Martha, and I would like to thank Jean Fagan Yellin and Dorothy Sterling for bringing this to my attention. A Fall River delegate to the 1838 women's antislavery convention described Martha Ball as "slightly colored," giving rise to the reasonable as-

another occasion, Ball's faction claimed that their fair to raise funds for the Samaritan Asylum "was largely patronized by our colored friends" since blacks felt "a deep interest in the welfare of this Infant institution."[38] Not to be outdone, Chapman reported the next year that the city's black abolitionists had turned out in support of her fair. "Beautiful it was," she wrote, "to see the white man forget his narrow and miserable prejudices and the colored man his wrongs, while their long silenced voices gathered around the same festive board in social and spiritual communion."[39]

The intense lobbying of African Americans by white BFASS leaders is understandable, for the black women in the organization enjoyed prominence

---

sumption that the Balls were African American. Official documents, however, uniformly indicate that the Balls were white. For example, while their father Joseph Ball was born in Jamaica, West Indies (which lends credence to the surmise that the Ball family was black), he was identified as white in the 1830 federal census. The sisters were also listed as white residents in the 1835 Boston city directory and again in the 1840 U.S. Census, and no biographical or obituary sketch on either of them mentions their race. The Massachusetts death certificates of the Ball sisters indicate that they were white as well. In addition, a *Liberator* advertisement that describes a school that may have been run by the Balls noted that it would "be conducted by two white young ladies, well qualified for the station" (April 26, 1834). Finally, I have not found any reference to the Balls' race in any of the correspondence or writings of their friends and colleagues. Though definitive proof is still lacking, I am convinced that although the Balls were very involved with the black community, they represented the white Baptist contingent in the women's organization. See Emma Willard and Mary Livermore, eds., *Woman of the Century* (New York, 1893), p. 50, for a biographical sketch on Martha. Obituaries for Lucy ran in the Boston *Transcript*, April 20, 1891 and the *Home Guardian* 53 (June 1891): 279–81. For material suggesting that the sisters were black, see *Report of a Delegate to the Anti-Slavery Convention of American Women, Held in Philadelphia, May 1838* . . . (Boston, 1838), p. 6; Dorothy Sterling, ed., *We Are Your Sisters: Black Women in the Nineteenth Century* (New York, 1984), pp. 114–15; and Shirley J. Yee, *Black Women Abolitionists: A Study in Activism, 1828–1860* (Knoxville, 1992), pp. 102–3.

38. *Liberator,* June 21, 1839.

39. Ibid., January 1, 1841. It appears that BFASS never successfully integrated, despite the efforts of some of its more advanced members. African American women signed the rolls, attended the meetings, and voted in elections, but they continued to sit in sections of the meeting halls reserved for blacks only. James and Lois Horton provide an account of an incident at an 1841 BFASS meeting during which an African American member, Charlotte Coleman, sat in the "white" section of the hall. Later she was chastised by white member Elisha Blanchard who reminded Coleman that "colored people were very well in their place" (*Black Bostonians,* p. 94). Susan Paul did assist at the fairs, but few other African Americans seemed to have followed her example. In fact, after Paul had been selected as a delegate to the 1837 women's antislavery convention, Anne Weston noted that although Paul had been chosen "because she was a favourable specimen of the coloured race," other African Americans did not consider her "as one of themselves" (Anne Warren Weston to Debora Weston, April 18, 1837). Although Paul was a leader in the black community, she apparently was not considered representative of it. This issue of racial integration within BFASS and other societies begs further study.

and economic standing in their own community. In fact, of the twenty-seven identifiable African Americans in the society, three were related to ministers and three to barbers, and others were married to waiters, tailors, blacksmiths, and boardinghouse operators. These were among the elite occupations available to blacks in antebellum Boston, where most African Americans worked as chimney sweeps, domestics, and day laborers.[40]

Until the controversies in BFASS arose, most black members were not particularly active in the organization and very few took a leading or policy-making role. Indeed, while black women cooperated with the white-controlled society, they were more intimately involved in their own ethnic organizations—such as the Colored Temperance Society, the Ladies of the Zion Church, and the African Baptist Church Singing Society—through which they provided direct assistance to Boston's black community. Because of their different priorities and concerns, most African Americans apparently remained neutral during the white women's debates that, to them, may have seemed irrelevant to their own work for racial freedom and equality. If they played a role in the society's division, it was as mediator rather than combatant, though they made themselves heard when they felt strongly about an issue. Thus even at the organization's final meeting, Mrs. J. C. Beman, wife of a prominent black minister, continued to appeal for solidarity: "The cause of my enslaved people is the cause of God," she declared, "and I hope this great and good body will be united in its advancement."[41]

Despite black members' efforts at reconciliation, BFASS had ceased to function as an organization by the fall of 1839 and was divided into two

40. I have identified the following African American women as members of BFASS in the 1830s: Arianna Adams, C. Barbadoes, Mrs. Jehiel C. Beman, Alice Burley, Alice Bush, Hannah Cutler, Eunice Davis, Bathsheba Fowler, Lydia Gould, Lavinia Hilton, Cecilia Howard, Anna Lawton, Eliza Logan Lawton, Chloe Lee, Mary Lewis (?), Anna Logan, Lavinia Nell, Louisa Nell, Susan Paul, Martha Ann Pero, Nancy Prince, Jane Putnam, Philis Salem, Adeline Saunders, Margaret Scarlett, Caroline Williams, and Julia Williams. In addition to information obtained in the secondary literature, the race of these women was established through a variety of official sources including the 1830 and 1840 federal censuses, Boston city directories (which in the 1830s distinguished between black and white residents), and church membership listings. The *Liberator* is a goldmine of information about the personal characteristics and activities of black and white abolitionists, and I am grateful to the family of the late Marilyn Baily for the use of the name index to that newspaper which she painstakingly compiled.

41. *Liberator,* "Extra" [April 1840]. For more on black women's benevolent organizations, see Anne Firor Scott, "Most Invisible of All: Black Women's Voluntary Associations," *Journal of Southern History* 56 (February 1990): 3–22; James Oliver Horton, "Freedom's Yoke: Gender Conventions among Antebellum Free Blacks," *Feminist Studies* 12 (Spring 1986): 51–76; and Yee, *Black Women Abolitionists.*

distinct factions with different priorities, allegiances, and activities. Once the society officially disbanded in April 1840, its members quickly regrouped. The proclerical forces organized the Massachusetts Female Emancipation Society and immediately affiliated themselves with the Reverend Amos Phelps's Massachusetts Abolition Society. Chapman's anticlerical contingent reconstituted BFASS, declaring that its dissolution had been illegal. Pressured into declaring their allegiances, the majority of African Americans demonstrated their support for Garrison and retained their ties to BFASS. Not surprisingly, though, the wives of black ministers, including Mrs. J. C. Beman and Julia Williams (who would marry the Reverend Henry Highland Garnet in 1841), aligned themselves with the Massachusetts Female Emancipation Society, as did several other African American women, including original member C. Barbadoes.[42]

Both BFASS and the Massachusetts Female Emancipation Society were short-lived. Chapman strove to keep BFASS functioning, but after 1840 its primary activity was the annual fair. Though the society continued to exist on paper well into the 1850s, most of its members participated in the Massachusetts and American antislavery societies, and the women's organization became a mere shell of its former self. As for the opposition, the Massachusetts Female Emancipation Society disappeared by the mid-1840s, with many of its former members shifting their attention to other reform and charitable associations, including the New England Female Moral Reform Society, the Seaman's Aid Society, and the First Baptist Sewing Circle. By 1845 Boston's separate female antislavery movement had all but disappeared.

Traditionally, historians have simply noted in passing the existence of women's antislavery organizations; only recently have they begun to document the important contributions women made to the movement. In searching for a feminist political tradition, however, historians have often underplayed the discord within the women's antislavery movement, considering it less significant than the development of a feminist consciousness

42. It seems that the African Americans in favor of the Massachusetts Abolition Society (and its auxiliary, the Massachusetts Female Emancipation Society) were interested in the "New Organization," as abolitionists called it, not simply because it was church based, but because its members were committed to political action. For example, the husbands of Mrs. Jehiel Beman and Julia Williams participated in the Liberty Party. For fine discussions of the role of African Americans in the divisions among abolitionists, see Yee, *Black Women Abolitionists*, pp. 100–104, and James Oliver Horton and Lois E. Horton, "The Affirmation of Manhood: Black Garrisonians in Antebellum Boston," in *Courage and Conscience*, pp. 127–53.

among some of antislavery's more prominent advocates.[43] Shirley Yee has suggested that racism and different abolition goals "prevented full interracial cooperation" and "precluded the possibility of creating a sisterhood between black and white women."[44] I would argue that white women also were divided by significant ideological and cultural barriers that made gender solidarity a temporary phenomenon at best.

As BFASS disintegrated, each faction developed persuasive explanations for the discord. The Chapman bloc attributed the divisions within the society to the controversies between male abolitionists, particularly to the conflict between laymen and ministers over the role of the clergy in the movement. As Caroline Weston recounted, "The clerical appeal had appeared in the summer of 1837 & there was trouble & discontent in the Boston Female Anti-Slavery Society, the members . . . having been tampered with by the disaffected clerical party." Chapman was equally convinced that the women's organization had been "infected with clerical abolition." According to her, "the difficulties in our Boston Female A.S. Society" were the result of the "grossest dishonesty" by the society's officers, who packed meetings with "sister church-members" to control the votes. Lydia Maria Child found the "scenes" during the society's final meetings "painful and disgusting." She, too, was convinced that the officers were "doing the work of [ministers] Phelps and Torrey, while they know it not."[45]

The women favoring the clerical wing of the abolition movement felt, as Martha Ball complained, that the Chapman bloc had "perverted" the original aims of BFASS by attempting "to carry their *peculiar views* along with them *in the Anti-Slavery car*." Because the "Boston F.A.S. Society do not think it right for them, as a body, to adopt the principles and measures of the Non-Resistance Society—to engage in the discussion of the Woman's Rights question, so called, and to encourage the no-human government doctrines," another disgruntled member explained, "a few restless, ambitious spirits have determined on our destruction."[46]

To the Chapman faction, the female supporters of clerical abolitionists were "at once ignorant, servile, tyrannical & fraudulent," women who had

43. See Blanche Glassman Hersh, *The Slavery of Sex: Feminist-Abolitionists in America* (Urbana, Ill., 1978); Ellen Carol DuBois, *Feminism and Suffrage: The Emergence of an Independent Women's Movement in America, 1848–1869* (Ithaca, 1978); and Keith Melder, *Beginnings of Sisterhood: The American Woman's Rights Movement, 1800–1850* (New York, 1977).

44. Yee, *Black Women Abolitionists*, p. 111.

45. For quotations, see Caroline Weston to Samuel Joseph May, October 21, 1871, BPL; Maria Weston Chapman to Elizabeth Pease, April 20, 1840, BPL; Lydia Maria Child to Lydia B. Child, December 12, 1839, in *Lydia Maria Child: Selected Letters*, pp. 125–26.

46. Martha V. Ball to Elizabeth Pease, May 6, 1840, BPL; *Liberator*, November 15, 1839.

paralyzed the society with bureaucratic maneuvering and behind-the-scenes plotting. The society's officers, on the other hand, believed that Chapman and her allies were "shameful and boisterous beyond description," and had repeatedly disrupted society meetings by "hissing, stamping, clapping, shouting, etc., etc., women though they were," finally making continued association impracticable.[47]

In locating the causes of BFASS's demise, its members focused on the ideological differences separating them. A close examination of the organization's socioeconomic composition, however, reveals that the society's division was a class-based phenomenon as well. For example, the white women favoring the proclerical policies of the society's officers frequently came from the city's emerging middle class. Dubbed by Anne Weston as "boarding house abolitionists," most of them were related to small proprietors, clerks, minor city officials, and artisans. In fact, excluding Quakers, all but three of the individuals associated with these occupational categories sided with the proclerical board in 1839 and 1840.[48] The middle-class group also included many of the organization's working women—teachers, boardinghouse operators, social workers, and shopkeepers. Several of the society's officers were working women themselves: Lucy Ball, Martha Ball, and Julia Williams were teachers; Mary Parker and Lydia Fuller ran boardinghouses; and Abigail Ordway was a milliner and agent for the Salem Female Anti-Slavery Society. As I noted earlier, these middle-class women were typically members of local Congregational and Baptist churches. In fact, 85 percent of the Congregationalists and all but two or three of the white Baptists in the organization favored the proclerical position taken by the board. Not surprisingly, nearly all of the ministers' wives (twenty of twenty-three) supported the clerics; indeed, only the wives of the Unitarian and Episcopalian ministers voted for positions espoused by the Chapman faction.[49]

In contrast to the middle-class contingent in BFASS, the white women supporting Maria Weston Chapman represented some of the wealthiest

47. Thankful Southwick, Maria Weston Chapman, and Lydia Maria Child to Sarah Pugh and the Philadelphia Female Anti-Slavery Society, January 14, 1840 [1841], BPL; Massachusetts Abolition Society, *The True History of the Late Division in the Anti-Slavery Societies* (Boston, 1841), p. 40.

48. Though middle class in background and orientation, some of the women in this group became quite prosperous. Judith Shipley's husband, for example, was a successful baker, while Emma Smith, Susan Sears, and Mrs. Rayner were married to early land developers. Mary Gilbert's husband manufactured pianos, and in 1850 the Gilberts were taxed on over $160,000 in assets.

49. Most BFASS members were active in Boston's "free" churches (no pew fees), the First Free Congregational Church and the Baptists' Tremont Temple.

and most socially prestigious families in Boston. At least twenty-five of these "fashionables," as Anne Weston styled them, were connected with Boston's mercantile elite, a group that included Chapman, whose husband owned a prosperous ship chandlery on the exclusive Central Wharf, and women from the May, Shaw, Jackson, and Cabot dynasties. Henrietta and Catherine Sargent, Rebecca Louge, and Hannah Tufts were connected to prominent banking and manufacturing families, and Ann Phillips, Louisa Sewell, and Louisa Loring had married into Boston's legal/political establishment. Unlike the Congregational and Baptist middle class, these elite women were predominantly Unitarian, though several wealthy Quakers, Episcopalians, and Universalists also aligned themselves with this faction.[50]

The elite women understood established forms of politics and power, and as a result, they were the society members who carried out their antislavery projects in the public sphere, adapting male styles of political action to their own ends. Anne Weston, daughter of a prosperous sea captain and Weymouth landowner, organized the society's petitioning, and she depended upon the cooperation of her well-connected family and friends to make the campaign succeed. The upper-class women who helped Weston petition (most notably her sisters, Lydia Maria Child, the Sargents, and the Southwicks) also attended court and legislative sessions and, after 1837, began public lecturing and political organizing themselves. Even the society's fair, which after 1834 was managed by Anne's sister, Maria, became a female version of more ambitious, profitable male fund-raisers. As Chapman explained in 1840, she saw "no reason why this effort [her fair] should not emulate the Mechanics Fair in attraction and productiveness."[51]

Because many of the projects designed by upper-class women were more public than private and were unconventional for females, most middle-class women in the society chose not to participate in them. For example, Congregational and Baptist women in the society remained aloof from Chapman's fair, probably because they were uncomfortable with such an openly

50. Lydia Maria Child, Maria Weston Chapman, and other BFASS Unitarians pressured prominent Unitarian minister William Ellery Channing to commit himself to their antislavery platform. See, for example, Lydia Maria Child to Henrietta Sargent, November 13, 1836, *Lydia Maria Child: Selected Letters*, pp. 56–57, and William Ellery Channing to Lydia Maria Child, March 12, 1842, Antislavery Collection, Cornell University, Olin Library, Department of Rare Books.

51. *Liberator*, March 13, 1840. For an interesting and somewhat different interpretation of the politicization of women abolitionists, see Nancy Hewitt, "The Social Origins of Women's Antislavery Politics in Western New York," in Alan M. Kraut, ed., *Crusaders and Compromisers: Essays on the Relationship of the Antislavery Struggle to the Antebellum Party System* (Westport, Conn., 1983), pp. 205–33.

materialistic, secular enterprise. As one society member explained: "Great objections were at first felt to adopting the Fair as a Society measure, in consequence of conscientious scruples on the part of the members. Some considered it [the sale] inconsistent with a Christian profession, and others were strongly prejudiced against fairs by the manner in which they had seen them conducted." Chapman and her allies agreed: the majority of the women in BFASS "had little or nothing to do with the Fairs, but to take the credit of them."[52]

While the elite women in BFASS emulated male styles of political protest and public action, middle-class members worked for the abolition movement in ways more consistent with their own cultural backgrounds and religious traditions. Obviously, they considered their antislavery activities to be church based and under the direction of abolitionist ministers. In addition to antislavery, therefore, they participated in other church-sponsored reform and charity groups, such as the Women's Union Missionary Society to convert the Jews and the Ladies Baptist Bethel society for the aid of sailors. In 1841, at least fifteen middle-class women abolitionists helped form the Boston Baptist Sewing Circle, an organization affiliated with the First Baptist Church and dedicated to sewing garments for indigent ministers and needy children.[53]

Middle-class women also preferred reform activities that were geared toward the needs of women and children. Nationally they fought slavery as a crime against women and the family; locally, they taught in black schools and ran the Samaritan Asylum orphanage. More than fifty middle-class BFASS members belonged to the New England Female Moral Reform Society, an organization that assisted prostitutes and unemployed or homeless women in the 1840s and 1850s.[54] Others joined the Children's Friend Society, the Home Education Society, and the Golden Rule Society, benevolent organizations that, again, aided needy women and children. In short, whereas the more politically oriented elite women in the society were petitioning, lecturing, and publishing political tracts, Boston's middle-class

---

52. *Liberator,* "Extra" [April 1840]; July 5, 1839.

53. For material on the Boston Baptist Sewing Circle, see the reports of this organization in the Special Collections Department at the Andover Newton Theological School, Newton-Centre, Massachusetts.

54. Valuable insight into the New England Female Moral Reform Society can be found in their monthly journal, the *Friend of Virtue,* which began publication in 1838. Boston Female Anti-Slavery Society member Rebecca Eaton was the magazine's founding editor; Martha Ball assumed the editorship in 1873. For an excellent study of this group, see Barbara Meil Hobson, *Uneasy Virtue: The Politics of Prostitution and the American Reform Tradition* (New York, 1987).

abolitionists, especially after 1840, preferred female-oriented reform and benevolent activities that remained under the aegis of local charities and churches.[55]

Despite their competing philosophies regarding women's political action, both factions of BFASS were represented at the first two women's antislavery conventions in 1837 and 1838.[56] During the sessions, however, they reprised the roles they had played in Boston, dramatizing their ideological and cultural differences. Boston's elite women, including Maria Chapman, Lydia Child, Anne Weston, Henrietta Sargent, and Thankful Southwick, participated actively in the conventions' proceedings, serving on committees, delivering lectures, offering resolutions, and helping to write important addresses. The antislavery platform that they developed included repudiating the "anti-republican and anti-christian" American Colonization Society, boycotting proslavery churches, purchasing free-labor goods, and defying customary segregation by seating themselves in areas designated for blacks only.[57] These political tactics required acts of public protest which resembled the methods developed by their male counterparts. Indeed, by calling for racial integration, these women abolitionists actually moved beyond their male colleagues and established a political agenda of their own.

Though members of the proclerical faction of BFASS attended the conventions, too, these women—including whites Mary Parker, Martha Ball, Catherine Sullivan, Lydia Fuller, and African American Julia Williams—were relatively quiet during the sessions. No middle-class member spoke during the 1837 meeting, and Parker, as presiding officer, was not in a position to offer any resolutions herself. Two white middle-class Bostonians, Abigail Ordway and Catherine Sullivan, did propose resolutions at the 1838 convention: Ordway urged every mother to "instruct her children in the principles of genuine abolition," and Sullivan resolved that women's antislavery agenda include the "general promotion of peace, moral reform, tem-

---

55. For a detailed analysis of the socioeconomic and cultural differences separating BFASS factions, see my book *Strained Sisterhood: Gender and Class in the Boston Female Anti-Slavery Society* (Amherst, 1993).

56. The lasting animosity that the Westons felt for their opponents, the Balls, is expressed in an 1849 letter written by Anne Weston to Sydney Howard Gay: ". . . you are aware that when a person has a perfect repugnance for another, there is nothing so dreadful as any show of regard. I have not yet forgotten the very cruel advantage that Miss Ball took of my inferior stature in Phil'ia so many years ago by *kissing* me when we met" (Anne Warren Weston to Sydney Howard Gay, August 10, 1849, Sydney Howard Gay Collection, Columbia University Libraries, Manuscript Collections).

57. *Proceedings of the Anti-Slavery Convention of American Women . . . 1837* (New York, 1837), p. 13.

perance, the circulation of the Scriptures, [and] the education of youth."[58] These public statements underscore how completely this contingent saw antislavery as part of a wider network of female reform to be carried out in homes and churches.

When BFASS was functioning well, its members congratulated themselves on the nonsectarian and interracial character of their association. As Caroline Weston later recalled, the grim reality of slavery as exposed by antislavery pioneers "raised the fear and indignation of all classes" and united this coalition of upper- and middle-class whites and elite blacks despite social ostracism, personal insult, and mob violence.[59] Yet on a daily basis, BFASS was assuredly not united. Most middle-class women worked on customary female benevolent projects; those from the upper class engaged in public acts of political protest. Although many of the society's African Americans lent their support to the Garrisonian faction, they reserved their full energies for black-sponsored organizations and projects.[60]

Historians have credited BFASS's activities and the controversies they engendered with creating the political climate that fostered the nineteenth-century women's rights movement. A permanent women's united front, however, in which gender concerns overrode the economic, religious, and racial differences of its participants, remained elusive. After several intensely productive years, BFASS disintegrated, and its members rejoined their male counterparts in organizational structures more compatible with their respective sociopolitical orientations. In the final analysis, the personal predispositions of BFASS members arising from class, religious, and racial backgrounds proved far more powerful than the bonds of womanhood.

58. *Proceedings of the Anti-Slavery Convention of American Women . . . 1838* (Philadelphia, 1838), pp. 6, 9.

59. Caroline Weston to Samuel Joseph May, October 21, 1871, BPL.

60. Indeed, while African American women were divided in their allegiances to white abolitionists, they continued to work together within black organizations. See, for example, an 1843 notice issued by Chapman supporters Anna Logan and Arianna Adams announcing a fair to raise money for Zion church. The wife of its minister, J. C. Beman, supported the board of BFASS and later joined the Massachusetts Female Emancipation Society (*Liberator,* October 20, 1843).

{ 4 }

Priorities and Power

The Philadelphia Female Anti-Slavery Society

Jean R. Soderlund

Historians often cite the Philadelphia Female Anti-Slavery Society for its inclusion of white and African American women as leaders and members, its defiance of middle-class norms, and its nurture of the women's rights movement.[1] Although PFASS was in the forefront of the fight against slavery and its members vigorously asserted their partnership in that struggle, our understanding of the evolution of the group's membership and program over the long term remains limited. Study of the society has focused primarily on the 1830s, when members circulated antislavery petitions widely, held "promiscuous" public meetings to attract new members, and attempted to end racial discrimination. Compared with sister societies in

I received support for this research from the Transformation of Philadelphia Project (funded by the National Endowment for the Humanities) of the Philadelphia Center for Early American Studies and from the University of Maryland, Baltimore County. I am grateful to Gerda Lerner, Kathryn Kish Sklar, Michael Zuckerman, members of the Philadelphia Center seminar, and the editors of this volume for helpful criticisms of earlier drafts.
 1. Ira V. Brown, "Cradle of Feminism: The Philadelphia Female Anti-Slavery Society, 1833–1840," *Pennsylvania Magazine of History and Biography* (hereafter cited as *PMHB*) 102 (1978): 143–66; Carolyn Williams, "The Philadelphia Female Anti-Slavery Society and the Conventions of Anti-Slavery Women: The Challenge to Racism and Sexism in Antebellum America," paper presented at the Annual Meeting of the Organization of American Historians, Louisville, April 1991; Gerda Lerner, *The Grimké Sisters from South Carolina: Rebels against Slavery* (Boston, 1967); Lerner, *The Majority Finds Its Past: Placing Women in History* (Oxford, 1979); Amy Swerdlow, "Abolition's Conservative Sisters: The Ladies' New York City Anti-Slavery Societies, 1834–1840, " Chapter 2 in the present volume; Brown, "The Woman's Rights Movement in Pennsylvania, 1848–1873," *Pennsylvania History* 32 (1965): 153–65.

Boston and New York City in that decade, Philadelphia women showed more unified support for gender equality among abolitionists. But we know little about the activities of the Philadelphia society after 1840, when the Garrisonian movement for immediate abolition split on the issues of political activity and women's participation.[2] Nor do we know much about how the Philadelphia society contributed to the genesis of the woman suffrage movement, beyond Lucretia Mott's meeting with Elizabeth Cady Stanton in London in 1840 and their subsequent decision to hold the Seneca Falls convention.

This essay provides an analysis of the evolving policies and priorities of PFASS from its December 1833 founding to 1854, the year in which Philadelphia women hosted a women's rights convention. This study measures the group's ability to sustain its commitment to fight slavery and racial discrimination, and assesses its role in starting the movement for women's rights. Although the group never wavered in its opposition to slavery and prejudice, its strategy and methods changed dramatically. The society began as a team of energetic young women seeking new members and knocking on doors to obtain signatures for petitions; it eventually became a narrow, introspective circle of antislavery veterans who spent much of their time preparing for the annual fair. This transformation was complex, for the society did not abandon all of its early priorities. For example, although it ceased active efforts to recruit members, its leadership consistently included women of varied backgrounds. The African American women who helped to establish the organization remained among its core of leaders. And though the shift of emphasis from arranging antislavery lectures and circulating petitions to organizing the annual fair initially appears to be a retreat from the political arena to the private, in fact the society achieved significant political ends through the sale of sewn articles and other goods. Concentrating on the fair required less disregard of accepted gender roles than obtaining signatures on petitions; still, the Philadelphia society used the impressive proceeds of its fair to gain power within the abolitionist movement, especially the state society, which included women and men.

The alteration in the Philadelphia society must be understood within several contexts: the changes in the abolitionist movement on the national level and in Pennsylvania, the refusal of Congress to consider antislavery petitions, the rising level of racist attacks in Philadelphia, and the increas-

---

2. Swerdlow, "Abolition's Conservative Sisters"; Keith E. Melder, *Beginnings of Sisterhood: The American Woman's Rights Movement, 1800–1850* (New York, 1977), pp. 95–128; Aileen S. Kraditor, *Means and Ends in American Abolitionism: William Lloyd Garrison and His Critics, 1834–1850* (New York, 1969); and Ronald G. Walters, *The Antislavery Appeal: American Abolitionism after 1830* (Baltimore, 1976), pp. 3–18.

ing private responsibilities and age of society members. All these factors constricted the society's focus and sapped its ability to provide strong support in 1848 for the fledgling women's rights movement.

Before 1838, PFASS consciously tried to recruit women of diverse backgrounds. It sponsored public addresses by both black and white abolitionists, including Robert Forten, Robert Purvis, James Cornish, Dr. Edwin Atlee, Joshua Coffin, James Gibbons, Andrew Gordon, and George Thompson. Membership grew impressively. During 1834, the society's first year, twenty-nine women signed the constitution (table 1).[3] At least nine, and perhaps twelve, of these early members were African Americans. They included Charlotte, Margaretta, and Sarah Forten, the wife and unmarried daughters of abolitionist James Forten; and Harriet D. Forten Purvis, another Forten daughter and wife of Robert Purvis.[4] Of seventeen white women who joined in 1834, thirteen were Hicksite Quakers, including minister Lucretia Mott, a Nantucket native and wife of wool merchant James Mott; Esther Moore, who came to Philadelphia from the Eastern Shore of Maryland; and Lydia White, who ran a free produce grocery.[5] In 1835, sixty-

3. Philadelphia Female Anti-Slavery Society, Minute Books, 1833–1870 [hereafter cited as PFASS mins.], in Pennsylvania Abolition Society Papers, Historical Society of Pennsylvania [hereafter cited as HSP], microfilm edition [hereafter cited as PASP], Reel 30, list of members before minutes for January 9, 1845.

4. Biographical information on African American members is from U.S. manuscript censuses, 1840 and 1850; "Census Facts collected by Benjamin C. Bacon and Charles Gardner," 1838, vols. 1–4, PASP, Reel 26; *Wealth and Biography of the Wealthy Citizens of Philadelphia*, 2d ed. (Philadelphia, 1845); Emma Jones Lapsansky, "Friends, Wives, and Strivings: Networks and Community Values among Nineteenth-Century Philadelphia Afroamerican Elites," *PMHB* 108 (1984): 3–24; Julie Winch, *Philadelphia's Black Elite: Activism, Accommodation, and the Struggle for Autonomy, 1787–1848* (Philadelphia, 1988); Brown, "Cradle," p. 147; [Joseph Willson], *Sketches of the Higher Classes of Colored Society in Philadelphia* (1841; rpt. Philadelphia, 1969), pp. 16–18, 74, 96, 103–12; Rev. William Douglass, *Annals of the First African Church, in the United States of America, Now Styled the African Episcopal Church of St. Thomas, Philadelphia* (Philadelphia, 1862), pp. 107, 111, 137; William Still, *The Underground Railroad* (1872; rpt. New York, 1968), pp. 610–12, 711; Charles L. Blockson, *The Underground Railroad: First-Person Narratives of Escapes to Freedom in the North* (New York, 1987), pp. 227–51; Ray Allen Billington, ed., *The Journal of Charlotte Forten* (New York, 1953), pp. 7–27; Lerner, *Grimké Sisters;* Edward T. James et al., eds., *Notable American Women, 1607–1950*, 3 vols. (Cambridge, Mass., 1971), 1:511–12; Rayford W. Logan et al., eds., *Dictionary of American Negro Biography* (New York, 1982), pp. 234–35, 508; *McElroy's Philadelphia Directory for 1845* (Philadelphia, 1845).

5. Biographical data on white members are from a variety of sources including: William Wade Hinshaw, *Encyclopedia of American Quaker Genealogy* (Ann Arbor, 1938), vol. 2; Hinshaw card files at Friends Historical Library of Swarthmore College (hereafter cited as FHL); Records of Green Street Monthly Meeting and Spruce Street Monthly Meeting, FHL; Pamphlet Group 7, Emmor Kimber, FHL; Records of Old Swedes Church (Gloria Dei) and St.

Jean R. Soderlund

Table 1. PFASS membership, 1834–1848

Year	Number of members	African American	Hicksite	Orthodox[a]	African Episcopal	Other	Unknown
1834	29	9	13	3	6	1	6
1835	69	9	25	18	4	6	16
1836	13	0	4	2	0	1	6
1837	42	0	25	8	0	3	6
1838	9	0	5	2	0	0	2
1839	14	1	9	0	0	0	5
1840	9	0	5	2	0	1	1
1841	7	3	3	0	0	2	2
1842	7	2	3	0	0	1	3
1843	1	0	1	0	0	0	0
1844	4	0	3	0	0	0	1
1845	3	0	0	1	0	1	1
1846	0	0	0	0	0	0	0
1847	0	0	0	0	0	0	0
1848	8[b]	0	4	1	0	0	3
	215	24	100 (61%)[c]	37 (23%)	10 (6%)	16 (10%)	52

Sources: See notes 3, 4, and 5.
[a]Includes Friends who did not appear in the Quaker records after the 1827 schism.
[b]Includes 3 members not on the 1845 list.
[c]Percentage of 163 known.

nine new members, including at least nine African American women, signed the constitution. The society grew and reached beyond the Hicksite meetings and the African Episcopal Church of St. Thomas, to which most of the first members belonged. Although twenty-five of the new members

George's Methodist Episcopal Church, Philadelphia, in the Genealogical Society of Pennsylvania collections, HSP; U.S. manuscript censuses, 1840 and 1850; *Wealth and Biography of Wealthy Citizens of Phila.*; *Notable American Women*; *McElroy's Philadelphia Directory for 1845*; Brown, "Cradle"; Ira V. Brown, "'Am I Not a Woman and a Sister?': The Anti-Slavery Conventions of American Women, 1837–1839," *Pennsylvania History* 50 (1983): 1–19; Brown, "Miller McKim and Pennsylvania Abolitionism," *Pennsylvania History* 30 (1963): 56–72; Lerner, *Grimké Sisters*; Still, *Underground Railroad*, pp. 610–16, 649–59; Margaret Hope Bacon, *Valiant Friend: The Life of Lucretia Mott* (New York, 1980); Elizabeth Cady Stanton et al., eds., *History of Woman Suffrage* (New York, 1881), vol. 1; Dumas Malone, ed., *Dictionary of American Biography* (New York, 1933), 2:284, 6:506–7; Thomas Earle, ed., *The Life, Travels and Opinions of Benjamin Lundy* (1847; rpt. New York, 1969); and H. Larry Ingle, *Quakers in Conflict: The Hicksite Reformation* (Knoxville, Tenn., 1986).

were Hicksites, including Mott's daughters Maria Davis and Anna Hopper, eighteen were Orthodox Friends or Quakers who do not appear in the records of either branch after the 1827 schism. Furthermore, Mary and Susan Grew, who quickly became leaders, were daughters of abolitionist Henry Grew, a Baptist minister. Several other recruits had ties to St. George's Methodist Episcopal Church or to Gloria Dei.

The society continued to broaden its membership by sponsoring public addresses through 1836 and early 1837. In April 1837, however, they turned over the job of organizing open meetings to the Pennsylvania Anti-Slavery Society, and the number of recruits dwindled. The fledgling state society took over many tasks that the women had performed, and it hired agents to conduct antislavery meetings throughout Pennsylvania and to plan tours for visiting speakers. The state society, not the women's group, now dealt with the American Anti-Slavery Society; the women now contributed most of their funds to the state's outreach program rather than conducting one of their own.

But though PFASS relinquished its most effective means of adding to the roll, for several years it remained committed to gaining new members. As plans to establish the state society proceeded in January 1837, the Philadelphia women appointed a committee to seek recruits. Although encouraged by the fact that over one hundred members had already joined, they viewed their success with "penitence and humility" because they had not gathered even more hundreds "around [their] standard."[6] And, indeed, without dynamic speakers to draw and convince large audiences, the membership committee made little progress. After 1838, the burning of Pennsylvania Hall and other racist attacks must have discouraged sympathetic Philadelphians from joining. PFASS decided in March 1839 to make a special effort to attract African American members. They published an "invitation to our colored sisters to co-operate with us in our labors for the emancipation of the slave" and appointed black schoolteacher Sarah Mapps Douglass, among others, to a committee charged with extending this invitation to individuals.[7] In 1839, the committee recruited teacher Amelia M. Bogle and perhaps one other black woman; within the next few years, five more African Americans joined. Vice-president Huldah Justice recognized that the society had given up its best means of winning new members, for in January 1840 she suggested organizing a public meeting to attract recruits. But by then the momentum was lost and the women took almost a year to ar-

6. PFASS mins., January 12, 1837.
7. Ibid., March 14, 1839.

range the meeting. First they invited Sarah Grimké to speak, but after she declined on account of health, they engaged Charles Burleigh, agent of the state society. His words apparently had little effect, and the number of women joining each year continued to decline.[8]

By April 1841 the leadership was discouraged not only by falling recruitment but by poor attendance as well. When the society asked for advice on how to improve attendance at meetings, the board of managers said they were "unable to suggest any measures for reviving the interest once felt in the cause further than the faithful discharge of the duties & responsibilities resting upon each member" and thought the society should "consider the expediency of holding quarterly instead of monthly meetings." After the members rejected this advice, the board decided to cancel its own sessions. Officers believed that attending monthly meetings of both the board and of the society was excessive.[9] In November 1843 the society asked Mary Grew and Lucretia Mott to prepare a call to those who have "from various causes absented themselves from our meetings & withdrawn from active participation in our labors," but the situation had not improved two years later. As the secretary wrote in December 1845, "the smallness of our Meetings no cause of discouragement. Reformers will ever be a small minority as they are always progressing; they retrograde if they stand still. Two or three are strong in right principle—and always great while advancing."[10] Since 1842, as discussed below, the women's society had been moving toward a more restrictive ideological position, one that required members to accept the nonresistance doctrine of William Lloyd Garrison and Lucretia Mott. Members who believed in the efficacy of political action resigned, and with only eight recruits between 1843 and 1847 and normal attrition as people moved away, died, or lost interest, the society shrank significantly. Like other Garrisonians, the society chose to constitute a small coterie of moral reformers rather than scramble for new converts.[11]

Its declining recruitment and its reduced ability to spark new members into active participation reflected the organization's altered strategy in promoting abolitionist reform. In January 1845 the society prepared an annotated roll of members. This list, which was updated until early 1848, totalled 212 names. Of these, ninety-four were so deeply involved in the so-

8. Ibid., January 9, 1840; November 12, 1840; PFASS Board of Managers, Minute Books, 1833–1841, in PASP, Reel 30, December 3, 1840.

9. PFASS Board of Managers mins., April 1, 1841; October 11, 1841; PFASS mins., April 8, 1841.

10. PFASS mins., November 9, 1843; December 11, 1845.

11. Ellen DuBois, "Women's Rights and Abolition: The Nature of the Connection," in Lewis Perry and Michael Fellman, eds., *Antislavery Reconsidered: New Perspectives on the Abolitionists* (Baton Rouge, La., 1979), pp. 247–51.

The Philadelphia Female Anti-Slavery Society

Table 2. PFASS participants and officers, by religion

	Participants	Officers
	(Percentage of known)	
Hicksite	54 (64%)	29 (63%)
Orthodox[a]	21 (25)	11 (24)
African Episcopal	5 (6)	3 (7)
Other	4 (5)	3 (7)
Unknown	10	6
	94	52

Sources: PFASS mins.; see notes 4 and 5.
[a]Includes Friends who did not appear in the Quaker records after the 1827 schism.

ciety that they were appointed to four or more offices or committees.[12] Functionally, these ninety-four women were the society membership; the rest did little more than sign the constitution. The numbers indicate clearly that the society became less concerned with absorbing new members into the inner circle of leaders. From 1834 through 1837, 48 percent of those who signed up became active, whereas from 1837 to 1848 only 37 percent did so. After its initial four years, the group became cliquish, and more recruits remained outsiders. Furthermore, of the nine new members who did become active from 1841 to 1848, five had been part of the national antislavery network before joining: Sarah J. McKim, Gertrude Burleigh, Emily Winslow, Paulina S. Wright, and Rebecca Plumly. None of the five African American women who joined in the 1840s took an active part.

The Philadelphia Female Anti-Slavery Society did not set out to exclude African American women from leadership, nor did it favor members of one religion over another. In the 1840s, all new members found it more difficult to gain acceptance than in the past. Between 1833 and 1850, black women were 11 percent of all members, 9 percent of participants, and 12 percent of officers.[13] Hicksite women, who were about 60 percent of all members whose religion is known, were only slightly overrepresented among participants and officers (table 2). As the group ossified, so did its racial and religious composition. Of thirty participants who had joined in the 1830s and either resigned or stopped participating by 1842 (thirteen others died or moved away), only one was African American, 64 percent were Hicksite

12. PFASS mins., January 9, 1845. The list was annotated as to whether members had resigned, moved away, or died. Officers included the president, vice-president, corresponding secretary, recording secretary, treasurer, librarian, and other members of the board of managers.
13. These percentages approximate the proportion of African Americans in the city's population, which in 1840 was 11 percent. Leonard P. Curry, *The Free Black in Urban America 1800–1850: The Shadow of the Dream* (Chicago, 1981), p. 246.

and 32 percent were Orthodox or unspecified Quaker. Black women made up 10 percent of active members in 1838 and 13 percent in 1848. Hicksites were 65 percent of the participants in 1838 and 61 percent ten years later. The percentage of Orthodox and unspecified Quakers declined slightly.

Information about fifty-five of the ninety-four participants shows little difference between the wealth of those who were active in the 1830s and dropped out and those still participating in the late 1840s. All were from the middle and upper classes. The eight black activists represented the city's African American elite. Although most black women in Philadelphia were domestic servants, day workers, and clothes washers, four of the black participants belonged to families owning property worth over fifty thousand dollars (placing them in the top 1 to 2 percent of all Philadelphians), and the other four belonged to families in comfortable circumstances and pursued their own careers in teaching, millinery, shopkeeping, and wigmaking. Similarly, some of the forty-seven active white members were wealthy, including Lucretia Mott, her daughter Maria Davis, Huldah Justice, Susan Parrish, and Mary Needles. Fourteen belonged to the families of merchants, three to manufacturers' households, and seventeen were the wives, daughters, or sisters of professionals. A few had husbands, fathers, or brothers who were craftsmen, including a watchmaker, a currier, a tailor, a bookbinder, and a tinplate worker; one was a waterman. Like the black members, several of the white women had careers: one was a dressmaker, another a seamstress, two were shopkeepers, and three were teachers.

Although no significant differences in financial status divided the black and white women active in the early days from those active a decade later, differences did exist in their numbers, in their marital status, and in their average ages (table 3). The pool of activists numbered seventy-one in 1838, but a decade later only thirty-eight served regularly on committees and as officers. In 1838, 47 percent were under age 30 and 55 percent were single; ten years later just 14 percent were under age 30 and 38 percent were single.[14] The society grew less vital as its numbers dwindled and the abolitionist cadre matured.

The private lives of society members, as well as their public experiences as abolitionists, affected the modus operandi of the group. Like other women, they were expected to care for their families. Single women were called upon to assist ailing parents and other relatives, and those who married had growing families. For example, Sarah Pugh, who served many

14. For a comparison with members of New York and Boston societies to 1840, see Anne M. Boylan, "Timid Girls, Venerable Widows, and Dignified Matrons: Life Cycle Patterns among Organized Women in New York and Boston, 1797–1840," *American Quarterly* 38 (1986): 779–97, especially 786–91.

Table 3. PFASS participants by marital status and age, 1838 and 1848

	1838 Number of participants	1848 Number of participants
Marital Status		
Single	36 (55%)[a]	13 (38%)[a]
Married or widowed	30 (45)	21 (62)
Unknown	5	4
	71	38
Age		
15–19 years	4 (6%)	0
20–29	26 (41)	5 (14%)
30–39	13 (20)	20 (59)
40–49	11 (17)	3 (9)
50–59	9 (14)	4 (12)
60–69	0	2 (6)
70–79	1 (2)	0
Unknown	7	4
	71	38

Sources: PFASS mins.; see notes 4 and 5.
[a]Percentage of known

years as president, began her first term when she was an unmarried school-teacher in her late thirties, but by 1841 she had stopped teaching to care for her aging mother. During the 1840s and early 1850s, Pugh expressed her frustration in her diary: she felt unable to accomplish anything that she considered important.[15] Margaretta Forten, also unmarried, served as recording secretary, treasurer, and manager during the 1830s. When her father fell ill in 1841 she asked to be released from service; although James Forten died in 1842, she did not resume her participation in the society until 1844. Anna Hopper, Lucretia Mott's oldest daughter, joined the society in 1835, two years after marrying attorney Edward Hopper. In 1836, she gave birth to their first child, who died the following year, and by 1855 she had four more children. Although she lightened her organizational workload in 1845 and 1847 when two of her children were born, Anna Hopper was one of the group's most faithful activists. Her younger sister Maria, who also served frequently on committees, joined the society in 1835. She married Edward Davis the next year and between 1838 and 1850 had four children. Huldah Justice, who was married and the mother of a daughter when she joined in 1837, gave birth to five more children by 1848. Amy Matilda Cassey gave birth to five children between 1829 and 1844, and was widowed

15. *Memorial of Sarah Pugh, A Tribute of Respect from Her Cousins* (Philadelphia, 1888), pp. 30–40.

in 1848. Sarah McKim, who joined soon after she married Pennsylvania Anti-Slavery Society agent J. Miller McKim in 1840, had two children in 1842 and 1847. Though many of the women had Irish or African American live-in servants who spared them the worst household drudgery,[16] the young matrons' burdens of childbearing and child care, like the family responsibilities borne by their unmarried co-workers, curtailed their activities. Thus PFASS increasingly turned from its early ambitious efforts to collect thousands of signatures on petitions to its later work of organizing sewing circles for the annual fair.

Several other collective experiences affected the priorities of the organization from 1838 to 1848, including members' disappointment in their efforts to "elevate" the black population, the decision of Congress not to discuss their petitions, and the burning of Pennsylvania Hall. Meanwhile, like other Garrisonians, the women established new ideological criteria for membership that cost the group valuable support.

The society originally emphasized the need to assist free blacks as well as slaves, but gradually ceased efforts "to adopt such measures, as may be in our power to dispel the prejudice against the people of colour, [and] to improve their condition."[17] In June 1834, the women appointed a committee to assess the public education of African American students, and by the end of the year they had started their own school. At their request, Rebecca Buffum took charge and combined it with her own, but by March 1838 she had left the city and Sarah Douglass had taken over the institution.[18] Douglass asked the society to assume full financial responsibility because it did not yield sufficient income. The board of managers agreed, offered to pay Douglass a salary of three hundred dollars, and appointed Sarah Pugh and Mary Grew to procure any necessary furniture.[19]

For the next eleven years PFASS contributed financially to the school. Relations were sometimes strained, however, though Douglass was a member of society committees and served as recording secretary, librarian, and manager. The board of managers reprimanded Douglass for permitting stu-

16. U.S. manuscript census, 1850.

17. PFASS mins., December 14, 1833.

18. PFASS Board of Managers mins., June 2, 1834; December 1, 1834; January 26, 1835; September 1, 1835; March 1, 1838. Rebecca Buffum, daughter of Arnold and Rebecca Buffum of Rhode Island, went to Philadelphia to teach black children. She married Marcus Spring, a wealthy New York merchant who funded the Raritan Bay Union at Eagleswood, N.J., a community of abolitionists and reformers. Lillie Buffum Chace Wyman et al., *Elizabeth Buffum Chace, 1806–1899, Her Life and Its Environment* (Boston, 1914), 1:35, 45; *Two Quaker Sisters: From the Original Diaries of Elizabeth Buffum Chace and Lucy Buffum Lowell* (New York, 1937), p. xxviii.

19. PFASS Board of Managers mins., March 1, 1838; April 5, 1838.

dents to make up time when they had been absent because of sickness or foul weather. They also refused to pay the salary of an assistant she had recruited from among her students, and they threatened to move the school unless the landlord lowered the rent. By March 1840, Douglass had had enough of their meddling. After she announced that she would withdraw the school from the society's oversight, the board relented and resolved to appropriate $125 annually for the school's rent. Nine years later, however, they decided they could no longer afford the expense.[20] In 1849 the society brought in a considerably larger income than it had in the late 1830s when it paid both Douglass's salary and the rent. Nevertheless, the group cited lack of funds as its excuse to abandon its commitment to the education of African American children.

The Philadelphia women initiated and quickly dropped other efforts to ameliorate the condition of blacks. By 1841, the society's education committee, whose job was to visit black schools in the city and report on their condition, was defunct, primarily because members failed to make the visits.[21] Other efforts to promote "the moral and intellectual improvement of the people of color" included holding "scientific" lectures, planning to assist African Americans in their trades and businesses, establishing a serving school, and offering sewing lessons and literary and religious instruction. The women's society did little more than appoint committees to consider these proposals, however, and by 1842 they had decided that other societies to which some of their members belonged were better suited to the task of "improving" the black community.[22]

After 1837, PFASS also reduced its efforts to circulate petitions. The society had exercised this right since 1834, for it was the only recognized political tool that women could employ. They petitioned Congress to abolish slavery in the District of Columbia and prohibit the interstate slave trade; they pressed the Pennsylvania legislature to allow jury trials for suspected fugitives. Petitions remained a standard feature of the group's work from 1834 to the 1850s but, like antislavery societies elsewhere, the Philadelphia society prepared statements and collected signatures with ever less enthusiasm as the

20. Ibid., February 7, 1839; April 4, 1839; February 6, 1840; March 5, 1840; April 2, 1840; PFASS mins., April 9, 1840; February 8, 1849; March 8, 1849; April 12, 1849.

21. PFASS mins., January 4, 1838; January 9, 1840; January 14, 1841.

22. Ibid., May 14, 1835; March 10, 1836; May 12, 1836; January 12, 1837; February 9, 1837; July 14, 1837; June 13, 1839; July 11, 1839; October 8, 1840; June 9, 1842; June 23, 1842. The society had considerable interest in moral reform and temperance, and members were active in the Rosine Association, which worked with prostitutes, the Female Association of Philadelphia for the Relief of the Sick and Infirm Poor with Clothing, and the Association for the Relief and Employment of Poor Women. For the growing literature on women's benevolent and reform groups, see Bibliographical Notes to this volume.

years passed. The members were especially active during 1836, when thirty-three hundred women signed, and in 1837, when they gathered almost five thousand signatures. In that year, when the first Anti-Slavery Convention of American Women devised an elaborate plan for collecting signatures in every town and township, the Philadelphia women went to work immediately. They assigned one member to correspond with abolitionists in each county in eastern Pennsylvania and divided the city and Northern Liberties into districts, with a pair of members to canvass each. A convention circular urged them to visit every house and ask every individual to sign, "for when all the maids and matrons of the land knock at the door of Congress, our Statesmen must legislate."[23]

Enthusiasm for circulating petitions sagged partly because of the series of Gag Rules the House of Representatives passed in 1836. The mob burning of Pennsylvania Hall in May 1838 after an evening session of the second Anti-Slavery Convention of American Women also intimidated some members of the Philadelphia society. At its June 1838 meeting, Lucretia Mott asked that the preamble of the group's constitution be read, and then "commented with much feeling, thereby strengthening the hands and cheering the hearts of some who were well nigh fainting." When asked to solicit signatures, few members refused.[24]

Prompted more by personal reservations than by the 1838 riot, Sarah Pugh delayed assuming responsibility for collecting signatures. She refused to circulate petitions in 1838 but participated the following year. She wrote in her diary in December 1839: "I never undertook anything that was so entirely distasteful to me; but, as it is in many things, the anticipation was more than the reality. In our aristocratic district we were generally civilly received and heard, and as civilly refused with few words. We had many interesting conversations and opportunities for showing forth abolition truth."[25]

Nevertheless, by March 1840 the society's petition committee reported that they had obtained only 1,483 names on petitions to Congress, and the petition drive continued to slow as the number of members agreeing to canvass plummeted. For this "& other causes," the petition committee explained in 1841, they obtained only 678 signatures on the memorials to Con-

---

23. Lerner, *Majority Finds Its Past*, pp. 112–28; PFASS mins., October 13, 1836; January 12, 1837; February 9, 1837; May 18, 1837; June 8, 1837; July 14, 1837; January 4, 1838; Samuel McKean to Mary Grew, February 20, 1837, PFASS Correspondence, Incoming, PASP, Reel 31; Joan M. Jensen, *Loosening the Bonds: Mid-Atlantic Farm Women, 1750–1850* (New Haven, 1986), pp. 191–92.

24. PFASS mins., June 14, 1838; September 14, 1838; October 19, 1838.

25. *Memorial of Sarah Pugh*, p. 22.

gress. As late as February 1854 the society continued to memorialize Congress and the Pennsylvania legislature, but after 1846 the women solicited signatures from door-to-door much less frequently, if at all. They circulated some petitions, particularly those drawn up by the state society, but most of their own petitions were undersigned by only the president and secretary.[26]

The national debate over women's role in the abolition movement and the organization of the Liberty Party, which split the American Anti-Slavery Society in 1840, had an uneven impact on PFASS. On the one hand, the question of whether women should participate in the national or state groups was never an issue in the society. They supported fully Angelina Grimké's decision to become an antislavery agent, and in January 1837, when plans were proceeding to establish the Pennsylvania Anti-Slavery Society, the Philadelphia women appointed ten delegates to attend the organizing convention. On the other hand, no women were listed among the representatives at the state convention. Apparently, they were refused seats, but the women's delegation reported only that "owing to a variety of circumstances," none of them was present. In January 1838, however, at the next state convention, several women represented rural societies, and in the autumn one hundred of 254 members were women, including ten delegates from PFASS. In Pennsylvania, male abolitionists did not immediately welcome women, but they offered little resistance. In contrast, the battle over inclusion of women in the Massachusetts Anti-Slavery Society ended in schisms of both the Boston Female Anti-Slavery Society and the state organization. The Pennsylvania society did not publicly debate the issue of women's participation, and in 1841 it deplored the decision of the 1840 World's Anti-Slavery Convention in London to exclude women from participating.[27]

26. PFASS mins., March 12, 1840; February 11, 1841; 1842–1854. Judith Wellman found an even greater decline in women's petitioning in New York State; see "Women and Radical Reform in Antebellum Upstate New York: A Profile of Grassroots Female Abolitionists," in Mabel E. Deutrich et al., eds., *Clio Was a Woman: Studies in the History of American Women* (Washington, D.C., 1980), pp. 113–27.

27. PFASS mins., November 11, 1836; January 12, 1837; February 9, 1837; Pennsylvania Anti-Slavery Society, Minute Book, 1838–1846 (PASS mins.), in PASP, Reel 31. The call to the state organizing convention was signed by men only, twelve hundred in number, and did not mention women. The meeting discussed and adopted unanimously a resolution that "we hail with great encouragement, the efforts that are being made by females in the promotion of Universal Liberty, throughout our favoured land, and that we recognise in their sympathy and action, the influence they must exert in the great struggle for Human Rights." *Proceedings of the Pennsylvania Convention, Assembled to Organize a State Anti-Slavery Society, at Harrisburg, on the 31st of January and 1st, 2d and 3d of February 1837* (Philadelphia, 1837), pp. 3–5, 70–74, quotation on p. 70.

The issue of political action did create bitter dissension among Pennsylvania abolitionists, however, and this caused further diminution in the ranks of PFASS. In 1842 the society initiated new ideological standards for membership. Although the constitution stated simply that members should work for immediate emancipation and for improvement of the condition of African Americans, in May the society resolved "that in the work of abolishing slavery, we rely not on the efficacy of physical force, or political parties but on moral power, on the use of those weapons, which operate on the heart & on the conscience." Two years later it endorsed the Garrisonian doctrine "that abolitionists can consistently have no union with slave holders, by voting for officers who must swear to support the Constitution of the U.S."[28] Dissenters to the new rules against voting and working with political parties included Sarah Lewis, with whom Pugh had taught school, Mary and Phebe Earle, and Susan Grew. They did not resign immediately. Instead, they waited for the state organization to act, perhaps hoping that PFASS could be persuaded to adopt a more latitudinarian policy. But in 1845 when the state society banned voting, and in 1846 when it affirmed the doctrine of Garrisonian nonresistance, supporters of political action dropped out of PFASS.[29]

Thus, as the society matured it narrowed its ideology, stopped seeking new members, and reduced efforts to circulate petitions and to improve the condition of blacks. At the same time, the organization devoted itself increasingly to the sphere of antislavery work in which it had considerable success—the annual fair. In June 1835 the board of managers had suggested that the Philadelphia women follow the example of societies elsewhere and sew articles such as workbags and handkerchiefs on which to inscribe abolitionist mottoes. The society debated whether or not to hold a fair because some Quaker members questioned its propriety; they could expect criticism from other Friends for taking part in "profane babbling."[30] Nevertheless, they agreed to meet every Saturday afternoon at Mary Needles's house on the corner of 12th and Race. The following year, the members held their first fair and were pleasantly surprised when they raised

28. The society did not, however, approve motions in 1844 to require members to withdraw from churches "which are pro-slavery in their character or conduct." PFASS mins., May 19, 1842; May 15, 1844; September 12, 1844; October 10, 1844.

29. The opposition of the women's society to emancipating slaves by purchase, as in the case of Frederick Douglass, was the last straw for Mary Earle. PFASS mins., February 11, 1847; March 12, 1847; February 13, 1848.

30. PFASS Board of Managers mins., June 6, 1835; PFASS mins., June 13, 1835; Anna Davis Hallowell, ed., *James and Lucretia Mott: Life and Letters* (Boston, 1884), p. 397; quoted in N. Orwin Rush, "Lucretia Mott and the Philadelphia Antislavery Fairs," *Bulletin of Friends Historical Association* 35 (1946): 69.

$228.60.[31] The fair became more elaborate each year. In 1839, a committee met weekly from September to December to prepare items and make arrangements for the event, which was held from December 23 through Christmas evening. By charging a small admission and selling antislavery publications as well as their plain and fancy handiwork, the women netted about seven hundred dollars.[32]

As the fair became more profitable, its importance to the antislavery cause increased. The Philadelphia Female Anti-Slavery Society felt the weight of this responsibility and in 1842 suggested that the state society organize the event. The Pennsylvania Anti-Slavery Society affirmed its confidence in the women's group to manage this "department" of antislavery work and urged abolitionists throughout the state to provide assistance. In 1845, PFASS again considered, but this time rejected, a motion to transfer the fair to the state society.[33] From that point, though the Pennsylvania society appointed large committees of men and women from throughout the state to help prepare for the sale, the Philadelphia women gave it their management and their name.

By the mid-1840s, the Philadelphia society had made the fair its focus, and they coordinated the activities of antislavery women throughout southeastern Pennsylvania and southwestern New Jersey.[34] One rural Pennsylvania woman, Rebecca S. Potts, wrote in 1846 to encourage those "who cannot conveniently meet with a sewing circle—that we labor at all times as much as practicable for the benefit of the Fair—but especially appropriate one afternoon of every week for that purpose, and not suffer household duties to interfere." The Philadelphia society's fair committee appreciated Potts' support, adding "though it is pleasant for several to meet together to labor—yet a solitary worker may have the company of good and bright thoughts." The committee urged "friends in town and country . . . to make arrangements for working circles, etc., and enlist as many warm hearts and efficient hands as can be found in their respective neighborhoods. . . . All the usual articles of needle work will be in demand, and a much larger supply than heretofore of the products of the garden, the dairy, and the farm. We wish to fill one table with specimens of Natural History, in every variety, and another with pot flowers. Will the friends in the country prepare these for the occasion?"[35] The Philadelphia Female Anti-Slavery Society

31. PFASS mins., June 13, 1835; September 8, 1836.
32. Ibid., March 12, 1840.
33. PASS mins., August 1, 1842; PFASS mins., March 13, 1845.
34. PFASS mins., January 14, 1841; January 20, 1842; January 12, 1843; March 14, 1844; January 11, 1849; January 10, 1850; January 13, 1852; May 12, 1853; January 12, 1854.
35. *Pennsylvania Freeman*, April 16, 1846; July 2, 1846.

also coordinated men's preparations for the annual fair. Of the 110 people appointed in 1846 by the state society to assist with the sale, forty-two were men.[36]

The state society appointed large committees, and virtually the entire active membership of the Philadelphia women's society participated in the fair. Consequently, the event became bureaucratized. The fair committee now formed subcommittees and held social gatherings to entertain the scores of people involved. Writing on October 17, 1853, Sarah Pugh described the Fair Circle that "met at James and Lucretia Mott's this evening,—about sixty to tea, after which our number increased. . . . Quite a contrast, this brilliant scene, with our small number, eight or ten, who repaired to a school-room because it was central, each with her supper of nuts and cakes brought in pocket, eaten at twilight while we walked in the yard,—then a few more hours' work by the glimmer of candles."[37]

Fairs in the 1850s were elaborate occasions. In addition to the sale of needlework and farm products, they featured speeches by abolitionists William H. Furness, Joshua R. Giddings, Wendell Phillips, William Lloyd Garrison, and Charles Burleigh, and music by Joshua Hutchinson. In 1853, the admission fee was doubled over the previous year, but the fair still attracted so many people that some even failed to gain admission. The fair committee attributed the success to the "rare and desirable articles" offered for sale as well as to the attraction of eloquent speakers. Lucretia Mott and Mary Grew exhorted members in May 1853 to work for the success of the fair, underscoring the "importance of each individual, whether member of an Anti-Slavery Society or not, fulfilling in her own appropriate way her duty to the slave."[38]

The Philadelphia women had good reason to concentrate on the fair: its success and the funds it raised enabled them to secure power within the state antislavery society. According to one leader, the sale was "a means of keeping an interest alive among many who otherwise would care little & do less for the cause, . . . a means of pecuniary benefit, almost the only one of which women can avail themselves."[39] Over the eighteen years from 1836 to 1853, the women raised about $16,500 from the fair. Their annual take rose

36. Ibid., August 20, 1846.
37. Pugh also remarked that "more than half [of the Fair Circle] were faces new to me, having joined the movement within the last two years," but actually only twelve of the forty-four PFASS committee members had joined within the past two years, which Pugh had spent in Europe. *Memorial of Sarah Pugh,* p. 86; PFASS mins., April 8, 1847; January 13, 1852; February 10, 1853.
38. PFASS mins., January 13, 1852; May 12, 1853; January 12, 1854.
39. Ibid., January 20, 1842.

from an average of $540 in 1836–1844 to $1,170 in 1845–1852, and then shot up to $2,200 in 1853. PFASS donated $13,845 (about 85 percent) of this money to the Pennsylvania society. Their contribution rose from four hundred dollars in 1838, the second year the state group existed and the first year in which the Philadelphia women had a delegation, to eighteen hundred dollars in 1854.

Throughout this entire period, the women's society provided a large proportion of all funds donated to the state society, and their achievement was duly recognized. In October 1838, the report of the state executive committee observed that "if the amount of money contributed by every society in the state, bore the same proportion to the number of its members, as does that of one Female A. S. Society of 142 members, this state would probably have raised during the present year, not less than twenty or thirty thousand dollars for antislavery purposes." The following year the treasurer subsumed the Philadelphia society's donation under another category, but apparently the women objected and in succeeding years the treasurer's report faithfully itemized their contributions.[40]

From 1844 to 1849, funds raised by the Philadelphia women covered 17 to 22 percent of the state budget and accounted for 31 to 45 percent of donations.[41] During the 1844–1845 fiscal year, for example, PFASS contributed $650, whereas the Clarkson, Kennett, Chester County, East Fallowfield, and Buckingham-Plumstead abolitionist societies gave a total of $180 and individuals donated $1,239. Two years later, the Philadelphia women gave $1,200, whereas Clarkson, Kennett, Lundy Union, Columbia County, and Westfield Sewing Circle provided only $38 and individuals (including members of the Philadelphia women's society) subscribed for $1,447. In its 1851 annual report, the women's organization explained that "its operations have, for several years past been so intimately connected with those of the Pennsylvania Anti-Slavery Society, that it is impossible to present an entirely separate and distinct report of them. A large portion of the results of the labors of the Philadelphia Female Anti-Slavery Society, are to be found in the successful operations of the State Society." The antislavery fair, they pointed out, was their "especial charge" and should be considered "one of our most important instrumentalities."[42]

40. PASS mins., October 30–November 1, 1838; May 20–22, 1839.
41. Besides donations, the state society derived income from the sale of publications, subscriptions to the *Pennsylvania Freeman*, and rental of office space. Its publications program also accounted for much of its expenditures.
42. PASS mins., August 11, 1845; August 4, 1847; *Pennsylvania Freeman*, August 13, 1846; February 12, 1852.

By raising and contributing the fair money, Philadelphia women kept a high profile in the state organization and after several years took places in its leadership. The October 1838 state convention appointed Mary Earle and Sarah Lewis to the business committee, which prepared the meeting agenda, and named Mary C. Pennock to a committee on petitions. Though Philadelphia delegates numbered only ten of the one hundred women at this meeting, three of the four women assigned to committees were from the Philadelphia society. In 1841, Sarah Pugh and Lucretia Mott were elected to the state executive committee, and members of the Philadelphia women's group subsequently remained part of the state leadership, though they were outranked in offices and outnumbered by men on the executive committee. Pugh became treasurer in 1843, and the next year Mary Grew became corresponding secretary, the job she had held in the women's society since 1836. With Mott and Elizabeth Neall on the executive committee, PFASS held four of fifteen state offices.[43]

Mott, Grew, Pugh, and Neall achieved prominence in the Pennsylvania society because they were talented and dedicated abolitionists, but the importance of the financial strategy of the women's group cannot be ignored. The Philadelphia women not only channeled their own energies into the lucrative fair but increasingly directed the production of rural women as well. In the countryside, most antislavery societies were mixed by sex. The state organization chose only men from rural societies to serve as state officers; rural women received less significant appointments to committees. The Philadelphia Female Anti-Slavery Society tapped the womanpower of the countryside, fostering a network of sewing circles and harnessing its energy. They sold what the rural women produced and funneled the proceeds, or most of them, through their own treasury to the state society. Thus they accomplished three goals: they kept the women's contributions separate from the men's; they amassed many small donations into an impressive total; and they advanced their own position within the state organization.

By pursuing this strategy, PFASS members won a share of authority at the state level and significantly altered the character of their own society. Given the pecuniary benefits and the prestige and power within the state organization that the annual sale provided, one can argue that PFASS (like other women's organizations that held fairs) transformed female domestic skills into political activities. The shift from petition drives to sewing circles was not a regression from the political realm to women's domestic culture, but rather an expansion of politics. Nonetheless, the transition resulted in a sep-

43. PASS mins., 1837–1846.

aration of spheres within the Pennsylvania abolition movement. Though women continued to speak at conventions and to circulate the occasional petition, and although men assisted with the fair, the expectation by the mid-1840s was that women would concentrate on sewing circles and the annual sale while men canvassed for signatures, organized speaking tours, and managed publications. By the late 1840s, except for the leaders who helped make state policy—notably Mott, Pugh, and Grew—the Philadelphia society's abolitionist activity was confined largely to sewing and organizing the fair.

Mott, Pugh, and Grew were the same members of PFASS who after 1848 became most active in the women's rights movement. Although PFASS has been called the "cradle of feminism" and even stood for gender equality in the antislavery movement, the small group of 1848 seemed ill-prepared to spearhead a new movement. Of thirty-eight active members in that year, fifteen are known to have signed calls for or attended national women's rights conventions in the late 1840s and early 1850s—a significant percentage but a small number to launch the crusade in Philadelphia.[44] In 1851, Mott wrote to Elizabeth Cady Stanton that the city was too backward on the subject of women's rights "to bear such a glare as a national Convention would throw out." Because only a few radical Hicksites "whose names are cast out as evil" lent their support, "we must labor more in a smaller way. We want forerunners to come 'crying in the wilderness'. "[45]

Mott's fears were evidently unfounded, for in 1854, when Philadelphia hosted a women's rights convention, crowds thronged to witness the proceedings. According to one report: "a casual visitor would have been impressed with the number and character of this assembly, both among the actors and spectators. Every variety of age, sex, race, color, and costume were here represented. Bloomers were side by side with mouse-colored gowns and white shawls of the wealthy Quaker dames, and genteelly dressed ladies of the latest Paris fashion." The leadership was pleased with the "fair reports of the Press" and the convention's attentive and "intelligent" audiences; they believed that "in the spirit of harmony and fraternity which has prevailed amongst its members, we see evidence of the rapid progress of our cause."[46]

The 1854 Philadelphia women's rights convention, like those held elsewhere in the years before the Civil War, was successful in much the same way as the antislavery fairs. The conventions and the fairs both drew large

44. Stanton et al., eds., *History of Woman Suffrage*, 1:350–67, 375–86, 809–10, 820–25; *Pennsylvania Freeman*, April 15, 1852; May 6, 1852; May 27, 1852; June 12, 1852.
45. Mott to Stanton, September 11, 1851; quoted in Bacon, *Valiant Friend*, p. 144.
46. Stanton et al., eds., *History of Woman Suffrage*, 1:375, 386.

crowds who were willing to pay an admission charge to hear dynamic speakers. In both cases the strategy for converting others to the cause was similar. Rather than attempt to build large organizations, a small core of organizers and speakers presented their views to mostly passive audiences of local women and men. Historian Ellen DuBois has explained that the feminist leaders "saw their primary task as agitating public sentiment on the woman question. . . . Thus, they were not particularly concerned with the deliberate recruitment of new women, with differing levels of commitment to women's rights, into the work. Instead the movement relied on a small group of highly skilled and deeply committed women, willing to shoulder the opprobrium of 'strong-mindedness'."[47]

The antislavery women who organized both the fairs and the women's rights conventions consciously chose this strategy. If PFASS had relaxed its ideological standards, presumably it could have signed up many new members at its fairs—after Phillips and Garrison, for example, gave their stirring addresses[48]—just as the society had done twenty years before. But in five years of successful fairs from 1849 to 1853, only twenty women joined the society, an average of four per year. Similarly, in 1852, women's rights leaders rejected a motion to create a national association. Ernestine Rose proclaimed "organizations to be like Chinese bandages." Lucy Stone believed "that like a burnt child that dreads the fire, they had all been in permanent organizations, and therefore dread them." She "had had enough of thumb-screws and soul screws ever to wish to be placed under them again. The present duty is agitation."[49]

The women's rights leaders and abolitionists also surely feared to lose control to ideological opponents if they created a more inclusive organization. Susan B. Anthony and Elizabeth Cady Stanton experienced such a defeat in 1853 when the Woman's New York State Temperance Society ousted them from leadership.[50] Historians Suzanne Lebsock and Lori Ginzberg have described the rising trend in the 1850s toward mixed benevolent associations, with subsequent loss of authority by women.[51] By refusing to es-

---

47. DuBois, "Women's Rights and Abolition," p. 249.
48. *Memorial of Sarah Pugh*, p. 89.
49. DuBois, "Women's Rights and Abolition," pp. 249–51; Stanton et al., eds., *History of Woman Suffrage*, 1:540–42.
50. Stanton et al., eds., *History of Woman Suffrage*, 1:481–85, 493–99.
51. Suzanne Lebsock, *Free Women of Petersburg: Status and Culture in a Southern Town, 1784–1860* (New York, 1984), pp. 195–236; Lori D. Ginzberg, *Women and the Work of Benevolence: Morality, Politics, and Class in the Nineteenth-Century United States* (New Haven, 1990), pp. 109–29.

tablish a national society, leaders of the antebellum women's rights movement avoided domination by their male colleagues. Certainly PFASS was conscious of the advantages of autonomy. In 1853 Hannah J. Stickney, a past president, objected to the word "Female" in the society's name and another member suggested a merger with men to form a citywide organization, but the group rejected both motions. Mary Grew, longtime corresponding secretary, explained why she saw no reason to change the character of the organization. Over "the long course of varying experiences thro' which the Society had steadily kept its way," she argued, "it had ever been true to the highest form of antislavery principle professed by American abolitionists." The women had endured "hours of darkness and perplexity" and had not faltered "when openly to profess anti-slavery was perilous to property and life and reputation." Grew did not expect a combined organization to be any more efficient than the women's society had been, and for "the sake of the Past and the Present" she hoped that the group would remain unaltered.[52]

The Philadelphia Female Anti-Slavery Society had changed, however, over the previous two decades, though not in its commitments to abolish slavery, integrate its own leadership, and maintain its autonomy. In the 1830s, the young society had eagerly sought new members, canvassed door to door for thousands of signatures, supported a school for African American children, considered ways to improve opportunity for black Philadelphians, and imposed few ideological restraints upon its members. After 1837, in response to increasing personal responsibilities and such outside influences as the destruction of Pennsylvania Hall, imposition of the Gag Rule, and more rigid ideological positions in the abolitionist movement, the society followed a more narrow path. In requiring adherence to nonresistance, the Philadelphia women chose to be a tiny band of moral reformers rather than the organizers of a mass movement. The antislavery fair was ideally suited to this new strategy, for they could coordinate the work of many sympathizers (whose commitment was judged by their needlework rather than by the orthodoxy of their beliefs) and attract large crowds to hear abolitionist speakers. The Philadelphia leaders thus kept control of their organization and its ideology and at the same time raised significant sums of money, thereby solidifying their position within the larger abolitionist crusade.

When Stanton, Mott, and others initiated the women's rights movement, they followed a parallel course. Instead of establishing a national as-

---

52. PFASS mins., November 10, 1853.

sociation dedicated to attracting a large membership, they held annual conventions at which advocates could present their views. This design not only permitted intellectual flexibility but required minimal organizational effort from women who had substantial responsibilities at home.[53] The women's rights leaders were wiser than they knew. Later, after the Civil War, when women's rights leaders found the time and resources to set up organizations, the movement quickly divided over priorities and tactics.

53. For a prominent example, see Elisabeth Griffith, *In Her Own Right: The Life of Elizabeth Cady Stanton* (New York, 1984).

{ Part II }

Black Women in the
Political Culture of Reform

{ 5 }

The World the Agitators Made
The Counterculture of Agitation in Urban Philadelphia

Emma Jones Lapsansky

In 1837, as Philadelphians hurried along near Second and Market streets, banking, shopping, visiting, and newsgathering, they could watch the dismantling of the market and courthouse that had been a symbol of city authority, centrality, and stability since the founding of Pennsylvania. Indeed, the demolition of this building symbolized the demise of a familiar and traditional world. No Philadelphian, watching the old courthouse and marketplace come down, could grasp all of the implications of this era of change, but neither could any aware Philadelphian in that year have looked at the rapidly changing world without some anxiety.

Despite the lack of clarity about the causes of the tremors that shook the nineteenth-century Philadelphian's world—or perhaps because of the lack of clarity—many Philadelphians were fervent in their prescriptions for remedies to "the problem." The problem, as one historian has described it, was a "rapid succession of events during the three decades from 1830–1860 [which] test[ed] every element in Philadelphia's traditions by relentlessly overturning the commonplace modes of daily life. Methods of business and relationships among men which had sufficed since the first settling of Penn's town were suddenly transformed by an irresistible series of novel events. Speed, bigness, newcomers and money beat upon settled manners with a rain of harassment and opportunity."[1]

The peaceable kingdom that Penn had envisioned was coming apart, and Philadelphia's inhabitants were overwhelmed by "civilization." They ad-

---

1. Sam Bass Warner, *The Private City: Philadelphia in Three Periods of Its Growth* (Philadelphia, 1968), p. 49.

justed to their confusion by huddling in the relative safety of others "like themselves," shunning anyone or anything that reminded them of the instability of their world.[2]

But how to locate people "like themselves" when "like themselves" increasingly meant something other than family or neighbors? To be sure, old community traditions endured. Public celebrations were still held at the State House, with local residents of all ages, sexes, classes, races, and states of inebriation sharing the euphoria. The freezing of the river still brought anyone and everyone out to enjoy the winter, and when the arrival of the shad was announced in the papers, all manner of local citizens turned out to fish.[3] Yet in the 1830s, as "community" became an increasingly complex concept, these rituals acquired a new edge of tension, a hint of lawlessness and hostility that was echoed in street brawling and conflicts over public space which threatened to destroy the community rituals.

The once-friendly streets were now crowded with gangs and thieves and "foreigners," and—just as frightening—with women with new strident and sophisticated political voices. Certain Philadelphia women, uniquely positioned by geography, class, experience, family, and culture, were profoundly shaped by, and were powerful shapers of, the new world. Philadelphia, where many reform Quaker families lived, was also the locus of the largest northern free black population. Both groups, keeping step with the times, encouraged their women to embrace the opportunities of the new era.

The founding of the Philadelphia Female Anti-Slavery Society in 1833 had reflected some of the dynamics of this unsettling new world. This group of capable and strong-willed women, many of them Quaker, some of them black, challenged the traditional norms against biracial cooperation. In addition, the group broke the taboos against women speaking in public and took a hard-line reformist stand against slavery, one of the most controversial issues of the day. Respectable women, members of some of the city's most venerable families, joined these ranks, adding their powerful voices to the unsettling new demands.[4]

2. Ibid., chaps. 3–4. Michael Feldberg, *The Turbulent Era: Riot and Disorder in Jacksonian America* (New York, 1980), chap. 5.

3. One has only to peruse the announcements in the *Public Ledger* or to browse through collections of contemporary Philadelphia prints to get a sense of the bustling activity of the city and its port. Two good collections are Nicholas Wainwright, *Philadelphia in the Romantic Age of Lithography* (Philadelphia, 1970) and Philip Chadwick Foster Smith, *Philadelphia on the River* (Philadelphia, 1986).

4. See Ira Brown, "'Am I Not a Women and a Sister?': The Anti-Slavery Convention of American Women, 1837–39," *Pennsylvania History* 50 (1983): 1–19.

The Counterculture of Agitation in Philadelphia

Not only did Philadelphians face bewildering new kinds of public inter-actions, but as part of the modern city they encountered dramatic changes in the way public interactions were conducted as well. Informal attitudes toward time and appointments increasingly gave way to expectations of punctuality and regularity. The rigid and uniformly applied taskmasters of factories—time clocks—replaced the more individualized rhythms of cot-tage industries. Professional politicians, teachers, and financiers, concen-trating on "specializations," crowded out the old-style "gentleman" leader who had divided his time and resources among a range of endeavors. No segment of the community was spared. Women reported to scheduled jobs in shops and factories. Routinization redefined the lives of some young people in the form of public schools (Central High School opened in 1837), economic depressions devalued workers' security, high immigration brought competition to the workplace—unrest was endemic to every in-terest group, and the number of interest groups grew daily.[5]

In the changing cities of the northern states, black communities, ener-gized by newly organized institutions and new southern immigrants, worked to realize the self-determination that had been vaguely promised when a half-dozen northern states abolished slavery in the late eighteenth century. An integral part of American industrial society, the urban African American could not remain immune to the collateral effects of industrial-ization. In the 1830s and the 1840s, many individuals and groups in the black community offered their own solutions to urban problems. African American organizations multiplied, and they advocated self-help, self-improvement, self-education, and economic autonomy as ways to earn full citizenship in the emerging capitalist-industrial City of Brotherly Love.[6]

If the dismantling of the old marketplace symbolized the end of an era—the decline of the old face-to-face village—the year 1837 also brought signs of the new age, for in that year a group of Philadelphia's political radicals began to plan Pennsylvania Hall. Financed partly by funds raised by PFASS, the new building was necessary because women who espoused such radical

5. Warner, *Private City*, p. 61.
6. An enlightening list of such organizations can be found in [Joseph Willson], *Sketches of the Higher Classes of Colored People in Philadelphia, by a Southerner* (Philadelphia, 1841). Fuller discussion of these and other dynamics in nineteenth-century African American communities can be found in Julie Winch, *Philadelphia's Black Elite: Activism, Accommodation, and the Strug-gle for Autonomy, 1787–1848* (Philadelphia, 1988); James Horton, *Black Bostonians: Family Life and Community Struggle in the Antebellum North* (Boston, 1978); Leon Litwack, *North of Slavery: The Negro in the Free States, 1790–1860* (Chicago, 1961); Benjamin Quarles, *Black Abolitionists* (New York, 1969); and Richard Blackett, *Building an Antislavery Wall: Black Americans in the Atlantic Abolitionist Movement, 1830–1860* (Ithaca, 1983). For a good representation of the ideas of these leaders, see Dorothy Porter, *Early Negro Writing, 1760–1837* (Boston, 1971), pp. 79–250.

ideas as abolition could not find a public hall where they could meet to discuss and publicize their own remedy for the tensions of the new age: the elimination of slavery from American society.

As plans developed for the erection of Pennsylvania Hall, two children were born into two black reformist Philadelphia families. Their lives would exemplify the strategies and aspirations of African American reformers in the "new age." Into the family of African American patriarch James Forten was born a granddaughter, Charlotte Forten, who would eventually reinforce family alliances by marrying the nephew of two of the planners of Pennsylvania Hall. Into the family of another black patriarch, Jacob C. White, Sr., was born a son, Jacob C. White, Jr., who would become an early version of the "New Negro."

Charlotte Forten and Jacob White, Jr., were not yet toddlers when Pennsylvania Hall was burned to the ground. Yet the violent destruction of Pennsylvania Hall, immortalized in the folklore of their families and friends, was etched in their memories as they defined a direction for their adult lives.[7] Charlotte Forten trained herself to be a teacher and during the Civil War worked on the Sea Islands to educate freedmen. In this work she frequently lamented her sense of "unworthiness."

Jacob C. White, Sr., was a leader in the movement to define this new society. He owned the prosperous Lebanon Cemetery at the southern edge of the city, and he imbued his three sons with a passion for civic responsibility. By the time he was twenty years old, young Jacob White had adopted his father's social ambitions. The elder White had been a founding member of the short-lived Gilbert Lyceum, established by black leaders in 1841 "for the encouragement of polite literature" in the black community. He was also an avid participant in the Philadelphia station of the Underground Railroad and a leader in a half dozen other "uplift" efforts among his African American brethren. A successful entrepreneur, White had been able to give his children a sophisticated liberal education and a wide acquaintance with other similarly committed families. The intimate circle of the White family included Jesse Glasgow and his sons Jacob and Jesse, Jr., who in 1854 joined Jacob White, Jr., and his father in founding the Banneker Institute, a "young men's mutual instruction society." Jacob White, Jr., was an 1850s graduate of the Quaker-sponsored Institute for Colored Youth; he and the

7. Janice Sumler-Lewis, "The Fortens of Philadelphia: An African American Family and Nineteenth-Century Reform" (Ph.D. diss., Georgetown University, 1978); Harry C. Silcox, "Philadelphia Negro Educator, Jacob C. White, Jr., 1837–1902," *Pennsylvania Magazine of History and Biography* 97 (1973): 75–98; Margaret Hope Bacon, *Mothers of Feminism: The Story of Quaker Women in America* (San Francisco, 1986), p. 105.

Glasgow boys had been among the school's most talented and ambitious students.[8]

The parallel between the plight of African Americans and white women in the mid-nineteenth century has been frequently drawn, both by those groups themselves and by subsequent observers. The variables constituting that parallel, however, have received less attention. Specifically, the demands of the modernizing city required that, to "be seen as . . . responsible and moral human being[s]," both women and blacks adopt a theretofore unnecessary formality and rigidity about schedules and rules for public behavior. The new formality can be seen, for example, in the development of Philadelphia's Banneker Institute, which blazed an "untrodden path" of urban discipline for blacks. The goals and strategies of this organization—as well as its precarious existence and internal frictions—mirror the related circumstances of women's organizations in antebellum cities.

The inner circle of the institute were all men of the Glasgows' caliber—dedicated, self-directed, and motivated to improve the social and political possibilities of blacks. The catalyst and center of the organization of the Banneker Institute was Jacob C. White, Jr., and White's energy, enthusiasm, imagination, and contacts sustained the group for almost two decades. The goal of the institute's leaders was twofold. First, they sought to show other black brothers the rewards of conformity to urban capitalist discipline. Second, in "reflecting great credit on those who constitute this association,"[9] they hoped to present to the larger white world a cohesive unit of African Americans visibly capable of accepting full, productive citizenship in American society.

Seeking to display themselves in the best light, the leaders of the institute recruited men who they believed would share their ambitions and their belief that the first step in effective political action was self-education. Simultaneously, the institute's rules, regulations, and policies reflected and reinforced the lifestyle that the upwardly mobile black Philadelphian regarded as necessary to present a "respectable" public image and to meet the rigorous new demands of modern urban society.

The Banneker Institute maintained a library and sponsored an annual series of lectures on various political, economic, and cultural topics. It publicized its activities in local newspapers and broadsides, no doubt as much to make its presence known in the white community as to recruit the support of other African Americans. For nearly two decades, the group met

8. Harry C. Silcox, "Delay and Neglect: Negro Public Education in Antebellum Philadelphia, 1800–1860," *Pennsylvania Magazine of History and Biography* 97 (1973): 444–64.

9. Banneker Institute, Ms. Minute Books and Roll Books, 1854–1872, quotation from January 1854, Gardiner Collection, Historical Society of Pennsylvania.

with regularity and punctuality. The institute's leadership hoped that such a regimen would not only assure good order in their own lives but would also provide a model for less-privileged blacks and a standard for other Americans to admire.[10]

White, Glasgow, and Octavius V. Catto had all been children in Philadelphia during two decades of race riots in the 1830s and 1840s. They would have known of the attacks on the families and property of their middle-class friends and neighbors. These men knew the city streets were populated with roving gangs, unchecked by authorities, gangs that might, at any moment, unleash their frustration on African Americans. And if black men were acutely aware of the limitations on their opportunities, African American women, doubly shackled by race and gender, had even greater incentive to find ways to fulfill their ambitions.

For women, as well as for men, the energy for reform was often a multigenerational impulse. Charlotte Forten, like Jacob White, Jr., grew up in a dynasty of social activists. Two of her aunts, cultured and privileged women, had been active in the establishment of the interracial PFASS.[11] These women, along with Grace Douglass and her daughter Sarah, had been among the handful of black women who put their lives on the line in the spring of 1838 during the destruction of Pennsylvania Hall. For these women, the event had been pivotal, and they kept its memory so vivid that young Charlotte, almost two decades later, referred to it as a significant event in her own life.[12] By the 1850s, black men and black women in Philadelphia had analyzed the challenges of their society. Sometimes in harmony and tandem, sometimes in juxtaposition and opposition, each group began to develop strategies for fighting oppression.

In urban America of the mid-nineteenth century, power was being redistributed, and Philadelphia's women were out to get their share. Like their male counterparts, Philadelphia's women reformers were eager to join the new order. As early as the 1820s, Quaker women had organized to reform the prison system. By 1828, supported by a religious ethic that encouraged women's leadership, they had raised funds to expand the mission of the Female Prison Association of Friends (established in 1823) to include a women's House of Refuge, an alternative to squalid prison conditions.[13] Within a few years, Quaker and black women had recognized their com-

10. Ibid.

11. Ira Brown, "Anti-Slavery Convention," pp. 1–19.

12. Charlotte Forten, Ms. Diary, April 8, 1859, Moorland-Spingarn Collection, Howard University Library.

13. Bacon, *Mothers of Feminism*, pp. 139–41.

mon goals in the founding of PFASS, and by 1834 the Female Minervian Association was established. A literary organization consisting of about three dozen black women, the Female Minervian Association sponsored readings and recitations at its weekly meetings. In 1841 an observer reported that some women of this group had had their poetry published. A second black women's group, the Edgeworth Literary Association, had a similar agenda.[14]

Though such ambitious enterprises were not always wholeheartedly endorsed by the men of these families, the establishment of two exemplary organizations suggests that many men saw positive aspects to women having power. In 1841 the Gilbert Lyceum was established. Started by eleven blacks, five of whom had been founding members of PFASS, the Gilbert Lyceum was a literary and scientific club that counted both men and women among its founders. Similarly, by 1838 the Quaker-sponsored Pennsylvania Anti-Slavery Society enrolled men and women, both black and white. Lucretia Mott was one of its officers.[15]

Although the Banneker Institute admitted only men, they were not insensitive to the issues of their sisters. A few women—especially those who were directly related to members of the institute—appear from time to time in the institute's records as speakers or financial supporters. Sarah Mapps Douglass's talk on anatomy attracted a "tolerable" audience even on a rainy evening. Douglass, a teacher at the Quaker-sponsored Institute for Colored Youth, was married to minister William Douglass—also an invited speaker before the institute—and a relative of Banneker Institute member Joseph Bustill. Sarah Douglass and several other women appear on the rolls as "contributing members" of the institute, and other women are listed as performers or lecturers, including vocalist Elizabeth Bowers, poet Frances Ellen Watkins Harper, and ICY's first female head, Fanny Jackson Coppin.[16]

The women leaders of the generation of Jacob White, Jr., were no less ambitious than the men in their concern about the relationship between personal and group discipline. As Fanny Jackson Coppin commented: "I

14. Ibid., p. 107; Willson, *Higher Classes*, p. 109.
15. Bacon, *Mothers of Feminism*, p. 103. Founders of PFASS included Lucretia Mott, Sarah Pugh, Sarah Forten,* Harriet Forten Purvis,* Grace and Sarah Douglass,* Hetty Burr (*black). Willson, *Higher Classes*, p. 109. Founders of the Gilbert Lyceum included Joseph Cassey, Jacob C. White, John Bowers, Robert Purvis, Amy Cassey, Sarah Mapps Douglass, Grace Douglass, Hetty Burr, Harriet Purvis, and Amelia Bogle. For a fuller discussion of PFASS, see Ira Brown, *Mary Grew: Abolitionist and Feminist (1813–1896)* (Cranberry, NJ., 1991), pp. 14–22.
16. Banneker Institute, Ms. Minute Book, January 20, 1859, February 16, 1859, March 23, 1859, and May 18, 1859. Banneker Institute, Roll Book, 1854–1865.

never rose to recite in my classes at Oberlin but I felt that I had the honor of the whole African race upon my shoulders. I felt that, should I fail, it would be ascribed to the fact that I was colored."[17]

Born the same year as Jacob White, Jr., and Charlotte Forten, Coppin felt, as they did, the combination of fear, hope, and ambition instilled by a well-informed and public-spirited family. These young people responded to the challenge, pursuing self-development in the service of their race and judging themselves and their brothers and sisters harshly for any failings, real or imagined. Preparing to lead the struggle for equality, they also viewed themselves as missionaries to their less-fortunate brothers and sisters. Like many members of their cohort, White, Coppin, Forten, Catto, and Purvis assumed, at some point in their lives, the role of teacher, lecturer, or organizer of schools.[18]

What did these reformers hope to achieve? What was their ultimate goal? They had complex motives, including the desire to be perceived as frugal, temperate, "moderate," respectable, systematic, and disciplined, and to transmit these attitudes to yet another generation. Although this agenda strongly resembles the values of these reformers' Quaker allies, it also conforms significantly to the formality of the new urban discipline—including a commitment to formal and systematized education.[19] William Whipper, a respected black businessman, addressed the Colored Reading Society of Philadelphia for Mental Improvement and noted that "the age in which we live is fastidious in its taste. It demands eloquence, figure, rhetoric and pathos. . . . This is the golden age of Literature; men studious of change are constantly looking for something new."[20] Sarah Forten, Charlotte Forten's aunt, shared this dedication to a careful public presentation. "I have been looking over [my] . . . badly written letter and am almost ashamed to send it. . . . I recall with feelings of shame, Hannah More's advice to young ladies—wherein she recommends them 'never to write a letter in a careless or slovenly manner—it is a sign of ill breeding or indifference.' "[21]

17. Quoted in Dorothy Sterling, ed., *We Are Your Sisters: Black Women in the Nineteenth Century* (New York, 1984), p. 205.

18. Emma J. Lapsansky, "Feminism, Freedom, and Community: Charlotte Forten and Women Activists in Nineteenth-Century Philadelphia," *Pennsylvania Magazine of History and Biography* 113 (1989): 13, 17, 19.

19. For a discussion of some of the issues involved in these new urban styles, see Gary Cross, ed., *Worktime and Industrialization: An International History* (Philadelphia, 1988).

20. William Whipper, "Minutes and Proceedings of the First Annual Meeting of the American Moral Reform Society," in Porter, ed., *Early Negro Writing*, p. 209.

21. Sterling, *We Are Your Sisters*, p. 95.

The leaders of this movement hoped to create a self-conscious and cohesive black bourgeoisie, which by embracing the value of systematic networking and long-range goal setting, would adopt an agenda appropriate to their needs. Thus they hoped to construct a supportive community in a chaotic world.

Race and gender, ethnicity and class, modernity and tradition clashed as each was redefined. The dismantling of old buildings, the erection of new ones, the violent conflict over what these new buildings symbolized—these were the realities of the generation of Philadelphians born in the 1830s. Forten and White, and their families and friends, represent a generation struggling to reclaim order from the "irresistible series of novel events . . . speed, bigness, newcomers . . . [that] beat upon settled manners with a rain of harassment and opportunity."[22] Like many other city dwellers, they redefined community and fashioned values to meet the new demands of complex urban life.

22. Warner, *Private City*, p. 49.

{ 6 }

"You Have Talents— Only Cultivate Them"

Philadelphia's Black Female Literary Societies and the Abolitionist Crusade

Julie Winch

African American women in other northern cities had their own literary associations, but none flourished like those in Philadelphia. Boasting the largest and best-educated black community in the antebellum North, by 1836 Philadelphia was home to not one but three African American women's literary societies—the Female Literary Association, the Female Minervian Association, and the Edgeworth Literary Association.[1]

These societies were far more than coteries of middle-class ladies meeting to discuss the latest novels and write sentimental verses. The weekly meetings were intended to "improve the mental condition of all who feel disposed to participate" and membership was "not confined to any particular class."[2] Philadelphia's African American community comprised "in a gradual, moderate, and limited ratio, almost every grade of character, wealth, and . . . education." There were men and women who lived "in ease, comfort and the enjoyment of all the social blessings." Others could be seen "in the lowest depths of human degradation, misery and want." And then there were those "in the intermediate stages—sober, honest, industrious and respectable—claiming neither 'poverty nor riches,' yet maintaining,

---

1. By 1835 over 15,000 African Americans lived in the city and county of Philadelphia. The community supported 14 churches, 2 public halls, and over 60 benevolent societies, as well as a network of schools, temperance societies, and social reform organizations (*African Repository,* May 1835). For a discussion of literary societies in Philadelphia and elsewhere see Dorothy B. Porter, "The Organized Educational Activities of Negro Literary Societies, 1828–1846," *Journal of Negro Education* 5 (October 1936): 556–66.

2. *Liberator,* March 1, 1834.

by their pursuits, their families in comparative ease and comfort."[3] Although it is unlikely that the poorest women in the community had the skills, the leisure, or the means to participate in the activities of the associations (each assumed literacy and levied a modest fee to buy books and journals for its library), the literary societies had on their rolls women who had been forced to forgo formal schooling in order to work to support their families, as well as women from more prosperous backgrounds who had been tutored at home or sent to one of the city's private schools for black children. In a very real sense, membership in the literary societies united these women by cutting across class lines. As one of the wealthier and better-educated members wrote: "I look back with pleasure to the day when I became a member [of the Female Literary Association], it has brought me to see my own deficiencies and to have charity for my neighbors."[4]

Some African American men praised the work of the women's societies and occasionally addressed their meetings, but the attitudes of other men in the community obliged the women to organize independently. Keenly aware that "knowledge is power" and that "glorious" results might be expected if "this power [were] in the possession of the . . . freemen of colour,"[5] middle-class black men had already banded together to form literary and self-improvement organizations. In such exclusively male groups as the African Literary Society, the Reading Room Society, the Young Men's Literary Association, the Demosthenian Institute, and the Philadelphia Library Company of Colored Persons, they met regularly to debate issues of the day and refine their writing skills. Even when a society's constitution stated that it was founded for "the entire population of the City," women were barred from membership.[6] Not until 1841, with the founding

3. [Joseph Willson], *Sketches of the Higher Classes of Colored Society in Philadelphia by "A Southerner"* (Philadelphia, 1841), pp. 14–15.

4. Sarah Mapps Douglass to William Lloyd Garrison, December 6, 1832, Antislavery Manuscripts, Boston Public Library (hereafter cited as BPL). Members were also drawn from various religious denominations. The religious affiliations represented in the literary societies included St. Thomas's African Episcopal Church, Bethel African Methodist Episcopal Church, the First and Second African Presbyterian Churches, and the Society of Friends.

5. *Constitution of the Rush Education Society of Philadelphia* (Philadelphia, n.d.), pp. 1–2.

6. On the men's societies see *Poulson's American Daily Advertiser,* September 14, 1824 (African Literary Society); *Freedom's Journal,* June 20, 1828 (Reading Room Society); *Hazard's Register,* November 18, p. 186 (Philadelphia Library Company of Colored Persons); *Pennsylvania Freeman,* September 26, 1839 (Young Men's Library Association), and November 17, 1841 (Athenian Lyceum); and *Colored American,* February 2, 1839 (Young Men's Union Literary Association) and April 24, 1841 (Demosthenian Institute).

of the Gilbert Lyceum, did Philadelphia's African American community have a literary organization that admitted both men and women.[7]

Even if the male societies had invited females to join, however, at least some of the women might have chosen to keep to their own organizations. Issues of specific concern to them, some women felt, could best be raised in an exclusively female setting. Moreover, for those whose education had been restricted by poverty as well as by gender and race, a sense of inferiority and shame at being obliged to expose their ignorance, and a fear of being overawed by men may have prompted them to seek the companionship of other women. For the untutored, membership meant a chance to learn from their more highly educated sisters in a supportive atmosphere. For elite women, membership brought other opportunities. Within their own organizations they could develop leadership abilities, practice framing constitutions and bylaws, and hone their writing skills. Some of the most able officers of the women's antislavery conventions, such as Sarah Mapps Douglass and Hetty Burr, served their apprenticeship in Philadelphia's female literary societies.

Black women in Philadelphia did not suddenly find a voice with the formation of the literary societies. As soon as they realized that editors would publish their work, individual women had begun contributing poetry and prose to such journals as the *Liberator* and the *Genius of Universal Emancipation*. The twin concerns of abolition and the eradication of prejudice permeated these early writings. In a letter to the *Liberator* in 1831, for example, "Anna Elizabeth" suggested that "Females of Color" set aside the Fourth of July "as a day of humiliation and prayer,"[8] and "Ella" asked, "Why do our friends, as well as our enemies, call us 'negroes?'" explaining that she and others considered it "a term of reproach."[9]

Under the pen name "Ada," Sarah Forten, one of the daughters of wealthy businessman and community leader James Forten, became a regular contributor to the *Liberator*.[10] She politicized such popular literary

7. On the Gilbert Lyceum, see Porter, "Educational Activities," p. 563; *Sketches of the Higher Classes*, p. 110; and Box 2G, f. 13, Leon Gardiner Collection, Historical Society of Pennsylvania. Among the members of the Gilbert Lyceum were several women who had been active in the female literary societies, including Grace and Sarah Douglass, Harriet Forten Purvis, and Hetty Burr.

8. *Liberator*, June 18, 1831.

9. Ibid., September 24, 1831. For an earlier work by "Ella," a poem titled "A Christian's Dying Hour," see ibid., September 3, 1831.

10. On the identity of "Ada" see James Forten to William Lloyd Garrison, February 23, 1831 (Antislavery Manuscripts, BPL). For a listing of Sarah Forten's writings, see Jean Fagan Yellin and Cynthia D. Bond, comps., *The Pen Is Ours: A List of Writings by and about African-*

themes as sorrow at leaving home and family by treating them in relation to the plight of the slave.

> The mother, wife, or child he loved,
> He ne'er shall see again;
> To him they're lost—ay, dead indeed:
> What for him doth remain?[11]

Further, as the daughter of a Revolutionary War veteran, Forten reproached the nation for failing to recognize the similarities between colonized Americans and enslaved Africans and for failing to live up to the Revolution's ideals. In "The Slave" she observed that white Americans had apparently

> ... quite forgot,
> That bondage once had been their lot;
> The sweets of freedom now they know,
> They care not for the captive's wo[e].[12]

Turning to prose and signing herself "Magawisca," she warned white Americans that it was time to "awake from [their] lethargy" and remember that God "is just, and his anger will not always slumber. He will wipe the tear from Ethiopia's eye; He will shake the tree of liberty."[13]

Forten and the other African American women of Philadelphia, who published as "Anna Elizabeth," "Ella," "Sophanisba," "Zillah," "Woodby," "Bera," and "Zoe," were the moving force behind the founding of the Female Literary Association in September 1831. They were responding, in part, to a suggestion made by white abolitionist Simeon S. Jocelyn, who had been in Philadelphia a few weeks earlier to attend the black national convention. He had urged African American women to meet at each other's homes once a month for a "mental feast" of "moral and religious meditation, conversation, reading and speaking, sympathizing over the fate of the

---

American Women before 1910 (New York, 1991), pp. 257–61. On Forten and her sisters see Janice Sumler-Lewis, "The Forten-Purvis Women of Philadelphia and the American Anti-Slavery Crusade," *Journal of Negro History* 66 (Winter 1981): 281–88.

11. *Liberator,* March 19, 1831. See also ibid., January 22, 1831; January 29, 1831; and March 26, 1831.

12. Ibid., April 16, 1831.

13. Ibid., March 26, 1831. On a similar theme see "Ella's" poem, "Thy Thunder Pealeth O'er Us," ibid., August 9, 1834.

unhappy slaves, improving their own minds, &c &c."[14] Jocelyn had apparently envisaged something fairly informal, but the women in his audience set about giving their "mental feasts" an institutional framework. With a sophistication that they would later bring to the organization of the Philadelphia Female Anti-Slavery Society and the national antislavery conventions, the women crafted bylaws for their new society, defined the duties of each of the officers, and made provisions for elections. The main business of the society was to be transacted at weekly meetings "devoted to reading and recitation." To these each member could bring her work, unsigned or identified only by a nom de plume, and place it in a box. An officer would then read it, and the other members would offer their comments. In this way views could be expressed, and stylistic and grammatical corrections made, without embarrassment or personal affront.[15]

The secretary of the new society was Sarah Mapps Douglass, a dedicated teacher who earnestly wished to see more educational opportunities made available to African American women.[16] Eager to spur into action her "sisters of other Cities," she lost no time in forwarding to William Lloyd Garrison a copy of the society's constitution with a request that he publish it in the *Liberator*.[17] Garrison welcomed the formation of the society, observing that it gave him "a new weapon . . . to use against southern oppressors." He also reminded Douglass that the *Liberator* now had a "Ladies Department." He urged her to "occupy it as often as possible with your productions, and get others of your Society to do the same."[18]

The success of the Female Literary Association led to the creation of two more such groups in Philadelphia. In October 1834, taking as their patron

14. Ibid., July 21, 1832. See also ibid., December 8, 1832.

15. Ibid., December 3, 1831. On the proceedings at the weekly meetings see also ibid., June 30, 1832.

16. Sarah Mapps Douglass (1806–1882) was the daughter of affluent barber Robert Douglass, Sr., and Grace Bustill Douglass. As a child she attended Quaker meeting with her mother, but as an adult she was often critical of white Friends for their behavior toward African Americans. For many years she operated a successful private school in Philadelphia. Acquiring a basic medical training when she was in her fifties, she became a noted lecturer on matters of hygiene and female reproductive health.

17. The constitution was sent to Garrison at the members' request by Frederick A. Hinton, one of the agents for the *Liberator* in Philadelphia. When they did not see it in print the members directed their secretary, Sarah Mapps Douglass, to find out whether it was being deliberately suppressed (Sarah Mapps Douglass to William Lloyd Garrison, February 29, 1832, Antislavery Manuscripts, BPL). Garrison was obliged to confess that he had received it but had misplaced it. When it surfaced again he published it (Garrison to Douglass, March 5, 1832, Antislavery Manuscripts, BPL).

18. William Lloyd Garrison to Sarah Mapps Douglass, March 5, 1832, Antislavery Manuscripts, BPL.

the Roman goddess of wisdom, thirty women founded the Female Min-
ervian Association as a "school for the . . . promotion of polite literature."[19]
Two years later, another company of women, admirers of the British novelist Maria Edgeworth, affiliated as the Edgeworth Literary Association.
By 1838 these three organizations had a total membership of seventy-two.[20]
Although none of the societies could rival the all-male Colored Library
Company, which boasted 150 members and a library of six hundred books,
the very fact that they continued to flourish testifies to the determination
of these women to educate themselves.[21]

The energy and enthusiasm with which the members of these societies
sought "mental cultivation" did not, however, necessarily imply an open
rejection of traditional gender roles. By improving their minds they intended to become not less but more "womanly." Learning, they believed,
enabled them to avoid "bad desires and passions" and to look upon suffering with Christian resignation. As one member of the Female Minervian
Association told her sisters, they should seek "mental cultivation" because
it "beautifies and renders life a blessing [and] irradiate[s] the gloomy vale
of death."[22] Like their white contemporaries, they were told, and they accepted, that they were the guardians of society's moral values. Community
activist J. P. Clay reminded the women of the Edgeworth Literary Association that they wielded great power. With a sound education and a steadfast commitment to correct moral principles, they had the potential to
reform the nation. In "a country, where knowledge and virtue were generally diffused among the female sex," he asserted, men "would . . . be restrained from vice and error by the fear of being banished" from the
company of women.[23]

This sentiment was echoed by Garrison. In applauding the women who
had organized the Female Literary Association, he declared: "There is not
a glance of your eye, not a tone of your voice . . . but has a direct connexion
[*sic*] with the results of masculine actions and pursuits."[24] He repeated this

19. *Sketches of the Higher Classes*, pp. 107–8.

20. Some women probably belonged to more than one society, so the total number of individuals involved in the three organizations may have been less than seventy-two.

21. Pennsylvania Abolition Society, *The Present State and Condition of the Free People of Color
in the City of Philadelphia* (Philadelphia, 1838), p. 30; and "Schools, Benevolent Societies and
Literary Societies, 1838," PAS microfilm, reel 26, Historical Society of Pennsylvania. The president of the Colored Library Company was Robert Douglass, Sr., the father of Sarah Mapps
Douglass.

22. *Liberator*, December 8, 1832.

23. *Pennsylvania Freeman*, September 7, 1837.

24. William Lloyd Garrison to Sarah Mapps Douglass, March 5, 1832, Antislavery Manuscripts, BPL.

message in an address to the society when he visited Philadelphia. Deploring the fact that the schooling these African American women usually received was more likely "to debase the moral power, to enervate the understanding; and render them incapable of fulfilling the stations allotted them with becoming dignity," he looked to "the time when a complete reformation may be wrought therein" and "the female character raised to a just stand."[25]

The desire to raise "female character[s] . . . to a just stand" in order that they could perform their "womanly" roles more effectively was not simply imposed upon these women; it was explicitly endorsed by them. "A" insisted that when a woman was "virtuous and well-educated" she enhanced her worth to those in her immediate circle. "In the bosom of her family," she wrote, the educated woman "is revered for her judgment—her morality—her meekness. She rules only by the power of love." Her husband finds in her "not only the partner of his joys, but his counsellor—his guide—his comforter."[26]

Far from rejecting traditional womanly qualities, members of these literary societies praised them. In a letter to the *Liberator,* for example, "Zillah" exalted maternal love, self-sacrifice and forgiveness. She recalled hearing from a former slave how her mistress had "so far forgot her gentle nature" as to beat her for tending to her child instead of doing her work. The slave had stifled her desire to strike back for fear that her child might be punished in her stead. Years later, after gaining her freedom, she learned that her mistress, who had fallen upon hard times, wished her to return to help her. Friends of the former slave urged her not to go, but "woman-like, weeping that a lady should be so reduced, [she] obeyed the call."[27] "Zillah" judged that to be merciful, even toward one's enemies, and to express sorrow at their misfortunes, was "woman-like" and appropriate to one's "gentle nature." Whereas the slaveowner had betrayed her womanhood, her slave, with her love for her child and her willingness to forgive past wrongs, had proven herself a true lady.

"Zillah's" friend "Beatrice" thought "the cultivation of a woman's mind . . . all important, and far more so, than the adornment of the body." Exhorting her sister members of the Female Literary Association to greater intellectual feats, she declared: "You have talents—only cultivate them; you

25. *Liberator,* June 9, 1832.

26. Ibid., November 22, 1834.

27. Ibid., July 28, 1832. For a more extensive discussion of "womanly roles" in the northern black community see James O. Horton, "Freedom's Yoke: Gender Conventions among Antebellum Free Blacks," *Feminist Studies* 12 (Spring 1986): 51–76.

have minds—enrich them." She was convinced that "woman has a high destiny to fulfill" but agreed that a woman's destiny was not the same as a man's. "Though [woman] possess not the physical strength, nor ... the moral courage or ambition of man, yet she may have the wide field of the domestic circle to interest her."[28]

Yet these women's acceptance of their "sphere" was not as restricting as it might at first appear. To them, the "domestic circle" could indeed be a "wide field" encompassing far more than their immediate family, because they were prepared to use their "womanly qualities" to effect a fundamental moral and social reformation. Central to the decision of these African American women to organize literary societies was a sense of their responsibility to the entire black population of the United States, regardless of gender or status. The founders of the Female Literary Association acknowledged their duty "as daughters of a despised race ... to cultivate the talents entrusted to [their] keeping, that ... [they might] break down the strong barrier of prejudice, and raise [them]selves to an equality with those of [their] fellow beings who differ from [them] in complexion."[29]

Any attempt to deny African Americans an education was roundly condemned. For the benefit of "the [white] children who read the Liberator," "Zillah" wrote a short story about a crippled black girl forced to leave school because of the complaints of white classmates who envied her ability. With quiet resignation she stayed at home where she ruled her brothers and sister "by the law of love." She eventually died in great pain but strong in her religious faith. "Zillah" asked her "little readers, if [her] character ... appears the less lovely to them, because her complexion differed from theirs?"[30] Although willing to create a fictionalized black female victim to persuade young white children to reject racism, "Zillah" was capable of condemning adult bigotry. Deploring the persecution of abolitionist Prudence Crandall for opening a school for black women in Connecticut, she had no doubt that the teacher's sufferings were the result of the fears of "our enemies ... that education will elevate us to an equality with themselves." Those young women who had promised to attend Crandall's school should not be afraid. "We seldom walk abroad without being wounded by 'the cruel language of the eye;' and methinks for the sake of an education, we might be willing to bear not only scornful looks, but oppressive acts."

28. *Liberator,* July 7, 1832.
29. Ibid., December 3, 1831.
30. *Liberator,* August 18, 1832. On a similar theme see ibid., July 7, 1832, and *National Enquirer,* March 1, 1837. "Zillah" also wrote improving stories for African American children. See *Liberator,* September 1, 1832.

Moreover, "the time is fast approaching when an uneducated woman . . . will be little thought of."[31]

Members of all three societies believed that African American women should become educated so they could teach their children. "A" wrote in praise of the virtuous and well-educated mother who reared her "young buds of promise" to "become happy and useful here—happy and blessed hereafter."[32] "A" and her sisters did not merely believe that education should begin in the home or that women were intended to be teachers but that education involved the elevation of the entire race. They knew from their own experience how inadequate the provision of public school-ing was for black children. Further, they knew that fees at private schools exceeded the means of many parents, and that, even when tuition was free, children often had to be sent out to work.[33] If black women were not trained to teach their own children, the next generation might be con-demned to illiteracy.

For the members of the literary societies, female education involved far more than reading and writing. Women had to be able to transmit to their children sound moral principles, and that meant they themselves needed a new kind of education. To train a woman merely to be decorative was to leave her unprepared for life and unable to be an effective mother. "Zoe" was disturbed by the fact that so many young people were "sent into the world . . . ignorant and conceited . . . and wholly unable . . . to encounter difficulties with becoming fortitude."[34] In a letter in the same edition of the *Liberator* "Zoe's" friend "Bera" wrote that she believed firmly that "well educated people are the bulwark of national freedom: an ignorant commu-nity only can submit to the arbitrament of a despot." She considered the usual type of education sadly defective, however; parents, and especially mothers, must be made to see "that one more perfect is within their reach."[35]

After listening to a speech to the Female Minervian Association by a male guest in 1840, the white abolitionist Lucretia Mott concluded that some men "set a limit to the sphere of woman, which she may find it her

31. *Emancipator,* July 20, 1833. Her writings reveal little about the identity of "Zillah," other than that she was a teacher. See *Liberator,* July 7, 1832.

32. Ibid., November 22, 1834.

33. On the educational opportunities for African American children in Philadelphia see Harry C. Silcox, "Delay and Neglect: Negro Education in Philadelphia, 1800–1860," *Pennsyl-vania Magazine of History and Biography* 97 (October 1973): 444–64, and Edward J. Price, Jr., "School Segregation in Nineteenth-Century Pennsylvania," *Pennsylvania History* 43 (April 1976): 121–37.

34. *Liberator,* August 11, 1832.

35. Ibid.

duty to overstep."[36] By 1840 the whole issue of "woman's sphere" was being reexamined, and Mott herself was about to leave for the World's Anti-Slavery Convention in London, at which differences over the "appropriate" role of women would split the international abolition movement. The members of the literary societies were well aware of the nature of that debate, but in their pursuit of learning and in their efforts to widen their "domestic field" they also knew they had support from some of the men in their own community.

In 1834 John C. Bowers, a member of one of the men's literary societies, wrote the *Liberator* to praise the women's groups.[37] He observed that the women had done much to improve "their mental faculties—which object should be eagerly sought after . . . by every female." In his opinion, "a female soul, without education, is like marble in a quarry previous to being polished by the hands of the artist." Moreover, the determination of these women to educate themselves and demonstrate their intellectual abilities helped the entire black community. A steadfast opponent of the American Colonization Society, Bowers had no patience with those who argued that African Americans were intellectually inferior and should therefore be forced to leave the United States. When his "oppressed sisters" showed themselves capable of intellectual improvement they helped to refute the argument that no black person "can ever be elevated in this country."[38]

Three years later, in an impassioned speech on education before the American Moral Reform Society, Sarah Forten's younger brother, James Forten, Jr., acknowledged that "much opposition . . . existed in relation to females being educated on a more extensive scale than formerly." He blamed male jealousy, "for it appears . . . our sex startle at the idea of woman rising equal to them in . . . intellectual strength." Men must encourage women to become educated, "if . . . only to check that false pride and unpardonable vanity which we are too apt to assume towards" them. A moral principle was also at stake. "It is not for us to . . . cry aloud against persecution, and . . . play the part of persecutors."[39]

36. *Pennsylvania Freeman*, February 27, 1840. Mott observed that she often attended the society's meetings.

37. Bowers had a sister, Margaret, who was a member of PFASS. His wife, Mary, the daughter of community leader Cato Collins, taught in the Sunday School at St. Thomas's African Episcopal Church.

38. *Liberator*, August 30, 1834.

39. *Minutes and Proceedings of the First Annual Meeting of the American Moral Reform Society* (Philadelphia, 1837), in Dorothy B. Porter, ed., *Early Negro Writing, 1760–1837* (Boston, 1971), pp. 237–38.

A few men in the community urged the women to press still further for self-improvement. J. P. Clay suggested that the members of the Edgeworth Literary Association take up the study of astronomy. "All the arts and sciences that require no masculine arm to wield, are suitable and beneficial to [women], for to the female mankind is indebted for the first formation of the human mind . . . it is the power of education . . . that elevates the female sex to that dignity and usefulness in society for which they were formed." He looked to female influence to bring about "a new era . . . in the history of mankind."[40] Similarly, Joseph Willson, the putative author of *Sketches of the Higher Classes of Colored Society in Philadelphia by "A Southerner,"* praised the women for forming literary associations and advised them to emulate the male societies by holding "systematic debates." He was sure that "great improvement would result therefrom. It would . . . be the means of promoting conversational powers; and ease and fluency, in this respect, is an accomplishment certainly well worth the aim of all."[41]

Even if the women did not follow "A Southerner's" advice and hold "systematic debates," they did not focus on education and the cultivation of literary taste to the exclusion of political concerns. Many political issues occupied their attention. They spoke out repeatedly on colonization, on the erosion of fundamental civil rights, and on racial discrimination against free people.[42] In 1837 Sarah Douglass forwarded to the editor of the *Colored American* a poem by her "esteemed friend," "Ella."[43] Reading the phrase "land of oppression" in the *Colored American* prompted "Ella" to write a poem about the consequences of American racism.

> Among the free, the wealthy, those who seem
> To lead a happy life are many found
> Whose hearts are wrung, whose cheeks are often wet
> With bitter tears: they feel the air they breathe

40. *Pennsylvania Freeman*, September 7, 1837.

41. *Sketches of the Higher Classes*, pp. 30–31.

42. On the deep interest of the members of the Female Literary Association in the issue of African colonization see Sarah Mapps Douglass to William Lloyd Garrison, December 6, 1832, Antislavery Manuscripts, BPL.

43. "Ella" was, in fact, Sarah Mapps Douglass. On September 24, 1831, the *Liberator* published a letter by "Ella" describing racial proscription by "white Christians." It is almost identical to the account of prejudice among white Friends that Douglass wrote at the request of Sarah and Angelina Grimké (Sarah Mapps Douglass to William Basset, December 1837, Antislavery Manuscripts, BPL). Another letter, written in 1832 and signed "Ella," was addressed to a brother about to leave home. In 1832 Robert Douglass, Jr., Douglass's younger brother, left Philadelphia to embark on a career as an artist (*Liberator*, March 24, 1832). For other works by "Ella" see ibid., August 9, 1834; *National Enquirer*, October 8, 1834; *Liberator*, December 3, 1836; *National Enquirer*, March 11, 1837, January 11, 1838, and January 25, 1838.

Julie Winch

Is tainted with oppression: and it comes
Across their spirits with a sick'ning weight![44]

Throughout the antebellum era African Americans engaged in an intense
and often acrimonious debate over the merits of emigration, wrestling with
the issue of whether they should remain in the United States at all costs or
whether, in the face of prejudice and proscription, they should look for a
new home.[45] The women of Philadelphia were not content to sit on the
sidelines and leave the men to resolve the issue. Readers of the *Liberator*
could follow the spirited exchange between "Woodby" and "Zillah," who
objected to the views expressed by "A Colored Female of Philadelphia" in
a piece read at a meeting of the Female Literary Association and subsequently published in the *Liberator*.[46] "A Colored Female" argued that African Americans would find in Mexico all the rights they were denied in
the United States and endorsed emigration. "Zillah" adamantly responded
that no other country could offer such advantages as America. It was her
home, "and though she unkindly strives to throw me from her bosom, I
will but embrace her the closer, determining never to part with her while I
have life. "Woodby" rejoined that "A Colored Female" had not advocated
emigration but had merely said a place should be decided upon in case African Americans were forced to leave their native land. But "Zillah" answered: "Cease . . . to think of any other city of refuge. Listen to the voice
of our dear Redeemer!It says: 'Fear not . . . it is your Father's good pleasure
to give you the kingdom.'" On a related issue, a move to deprive black
Pennsylvanians of many of their basic rights, she found comfort in reflecting on how others had steeled themselves to suffer in a righteous cause, and
she looked forward to a day when she would see "black and white mingle
together in social intercourse, without a shadow of disgust appearing on
the countenance of either."[47]

44. *Colored American*, January 20, 1838.
45. For a discussion of the various responses to emigration within the Philadelphia community see Julie Winch, *Philadelphia's Black Elite: Activism, Accommodation, and the Struggle for
Autonomy, 1787–1848* (Philadelphia, 1988), pp. 26–69.
46. The exchange was published over a span of several months: *Liberator*, January 28, 1832;
July 21, 1832; August 18, 1832; see also the poem "My Country" by Sarah Forten, January 4, 1834.
47. Ibid., June 30, 1832. This was prompted by a move in the state legislature to limit the
mobility of black Pennsylvanians and prevent the migration of free people of color from the
south into Pennsylvania. Leaders of Philadelphia's African American community responded
with a series of petitions and the proposed law was not enacted. For other writings by "Zillah"
see "Moonlight," ibid., April 7, 1832, and "A Leaf From My Scrap Book," ibid., December 15,
1832.

The most frequent theme in the writings of the Philadelphia women was unity with the slave. Every August 1, the anniversary of Britain's abolition of slavery in her West Indian colonies, members of the various societies met to give thanks for what had already been accomplished and to pledge to end slavery in the United States. They prayed, read their own writings, listened to antislavery addresses, and feasted on bread and water. The money they would have spent on food was donated to the various antislavery organizations.[48]

Making common cause with the slaves was not, however, confined to one day a year. Repeatedly, in poems, short stories, and letters, these free Philadelphia women acknowledged how firmly tied their fate was to that of the slaves. Some attributed their zeal in the antislavery cause to their "mental feasts." Sarah Mapps Douglass, for example, confessed, "I had formed a little world of my own, and cared not to move beyond its precincts." It was true that "the wail of the captive sometimes came to [her] ear in the midst of [her] happiness ... but ... the impression was as evanescent as the morning dew." Meeting with other women and listening to them discuss the sufferings of the slaves had awakened her. "I started up, and with one mighty effort threw from me the lethargy which had covered me as a mantle for years; and determined, by the help of the Almighty, to use every exertion in my power to elevate the character of my wronged and neglected race." She asked fellow members of her organization, "Has this not been your experience, my sisters?"[49]

On the first anniversary of the Female Literary Association a member addressed the group, asserting that "as the free people of color become virtuous and intelligent, the ... condition of the slave will also improve." Each member must "sympathise [sic] in [the] woes" of the slaves and "rehearse their wrongs to her friends on every occasion, always remembering that our interests are one, that we rise or fall together, and that we can never be elevated to our proper standing while they are in bondage." Alluding to the mixed racial ancestry of many of the women in her audience, the speaker insisted that they must not be deluded into assuming they were "better" than the slaves. To those who would "persuade us that we are a superior race to the slaves, and that our superiority is owing to a mixture with the whites" they should answer "that the black man is equal by nature with the white, and that slavery and not his color has debased him."[50]

Two years later a member took the women to task for not always living up to their high ideals. "With all the persecutions ... we have had to en-

48. See, for example, *Pennsylvania Freeman*, August 31, 1836.
49. *Liberator*, July 21, 1832.
50. Ibid., October 13, 1832.

counter, we are estranged one from another." They must unite if they intended to end slavery.[51] Yet another "young lady of color" observed that the meetings of the various societies were designed to "remove that spirit of indifference . . . which . . . exists among us, and to unite us as a band of sisters in the great work of improvement." She feared that "we shall never be a religious people . . . until we drink more deeply of the cup of bitterness daily meted out to the slave." To those who asked what they could do to help the slaves she replied, "be united—cultivate your minds—pray."[52]

In describing the joys and consolations of religious faith, Sarah Mapps Douglass, signing herself "Sophanisba," expressed her deep sadness that "there is a portion of our sex, from whom these precious privileges . . . are withheld." She appealed to free women like herself to "bear on our hearts the sorrows, the ignorance, the degradation of our captive sisters . . . [and] make them the subject of our daily conversation, our daily prayers."[53] In another piece she spoke of "the grave as the leveller of distinctions [where] the despised black reposes in undisturbed serenity by the side of the lordly white . . . and the slave is free from his master." Although she was fortunate enough to be freeborn, moderately prosperous, and surrounded by a loving family, her "heart was filled with sorrow for [her] enslaved sisters." Condemning a system that kept so many in ignorance, she begged her "sister slave, fainting with toil and sickness in the burning sun," to have faith. God would ease her sufferings and the abolitionists would spare no effort on her behalf.[54]

The members of the literary societies followed the progress of abolition with an avid interest that is reflected in their writings. In a poem she sent to the *Liberator* in 1837, Sarah Forten likened the abolitionist onslaught to an avalanche sweeping all before it, including "prejudice, that Upas of the mind."[55] Again and again she and others praised people who devoted themselves to the cause.[56] In 1833, for example, the *Liberator* published Forten's poem "To the *Hibernia,*" celebrating the voyage of Garrison, "the Champion of the slave," to "old Britain's shores" to spread the antislavery

51. Ibid., March 1, 1834.
52. Ibid., December 8, 1832.
53. *Genius of Universal Emancipation,* February 1833, pp. 62–63. On the identification of "Sophanisba" as Sarah Mapps Douglass see Dorothy Sterling, ed., *We Are Your Sisters: Black Women in the Nineteenth Century* (New York, 1984), p. 112: and Yellin and Bond, *The Pen Is Ours,* pp. 252–57.
54. *Liberator,* August 4, 1832. For other writings by "Sophanisba" on religious faith and the abolitionist cause see ibid., July 14, 1832, and September 8, 1832.
55. Ibid., June 16, 1837.
56. See, for example, ibid., October 6, 1837.

message.[57] In "The Separation," written later that same year, she described her mixed emotions as abolitionists from all over the United States left Philadelphia after founding the American Anti-Slavery Society. She knew many of those who had attended the convention; some had dined at her home and discussed antislavery strategies with her and her family. Even though she regretted the departure of her "little band of friends," however, she rejoiced that they had gone to further the work of abolition.[58]

In the antislavery crusade women like Sarah Forten were far more than spectators. Their participation in the abolitionist movement paralleled their struggle for education and "mental cultivation." Through the Female Vigilance Association, Forten and her sisters, Sarah and Grace Douglass, Eliza Colly, Sarah McCrummill, Elizabeth White, and many of the other women active in the literary societies raised money to aid the hundreds of fugitive slaves who flocked to their city each year.[59] They clothed them, fed them, paid for their medical care, and sheltered them in their own homes until they could be sent on the next leg of their journey to Canada.[60] It was hardly coincidental that members of the literary societies also enrolled in the Philadelphia Female Anti-Slavery Society. The organization was interracial from its birth in December 1833.[61] Sarah McCrummill, the wife of community activist James McCrummill, and Margaretta Forten, a teacher and Sarah Forten's sister, were appointed to a committee to draw up a con-

57. Ibid., May 25, 1833. Sarah Forten's admiration of Garrison's work was shared by other members of the Female Literary Association. At their annual meeting in 1837 their secretary, Sarah Mapps Douglass, was instructed "to send [him] a letter . . . expressive of their sympathy in his late trials, and of their hearty approbation of the firm, manly, christian and consistent course he has ever pursued as editor of the Liberator" (*Liberator*, October 6, 1837).

58. *Liberator*, December 21, 1833. Sarah's older sister, Margaretta, wrote a poem on the same subject. See "To the Members of the Late Anti-Slavery Convention" in the *Emancipator*, January 14, 1834.

59. Grace Bustill Douglass (d. 1842), the mother of Sarah Mapps Douglass, was noted for her many private acts of charity in the African American community. Her father, Cyrus Bustill, was African American, and her mother, Elizabeth Morey Bustill, was of Native American and English descent. Cyrus Bustill had arranged for his daughter to be trained as a milliner, but her marriage to prosperous barber Robert Douglass relieved her of the necessity to work outside the home. Like Douglass, Elizabeth White had been trained in skilled trade (she was a tailor), but her husband's wealth meant she stayed at home and devoted herself to what the Pennsylvania Abolition Society census of 1838 termed her "own work." In contrast, Eliza Colly was obliged to take in washing to supplement her husband's income as a shoemaker. Sarah McCrummill, the wife of dentist James McCrummill, was a hairworker (she dressed and wove hair for wigs).

60. *Pennsylvania Freeman*, July 5, 1838; March 12, 1840.

61. On the early years of the organization see Ira V. Brown, "Cradle of Feminism: The Philadelphia Female Anti-Slavery Society, 1833–40," *Pennsylvania Magazine of History and Biography* 102 (April 1978): 143–66.

stitution. Among their sister members were at least two of the officers of the Female Literary Association, Sarah Douglass and Hetty Burr. Other African American members—Elizabeth Butler, Eliza Bias, Amy Cassey, Sarah Dorsey, Rebecca Hutchins, Margaret Bowers, Harriet Forten Purvis, Sarah Forten, Charlotte Vandine Forten, and Mary Wood Forten—all had shown a strong commitment to education and social reform. Although it is impossible to identify with any degree of certainty "Zoe," "Bera," and many of the others who wrote under such aliases, some of them were likely included in this group.[62]

As the female abolition movement gained momentum, the black women of Philadelphia extended their activities to the national level. In 1837 about half a dozen of them traveled to New York for the first women's antislavery convention. Grace Douglass, Sarah Mapps Douglass's mother, was elected one of the convention's six presidents and was appointed, with Angelina Grimké and Lydia Maria Child, to prepare the *Appeal to the Women of the Nominally Free States*.[63] This appeal drew upon the literary talents of the Philadelphia women as well as on their organizational abilities. An open letter describing the effect of prejudice on the individual was based, at least in part, on information supplied by Sarah Mapps Douglass, and an excerpt from "An Appeal to Woman," a poem by Sarah Forten, appeared on the front page of the pamphlet.

62. Margaretta Forten was the eldest daughter of wealthy sailmaker James Forten. For many years she ran a successful private school. Hetty Burr was the wife of community leader John P. Burr. Eliza Ann Bias had been born into slavery in Maryland. Once she was manumitted she and her husband, former slave James J. G. Bias, moved to Philadelphia. Bias established himself as a dentist and bleeder and Eliza Bias assisted him in his work. Elizabeth Butler, the wife of affluent hairdresser Thomas Butler, was the president of the Dorcas Society and an officer of the Female Vigilant Committee. Amy Matilda Cassey was the daughter of the Rev. Peter Williams, a New York minister and reformer, and the wife of Joseph Cassey, one of the few African Americans in antebellum Philadelphia to be accorded the title of "gentleman" in the city directories. Rebecca Hutchins (d. 1836) was the wife of affluent clothier Samuel C. Hutchins. In addition to her involvement in the literary societies, her obituary noted that she was active in several female benevolent organizations. Charlotte Vandine Forten, a freeborn native of Pennsylvania, was the second wife of James Forten and the mother of Margaretta, Harriet, and Sarah Forten. In 1831 Harriet Forten married Robert Purvis, a rich emigré from South Carolina and an outspoken abolitionist. Mary Virginia Wood married Robert Bridges Forten, James and Charlotte Forten's second son, in 1836. As for Sarah Dorsey, she cannot be identified with any degree of certainty because there were several African American families of the name of Dorsey in Philadelphia in the 1830s. Hetty Burr, Elizabeth Butler, Amy Cassey, Charlotte Forten, two of her daughters, and her daughter-in-law, did not work outside the home. The Pennsylvania Abolition Society census of 1838 recorded them as doing their "own work" or attending to "domestic duties."

63. *Proceedings of the Anti-Slavery Convention of American Women . . . 1837* (New York, 1837), pp. 3, 7, 15.

We are thy sisters,—God has truly said,
That of one blood, the nations he has made.
O, Christian woman, in a Christian land,
Canst thou unblushing read this great command?
Suffer the wrongs which wring our inmost heart,
To draw one throb of pity on thy part!
Our 'skins may differ,' but from thee we claim
A sister's privilege, in a sister's name.[64]

Eighteen thirty-eight saw even greater participation by the Philadelphia women when the second Anti-Slavery Convention of American Women met in their own city. Sarah Mapps Douglass, secretary of the Female Literary Association, was the convention's treasurer and, with the association's president, Hetty Burr, she served on the business committee. Other black abolitionists from Philadelphia attended as delegates or as corresponding members.[65] The following year, even more of the women took part in the third and final separate female antislavery convention.[66]

The formation of literary societies by the black women of Philadelphia was an integral part of the antislavery crusade. The poetry and prose they produced testifies to their understanding of their role not only in the abolitionist cause but in several interconnected reform movements. As women, they shared with their white sisters a duty to educate themselves so that they could be effective both within their families and in the larger society as guardians of moral values. As free black women, they assumed at least part of the burden of improving their own community and of disabusing whites of notions of the intellectual inferiority of black people. Further, as black women, they drew on their talents and energies to make common cause with the slaves. On one level, they acknowledged a moral obligation

64. This is one verse of her poem, "An Appeal to Woman," which appeared first in the *Lowell Observer* and was then reprinted in the *Liberator,* February 1, 1834.

65. *Proceedings of the Anti-Slavery Convention of American Women . . . 1838* (Philadelphia, 1838), pp. 3, 4, 12, 14. The black women delegates from Philadelphia were Grace and Sarah Douglass, Elizabeth K. Dorsey, Hetty Burr, and Harriet Forten Purvis. There were others, like Sarah and Margaretta Forten, who attended but were not listed as delegates. Elizabeth K. Dorsey was a member of one of the various Dorsey families in the African American community. Amelia Bogle, the daughter of caterer Robert Bogle, ran a private school.

66. *Proceedings of the Third Anti-Slavery Convention of American Women . . . 1839* (Philadelphia, 1839). pp. 13–14. Five African American women from Philadelphia were listed as delegates—Grace and Sarah Douglass, Harriet Forten Purvis, Hannah Purnell, and Eliza Colly. Four more were corresponding members—Sarah Dorsey, Hetty Burr, Amelia Bogle, and Elizabeth Butler.

to work for the freedom of every member of their "aspersed race."[67] On another, they knew only too well that the very existence of the "peculiar institution" compromised their own freedom. In Sarah Forten's words:

> Can the names of our fathers who perished in fight,
> Be hallowed in story, midst slavery's blight? . . .
> Speak not of "my country," unless she shall be,
> In truth, the bright home of the "brave and the free."[68]

67. *Liberator,* December 8, 1832.
68. Ibid., January 4, 1834.

{ 7 }

Benevolence and Antislavery Activity among African American Women in New York and Boston, 1820–1840

Anne M. Boylan

The formation of women's antislavery societies in the 1830s brought black and white women together in an unprecedented fashion. Although white women's benevolent groups had existed since the 1790s, almost none accepted African Americans as clients, let alone as members. Instead, white women generally restricted their organizations to serving "the virtuous poor" of their own race and religion. When free black women organized independent associations, beginning in the 1820s, the realities of white racial exclusivity and desperate need among the black poor guaranteed that they would have neither white clients nor white members. Interracial antislavery societies represented a new departure in the history of both black and white women's organizing.[1]

For comments on an earlier version of this essay, I am grateful to Robert Gross, Peter Kolchin, Joanne Meyerowitz, and especially Jean Fagan Yellin.

1. For a general introduction to the history of women's organizations, see Eleanor Flexner, *Century of Struggle: The Woman's Rights Movement in the United States* (Cambridge, 1959), pp. 41–61; Mary Bosworth Treudley, " 'The Benevolent Fair': A Study of Charitable Organization among American Women in the First Third of the Nineteenth Century," *Social Service Review* 14 (September 1940): 509–22; two articles by Anne Firor Scott: "On Seeing and Not Seeing: A Case of Historical Invisibility," *Journal of American History* 71 (June, 1984): 7–21; and "Most Invisible of All: Black Women's Voluntary Organizations," *Journal of Southern History* 66 (February 1990): 3–22; and Lori D. Ginzberg, *Women and the Work of Benevolence: Morality, Politics, and Class in the Nineteenth-Century United States* (New Haven, 1990).

The ideal of cross-racial cooperation to end slavery often proved elusive, and attempts to achieve it were extremely controversial.[2] Occasionally, they evoked violent reactions among northern whites, such as the 1835 mobbing of the Boston Female Anti-Slavery Society and the burning of Pennsylvania Hall during the Anti-Slavery Convention of American Women in 1838. What enraged the rioters in these instances was the behavior of white female abolitionists, not black. When white female abolitionists engaged in public agitation and figuratively embraced free black women, their opponents conceived images of racial "amalgamation" and presumed their loss of all claims to feminine virtue. Although some women's societies, such as the Ladies' New York City Anti-Slavery Society, tried to sidestep controversy by choosing only white officers, most women's antislavery groups defied public opinion on this matter. African American women were active members and leaders of many female antislavery societies and of the three antislavery conventions of American women held between 1837 and 1839.[3]

Nevertheless, ideals of feminine respectability were very powerful in the antebellum North, and they took a toll on black women. Unlike white women, who enjoyed the presumption that they were "virtuous" until proven otherwise, free black women were uniformly slandered as "degraded" (that is, sexually promiscuous) because of their race. By forming their own organizations African American women could challenge the slander and also create an autonomous organizational tradition. Yet such activity also exposed them to the scrutiny of whites and heightened the expectations of African American men that women could do much to uplift the entire race. The organizational experiences of free black women in New York and Boston during the 1820s and 1830s illustrate their enormous resourcefulness in meeting family and community needs and their vulnerability in the face of white racial attitudes and gender conventions. Even within mixed-race groups such as female antislavery societies, their participation was constrained by attitudes and conventions that they had little power to control.

2. On the difficulties black abolitionists faced within the abolitionist movement, see Lawrence Friedman, *Gregarious Saints: Self and Community in American Abolitionism, 1830–1870* (New York, 1982), pp. 160–95; and Gerda Lerner, "Black and White Women in Interaction and Confrontation," in her book *The Majority Finds Its Past: Placing Women in History* (New York, 1979), pp. 94–103.

3. See the essays in this volume by Amy Swerdlow (Chapter 2), Debra L. Hansen (Chapter 3), and Jean R. Soderlund (Chapter 4). On the issue of racial "amalgamation" and women's virtue, see Jean Fagan Yellin, *Women and Sisters: The Antislavery Feminists in American Culture* (New Haven, 1989), pp. 45–50.

Antislavery Activity among African American Women

African Americans began to organize for mutual assistance and benevolent purposes immediately after the first emancipations in the Northeast. (In Boston, emancipation came overnight, as a 1783 judicial decision ended slavery in Massachusetts; in New York, it was a long, slow process that began in 1799 but was not completed until 1827.) Migration patterns, together with the end of slavery, brought increased numbers of free blacks into urban areas, creating the bases for the formation of separate black churches and institutions. By 1841, when a survey counted some thirty-three black benevolent societies, New York had a free black population of over sixteen thousand. Boston's considerably smaller African American population (about two thousand in 1840) supported at least three churches and a coterie of organizations. Free black women initially devoted themselves to aiding the fledgling churches that relied on their work and fund-raising abilities and to supporting the masonic orders and mutual aid societies that free black men had begun to create in the 1780s and 1790s.[4] By the 1820s, however, separate women's groups had begun to multiply.

These organizations resembled the myriad societies formed by other Americans, black and white, female and male. Their organizers wrote constitutions and bylaws, chose officers, met regularly, raised funds, and established programs. But the proliferation of such groups in the 1820s and 1830s suggests that black women, like white women, experienced a consciousness of gender that made separate organizations seem desirable. African American women's groups fell into the same broad categories of benevolence and reform as white women's (although, as we shall see, the distinction between benevolent and reform activity often evaporated quickly). Benevolent societies concentrated on the needs of black women and children, particularly widows and orphans, or did fund-raising for religious purposes. New York's Female Branch of Zion, attached to the African Methodist Episcopal Zion Church, aided sick church members, buried the dead, and helped support the orphaned children of deceased members. A second Zion Church group, the United Daughters

4. Dorothy Sterling, ed., *We Are Your Sisters: Black Women in the Nineteenth Century* (New York, 1984), pp. 104–8; Linda Perkins, "Black Women and Racial 'Uplift' Prior to Emancipation," in Filomena Chioma Steady, ed., *The Black Woman Cross-Culturally* (Cambridge, Mass., 1981), pp. 317–34; Rhoda G. Freeman, "The Free Negro in New York City in the Era Before the Civil War" (Ph.D. diss., Columbia Univiersity, 1966), p. 240; James Oliver Horton and Lois E. Horton, *Black Bostonians: Family Life and Community Struggle in the Antebellum North* (New York, 1979), pp. 28–35; Gary B. Nash, "Forging Freedom: The Emancipation Experience in the Northern Seaport Cities, 1775–1820," in Ira Berlin and Ronald Hoffman, eds., *Slavery and Freedom in the Age of the American Revolution* (Charlottesville, 1983), pp. 3–48; Scott, "Black Women's Voluntary Associations," pp. 3–7. See chapter appendix for a list of New York and Boston groups.

Anne M. Boylan

of Conference, raised money to support the ministry, as did the Female
Education Society at the First Colored Presbyterian Church. Reform organizations, such as temperance and antislavery groups, sought broad
social change.[5]

But most black women's benevolent organizations addressed the needs of
members and their families as well as those of the church and other community institutions, thus differing from comparable white women's groups.
Literary and educational societies were important sources of self-education
and self-improvement, although some also raised funds for children's education or promoted the training of young black men as ministers. Members
of Boston's Afric-American Female Intelligence Society, for example, met
to discuss literature or their own essays, thus improving their reading, writing, and speaking abilities. That the group's president, Elizabeth Riley,
signed legal documents with a mark, not a signature, suggests how re-
sourceful and how needy some organizers of literary societies could be. The
society also collected books for a library and brought in guest lecturers for
the members' edification. Mutual aid societies, by far the most common organizations of free black women, united individuals who contributed small
sums on a regular basis in return for sickness or death benefits. The payment of seventy-five cents every three months entitled members of New
York's Abyssinian Benevolent Daughters of Esther Association to two dollars per week sick benefits for up to six months. Offering a small measure
of insurance against illness or other personal catastrophe, mutual benefit
societies were far more numerous among black than among white women.[6]
By creating such groups, African American women expressed a belief that
they alone could meet certain needs, particularly women's needs, and they

5. On the Female Branch of Zion, see *Colored American*, June 3, 1837, p. 4; on the United
Daughters of Conference, see *Colored American*, December 9, 1839, p. 3; on the Female Education Society, see *Colored American*, October 31, 1840, p. 2; on women's temperance societies,
see Donald Martin Jacobs, "A History of the Boston Negro from the Revolution to the Civil
War" (Ph.D. diss., Boston University, 1968), p. 119.

6. On literary societies, see Dorothy B. Porter, "The Organized Educational Activities of
Negro Literary Societies, 1828–1846," *Journal of Negro Education* 5 (October 1936): 555–76; on
the Afric-American Female Intelligence Society, see Gerda Lerner, *Black Women in White
America: A Documentary History* (New York, 1972), pp. 437–40; on Elizabeth Riley's signa-
ture, see the legal documents transcribed in Carol Buchalter Stapp, "Afro-Americans in
Antebellum Boston: An Analysis of Probate Records" (Ph.D. diss., George Washington Uni-
versity, 1990), pp. 522–42; on the Abyssinian Benevolent Daughters of Esther Association, see
Daniel Perlman, "Organizations of the Free Negro in New York, 1800–1860," *Journal of Negro
History* 56 (July 1971): 187. See also Freeman, "The Free Negro in New York City," pp. 240–42.
On white working-class mutual aid societies, see Ruth M. Alexander, "'We are Engaged as a
Band of Sisters': Class and Domesticity in the Washingtonian Temperance Movement, 1840–
1850," *Journal of American History* 75 (December 1988): 763–85.

also showed faith in their collective ability to address the enormous problems faced by all free blacks.

Such beliefs fit the dominant gender conventions of northern free blacks in the early nineteenth century. As James Oliver Horton has noted, these conventions emphasized differences between the sexes, not similarities. Newspapers, sermons, and organizations, the major sources of prescriptive attitudes, propounded the message that women were, in Horton's words, "the gentler sex, naturally more moral, more loving, more caring than men." Yet the admonitions to free black women—to guide but not nag men, to take a secondary role in family and community life, and to be nurturing and submissive—resonated differently from similar warnings directed to white women, because black men's ability to be providers and patriarchs was severely compromised by racial discrimination. Except in menial occupations or in a few trades where black men had a foothold, jobs were hard to come by. For women, the range of occupations was even narrower; in addition, they faced uneven sex ratios (women outnumbered men in both cities) and high rates of widowhood. Education was no guarantee of occupational success, and hard-won economic prosperity could be wiped out overnight, as New York's African Americans discovered in 1834 when white mobs who descended upon their neighborhoods made property holders specific targets of their fury. Unable to take women's dependence upon men as a given, free black women had to assume multiple roles as wage earners, educators, and community builders. At the same time, they believed it necessary to bolster black men's tenuous claims to social power whenever possible.[7]

To be sure, some black women's organizations bowed to gender conventions. A few groups owed their existence to men's sponsorship, as did some white women's missionary societies. New York's African Dorcas Association, formed in January 1828 to provide clothing for pupils in the city's African schools, developed at the prompting of the Manumission Society, a white men's group that sponsored the schools. A black minister chaired the African Dorcas Association's initial meeting, and Charles C. Andrews, a

---

7. James Oliver Horton, "Freedom's Yoke: Gender Conventions among Antebellum Free Blacks," *Feminist Studies* 12 (Spring 1986): 55–59. On the economic conditions of free blacks, see Freeman, "Free Negro in New York City," pp. 268–311; Shane White, " 'We Dwell in Safety and Pursue our Honest Callings': Free Blacks in New York City, 1783–1810," *Journal of American History* 75 (September 1988): 457–61; Vivienne L. Kruger, "Born to Run: The Slave Family in Early New York, 1616 to 1827" (Ph.D. diss., Columbia University, 1985), pp. 887–956; and Suzanne Lebsock, *The Free Women of Petersburg: Status and Culture in a Southern Town, 1784–1860* (New York, 1984), pp. 87–111. On the 1834 riots, see Paul A. Gilje, *Mobocracy: Popular Disorder in New York City, 1763–1834* (Chapel Hill, 1987), chap. 6.

white teacher in the African boys' school, presented the women with a written constitution for their approval. Although the female members elected their own officers and met weekly to sew at the home of their president, Margaret Francis, seven black ministers, one from each African church in the city, formed an advisory committee that scrutinized their activities. The advisory committee (with the aid of three white businessmen) not only received all donations for the Dorcas Association but had the authority to call annual meetings as well.[8] Boston women also observed convention when they met with male temperance advocates in 1833. After an address from a male speaker, "the ladies retired to the School Room for the purpose of forming a Temperance Society," reported the *Liberator,* "and the gentlemen remained in the House for the same purpose."[9]

Both these women's groups followed accepted practices for mixed-sex audiences. Similarly, when New York's Female Assistant Benefit Society met in 1838, its officers and members merely sat in the audience while the featured speaker, a young Henry Highland Garnet (later to be famous as a black nationalist orator), delivered a speech. Sharing the podium with Garnet were three other African American men: Henry Watson, who chaired the meeting, the Rev. J. D. Richardson, who offered the prayer, and F. Reynolds, who read the group's constitution. (It was the women, though, who had raised $360 that year and made 765 charitable visits.)[10] Using the services of male "advisors," as the African Dorcas Association did, was also a common practice among white women's benevolent groups; many institutionalized the practice by appointing formal "Committees of Gentlemen" during the 1830s, 1840s, and 1850s.[11]

Gender conventions and ritual practices aside, however, the deferential posture evident in these examples was unusual. More often, black women defied stereotypes of female behavior and the pronouncements of powerful men about how to channel female humanitarianism. Among white women, only reform group members such as antislavery and antiprostitution crusaders, whose numbers were small compared with the mass of organized women, exhibited similar defiance. (And even some of those women sub-

8. *Freedom's Journal,* February 1, 1828, p. 179; February 15, 1828, p. 187; March 7, 1828, p. 197; February 7, 1829, p. 355. Charles C. Andrews, *The History of the New-York Free-Schools, from Their Establishment in 1787 to the Present Time* (1830; rept., New York, 1969), p. 105. See also Freeman, "Free Negro in New York City," pp. 331–32.

9. *Liberator,* April 20, 1833, p. 63.

10. *Colored American,* March 15, 1838, pp. 2–3.

11. See Anne M. Boylan, "Women in Groups: An Analysis of Women's Benevolent Organizations in New York and Boston, 1797–1840," *Journal of American History* 71 (December 1984): 507, n. 16.

mitted to such critiques of female public speaking and political activity as that of the Congregational Association in 1837.) In black women's circles, however, inviting women to speak or hosting both male and female speakers was accepted practice. The 1832 anniversary orator of the recently organized Afric-American Female Intelligence Society was Maria W. Stewart. The following year, the group heard from the Congregationalist minister Amos A. Phelps, whose wife, Charlotte Brown Phelps, was the first president of BFASS. In announcing their fifth annual gathering, New York's Daughters of Abyssinia specified that "the meeting will be addressed by several distinguished speakers, both male and female." This pointed announcement came in September 1837 on the heels of the Congregational Association's critique of women's public speaking and four months after the group's participation in the first Anti-Slavery Convention of American Women. These women clearly did not intend to be constrained by white ministerial rules. Black women's benevolence, unlike white women's, often blended seamlessly with reformist work aimed at ending slavery. In yet another challenge to established rules, at least one organization, the Boston Mutual Lyceum, organized in 1833, had a mixed-sex membership. In this literary society, one of the two vice-presidents and two of the five managers were women.[12]

Black women's own visions for their organizations can be viewed most clearly through the names they chose, the programs they pursued, and the rules they established. Given the importance of naming in African and African American cultures, we can assume that organizational names were not chosen lightly. Like black men, free black women commonly selected "African" for association titles (African Dorcas Association, Afric-American Female Intelligence Society), although "colored" (as in Colored Female Charitable Society) came into more frequent use in the 1830s among both women and men as a protest against efforts to colonize slaves and free blacks in Africa. The term "African" expressed racial pride, "Afric-American" proclaimed an American identity in the face of colonization

---

12. On white women's groups, see Ginzberg, *Women and the Work of Benevolence*, pp. 67–97; and Anne M. Boylan, "Women and Politics in the Era before Seneca Falls," *Journal of the Early Republic* 10 (Fall, 1990): 363–82. On Stewart's address see *Liberator*, April 28, 1832, pp. 66–67. For this and other speeches, see Marilyn Richardson, ed., *Maria W. Stewart: America's First Black Female Political Orator: Writings, Essays, Speeches* (Bloomington, Ind., 1988). On the Daughters of Abyssinia, see *Colored American*, September 9, 1837, p. 3; and on the Boston Mutual Lyceum, see *Liberator*, August 31, 1833, p. 139. See also Dorothy Sterling, ed., *Turning the World Upside Down: The Anti-Slavery Convention of American Women, Held in New York City, May 9–12, 1837* (New York, 1987), p. 22.

efforts, and "Abyssinian" (as in Abyssinian Benevolent Daughters of Esther Association) harked back to a glorious past while also echoing the name of New York's premier black Baptist church, Abyssinian Baptist.[13]

Unlike black men, who favored classical names for their groups, such as New York's Phoenix Society, New York's and Boston's Philomathean societies, or Boston's Adelphic Union, black women chose gender-conscious titles. Many contained allusions to the Old Testament (for example, New York's Daughters of Israel), reflecting the singular importance of the story of Israel's captivity and deliverance in black Christianity. Others infused a specifically female element into black Christianity by recalling the notable women of the Old Testament. The Abyssinian Benevolent Daughters of Esther Association in New York had a name calculated to bring to mind the courageous actions of Esther (also called Hadassah in the Book of Esther), who in saving the Jews from annihilation became a symbol of heroic resistance against persecution. Such names conveyed an image of black womanhood that was strong and redemptive.[14]

Only occasionally did black women choose New Testament names or names without distinctive racial content. The title of the African Dorcas Association recalled the woman described in the New Testament as "full of good works and acts of charity," whose name white women also employed for sewing societies. It is likely, however, that the men who created this group, not the women themselves, chose its name.[15] Boston's Garrison Society, a literary group, and New York's Juvenile Daughters of Rush, an African Methodist Episcopal Zion Church organization, honored individual men by their titles: William Lloyd Garrison, the white abolitionist, and Christopher Rush, the black Zion Church supervisor.[16] New York's Female

13. On the issue of naming, see Sterling Stuckey, *Slave Culture: Nationalist Theory and the Foundations of Black America* (New York, 1988), pp. 198–211; and Gary B. Nash, *Forging Freedom: The Formation of Philadelphia's Black Community, 1720–1840* (Cambridge, Mass., 1988), pp. 210–11. On the use of "colored" during the 1830s, see Horton and Horton, *Black Bostonians*, p. 91. On black protests against colonization, see C. Peter Ripley, ed., *The Black Abolitionist Papers, Vol. 3: The United States, 1830–1846* (Chapel Hill, 1991), pp. 3–8. New York's Daughters of Abyssinia (sometimes called the Rising Daughters of Abyssinia) undoubtedly was also affiliated with Abyssinian Baptist. See *The Articles of Faith, Church Discipline, and By-Laws of the Abyssinian Baptist Church in the City of New York, April 3, 1833* (New York, 1833), pp. 2–7.

14. On black Christianity, see Albert J. Raboteau, *Slave Religion* (New York, 1978), and Lawrence Levine, *Black Culture and Black Consciousness* (New York, 1977). On organizational titles, see Porter, "Negro Literary Societies," pp. 555–76; Horton and Horton, *Black Bostonians*, pp. 28–35; and Nash, *Forging Freedom*, p. 210.

15. Acts 9:36; *Freedom's Journal*, February 1, 1828, p. 179; Porter, "Negro Literary Societies," p. 569.

16. See Christopher Rush, *A Short Account of the Rise and Progress of the African Methodist Episcopal Church in America* (New York, 1843), p. 119.

Mite Society and Female Assistant Benefit Society carried names that might just as well have belonged to white women's organizations, as did the Female Literary Society. But even without racial markers, black women's groups were usually easy to distinguish from white women's groups. A title such as "Society for Employing the Female Poor" or "Association for the Relief of Respectable, Aged, Indigent Females" invariably designated a white women's organization. Black women did not use organizational titles to set themselves off from potential clients (although they were not averse, as we shall see, to establishing morality tests for membership). Instead, black women's associations blended benevolence, mutual aid, self-improvement, community service, and social reform in ways that defied easy categorization. As a result, black women's benevolence reflected their special situation as women within highly vulnerable free black communities.

Even groups that on the surface appeared to be strictly benevolent in focus sustained this unique character. The African Dorcas Association, with its Wednesday sewing meetings and numerical accountings of garments distributed, looked for all the world like any other "fragment" society, dispensing aid to people of a different social class. But the association's benevolence was directed toward the members' neighbors and friends and toward their children's schoolmates, not toward an abstract category of "the poor." Maria De Grasse, one of the association's managers in 1828, undoubtedly could afford to clothe her fifteen-year-old son Isaiah for classes at the African Free School. Her husband, George De Grasse, ran a provisioning business on Orange Street, and Maria, like most women in the free black community, probably did remunerative work too. Her labor for the association aided those of Isaiah's classmates who could not afford decent clothing. But Maria never knew when she might need help herself; she had a three-year-old son, John, who would soon attend the African Free School and might some day need clothing. Economic security was often evanescent for families like the De Grasses; endemic racial discrimination and a volatile economy meant that running a business or even owning property seldom offered protection from destitution. Maria De Grasse's work for the African Dorcas Association could be termed "benevolent," but among women whose middle-class status was extremely tenuous, benevolence often resembled mutual assistance.[17] The resemblance existed in other benevolent

17. Information on Maria Van Surly De Grasse and her family has been pieced together from the following sources: *Freedom's Journal*, February 15, 1828, p. 187; "John Van Surly De Grasse," in Rayford W. Logan and Michael R. Winston, eds., *Dictionary of American Negro Biography* (New York, 1982), p. 169; *Longworth's New-York Directory* (New York, 1831, 1838);

Anne M. Boylan

organizations as well, such as New York's Female Mite Society and Female Assistant Benefit Society, or Boston's Colored Female Union Society and Colored Female Charitable Society.[18]

Black women's literary societies combined not only benevolence and mutual aid but also abolitionism and self-improvement. In addition to buying books for a library and engaging lecturers like Maria W. Stewart, Boston's Afric-American Female Intelligence Society made provisions to aid members experiencing "any unforeseen and afflictive event" by agreeing to visit them when sick and furnish monetary assistance ("one dollar a week out of the funds of the Society as long as consistent with the means of the institution"). Members of New York's Ladies Literary Society, while seeking to "acquir[e] literary and scientific knowledge" for individual and collective advancement, used their resources to raise funds for the New York Vigilance Committee, a men's group that assisted runaway slaves. At the 1837 Anti-Slavery Convention of American Women in New York, the society pledged five dollars to support a petition campaign directed at the abolition of slavery in Washington, D.C. The women of Boston's Garrison Society, a literary group, made sure that African American girls learned their multiple responsibilities early. By sponsoring a Garrison Juvenile Society, the women encouraged schoolchildren to do useful sewing, save (in the words of a sympathetic white observer) "the money they would otherwise have spent for candy, &c.," and promote "the 'improvement of the mind' and the cultivation of the virtues of industry, fidelity, frugality, self-respect, propriety of deportment, &c., &c." To do so, the women knew, was to

Andrews, *African Free Schools*, pp. 65–68; and William C. Nell, *The Colored Patriots of the American Revolution* (Boston, 1855), pp. 316–17. Available sources indicate that Maria De Grasse was "German" but likely of mixed-race ancestry; George De Grasse was born in Calcutta and naturalized in 1804. The family lived as free blacks in New York City. Isaiah De Grasse, who later became pastor of St. Matthew's (Episcopal) Free Church, was light-skinned enough that, according to Theodore Dwight Weld, "strangers to his *Parentage* would never from his complexion, features or hair ever *suspect* his African descent" (Gilbert H. Barnes and Dwight L. Dumond, eds., *Letters of Theodore Dwight Weld, Angelina Grimké Weld and Sarah Grimké, 1822–1844*, 2 vols. [New York, 1934], 1: 446). Isaiah referred to himself in an 1828 essay as "but a poor descendant of that injured people [the African race]"; *Minutes of the Adjourned Session of the Twentieth Biennial American Convention for Promoting the Abolition of Slavery, and Improving the Condition of the African Race* (Philadelphia, 1828), p. 67. Andrews (*African Free Schools*) gives Isaiah's age in 1828 as fifteen as does Isaiah's 1828 essay, but his 1841 death notice in the *New York Evening Post* gives his age as twenty-three. The newspaper is doubtless in error; he became pastor of St. Matthew's in 1838, and died as a missionary in Jamaica, and it is therefore unlikely that he was only twenty-three in 1841.

18. *Colored American*, February 18, 1837, p. 3 and October 14, 1837, p. 3; *Liberator*, December 29, 1832, p. 207, and September 5, 1835, p. 143.

counteract negative stereotypes of free blacks and aid the cause of emancipation, because self-improvement promoted the welfare of all African Americans. Indeed by the late 1830s even church fund-raising groups connected their efforts to the attack on slavery by carefully advertising that all items sold at church fairs would be "the product of FREE LABOR."[19]

The intertwined concern with self-improvement, mutual aid, and abolitionism so typical of literary societies was also evident in the lives of individual members. Henrietta Green Regulus Ray, president of the New York Ladies Literary Society from its inception until her death in 1836 at the age of 28, had also served as secretary of the African Dorcas Association; several members, including Maria W. Stewart, who joined after her arrival from Boston, and Matilda and Sarah Jennings, were also active in abolitionist causes.[20] In Boston, the lives of Jane Putnam, Margaret Scarlett, Susan Paul, and Lavinia Hilton exhibited similar patterns of involvement. They all were officers in a women's temperance society founded in 1833; Putnam and Hilton also served as officers of the Garrison Society and lent support to abolitionist activities, and Scarlett and Paul helped lead BFASS. Indeed, during her brief life (she died of tuberculosis at age 32), Susan Paul pursued a teaching career (including managing a well-known African American children's choir) helped support her deceased sister's four children, and held offices in the women's temperance group, BFASS, and the 1838 Anti-Slavery Convention of American Women. She also assumed personal responsibility for combatting racial prejudice by, for example, publicly reporting her humiliation at the hands of a white coach attendant who refused to take her as a passenger. Jane Putnam and Margaret Scarlett opposed discrimination, as well, by signing a petition protesting segregated schooling in Boston.[21]

19. Lerner, *Black Women in White America*, pp. 438–39; Porter, "Negro Literary Societies," pp. 555–76; *Emancipator,* November 24, 1836, p. 119, and July 7, 1836, p. 40; Sterling, ed., *Turning the World Upside Down*, p. 22; *Colored American,* May 3, 1838, p. 3. On the connections between Philadelphia's literary societies and the abolitionist movement, see the essay by Julie Winch, Chapter 6, in this volume.

20. *Colored American,* December 23, 1837, p. 3; "Charles B. Ray," in Logan and Winston, *Dictionary of American Negro Biography,* pp. 515–16; Sterling, *We Are Your Sisters,* pp. 112–13. Henrietta Ray had married the abolitionist Charles B. Ray in 1834, after the death of her first husband, Laurent (Lawrence) Regulus. See "Henrietta Green Regulus Ray," in Darlene Clark Hine, ed., *Black Women in America: An Historical Encyclopedia* (Brooklyn, N.Y., 1993). On the Jennings family, see John H. Hewitt, "The Search for Elizabeth Jennings, Heroine of a Sunday Afternoon in New York City," *New York History* 62 (October, 1990): 387–415.

21. On the temperance society, see *Liberator,* April 20, 1833, p. 63. On Susan Paul, see Milton Meltzer and Patricia Holland, eds., *Lydia Maria Child: Selected Letters, 1817–1880* (Amherst, 1982), pp. 66, 69–70; Jacobs, "A History of the Boston Negro," pp. 119, 130; and Paul's letter to the *Liberator,* April 5, 1834, p. 55. On the school petition, see Jacobs, "History of the Boston

Anne M. Boylan

Both in naming their organizations and in undertaking specific organizational programs, African American women behaved differently from their white counterparts. Black benevolent societies, unlike white, provided services to family, friends, and neighbors, as well as to strangers. Well aware that this month's dispenser of aid might be next month's recipient, black women's groups did not, like middle-class white women's organizations, assume that those who gave and those who received would come from different social classes. And because self-help could not be separated from the advancement of their race, members of black mutual aid societies did not, like the working-class white women who formed such societies, restrict themselves primarily to mutual assistance.[22]

Yet in their membership rules and practices, African American women were neither inclusive nor democratic. Many groups adopted exclusionary practices that reinforced existing status distinctions within the free black community.[23] Requiring high dues was one such practice. Members of Boston's Afric-American Female Intelligence Society were assessed twelve and a half cents per month, or one dollar and fifty cents per year, an amount well beyond the pocketbooks of most free black women. Moreover, missing a monthly meeting brought a fine of six and a quarter cents. New York's Abyssinian Benevolent Daughters of Esther Association levied dues of seventy-five cents per quarter, or three dollars per year, an amount comparable to the annual subscription fee for most white women's groups. Dues were necessary, of course, if the organizations were to have any funds to dispense, but those charging high dues clearly limited their membership to the more affluent women in the community. In this way, such groups, although taking a less hierarchical approach to benevolence than white women's organizations, still established class standing as a precondition for joining.

Negro," pp. 126–27, and Horton and Horton, *Black Bostonians,* pp. 71–74. The husbands of Margaret Scarlett (John E.), Lavinia Hilton (John T.) and Jane Putnam (George), were leaders in temperance and abolitionist activity; for brief sketches of John Hilton and John Scarlett, see Ripley, *The Black Abolitionist Papers,* pp. 305–7, 307n. On George Putnam, see Horton and Horton, *Black Bostonians,* p. 84; on Jane Putnam's support for the Boston Vigilance Committee, see Horton and Horton, *Black Bostonians,* p. 66; on Lavinia Hilton's work for the 1844 antislavery fair, see *Liberator,* February 16, 1844. See also Shirley J. Yee, *Black Women Abolitionists: A Study in Activism, 1828–1860* (Knoxville, Tenn., 1992), pp. 103, 132.

22. On working-class white women's societies, see Alexander, "We Are Engaged as a Band of Sisters," pp. 776–80; and Jay P. Dolan, *The Immigrant Church: New York's Irish and German Catholics, 1815–1865* (Baltimore, 1975), pp. 135–37.

23. See Emma Jones Lapsansky, "Friends, Wives, and Strivings: Networks and Community Values among Nineteenth-Century Philadelphia Afroamerican Elites," *Pennsylvania Magazine of History and Biography* 66 (January 1984): 3–24.

Why they did so must be understood in the context of other forms of exclusion practiced by the organizations. Most common were ritual announcements that members must be "of good moral character," but some societies were very specific in their strictures. New York's Abyssinian Benevolent Daughters of Esther Association excluded from membership "any person addicted to inebriety or having a plurality of husbands," and refused to provide aid to members who became ill as a result of "immoral conduct." Nor could pregnancy be used to claim any benefits. In a similar fashion, Boston's Afric-American Female Intelligence Society warned that sick benefits would be denied to members "who shall rashly sacrifice their own health." Such scrutiny of other women's characters and personal circumstances also existed in middle-class white women's groups, but it was characteristically applied to an organization's clients, not its members.[24]

These regulations revealed a focus on propriety and appearances in the thinking of organizational leaders, as well as very practical concerns about guaranteeing the solidarity and financial stability of the organization. Because free African American women leaders, like their male counterparts, usually had some access to property and education, they felt the need to protect scarce resources amid desperate poverty. They therefore developed criteria to measure their own and others' social class standing. By clarifying the attributes potential members would need in order to join the organization, group regulations defined middle-class behavior, including monogamy, education, temperance, religion, and self-control. Middle-class white women stipulated such detailed standards only for potential clients. For example, white widows expecting assistance from the New York Society for the Relief of Poor Widows with Small Children were required to be "of fair character" (a quality determined by a home visit from one of the society's managers), to put children over ten years of age out to service, to abstain from liquor, and to avoid "vicious habits."[25] Only working-class white women who formed temperance mutual aid societies

24. Constitution of the African Dorcas Association in *Freedom's Journal*, February 1, 1828, p. 179; Constitution of the Abyssinian Benevolent Daughters of Esther Association quoted in Perlman, "Organizations of the Free Negro in New York," p. 187; Constitution of the Afric-American Female Intelligence Society in Lerner, *Black Women in White America*, pp. 438–40.

25. For some useful information on literacy and property holding by black Bostonians, see Stapp, "Afro-Americans in Antebellum Boston." The quotation is from *The By-Laws and Regulations of the Society for the Relief of Poor Widows with Small Children . . . Together with the Annual Reports for 1814, 1815, and 1816* (New York, 1817), pp. 6–7, 26. See also Christine Stansell, *City of Women: Sex and Class in New York, 1790–1850* (New York, 1986).

in the 1840s imposed similar standards of conduct on their own members; they hoped to protect their organizations from economic disaster and to promote female unity.[26]

But there were other reasons why organized black women felt they had to be extremely careful about appearances and behavior. They knew that racist stereotypes made them, like their slave sisters, vulnerable to sexual and moral debasement. How could they counteract white stereotypes except by careful attention to their own dress, language, and behavior, and by policing the behavior of their sons, brothers, and husbands? "Sensible of the gross ignorances under which we have too long labored," commented the founders of Boston's Afric-American Female Intelligence Society, the group would work "for the diffusion of knowledge, the suppression of vice and immorality, and for cherishing such virtues as will render us happy and useful to society."[27] Prescriptive literature written by black men (themselves people of education and property) reinforced the expectation that women would explode negative white stereotypes of free African Americans. "We are all . . . branded with the epithets of vicious, degraded, and worthless," wrote an editorialist in the first issue of the New York *Weekly Advocate;* it was up to women to "exert all their power to disabuse the public mind of the misrepresentations made of our character."[28] That they should do so by adopting certain standards of public behavior was clear from the praise and scorn handed out to two groups by the editors of New York's *Freedom's Journal* in 1829. Commending the African Dorcas Association, Samuel Cornish and John Russwurm noted that "they have no annual processions; they have no blazing banners, pharisee-like to proclaim to the world the nature of their work." Unlike the Daughters of Israel, a mutual relief organization that evoked the ire of Cornish and Russwurm for organizing "a female procession, dressed in the full costume of their order," the African Dorcas Association conducted its business in an unobtrusive and decorous fashion.[29]

Concern about public perceptions shaped the exclusionary rules that some organizations adopted. Intended for the gaze of outside observers as well as for potential members, behavioral rules might deflect the prying white eyes that were ever ready to judge, evaluate, and condemn black

26. Alexander, "We Are Engaged as a Band of Sisters," pp. 778–80.
27. Lerner, *Black Women in White America*, p. 437.
28. *Weekly Advocate*, January 7, 1837, pp. 1–2. On the newspaper's history, see Freeman, "Free Negro in New York City," pp. 175–76.
29. *Freedom's Journal*, January 9, 1829, p. 319; August 15, 1828, p. 166.

actions.[30] But as women, organization members also faced potential hostility from within their own community, as Maria W. Stewart discovered when she spoke in public on religious subjects. Despite the long tradition of "women preaching and mixing themselves in controversies," she conceded, she was wearied by the "prejudice," "opposition," and "contempt" she had encountered from her own people.[31] Because they assumed responsibility for racial "uplift" and community maintenance, members of black women's organizations felt pressure to prove their respectability, both from white racial hostility and from black gender conventions. Unlike white women, especially of the middle class, black women could not presume that they would be seen as "virtuous" simply because they were women. Unlike black men, they had no special claim on leadership roles among their own people.[32]

The experiences of these free black women illuminate the complex ways in which race and gender intertwined to shape their autonomous organizations. On the one hand, African American women flouted the conventions of feminine respectability that so often restricted white women: by speaking in public, forming mixed-sex organizations, or combining benevolent and reform activities. Just as they assumed multiple roles in family and community life, free black women created organizations that were more multi-faceted than comparable white groups.[33] Both Margaret Scarlett, for example, who belonged to Boston's black women's temperance society and to the Boston Female Anti-Slavery Society, and Hester Lane, former slave, manager of the African Dorcas Association, and nominee for the Executive Committee of the American Anti-Slavery Society, readily combined benevolence with reform work.[34] But in their dealings with whites, these same women often had to prove the respectability of their

30. For discussions of black women's strategies in protecting themselves from hostile scrutiny, see Deborah Gray White, "Mining the Forgotten: Manuscript Sources for Black Women's History," *Journal of American History* 74 (June, 1987): 237–42, and Darlene Clark Hine, "Rape and the Inner Lives of Black Women in the Midwest: Preliminary Thoughts on the Culture of Dissemblance," *Signs: Journal of Women in Culture and Society* 14 (Summer, 1989): 912–21.

31. Richardson, *Maria W. Stewart*, pp. 69–70.

32. See Horton, "Freedom's Yoke," pp. 58–59.

33. On the existence of separate organizational networks among white women in the antebellum years, see Nancy A. Hewitt, *Women's Activism and Social Change: Rochester, New York, 1822–1872* (Ithaca, 1984); and Boylan, "Women in Groups," pp. 497–523.

34. On Stewart, see Richardson, *Maria W. Stewart*, p. xiv, and Sterling, *We Are Your Sisters*, pp. 153–58; on Lane, see Freeman, "Free Negro in New York City," p. 193, and *Freedom's Journal*, February 15, 1828, p. 187.

characters; in their dealings with African American men, they sometimes had to accept subordinate roles. In 1838, for example, the all-male New England Temperance Society of Colored Americans refused to consider admitting women to membership because the society's president, John T. Hilton, whose wife Lavinia was treasurer of a Boston women's temperance group, opposed the proposal.[35]

When black women's organizational activities intersected with white women's, the power of both racial prejudice and ideals of feminine respectability became clear. In New York, white women ran Sunday schools and infant schools for black children, as well as the Colored Orphan Asylum and the Ladies' New York City Anti-Slavery Society. Despite the financial support provided to the orphanage and to the 1837 Anti-Slavery Convention of American Women by individuals and by black women's church groups, the leadership of both the Association for the Benefit of Colored Orphans and the women's antislavery society remained in white hands. Indeed, as Amy Swerdlow has noted, LNYCASS was so hostile to black involvement that Angelina Grimké privately condemned its "sinful prejudice" in having "hardly any colored members . . . [and not admitting] any such in the working S[ociet]y" and publicly alluded to the society's color prejudice in her *Appeal to the Women of the Nominally Free States*. Grimké considered "forming an Anti Slavery Socety [*sic*] among our colord sisters & getting them to invite their white friends to join them"; eventually, black women pursued precisely that course, forming the Manhattan Abolition Society in 1840.[36] In Boston, by contrast, African American women were active as members, officers, and fund-raisers for the female antislavery society and the Samaritan Asylum for Colored Children. The differences between Boston and New York are explicable not by external factors such as antiabolitionist mobs, which existed in both cities, but by the attitudes of white women abolitionists. Where the white leaders of female antislavery societ-

35. *Liberator,* November 9, 1838, p. 180.
36. Freeman, "Free Negro in New York City," pp. 243–46; Association for the Benefit of Colored Orphans, *First Annual Report* (New York, 1837); Swerdlow, Chapter 2 in this volume; letters of Angelina Grimké to Jane Smith, April 3 and 17, 1837, in Larry Ceplair, ed., *The Public Years of Sarah and Angelina Grimké: Selected Writings, 1835–1839* (New York, 1989), pp. 126, 129; Angelina E. Grimké, *An Appeal to the Women of the Nominally Free States,* quoted in *Turning the World Upside Down,* pp. 30–31. New York's African American leaders were, on occasion, quite critical of policies at the Colored Orphan Asylum. In 1838–1839 for example, the editors of the *Colored American* denounced the orphanage's white physician for his treatment of black children. In 1841, he was replaced by a black physician. Similarly, in 1839, black New Yorkers criticized the firing of a black matron from the orphange and the hiring of a white matron in her place. See *Colored American,* December 22, 1838, p. 2; January 19, 1839, p. 2; January 26, 1839, p. 2; and February 2, 1839, p. 3.

ies cultivated the involvement of black women (as in Boston and Philadelphia), black women abolitionists participated; where white women abolitionists were fearful of or hostile to black involvement (as in New York), black women were excluded. Either way, African American women's participation depended in part on white sufferance.

Even white abolitionists who were very supportive could be judgmental of their black co-workers. Anne Warren Weston's comment that Susan Paul had been chosen to represent BFASS at the first Anti-Slavery Convention of American Women because she was "a favorable specimen of the coloured race" revealed Weston's class and color prejudices.[37] On occasion, African American women themselves made similar judgments, arguing that the most "worthy," "industrious," "respectable," or "wealthy" among them suffered the most from racism. Rather than challenge critics who classed all black women as degraded, both white and black women sometimes tacitly accepted their critics' terms by attempting to prove their virtue.[38]

Issues of gender, race, and social class shaped the work of all women's organizations in the early nineteenth century. In varying ways, black and white women's organizations confronted questions of how much they could do, whom they would assist, and whom they would accept as members. African American women's decisions molded multifaceted instruments of benevolence, mutual assistance, self-help, and social reform that differed materially from the single-focus groups of white women. Excluded by virtue of their race from white conventions of feminine respectability, African American women were more adventurous in speaking out on public issues, combining abolitionism with community uplift, and challenging the pronouncements of male leaders. Nevertheless, in their relations with African American men and in their interactions with white women abolitionists, black women activists encountered barriers of gender, class, and color that also affected their organizations. African American women never endorsed standards of feminine respectability as fully as did white women. But insofar as they adopted those standards in order to establish their claim to feminine virtue, they found themselves constrained by narrow definitions of appropriate behavior.

37. Anne Warren Weston quoted in Debra Gold Hansen, *Strained Sisterhood: Gender and Class in the Boston Female Anti-Slavery Society* (Amherst, 1993), p. 19. See also Hansen, Chapter 3 in this volume.

38. See *Lydia Maria Child: Selected Letters*, p. 69; Grimké, *Appeal to the Women of the Nominally Free States*, quoted in *Turning the World Upside Down*, p. 30; and letter of Sarah Forten in Sterling, *We Are Your Sisters*, p. 124. Jean Fagan Yellin discusses the pitfalls of Victorian respectability for both white and black abolitionists in *Women and Sisters*, pp. 91–96.

Anne M. Boylan

Appendix

Between 1827 and 1841, according to my analysis of the sources listed below, African American women in New York founded at least seventeen associations, in Boston, five.

The New York organizations and founding dates are:

African Dorcas Association, 1827–1828
Daughters of Israel, 1820s
Female Branch of Zion, 1832
Daughters of Abyssinia (also called Rising Daughters of Abyssinia), 1832
Female Mite Society, 1833
Ladies Literary Society (also called Female Literary Association), 1834
Female Baptist Association (of the Abyssinian Baptist Church), 1834
United Daughters of Conference (of the African Methodist Episcopal Zion Church), c. 1836
Juvenile Daughters of Rush (for younger women; an offshoot of the United Daughters of Conference), 1837
Female Assistant Benefit Society, 1838
Women of the First Presbyterian Church of Color (a fundraising society that may have been the same as the Female Education Society), 1838
Abyssinian Benevolent Daughters of Esther Association, c. 1839
Female Education Society of the First Presbyterian Church of Color, 1840
Tappan Female Benevolent Society, 1840
Manhattan Abolition Society, 1840
Female Trading Association, 1841
Colored Female Vigilance Committee, 1841

During the same period, whites (both male and female) founded organizations to benefit blacks, including the African Infant School, 1827; the Ladies' New York City Anti-Slavery Society, 1835; the Association for the Benefit of Colored Orphans, 1836; the Female Wesleyan Anti-Slavery Society, 1836; and the Society for the Relief of Worthy, Aged, Indigent Colored Persons, 1839.

The Boston African American women's groups are:

Colored Female Union Society (of the Belknap Street Baptist Church), 1830
Afric-American Female Intelligence Society, 1832
Colored Female Charitable Society, 1832

Women's temperance society (formal name unclear), 1833
Garrison Society, 1833

In addition, African American women belonged to at least one mixed-sex group, the Mutual Lyceum, 1833, and to several integrated women's groups, including BFASS and the Samaritan Asylum for Indigent Colored Children, 1834.

Sources: *Freedom's Journal*, 1827–1829; *Colored American*, 1837–1841; *Liberator*, 1831–1840; Daniel Perlman, "Organizations of the Free Negro in New York, 1800–1860," *Journal of Negro History* 56 (July, 1971): 185–87; James Oliver Horton and Lois E. Horton, *Black Bostonians: Family Life and Community Struggle in the Antebellum North* (New York, 1979), pp. 28–35, 71–74; and William J. Walls, *The African Methodist Episcopal Zion Church: Reality of the Black Church* (Charlotte, N.C., 1974), pp. 133–34.

{ 8 }

Difference, Slavery, and Memory

Sojourner Truth in
Feminist Abolitionism

Nell Irvin Painter

The issue of race is always present in American culture, especially in large areas such as women's rights. Understandably, Americans often try to avoid the issue, for race can still sabotage analysis of terms as essential as the nineteenth-century formulation of *woman*. When race is acknowledged in discussions of American culture, the significance of the whole and the parts alters, subtly or drastically. Words and phrases acquire additional connotations, and lines of reasoning may twist imperceptibly. Large parts of social equations may disappear, as other parts are enhanced. Often the undeniable importance of race makes it too facile an explanation; it seems to provide answers that are too easy to hard questions.

In American antislavery feminism few of the principals who have been remembered were of African descent, but the movement was tethered both to the racially charged institution of slavery and to notions of gender that are deeply but subtly influenced by race. If the need for a black presence was felt in the early histories of American feminism, merely quoting the speeches of Sojourner Truth, an unforgettable black woman who frequented the halls where women organized for the abolition of slavery and the achievements of their own rights, apparently filled that need. With the flowering of black women's studies, however, merely quoting Sojourner

I gratefully acknowledge the support of the Center for Advanced Study in the Behavioral Sciences, Stanford, California, National Endowment for the Humanities, grant #FC-20060-85, and the Andrew W. Mellon Foundation and the counsel of Phillip Lapsansky, Jean Fagan Yellin, Dorothy Sterling, and Glenn Shafer.

Truth no longer substitutes for carefully analyzing Truth's persona and her place in the history of American reform.

A former slave from the Hudson River valley in New York, Sojourner Truth (ca. 1797–1883) appeared often on the antislavery and women's rights lecture circuits in the 1850s, 1860s, and 1870s. She is still one of the two most famous nineteenth-century black women; the other, Harriet Tubman, was also a mature, dark-skinned, unlettered former slave. Since Truth's heyday as an abolitionist and women's rights advocate, she has symbolized the connection of sex and race in liberal reform. The line most closely associated with her persona—"and ar'n't I a woman?"—demands that the category of "woman" include those who are poor or not white.

This message bears repeating on a regular basis, particularly as feminists seek to make their movement more broadly representative. The very fact that Truth's message has remained pertinent for so long inspires investigation into her place in feminist abolitionism and the function of her public persona in the history of American reform. The women's rights conference in Akron, Ohio, in 1851, at which Truth gave her most famous speech and at which she first gained prominence as a feminist, will serve here as the touchstone of my analysis.

As attractive as the scene in Akron has become to modern readers, its meaning is no longer as straightforward as it had seemed. Reexamining the meeting at Akron and Truth's own personal history in light of recent scholarship on feminist abolitionists raises new questions about the use of a naive persona among Americans who are educated, particularly when the naif is black and the educated are white. Was Sojourner Truth unique in 1851? What made her remarkable and how intentionally created was her persona? Why is Truth remembered while other black women reformers have mostly been forgotten? Could nineteenth-century black women feminist abolitionists be "woman"?

Comparing Truth with antislavery female leadership and the rank and file, I reconsider the prophetic persona of Sojourner Truth—a persona that Truth herself invented and that educated white women helped elaborate and preserve in American memory. I employ two different strategies. First I present a narrative history of Sojourner Truth; because Truth's life is less well known than her persona, this section runs long. In the second part of my essay, I analyze the discursive approaches that preserved Truth's place in cultural history.

Even though black women had already been active in women's reform for decades, the Ohio women's rights convention held in Akron in May 1851 is primarily remembered today, as in the nineteenth century, as the occasion when Sojourner Truth inserted black women into women's reform and reclaimed physical and emotional strength for all women. As was often the case, Truth was the only black person present. This was an event of enormous rhetorical and symbolic, as well as historical, importance. Not surprisingly, therefore, the only report that has been widely reprinted features Truth prominently. Its author was Frances Dana Gage, a white antislavery writer and lecturer from McConnelsville, Ohio, who chaired the meeting.[1]

By Gage's account, Truth stood out immediately. "A tall, gaunt, black women in a gray dress and white turban, surmounted with an uncouth sunbonnet," Truth made an unusual entrance and took an unorthodox seat. She "march[ed] deliberately into the church, walk[ed] with the air of a queen up the aisle, and [sat] upon the pulpit steps." During the first day, Gage writes, Truth said nothing. On the second day, several ministers in the audience vehemently denied women's claim to equal rights, arguing that women lacked intelligence, that Jesus Christ was a man, and that Eve, who had tempted man into original sin, was a woman. Throughout this onslaught, Gage reported, none of the white women in the convention was brave enough to counter the charges. As respectable white women cowered, silenced by the Pauline prohibition against women's public speech, scoffers and small boys in the gallery enjoyed the women's chagrin.

Then, said Gage, Sojourner Truth acted: "This almost Amazon form, which stood nearly six feet high, head erect, and eye piercing the upper air" instantly riveted everyone's attention. Whereas the white women organizers of the meeting failed to respond to the ministers' denunciation of women's rights, Truth, an uninvited participant, spoke for all the women in phrases that effectively silenced the male opposition. Gage recalled Truth's words:

> Wall, chilern, whar dar is so much racket dar must be somethin' out o' kilter. I tink dat 'twixt de niggers of the Souf and de womin at de Norf, all talkin' 'bout rights, de white men will be in a fix pretty soon. But what's all dis here talkin' 'bout?
>
> Dat man ober dar say dat womin needs to be helped into carriages, and lifted ober ditches, and to hab de best place everywhar. Nobody eber helps me into carriages, or ober mud-puddles, or gibs me any best place! And ar'n't I a woman? Look at me! Look at my arm! (and she bared her right arm to the shoulder, showing her tremendous muscular power). I have ploughed, and planted, and gathered into

1. For more information on Frances Dana Gage (1808–1884), see Edward T. James, Janet Wilson James, and Paul S. Boyer, eds., *Notable American Women* (Cambridge, Mass., 1971), 1:2–4.

barns, and no man could head me! And ar'n't I a woman? I could work as much and eat as much as a man—when I could get it—and bear de lash as well! And ar'n't I a woman? I have borne thirteen chilern, and seen 'em mos' all sold off to slavery, and when I cried out with my mother's grief, none but Jesus heard me! And ar'n't I a woman?

Subduing what Gage terms the "mobbish spirit of the day," Truth reversed this tide of denigration. Her speech brought "roars of applause" and turned a rout into triumph.[2]

Modern readers generally focus on one aspect of this report, Sojourner Truth's demand that poor, black women like herself be included with people classed as women. Some women are workers, Truth says, making the ability to work a womanly characteristic. Truth reminds her audience that although women belong to different classes and races, they nonetheless remain women, no matter what their material condition.

But Gage has still more to say about Sojourner Truth in this setting. Composing the rhetorical formula that made Truth's theme so memorable, Gage also delivers an important message about Truth's relative efficacy. Gage underscores Truth's authority by contrasting the timidity of the white women who had organized the meeting with the fearless Sojourner Truth. Summing up the symbolic significance of the scene, critic Jean Fagan Yellin says that Gage paints the black woman as the "powerful rescuer" of the powerless white women.[3]

The seat that Truth assumed—on the steps of the pulpit rather than in the pews—manifests the degree to which she stood (or rather sat) apart from the rest of the gathering. This physical placement hints at a distinction separating Truth from her feminist abolitionist peers that exceeds racial difference. Truth not only looked different from the white women, she appeared stronger as well. In the midst of the long quotation in dialect, Gage interrupts Truth's exotic phrasing to insert her own stage business in standard English, again contrasting two modes of expression and being. Gage does not explain how Truth came to exercise such power, leaving the cu-

2. [Olive Gilbert and Frances W. Titus], *Narrative of Sojourner Truth; A Bondswoman of Olden Time Emancipated by the New York Legislature in the Early Part of the Present Century; with a History of Her Labors and Correspondence Drawn from Her "Book of Life"* (Battle Creek, Mich., 1878, rpt. New York, 1968, and Salem, N.H., 1990), pp. 131–35. This narrative went through several reprintings and three main editions: the first, in 1850; the second, which added material from Truth's scrapbook in 1875/1878; and the third, which added a memorial section in 1884, after her death.

3. Jean Fagan Yellin, *Women and Sisters: The Antislavery Feminists in American Culture* (New Haven, 1989), p. 81.

rious reader to search out her own explanations. Truth's prior experience would seem a likely place to start, for compared with other women in the church that day she apparently traveled a singular life's road to Akron.

Sojourner Truth was born Isabella, in Hurley, Ulster County, New York, a region dominated culturally and economically by the descendants of nineteenth-century Dutch and French Huguenot settlers. Her parents, although not of African birth, seem to have been of unmixed African descent. The family's first language was Dutch. Isabella's earliest religious instruction came from her mother, who taught her to distinguish right from wrong and to believe in the existence of God ("a great man" who lived "high in the sky" and who could see everything that happened on the earth). As a young woman Isabella made a sanctuary on an island in the middle of a stream, where she went to talk with God and repeat the Lord's Prayer, which her mother had taught her.[4]

Separated from her parents as a child, Isabella worked for several owners before gaining her freedom under New York state law in 1827. While still enslaved, she married a fellow bondsman named Thomas, with whom she had five children. Her last year in servitude was charged with emotional events and spiritual development. Her son Peter was sold South illegally, and Isabella took the extraordinary step of going to court to sue successfully for his return. At about this same time, Jesus appeared to her in a vision, and Isabella experienced a conversion. As related in the *Narrative of Sojourner Truth:* "Her heart was now full of joy and gladness, as it had been of terror, and at one time of despair. In the light of her great happiness, the world was clad in new beauty, the very air sparkled as with diamonds, and was redolent of heaven."[5] Although this language recalls that of the founder of Methodism, John Wesley, in his Aldersgate experience, Truth was not connected to any church until 1827, when she began attending a Methodist church in Kingston, Ulster County. There she met a teacher, a Miss Grear, with whom she journeyed to New York City in about 1829. Isabella took her son Peter with her but left her daughters and husband in Ulster County.

In New York City, Isabella attended two Methodist churches, the white John Street Church and the black Zion African Church, formed in the 1790s by black members of John Street Church who had experienced racial discrimination. She also attended camp meetings, at which she preached and effected many conversions. Isabella's ability as a preacher earned her great respect in various Methodist circles, including that of a dissident Methodist

4. *Narrative of Sojourner Truth*, pp. 59–60.
5. Ibid., p. 68.

merchant, James Latourette. Considering Truth's later history, the Latourette connection is worth noting. Latourette, who had left the Methodist Church in the mid-1820s, wanted to take it back to its uncorrupted
roots, and he opposed both the consumption of alcoholic beverages and
the institution of slavery. Latourette's disciples became itinerant preachers
who were not connected with any formal church.[6] By the early 1830s, at
least, Isabella was associated with several brands of unconventional and
revivalist religion.

At the behest of Mrs. Latourette, Isabella attended prayers at the
Magdalen Asylum, a controversial mission for prostitutes, one of whose
founders was Arthur Tappan, who later became a prominent abolitionist.
At the Magdalen Asylum Isabella met and soon joined the household employ of Elijah Pierson, a wealthy widower subject to religious enthusiasms.
While working at Pierson's house and participating in Pierson's own brand
of religious exercises, Isabella encountered Robert Matthews, an itinerant
preacher from upstate New York who further influenced her spiritual evolution. Matthews, born about 1788, was of Scottish descent. Originally a
Washington County Presbyterian, he had joined the Dutch Reformed
Church in Albany and like many New Yorkers had been powerfully affected
by Charles Grandison Finney, the foremost preacher of the Second Great
Awakening. Matthews did not become a follower of Finney, but Finney's
preaching made him feel that his religion was hollow and encouraged him
to redirect his thinking. Matthews was already known for his street-corner
exhortations when he had a millenarian revelation one morning in Albany
in 1830. As he was shaving, he discovered his great truth: no man who
shaved could be a true Christian. He let his beard grow, proclaimed himself
a Jew, took the name Matthias, and began to prophesy God's destruction of
the city of Albany. Matthias left his family and traveled to Rochester and
through Pennsylvania. In 1832 he reached New York City.

In New York, Matthias visited Pierson's home, where he met Isabella.
Isabella, as much as Pierson, recognized Matthias's prophetic gift and became his follower. After Pierson and Matthias discovered that they had had
matching visions, Matthias renamed Pierson "Elias the Tishbite," and Pierson and another wealthy merchant underwrote the formation of a commune led by Matthias. Isabella belonged to this "kingdom," which was

---

6. Gilbert Vale, *Fanaticism; Its Source and Influence, Illustrated by the Simple Narrative of Isabella, in the Case of Matthias, Mr. and Mrs. B. Folger, Mr. Pierson, Mr. Mills, Catherine, Isabella,
&c. &c.* (New York, 1835), p. 18; Whitney R. Cross, *The Burned-Over District: The Social and
Intellectual History of Enthusiastic Religion in Western New York, 1800–1850* (Ithaca, 1950), p. 240.

housed first in New York City, then in the Hudson River town of Mount Pleasant (now Ossining).[7]

Matthias's kingdom was organized along authoritarian lines, with the prophet retaining the power to make all important and many trivial decisions. He also dictated its theology, which was rather informal and had much in common with other new religions emerging in upstate New York at the time, such as Mormonism and Millerite Second Adventism. Matthias taught his followers—all of whom, except for Isabella and a white woman who shared the housework of the establishment, were middle-class and relatively well educated—that he possessed the spirit of God, that there were good and evil spirits, and that the millennium was imminent. The almost corporeal existence of spirits was also a central tenet of the kingdom. Matthias and his followers did not believe in doctors, reasoning that illness was caused by evil spirits that must be cast out. Members of the kingdom fasted often and followed a diet that emphasized fresh fruit and vegetables and prohibited alcohol.[8]

Like many of the religious cults and utopian communities of the 1830s and 1840s, Matthias's kingdom foundered on the confusion between spiritual and carnal passion. After Pierson's death under suspicious circumstances, Matthias was tried and acquitted of Pierson's murder. The kingdom dissolved, and Matthias moved west. Isabella, his supporter throughout, remained in new York City for nearly a decade longer, taking in washing and doing household work as she had since her arrival in the city.

According to her *Narrative*, Isabella became exasperated with her life in New York City in 1843, particularly with the money grubbing and suffering that followed the severe economic panic of 1837. As the depression deepened and competition among the destitute grew more stark, Isabella, a poor woman herself, was appalled by her own lack of charity toward those more in need. Then God spoke to her, commanding her to quit the city and take a new name. On June 1, 1843, she renamed herself Sojourner Truth, left New York, and set out, as God instructed her, toward Brooklyn and eastern Long Island.

It is no accident that Truth took to the roads to preach in the year 1843. That year marked the apogee of Millerism, a mass movement in the Northeast that prophesied the arrival of the second Advent of Christ in mid-1843 (later readjusted to sometime between June 1843 and June 1844). William

7. Vale, *Fanaticism*, pp. 19–41.
8. *New York Courier and Enquirer*, April 17, 1835; *New York Sun*, April 20, 1835.

Miller was a farmer from Vermont and northern New York whose evolution closely paralleled (and perhaps inspired) that of his neighbor, Robert Matthews. Aroused by one of Finney's revivals, Miller had begun in 1831 to preach that the world would end in 1843. His message reached hundreds of thousands of people from Maine to Michigan in a series of widely distributed periodicals and through the teachings of scores of itinerant preachers who held forth at frequent and massive camp meetings. In 1843 northerners were particularly receptive to unlettered, itinerant preachers of many sorts, and hundreds of the faithful heeded God's command to preach their message to others. Isabella chose her new name well, for "sojourner" means itinerant, and telling the truth, she said, was her mission.

Once launched, Truth was able to reach large audiences immediately, for excited Millerites staged a series of camp meetings and invited her to preach. Millerites were used to listening to itinerant preachers, including women, so Truth found a ready welcome when she spoke up at those outdoor meetings. As in the early 1830s when she was preaching in and around New York City, Truth acquired a reputation as a gifted preacher and singer. Her audiences were not necessarily all convinced Second Adventists, for all denominations of northern evangelical Protestants were agitated in 1843, whether they expected the literal end of the world or not.[9]

Although Truth may not have shared all the Millerites' expectations or their frenzy in moments of extraordinary agitation, they did not hesitate to recommend her good preaching to their brethren. Through invitations extended at Second Advent meetings at which she preached, Truth followed a Millerite network on Long Island and then crossed into Connecticut. Walking up the Connecticut River Valley from New Haven to Hartford and Springfield, Massachusetts, she made her way finally to the utopian Northampton Association, where for the first time she encountered Garrisonian abolitionism.

It might first seem odd that Millerites steered Truth to the Northampton Association. Expecting the world to end momentarily, Millerites in 1843 were completely preoccupied with preparations for the millennium. Many of them, however, had once been active in moral reforms such as abolitionism, and the connection between Millerite millennialism and utopianism was also close.[10] The people in the Northampton Association were

9. Ruth Alden Doan, "Millerism and Evangelical Culture," in Ronald L. Numbers and Jonathan M. Butler, eds., *The Disappointed: Millerism and Millenarianism in the Nineteenth Century* (Bloomington, Ind., 1987), pp. 118–22.

10. Michael Barkun, *Crucible of the Millennium: The Burned-Over District of New York in the 1840s* (Syracuse, 1986), pp. 8, 31, 97–98; Ronald D. Graybill, "The Abolitionist-Millerite Connection," in Numbers and Butler, eds., *The Disappointed*, pp. 139, 146.

not particularly enthusiastic about their religion, especially considering the agitation that characterized the time, but they did have radical plans to regenerate the nation. Through the cooperative production of silk, they wanted to initiate the reformation of the political economy. Not only was slavery a blot on the American polity, but the economy, still depressed after the Panic of 1837, also seemed out of joint.

The Northampton Association attracted reform-minded visitors, abolitionists and supporters of women's rights like William Lloyd Garrison and Frederick Douglass. One of the Northampton Association's founders, George Benson, was Garrison's brother-in-law. While living in Connecticut in the mid-1830s, Benson had defended the Quaker school mistress Prudence Crandall after townspeople and the state legislature persecuted her for having admitted black girls to her school. Like Benson, the other members of the association were idealists, and they broke with community norms by allowing blacks access to their community.

In the Northampton Association Sojourner Truth encountered well-educated people whose main concerns were social rather than religious. She embraced abolitionism and women's rights and began to address antislavery audiences more often than camp meetings. In the late 1840s, after the Northampton Association dissolved, she joined the antislavery lecture circuit, speaking and selling signed postcards and *The Narrative of Sojourner Truth*, which she had dictated to Olive Gilbert, a Connecticut abolitionist, and published herself in 1850. Her sale of the book to antislavery and women's rights audiences allowed her to support herself and to pay off the mortgage of her home in Northampton. In 1851 she went to the women's rights convention in Akron primarily to sell her book, and Frances Dana Gage reports that indeed she did a brisk business on the first day.

When Truth and white feminist leaders met in Akron in 1851, the outspokenness of the one and the silence of the others might have seemed natural, given the very different routes they apparently had traveled. Feminist abolitionists had begun to seek their own rights within the antislavery community, but Truth had come out of religious cults and an itinerant ministry.[11] Like the prophet Matthias, she had changed her name when God told her to preach her truth. Like the Millerites, she gloried in massive outdoor camp meetings. And like other black women preachers, she heeded her inner spiritual voice and spoke up when the spirit moved her.

Although Truth may have been an unusual character in Akron, she was only one of several black female preachers active in the antebellum North.

11. Ellen Carol DuBois, *Feminism and Suffrage: The Emergence of an Independent Women's Movement in America, 1848–1869* (Ithaca, 1978), p. 24.

They, too, published autobiographies: Jarena Lee in 1839 and 1849; Zilpha Elaw, who preached in England for five years, in 1846; and Nancy Prince in 1850, the year Sojourner Truth's *Narrative* appeared. Nancy Prince was no stranger to women's rights or antislavery circles; indeed she spoke at the fifth national women's rights convention in Philadelphia in 1854. These northern women came out of the African Methodist Episcopal (AME) Church and reached wide audiences with messages of conversion and sanctification similar to Sojourner Truth's. Rebecca Cox Jackson also began in the AME Church and went on to become a Shaker eldress. If not for Truth's residence in the Northampton Association and her well-publicized advocacy of what we now consider secular reforms, she would belong wholly to this tradition of black women preachers.[12] But she built an enduring reputation on the antislavery feminist circuit over the years, and white women rather than black were her companions and filled her audiences.

Not only Truth's religious history but also her socioeconomic background would seem to contrast starkly with that of most other women at the Akron meeting. Whereas Truth had grown up as poor as could be, a slave on a farm in upstate New York, many antislavery women leaders— white women like Lucy Stone and Abby Kelley, and black women like Sarah Mapps Douglass and Frances Ellen Watkins Harper of Philadelphia—came from urban backgrounds. Also, like Stone, Kelley, Douglass, and Harper, leading antislavery women were from middle- and upper-middle-class families and consequently had a good deal more education and money than most of their female contemporaries, including Sojourner Truth. And like Frances Dana Gage, many had grown up in reform-minded homes and had long been exposed to discussions of moral reform (e.g., temperance) and politics.[13]

Many feminist abolitionists came to advocate women's rights after experiencing frustration in their antislavery work, but they found that acting on their convictions did not come easily. Often antebellum women who became feminists were not able effortlessly to move into the public realm.

12. William L. Andrews, ed., *Sisters of the Spirit: Three Black Women's Autobiographies of the Nineteenth Century* (Bloomington, Ind., 1986), pp. 2–3; Elizabeth Cady Stanton, Susan B. Anthony, and Matilda Joslyn Gage, *History of Woman Suffrage*, 6 vols. (Rochester, N.Y., 1889–1922, rpt. New York, 1970), 1:384; Nellie McKay, "Nineteenth-Century Black Women's Spiritual Autobiographies: Religious Faith and Self-Empowerment," in Joy Webster Barbre et al., eds., *Interpreting Women's Lives: Feminist Theory and Personal Narratives* (Urbana, 1989), pp. 137–54.

13. Blanche Glassman Hersh, *The Slavery of Sex: Feminist-Abolitionism in America* (Chicago, 1978), pp. 17, 121–36.

As Elizabeth Cady Stanton discovered, women raised to stay at home had to overcome shyness, inexperience in public speaking and in presiding over meetings, familial and community hostility, and the pressures of housekeeping and childrearing. These conditions explain Frances Gage's nervousness chairing the 1851 Akron meeting where Sojourner Truth spoke up.[14]

In common with women preachers through the ages, Truth had surmounted these barriers long ago. In the 1820s she had left her husband and four of her five children in Ulster County; by 1851 all her children lived apart from her and consumed none of her time and energy. She had already addressed camp meetings by the score. As an independent and, as she said, self-made woman, Truth could speak out in 1851 with the self-confidence that came from long experience. But did these experiences truly distinguish Truth from other women's rights abolitionists? Not necessarily.

A closer look at other antislavery feminists and at the 1851 meeting in Akron blurs easy distinctions. Two of the most salient figures at the Akron convention, Gage and journalist Jane Swisshelm, were better educated than Truth, but had, like Truth and many other early nineteenth-century Americans, grown up on farms. But if access to education separated Truth, who was illiterate, from other women who were journalists and school teachers, religion united them. Quakers, who recognized the right of women to preach, often supplied the common thread. Abby Kelley, Amy Post, and Sarah and Angelina Grimké, among feminist abolitionists, were or had been Quakers. Others, particularly those who lectured in public, shared with Truth a penchant for Quaker dress and close association with Quakers. Like Truth, other female leaders conceived of their mission in religious terms yet were deeply critical of organized churches and clergy. In 1854, Lucretia Mott spoke for all women's rights advocates: "It is not Christianity, but priestcraft that has subjected woman as we find her."[15] Their belief in the cause of the slave as a religious duty led antislavery feminists to lecture and write messages such as Angelina Grimké's 1836 *An Appeal to the Christian Women of the South*. (Like Truth, Angelina Grimké had been caught up in the Millerite fervor of 1843.)[16]

Just as the contrast between Truth's religious beliefs and experience as a public speaker and those of the female antislavery leadership does not hold up well under closer examination, distinctions of education, religiosity, and

14. DuBois, *Feminism and Suffrage*, pp. 24–25.

15. Stanton et al., *History of Woman Suffrage*, 1:380.

16. Gerda Lerner, *The Grimké Sisters from South Carolina: Pioneers for Women's Rights and Abolition* (New York, 1967), pp. 306–8.

style are even more difficult to sustain when we compare Sojourner Truth with the rank and file of the women's rights and antislavery movements. Throughout New England, upstate New York, and the old Northwest, the farming and working people who opposed slavery were also camp meeting followers, adherents of strenuous, evangelical religion, utopian communitarians, and devotees of spirit rappers and water cures. Truth's speeches to various overlapping communities of reformers were carried in a variety of periodicals. What at first glance appear to be discrete worlds of reform were fractured yet extensively overlapping. Women's rights supporters were likely to oppose slavery, criticize the clergy, follow the Graham diet, believe William Miller, and place more faith in the dictates of spirits than of medical doctors. And Sojourner Truth was a familiar presence among all these predominantly white reform communities.[17]

It was not so much that Truth had followed one, singular, brave, and public route to Akron while the white women had traveled a more private, fearful one. Truth had her road, Gage had hers, and other women had theirs. All these myriad avenues—through camp meetings, utopian communities, abolitionism, journalism, and temperance—led to women's rights. How, then, was Frances Dana Gage able to draw so clear a distinction between Truth and the white women in Akron? Answering this question requires an examination of discourse rather than personal narrative.

Frances Dana Gage's report of Sojourner Truth's speech is usually taken as a faithful transcript, as though what Gage wrote exactly captures the tenor of the meeting, the actions of the preachers, the chagrin of the organizers, and the wording of Truth's remarks. Gage's report, the most dramatic account of the meeting, has become definitive, but it is not the only one. The secretary of the meeting, a journalist friend of Sojourner Truth's named Marius Robinson, was the president of the Western Anti-Slavery Society. He published lengthy accounts of the proceedings for the news-

17. Recent feminist scholarship refigures the categorization of women's reform. Nancy Hewitt's *Women's Activism and Social Change: Rochester, New York, 1822–1872* (Ithaca, 1984), a study of women's activism in Rochester (a city in which Sojourner Truth had very good friends and spent a great deal of time), outlines three communities of women's reform, all of which were tinged more or less with Protestant Christianity. Mary P. Ryan, *Cradle of the Middle Class: The Family in Oneida County, New York, 1790–1865* (New York, 1981), testifies to the unrestricted reach of antislavery societies in Oneida and Utica, New York, in the 1830s. Ann Braude, *Radical Spirits: Spiritualism and Women's Rights in Nineteenth-Century America* (Boston, 1989), illustrates the tight relationship between spiritualism and other social reforms like women's rights at midcentury. Jean Fagan Yellin's *Women and Sisters: The Antislavery Feminists in American Culture* (New Haven, 1989), focusing on the iconography of women's abolitionism, traces the racial heterogeneity in feminists' cultural productions.

paper he edited, the Salem, Ohio, *Anti-Slavery Bugle*. Although they acknowledge the power of Sojourner Truth's remarks, Robinson's reports also give voice to the other participants.

The picture of the Akron meeting that emerges from the pages of the *Bugle* contradicts Gage in several regards, starting with the call to the conference, which ran in several reform newspapers in the spring of 1851 and appealed to "all the friends of Reform, in whatever department engaged." The call cited four evils that women's rights would combat: war, intemperance, sensuality, and slavery. Rather than fearing contamination by the antislavery cause, as Gage asserts, the organizers deliberately reached out to abolitionists.[18]

Robinson reports the women's spirited discussions, citing particularly the frequent contributions of the fervent Pittsburgh journalist, Jane Swisshelm, and of Emma Coe, a popular women's rights lecturer from Michigan. At one point a Mr. Sterling protested that men were talking too much and recommended their restraint. Mary A. W. Johnson dissented, reminding everyone that men as well as women were welcome to the floor. Robinson sums up approvingly: "The business of the Convention was principally conducted by the women." He features the speeches of Gage and Truth in separate articles, for Gage had delivered an effective keynote, and Truth's was "one of the most unique and interesting speeches" of the convention, thanks to "her powerful form, her whole-souled, earnest gestures, and . . . strong and truthful tones." But according to Robinson, the other women in attendance were neither, as Gage would have them, silent nor discomfited. The meeting included enough other women with public speaking experience that Sojourner Truth did not stand out only for that reason.[19] Accounts in other newspapers also emphasize the liveliness of the proceedings and mention Frances Dana Gage, Emma Coe, and Jane Swisshelm by name.[20]

Frances Dana Gage, who often published comentary and fiction under the pen name of Aunt Fanny, was a far more creative and experienced writer than Marius Robinson. She dramatized Sojourner Truth's presence much better than he did. In Gage's scenario, the featureless organizers of the convention "tremble" when Truth appears in all her physical strength.

18. Salem, Ohio, *Anti-Slavery Bugle*, March 29, April 2 and 5, 1851. In the spring of 1851, Oliver Johnson was editing the *Bugle*. Marius Robinson succeeded him at midyear.

19. Ibid., June 7, 14, and 21, 1851.

20. For example, the New York *Anti-Slavery Standard*, June 26, 1851, and the Rochester *Daily American*, June 4, 1851.

Whereas Robinson mentions merely Truth's "powerful form," Gage supplies a vivid image of "this almost Amazon form, which stood nearly six feet high, head erect, and eyes piercing the upper air like one in a dream," whose first words produce "a profound hush." Gage's Truth bares a tremendously muscular right arm, pulls herself up to her full six feet, and has a voice like thunder. The words that Gage quotes Truth speaking are commanding, and they emanate from a superhuman body.

Gage's sketch of Truth, first published in 1863, was influenced by another writer of far greater renown whose portrait of Truth had already reached a vast audience. Harriet Beecher Stowe was famous as the author of *Uncle Tom's Cabin* and other novels and stories when she published "Sojourner Truth, The Libyan Sibyl" in the April 1863 issue of the *Atlantic Monthly*. Stow made some mistakes. She thought, for instance, that Truth was dead. Such errors did not prevent the essay from becoming the most popular rendition of Truth at midcentury. For the next twenty-five years, other Truth biographers, including Gage, repeated (sometimes with variations, as was the case with Gage) the Libyan Sibyl appelation that Stowe had used.[21]

Stowe places less emphasis than Gage on Truth's physical presence and accentuates the exotic nature of Truth's persona: "No pen, however, can give an adequate ideal of Sojourner Truth. This unlettered African woman, with her deep religious and trustful nature burning in her soul like fire, has a magnetic power over an audience [that is] perfectly astounding." Whereas Gage's Truth is a voice in a powerful body, Stowe's Truth is an amusing native, an African whose insight gushes, untamed, out of her nature. Stowe contrasts the untutored Truth with the eminent clergymen who are her houseguests. Gage uses a similar strategy of opposition, contrasting potent Truth with insipid white women. Both quote Truth speaking in dialect while white characters speak cultured, standard English. Truth emerges from both essays as a colorful force of nature profoundly different from lackluster (white) people like the authors.

Other descriptions of Truth also stress her singularity. Frederick Douglass called her a "strange compound of wit and wisdom, of wild enthusiasm and flint-like common sense." She was, he said, "a genuine specimen of the uncultured negro" who cared nothing for "elegance of speech or refinement of manners. She seemed to please herself and others best when she

---

21. Harriet Beecher Stowe, "Sojourner Truth, the Libyan Sibyl," *Atlantic Monthly* 11, no. 66 (April 1863): 480. My analysis of Stowe's essay differs from Jean Yellin's excellent discussion in *Women and Sisters*, pp. 81–87, in that Yellin stresses the transcendent passivity and mystery of Stowe's "Libyan Sibyl."

put her ideas in the oddest forms."[22] The newspapers reprinted in the second part of the 1875/78 and 1884 editions of *The Narrative of Sojourner Truth* also underscore her differentness, portraying her as "this interesting and decidedly original character," "unique, witty, pathetic, sensible," "a child of nature, gifted beyond the common measure, witty, shrewd, sarcastic, with an open, broad honesty of heart, and unbounded kindness."[23]

Sojourner Truth's appeal was at once broader than race and deeply rooted in Americans' notions about the connection between blackness and slavery. Educated Americans have long been attracted to naifs, whether or not of African descent. Truth's unaffected religiosity gave her access to large American audiences. The prophetic, evangelical style that Truth employed has struck Americans as embodying more authenticity and more fundamental truth than the more educated rhetoric derived from the law and from written sermons. Truth's mode of expression owes much to late eighteenth- and early nineteenth-century Methodists, who invented the art of preaching—as opposed to sermonizing—and within fifty years grew into the largest American denomination. Nineteenth-century Americans were susceptible to inspired preaching, and Truth was first and foremost a preacher who gloried in divine inspiration. Elaborating on the Bible more than on the news from Washington, Sojourner Truth's message was thoroughly steeped in biblical imagery, and her text was intimately familiar to all her fellow citizens. To those numerous nineteenth-century Americans whose basic education had come from the Bible and whose religion was evangelical, Sojourner Truth would have been a persuasive purveyor of enduring and fundamental wisdom.

Truth was unforgettable for two reasons. First, she was a forceful speaker—like Frances Dana Gage, Frances Ellen Watkins Harper, Emma Coe, Nancy Prince, and Jane Swisshelm. Second, she presented herself as a woman who had been a slave; she made her persona as different from the educated white women who made her famous as they thought it possible to be. Even though the opportunities for women to speak in public were relatively circumscribed and always controversial in the first half of the nineteenth century, as a woman speaker Truth had many peers. Actresses were seldom considered entirely respectable; spiritual mediums spoke only while in a trance. But women preachers, Quakers or not, spoke in churches and camp meetings. Women lecturers like Emma Coe talked about great American women in schoolhouses, churches, and meeting halls. Sojourner Truth

22. Frederick Douglass, "What I Found at the Northampton Association," in Charles A. Sheffeld, ed., *History of Florence, Massachusetts. Including a Complete Account of the Northampton Association of Education and Industry* (Florence, Mass., 1895), pp. 131–32.
23. *Narrative of Sojourner Truth*, pp. 201, 221, 227.

had addressed audiences in each of these venues and had been recognized as a fine performer for twenty years before she went to Akron.

Truth had also crafted a persona that appealed enormously to educated white Americans. Her manipulation of the imagery of slavery and difference recommended her to talented publicists who guaranteed her place in the history of antislavery feminism. Gage's portrait, emphasizing Truth's body, reinforces notions that Truth herself asserted: that her experience in slavery—in which she worked like a man, suffered the loss of many children through sale, and felt a mother's grief but had no solace—lent her a potency that the white women at the meeting in Akron lacked, no matter how well they had been educated.

Unquestionably Sojourner Truth constructed her public persona to establish that what had happened to her—her enslavement—rather than her reason lent her a unique wisdom. She always reminded audiences that she had been a slave and that she remembered what slavery meant. If Gage quotes her accurately in 1851 when she says she lost thirteen children, Truth had appropriated her mother's sad experience of bearing and losing to slavery more than ten children. In fact, Sojourner Truth had five children, one of whom was sold away from her but whom she recovered. By the 1870s Truth had added a decade to her time as a slave. She knew full well that her experience in slavery authenticated her being and reinforced her message, whether she was speaking antislavery, women's rights, or freedmen's relief. And indeed, taking their cue from Truth, most readers conclude with Gage that Truth embodied some fundamental characteristic of blackness rooted in slavery, some power of race in rhetorically concentrated form.

Black slavery, Truth realized, was more memorable than black freedom for most Americans. Even the relatively enlightened communities of abolitionists focused more easily on abuses against the enslaved than on discrimination against the free. Again and again, free blacks in the antislavery movement had to remind their colleagues of their own situation, for the cause of the slave seemed so much more romantic and attractive. For many white abolitionists (William Lloyd Garrison, the Grimké sisters, and Abby Kelley were exceptions), free blacks existed in a conceptual limbo in which they were unseen or uninteresting or distasteful. Whereas other black women abolitionists became as much as possible like educated Americans, Truth emphasized her otherness by reciting her experiences as a slave. Widening the distance between herself and her audiences, Truth took maximum advantage of being exotic.

Truth resisted or ignored the temptation, as Frederick Douglass did not, to create an educated persona to display the benefits of freedom. Douglass recalled her poking fun at him as he remade himself: "[Truth] seemed to feel it her duty to trip me up in my speeches and to ridicule my efforts to speak and act like a person of cultivation and refinement." Douglass, like most other African American abolitionists, made one choice; Truth made another. As historian Carleton Mabee has noted, she remained illiterate despite many efforts to instruct her as an adult. Other former slaves, like Douglass and J. W. C. Pennington, associated literacy with freedom and presented themselves to the public as educated people.[24] Truth claimed that God inspired her, and she disdained education in lecturers or clergy. By stressing the inspirational aspect of her speaking gift and downplaying self-conscious preparation, she dispensed with any need for education, the very attainment that many other blacks in the antislavery movement most prized.

Truth also used her body in ways that women who were not actresses did not dare. Old and black and modestly dressed, she obliterated the sexual aspect of womanliness that youth, beauty, and lightness of skin would have accentuated. Yet Truth intentionally exhibited her body, and her American public recorded the occasions. She showed her arm in its full length 1851 and bared her breast in 1858, defining her womanliness and, miraculously, representing the essence of worker and mother rather than that of whore. Here her age, color, and naiveté served her well, for the figure of the light-skinned, ladylike Negro woman symbolized the enslaved fancy girl, whose sexuality—which could be bought and sold—was her most salient characteristic.

Sojourner Truth was not selling herself, at least not literally. But her gestures, sensational for the time, definitely enhanced her career. Truth followed a practice that was (and still is) common on American lecture circuits. Like Frederick Douglass and others who had published their autobiographies or other writing, she sold her books to reform-minded audiences whose curiosity had been whetted by her personal appearance. This tactic worked equally well for Frances Ellen Watkins Harper, a black teacher and poet who joined the antislavery lecture circuit in the 1850s. The free-born Harper toured under the auspices of the Maine Anti-Slavery Society, selling not a slave narrative but two volumes of poetry, *Forest Leaves* (1845) and *Poems on Miscellaneous Subjects* (1853).

Harper gained considerable respect as both poet and lecturer before the Civil War. After emancipation she taught in the South, and after Reconstruction she headed the Colored Division of the Woman's Christian Tem-

---

24. Douglass, "What I Found at the Northampton Association," p. 132; Carleton Mabee, "Sojourner Truth, Bold Prophet: Why Did She Never Learn to Read?" *New York History* 86 (January 1988): 55–77.

perance Union. In 1892 she published *Iola Leroy*, one of the earliest novels by an African American. For nearly half a century, Harper was active in the various reform movements that attracted the support of American women. Scholars like Hazel Carby, Frances Smith Foster, and Bettye Collier-Thomas have investigated her life and work.[25] Besides Frances Harper, Sojourner Truth had several other black women contemporaries in feminist abolitionism. Two pioneers of black women's history, Gerda Lerner and Dorothy Sterling, have edited documents that illuminate the lives of antislavery feminists such as Sarah Mapps Douglass (the most active black member of the Philadelphia Female Anti-Slavery Society, correspondent of Sarah Grimké's for forty years) and Sarah Parker Remond (born into an antislavery family in Salem, Massachusetts, an antislavery lecturer in New England and Great Britain in the 1850s). Marilyn Richardson has republished the speeches and essays of the Boston lecturer Maria Stewart. A popular speaker in the early 1830s, Stewart formulated phrases that Sojourner Truth came close to echoing: "What if I am a woman; is not the God of ancient times the God of these modern days?"[26]

The names of Harper, Douglass, Remond, and Stewart occasionally appear in passing in histories of abolitionism and in the three volumes of *The History of Woman Suffrage*. Although they are now becoming better known and their work is being reprinted, none has her portrait on a postage stamp, as has Sojourner Truth since 1986. Their lives and works remain the stuff of scholarly research, not of popular legend. Why this invisibility? On the one hand, as mostly light-skinned, ladylike women of African descent, they resembled too closely the stereotypical enslaved fancy girl; on the other hand, they were too much like their white women peers to seem memora-

25. For Harper, see Dorothy Sterling, ed., *We Are Your Sisters: Black Women in the Nineteenth Century* (New York, 1984), pp. 159–64. See also Hazel Carby, *Reconstructing Womanhood: The Emergence of the Afro-American Woman Novelist* (New York, 1987); Frances Smith Foster, ed., *A Brighter Coming Day: A Frances Ellen Watkins Harper Reader* (New York, 1990); and Bettye Collier-Thomas, *Frances Ellen Watkins Harper: Abolitionist and Feminist Reformer* (Chapel Hill, forthcoming).
26. Gerda Lerner, ed., *Black Women in White America: A Documentary History* (New York, 1972); Sterling, *We Are Your Sisters*, pp. 126–33, 175–80; Marilyn Richardson, ed., *Maria W. Stewart, America's First Black Woman Political Writer: Essays and Speeches* (Bloomington, Ind., 1987), p. 68. See also Dorothy B. Porter, "Sarah Parker Remond, Abolitionist and Physician," *Journal of Negro History* 20 (July 1935): 287–93; Ruth Bogin, "Sarah Parker Remond: Black Abolitionist from Salem," *Essex Institute Historical Collections* 110 (April 1974): 120–50; R. J. M. Blackett, *Building an Anti-Slavery Wall: Black Americans in the Atlantic Abolitionist Movement, 1830–1860* (Baton Rouge, 1983); R. J. M. Blackett, *Beating against the Barriers: Biographical Essays in Nineteenth-Century Afro-American History* (Baton Rouge, 1986); and Dorothy Sterling, *Black Foremothers: Three Lives*, 2d ed. (New York, 1988).

ble. But mostly, because they were very obviously free, the exotic character of the slave-woman victim has obliterated their existence. Educated, free black women have come very close, in fact, to vanishing entirely from the annals of antislavery and women's rights. To explain this near disappearance we must return to the phrase associated with Sojourner Truth: "and ar'n't I a woman?" Truth—and Stewart, Harper, Douglass, and Remond—saw themselves as women; their own womanly identity was secure. But the culture in which they lived seldom accorded them complete female identity. Even Frances Dana Gage quotes Truth presenting her statement in the form of a question, which she does not answer straightforwardly. Gage does not let Truth proclaim "Yes, I *am* a woman!" Instead, the rhetorical query leaves room for doubt. Most Americans in the middle of the nineteenth century would not even have thought to formulate such a question regarding black women or poor women of any race; as *woman*, these figures would have been invisible.

Had the question been posed, however, the short answer would most likely have been No. One of the era's most prominent antislavery feminists provides an example. In 1863, as several antislavery feminists were launching a petition drive to enact an amendment to the United State Constitution prohibiting slavery, Susan B. Anthony wrote to Elizabeth Cady Stanton that she planned to field teams of lecturers who would rally public support. Each team would consist of three people: "a *white* man, *black* man & a woman." Another women's rights advocate, Jane Swisshelm, followed the logic of her time when she spoke of "woman's rights" as opposed to the rights of "colored men." Swisshelm, like many of her colleagues in feminism, also deleted working-class women from the collectivity she called "woman." Certainly, white women's rights supporters were far from unified when they defined *woman*, and Parker Pillsbury and Frances Dana Gage insisted on including women who were black. By and large, however, the women who spoke up for "woman" did not have poor white women and women of color in mind.[27]

This way of thinking has proved amazingly durable. Nineteenth- and early twentieth-century human sciences like anthropometry and phrenology routinely paired white women and men of color, as though women of color did not, need not, exist. The white woman/black man parallel that ignores black women inspired Gloria T. Hull, Patricia Bell Scott, and Barbara Smith to include it in the subtitle of their 1982 anthology of black

27. Anthony quoted in Dorothy Sterling, *Ahead of Her Time: Abby Kelley and the Politics of Antislavery* (New York, 1991), p. 338, emphasis in original; Pittsburgh *Saturday Visiter,* November 23, 1850.

women's writing, "All the Women Are White, All the Blacks Are Men, But Some of Us Are Brave." Describing her experiences in the Harvard Law School in the 1970s, Patricia Williams recalls feeling utterly invisible.[28] With educated white women as *woman* and black men as *the slave*, free, articulate black women simply vanished. What little social category existed for black woman was reserved for the slave: if dark-skinned, as mother; if light-skinned, as sexual victim. Even to their compatriots in reform, educated free black women were not engaging enough to attract publicists who had a keen eye out for drama, like Frances Dana Gage and Harriet Beecher Stowe.

Sojourner Truth, in contrast, purposefully anchored herself in slavery. She employed a naive persona, which until the second half of the twentieth century was the most certain means for a black woman to secure individual recognition in American public life. In the twentieth century, Mary McLeod Bethune and Zora Neale Hurston used the naive persona to advance their interests with powerful white Americans in politics, education, and the arts. All three women came under criticism from other blacks for reinforcing unfortunate stereotypes of the-black-as-ignorant-primitive at the same time that they struck educated whites as quaintly and picturesquely charming.

Sojourner Truth asked whether she were a woman, without making herself into one at the time. She and other black women who employed her strategy did not erase the barrier between themselves and *woman*. Not-*woman*, they seemed to be something else—authentic, powerful, native—that was memorable. To appear in the eyes of most Americans to be both memorable and *woman* at the same time was not possible for nineteenth-century black women. Black women's individual experience had either to be reconstructed as something emblematically Negro—that is, as enslaved—or to be erased. In the nineteenth century, Frances Dana Gage did not let Sojourner Truth answer her own rhetorical question unequivocally, because for most of their compatriots, if not for themselves, blackness was exiled from the category of *woman*.

28. Nancy Leys Stepan, "Race and Gender: The Role of Analogy in Science," in David Theo Goldberg, ed., *Anatomy of Racism* (Minneapolis, 1990), p. 47; Gloria T. Hull, Patricia Bell Scott, and Barbara Smith, eds., *But Some of Us Are Brave: Black Women's Studies* (Old Westbury, N.Y., 1982); Patricia J. Williams, *The Alchemy of Race and Rights: Diary of a Law Professor* (Cambridge, Mass., 1991), pp. 55–56, 222.

{ Part III }

Strategies and Tactics

{ 9 }

The Female Antislavery Movement

Fighting against Racial Prejudice and Promoting Women's Rights in Antebellum America

Carolyn Williams

The character of American antislavery organizations, exclusively white and male from their origins in the late eighteenth century, began to change in the 1830s. In 1833, Lewis and Arthur Tappan and other New York abolitionists who planned the meeting invited African American men to participate in the founding convention of the American Anti-Slavery Society in December of that year. Male abolitionists, like other men of this era, generally accepted the "cult of true womanhood," which prescribed separate spheres for each gender. Women, therefore, were asked to attend the conference only as witnesses. The invitation to women was prompted by the valuable contributions of such activists as Elizabeth Chandler and Prudence Crandall to the struggle against slavery and racial prejudice.[1] Once at the convention, however, the women guests, particularly Lucretia Mott, took an active role that culminated not only in the incorporation of women into previously male organizations as equal members but also in the emergence of an autonomous American feminist movement, the first in the world.

Two organizations, the Boston Female Anti-Slavery Society, founded in late 1832, and the Philadelphia Female Anti-Slavery Society, which started

1. The following works illuminate the contributions of American Quakers Chandler and Crandall to the antebellum abolitionist movement: Benjamin Lundy, *The Poetical Works of Elizabeth Margaret Chandler with a Memoir of Her Life and Character* (Philadelphia, 1839); Edmund Fuller, *Prudence Crandall: An Incident of Racism in Antebellum America* (Middletown, Conn., 1971); Philip S. Foner, *Three Who Dared: Prudence Crandall, Margaret Douglass, Myrtilla Miner: Champions of Antebellum Black Education* (Westport, Conn., 1984); and Susan Stane, *A Whole Souled Woman: Prudence Crandall and the Education of Black Women* (New York, 1990).

immediately after the founding convention of the American Anti-Slavery Society, were principal agents in promoting women's equal inclusion in the abolitionist campaign and in creating a women's rights campaign. These women's organizations (particularly PFASS) were also crucial to the assault on racial prejudice within abolitionist circles.

One way BFASS, PFASS, and other women's organizations fostered the growing feminist movement was to promote the national organization of antislavery women. Conventions first suggested by the Boston society and held in 1837, 1838, and 1839 in New York and Philadelphia sponsored the initial wave of collective feminism. Women began to articulate their own oppressed condition and to construct an argument for their full and equal participation in the abolitionist movement and in society at large. From the antislavery conventions of the 1830s arose a women's community committed to overturning racial and sexual oppression.

The women of PFASS took the lead and worked for nearly forty years to eradicate racial barriers. The organization began in 1833, when the antebellum American abolitionist movement first dedicated itself to the immediate eradication of slavery and racial prejudice. It disbanded in 1870, several months after the passage of the Fifteenth Amendment enfranchised male African Americans.

Throughout the nearly four decades of its history, the feminist abolitionist Lucretia Mott was the guiding figure of PFASS.[2] Although we tend to associate her with Philadelphia, Lucretia Mott was a native of New England. She was born into the Quaker community in Nantucket and educated in schools in Boston and upstate New York. While attending Nine Partners, a Quaker boarding school open to males and females, the young Lucretia Coffin heard the frequent speeches of one of the school's founders, Elias Hicks, whose views would shape her subsequent responses to religion and reform.

Hicks, an itinerant minister born in New York, condemned slavery and racism. He delineated how those not directly involved in slavery helped perpetuate the institution by their racial prejudice and the use of slave-produced goods. He also asserted the importance of individual moral initiative, unimpeded by deference to any authority or hierarchy. Controversy over the teachings of Hicks combined with other doctrinal disputes to disrupt the American Quaker community in the early nineteenth century, dividing the Society of Friends into two factions, Orthodox and Hicksite

2. Margaret Hope Bacon presents an important study of the life and reform career of Lucretia Mott in *Valiant Friend: The Life of Lucretia Mott* (New York, 1980).

Quakers, in 1827–1828. In the 1830s most Pennsylvania Quakers active in the new wave of abolitionism identified with the Hicksite faction. Indeed, Lucretia Mott and other Hicksite Quaker women composed the majority of PFASS. Hicks's emphasis on the centrality of individual conscience was particularly compatible with the early feminist insistence on the equal moral natures of the sexes.

The issue of including women in organized abolitionism first surfaced during the founding convention of AASS. Although they did not receive formal invitations during the planning stage of the convention, a few local women were asked at the last minute to witness the momentous proceedings. Lucretia Mott and several other Philadelphia women accepted the hastily extended invitation to attend the convention as guests.

Mott was foremost among the Pennsylvania women who made an impression on the men involved in antislavery activities in the area. She acted on the advice of Elias Hicks and of English Quaker Elizabeth Heyrick, who formally articulated the new concept of immediatism, and early advocated the boycotting of slave-produced goods as a main tactic in the fight against slavery. Consequently, Mott joined with other Quaker women in Philadelphia to form a free produce society to boycott slave-produced goods in the city.[3]

During the three days of the convention "a number of excellent women, most of them of the 'Society of Friends,' were in constant attendance" at the various meetings.[4] Women were content at first to be silent witnesses, but soon Mott, Esther Moore, and Lydia White, all Hicksite Quakers from Philadelphia, took part in several of the debates throughout the three-day convention. Lucretia Mott spoke first and most extensively. One participant, the young divinity student and abolitionist James Miller McKim, expressed the reaction of men who were not Quakers when he said, "I had never before heard a woman speak at a public meeting." Miller went on to explain that despite the surprising spectacle, Mott's speech generated no offense. According to McKim, "she said but a few words, but these were spoken so modestly, in such sweet tones, and yet withal so decisively,

3. Elizabeth Heyrick presented her views on abolitionism and women's participation in this reform in the pamphlets *Immediate Not Gradual Abolition or an Inquiry into the Shortest, Safest and Most Effectual Means of Getting Rid of West Indian Slavery* and *Apology for Ladies Anti-Slavery Associations*, first published in London in 1824 and 1828, respectively. For information on Heyrick see Kenneth Corfield, "Elizabeth Heyrick: Radical Quaker," in Gail Malmgreen, ed., *Religion in the Lives of English Women, 1860–1930* (London, 1986), pp. 41–67.

4. *Proceedings of the American Anti-Slavery Society Convention Assembled at Philadelphia, Dec. 4, 5, and 6, 1833* (New York, 1833), p. 4.

that no one could fail to be pleased. And no one did fail to be pleased. She apologized for what might be regarded as an intrusion; but she was assured by the chairman and others that what she said was very acceptable."[5]

Although Mott made a contribution to the statement of purpose of the new organization drafted by Garrison,[6] she was not asked to sign the declaration. Lucretia Mott later observed, "I do not think it occurred to any one of us at the time, that there should be propriety in our signing the document." Women were, however, encouraged to form their own organizations. The convention expressed "great confidence in the efficacy" and the exertions of women abolitionists, and "all the ladies of the Land [were] respectively and earnestly invited . . . to form Anti-Slavery Societies in every state, County, and Town in the Union."[7]

Lucretia Mott and the other women attending the convention responded by inviting women interested in the cause to meet the following week in the schoolroom of a local Quaker teacher, Catharine McDermott. More than one hundred women, mostly Hicksite Quakers and a few African American women, attended. Because none of the women felt comfortable chairing a meeting based on parliamentary procedure, a local African American minister and dentist, James McCrummill, was asked to preside. Two recent delegates from New England to the founding convention of AASS, Samuel J. May and Nathaniel Southard, delivered remarks to the meeting.

May, a Unitarian minister, fortified the group by pointing "out the important assistance that might be rendered by the [female] sex, removing the great evil of slavery." Samuel May had recently witnessed dramatic events that illustrated the valor and commitment of a woman to the cause of African Americans. He had become a strong supporter of Connecticut teacher Prudence Crandall, who in 1832–1833 captured the attention of the abolitionist community when she attempted to provide education for young black women. The community of Canterbury persecuted Crandall and her

5. Anna M. Hallowell, ed., *James and Lucretia Mott: Their Lives and Letters* (Boston, 1884), p. 113.

6. On hearing the preliminary wording of the section of the Declaration—that is, "We plant ourselves on the truths of Divine Revelation and on the Declaration of Independence as an Everlasting Rock"—Mott believed that a mistake had been made in the arrangement of the wording of the phrase; that the author surely meant that Divine Revelation was the Everlasting Rock. After a brief delay in which she realized that no one else caught the error, Mott rose and suggested the words be transposed. Mott recalled, "I remember one of the younger members [J. Miller McKim] turning to see what woman there was there who knew what the word 'transpose' meant" (Hallowell, *James and Lucretia Mott*, pp. 113, 115).

7. *Proceedings*, p. 23.

students, put Crandall in jail and destroyed the school. May would later say of Prudence Crandall, "I shall never forget that woman. It was an event that sent deep into my soul that reverence which I now feel for women."[8]

Five days after the initial meeting the Philadelphia Female Anti-Slavery Society was formally established. Membership was open to "any Female united" in the views espoused by the organization and who contributed to the funds. The women who made up PFASS largely came from merchant and artisan families of the city. Teaching was the most common occupation among the membership. Other women worked in the sewing crafts or were merchants. Lydia White, for example, one of the founding members, operated a free produce store in Philadelphia in the late 1820s and 1830s.

Although most members of PFASS were followers of Elias Hicks, some Orthodox Friends and others who were not Quakers made invaluable contributions to the organization. Sarah Pugh, who served as president for most of the years 1838–1866, was originally affiliated with the Orthodox Quakers. Mary Grew, the most outstanding non-Quaker PFASS activist, was a member of a prominent Baptist family from New England. The corresponding secretary of the society from 1834 until 1870, Grew wrote the annual reports that chronicled its progress.[9] Mott, Pugh, and Grew became leading figures in the feminist campaign that arose from the nineteenth-century abolitionist movement.

Consistent with the new commitment to interracial solidarity, women abolitionists in Philadelphia also welcomed a few African Americans into

8. For important discussions of Samuel May see Jane H. Pease and William H. Pease, "The Gentle Humanitarian: Samuel Joseph May," in their *Bound with Them in Chains: A Biographical History of the Antislavery Movement* (Westport, Conn., 1972), pp. 276–307, and Donald Yacovone, *Samuel Joseph May and the Dilemmas of the Liberal Persuasion, 1797–1871* (Philadelphia, 1991). May left an account of the antislavery movement titled *Some Recollections of Our Anti-Slavery Conflict* (Boston, 1869).

9. When the Society of Friends in Pennsylvania split into Orthodox and Hicksite groups, Sarah Pugh refrained from identifying with either faction. She recorded in her diary in October 1838, "I join not the ranks of the other [Hicksite] party, for however much I admire some of their principles, and love many of their members, I am not a sectarian." In the same diary entry she articulated sentiments compatible with the views of Elias Hicks: "May we not believe with the apostle 'that of every nation, tongue and people, they that fear God and work righteousness will be accepted by him?'" Although she continued to adhere to the nonsectarian position, apparently later in life Pugh became more closely identified with the "other party" that claimed so many of the ones she long loved and toiled with in "righteousness." Pugh is buried in the Hicksite graveyard in Philadelphia. *Memorial of Sarah Pugh: A Tribute of Respect from Her Cousins* (Philadelphia, 1888), p. 11. For biographical sketches of Pugh and Mary Grew, see Edward T. James, ed., *Notable American Women, 1607–1950: A Biographical Dictionary*, 3 vols. (Cambridge, Mass., 1971), 2:91–92, 3:104–5. See also Ira V. Brown, *Mary Grew: Abolitionist and Feminist, 1813–1896* (Selinsgrove, Pa., 1991).

PFASS. Although the number of black members remained small over the years, the African American women became a highly visible and active part of the organization. Black women were among the founding members of PFASS and among the most active participants in its myriad projects, serving as officers, members of the executive board, and delegates representing the society at various functions.

From the founding meeting, Forten-Purvises and Douglasses, two leading African American families of Philadelphia, were active in PFASS. Three generations of Forten women served in the organization. Charlotte Forten, a social reformer and the prominent hostess of elite black Philadelphia society, her daughters Margaretta, Sarah Louise, and Harriet, and her daughter-in-law Mary Woods Forten, were active PFASS members. Harriet Forten, along with her husband Robert Purvis, participated in the Underground Railroad in the region. Mary Woods Forten was the mother of Charlotte L. Forten, who would make her mark as an important abolitionist writer and teacher during the Civil War era. The last Forten woman to join PFASS was Harriet Purvis, the daughter of Harriet and Robert Purvis.[10]

Grace and Sarah Douglass were known in Philadelphia for establishing various reform and literary societies of African American women.[11] Grace Douglass was also a founding member of PFASS. She attended the monthly meetings of the organization until her death in 1842. Through the years she served as a delegate of the society to several conventions, including the annual women's antislavery conventions of 1837–1839. Grace Douglass's daughter, Sarah, was a diligent PFASS member, at various times serving on the board of managers, on the fund-raising fair committees, and as librarian and recording secretary. Most important was Sarah Douglass's work to aid African Americans by providing educational opportunities for black chil-

10. The lives and reform activities of the members of the Forten-Purvis and Douglass families of Philadelphia are discussed in Esther Douty, *Forten the Sailmaker: Pioneer Champion of Negro Rights* (Chicago, 1968); Ray Allen Billington, "James Forten, Forgotten Abolitionist," *Negro History Bulletin* 30 (May 1967): 31–36; Janice Sumler-Lewis, "The Fortens of Philadelphia: An Afro-American Family and Nineteenth-Century Reform" (Ph.D. diss., Georgetown University, 1978); Sumler-Lewis, "The Forten-Purvis Women of Philadelphia and the American Anti-Slavery Crusade," *Journal of Negro History* 66 (1981): 281–88; Anna Bustill Smith, "The Bustill Family," *Journal of Negro History* 9 (1925): 638–44; the biographical sketch of Sarah Douglass in *Notable American Women*, 1:511–13; and the introductory remarks to primary materials presented in Dorothy Sterling, ed., *We Are Your Sisters: Black Women in the Nineteenth Century* (New York, 1984), pp. 119–33.

11. *Notable American Women*, 1:511–13. See the essay by Julie Winch, Chapter 6, in this volume.

dren and adults in Philadelphia.[12] In the 1830s and 1840s Sarah Douglass ran a school for African American children in the city which for several years PFASS helped sponsor.[13]

The prominence of these women of African descent testified both to the profound commitment of the white women to racial equality and cooperation and to the determination of the black women to help mold a multiracial America. Moreover, their presence gave PFASS a special advantage in the fight against racism. Black PFASS members offered personal insight into the nature and extent of the racial prejudice that plagued the lives of antebellum free blacks, and the abolitionists used their poignant testimony to raise white consciousness abut the problem of racism.

The black members of PFASS were part of an African American elite whose education, employment, and wealth distinguished them from the majority of oppressed blacks.[14] This elite set out to demonstrate through their exemplary behavior as well as their respectable and prosperous appearance that African Americans were worthy of the esteem and acceptance of white Americans. In this era of "the cult of true womanhood" the burden on black women was particularly heavy.[15] In elite families like the Fortens and Douglasses, women were expected both to epitomize ladylike gentility and to work tirelessly in the campaign to liberate the slave and elevate the free black.[16]

The African American elite of Philadelphia occupied a precarious position. The more respectable and affluent they appeared, the more they generated the suspicion and hostility of overtly racist whites. Middle- and

12. William L. Lang delineates the attitudes of abolitionists regarding black education in "Black Bootstraps: The Abolitionist Educators' Ideology and the Education of the Northern Negro, 1828–1860" (Ph.D. diss., University of Delaware, 1974). Frederick Cooper demonstrated that many African Americans shared this outlook in "Elevating the Race: The Social Thought of Black Leaders, 1827–40," *American Quarterly* 24 (December, 1972): 602–25.

13. Sterling, *We Are Your Sisters*, pp. 127–29.

14. Emma Jones Lapsansky analyzes the African American elite in nineteenth-century Philadelphia in "Friends, Wives, and Strivings: Networks and Community Values among Nineteenth-Century Philadelphia Afro-American Elites," *Pennsylvania Magazine of History and Biography* 108 (1984): 3–24. For a more comprehensive study of the antebellum leaders, particularly their reform activities, consult Julie Winch, *Philadelphia's Black Elite: Activism, Accommodation, and the Struggle for Autonomy, 1787–1848* (Philadelphia, 1988).

15. Barbara Welter examined this ideal of American womanhood in "The Cult of True Womanhood, 1820–1860," *American Quarterly* 18 (Summer 1966): 151–74.

16. In "Friends, Wives, and Strivings," Emma Lapsansky briefly examines the expectation regarding more privileged African American women. In her diary, Charlotte Forten illustrates the enormous responsibilities black women from leading families bore; see Brenda Stevenson, ed., *The Journals of Charlotte Forten Grimké* (New York, 1988).

upper-class whites who regarded blacks as inherently inferior perceived the efforts of elite African Americans as attempts at "amalgamation" (the mixing of the races), a prospect they, like most whites, abhorred. Lower-class whites resented the seeming airs of superiority and the wealth of the more privileged blacks.[17]

The few wealthy African Americans did all they could to cushion the shock of racial prejudice. Sarah Forten, whose father possessed sufficient wealth to shield his family from some of the harsher aspects of racial hatred and humiliation, described her family's position as protecting them "from falling under the weight of [the] evil of [racism]." The Fortens felt it "but in a slight degree compared with many others." "We are not," Sarah Forten wrote in 1837, "disturbed in our social relations—we never travel far from home and seldom go to public places unless quite sure that admission is free to all—therefore, we meet none of these mortifications which might otherwise ensue."[18]

Despite elaborate precautions to preserve their dignity, however, neither the Fortens nor other privileged African Americans could avoid racism altogether, and even relatively mild expressions of racial animosities and humiliations took their toll. Charlotte Forten's granddaughter and namesake, Charlotte, elaborated on the struggle against bitterness that blacks in this position experienced:

> These [minor racist snubs] are but trifles, certainly [compared] to the great public wrongs which we as a people are obliged to endure. But to those who experience them, these apparent trifles are most wearing and discouraging; even to the child's mind they reveal volumes of deceit and heartlessness, and early teach a lesson of suspicion and distrust. Oh! it is hard to go through life meeting contempt with contempt, hatred with hatred, fearing with good reason to love and trust hardly any one whose skin is white,—however lovable, attractive and congenial in seeming.[19]

Often even those whites sympathetic to the plight of African Americans displayed racism. Many reformers regarded blacks not as equals, but as wards; paternalism was the prevailing attitude. When Angelina Grimké in-

---

17. Emma Lapsansky demonstrates how these sentiments contributed to the rising tide of violence against African Americans in the antebellum period in "'Since They Got Those Separate Churches': Afro-Americans and Racism in Jacksonian Philadelphia," *American Quarterly* 32 (Spring 1980): 54–78.

18. Sterling, *We Are Your Sisters*, p. 125.

19. Stevenson, *The Journals of Charlotte Forten Grimké*, p. 140.

vestigated for PFASS the impact of racial prejudice, she sought Forten's views on the subject. Sarah Forten remarked on the extent of prejudice even among the allies of blacks, "No doubt but there has always existed the same amount of prejudice in the minds of Americans toward the descendants of Africa. Even our professed friends have not yet rid themselves of it. To some it clings like a dark mantle obscuring and choking up the avenues of higher and nobler sentiments."[20]

Angelina and Sarah Grimké, who enjoyed an intermittent association with PFASS, did more than anyone else to expose racism to the community of abolitionist women in the 1830s.[21] These aristocratic South Carolinians also forged a substantial link between abolitionism and feminism during their brief, controversial appearance in the public arena.[22] In emigrating from their native Carolina, the Grimké sisters fled not only the horrors of black bondage but also the genteel imprisonment of white women within plantation society. Their own daily contact with blacks under the racist regime of slavery allowed the Grimkés to focus on the humanity of blacks as they struggled against nearly impossible odds. Unlike many white abolitionists, the Grimké sisters regarded blacks as people rather than as abstract symbols of oppression and degradation.

Outside the slaveholding regions many whites had very little contact with African Americans. Black people lived in northern cities, but there was only fleeting contact between the races compared with the daily, sustained nature of southern race relations. As a result, northerners often felt both a horror and disapproval of slavery as an institution, and a revulsion—or at least a feeling of discomfort—when actually confronted with blacks on a personal level. While gathering information regarding racial discrimination among Quakers in America for British members of the Society of Friends in 1839, Sarah Grimké reported that a Massachusetts Quaker woman admitted that in her household the black hired hand was given separate dishes. The family "would no more have thought of using them, than if a cat or dog had eaten with them—Such said she are the prejudices I was educated in, I have found it hard to overcome them."[23]

20. Sterling, *We Are Your Sisters*, p. 125.

21. For an important account of the Grimkés' contributions to the fight against antebellum racism see Gerda Lerner, "The Grimké Sisters and the Struggle against Race Prejudice," *Journal of Negro History* 48 (1963): 277–91.

22. Larry Ceplair presents an illuminating study of the controversial careers of the Grimké sisters in the late 1830s in *The Public Years of Sarah and Angelina Grimké: Selected Writings, 1835–1839* (New York, 1989).

23. Sarah Grimké, "Letter on the Subject of Prejudice against Colour amongst the Society of Friends in the United States," Antislavery Collection, Boston Public Library.

Lucretia Mott was among the very small minority of northern whites who attempted to bridge the social and psychological gap between the two races. Her interest in African Americans transcended the formal boundaries of reform activities and translated into personal relationships. When she became active in abolitionist activities, Lucretia Mott participated on a regular basis with black people both on formal and social occasions, acquiring an important and unusual perspective on the "race question." In October 1833 she wrote to a relative in her native Nantuckett, "Since slavery has become my hobby I have had 6 appointed meetings for the people of colour in their several places of worship & expect to have 3 more which will embrace all." Shortly after helping establish PFASS, Mott wrote to white Pennsylvania abolitionist James Miller McKim, "We passed an evening with [William Lloyd Garrison and other visiting abolitionists] at our friend James Forten's."[24] The following excerpt from an 1838 letter reveals Mott's understanding of the impact of racism: "We cannot succeed in persuading the colored people who reside here that their interests would be promoted by scattering themselves more thru the country—they are a gregarious people & natural enough that they should be so while we exclude them from all other society than their own."[25]

It was the Grimké sisters, however, armed with the information and insight of black women friends, who extensively and potently addressed the issue of racism in the white antebellum North. The Grimkés' introduction to Philadelphia blacks began with their friendship with Grace and Sarah Douglass, whom they first saw at Quaker services in the city. Later, participation in PFASS widened the Grimkés' circle of African American acquaintances and deepened their knowledge of the black experience. While on their first lecture tour in New York, Angelina and Sarah Grimké observed how racism infected even abolitionist circles. African Americans were virtually excluded from white women's antislavery organizations in that city.[26]

Consequently, when they learned that the first national convention of antislavery women was scheduled for New York, the Grimkés made a

24. Mott to Phoebe Willis, March 18, 1832; and Mott to J. Miller McKim, February 5, 1834, Mott Correspondence, Friends Historical Library, Swarthmore College.

25. Mott to Willis, November 7, 1838, Mott Correspondence, Friends Historical Library.

26. In her biographical study of the Grimkés, Gerda Lerner discusses the relationship between the South Carolina sisters and African Americans, particularly Grace and Sarah Douglass. *The Grimké Sisters from South Carolina: Pioneers for Woman's Rights and Abolition* (New York, 1975), pp. 129–33, 156–60, 241, 256. Also see Lerner, "The Grimké Sisters," and Katharine Du Pre Lumpkin, *The Emancipation of Angelina Grimké* (Chapel Hill, 1974), p. 74.

special effort to encourage African American women to attend. Several black members of PFASS did come, and they played major roles: Grace Douglass was one of the seven vice-presidents, and Sarah Douglass was on the committee to draw up the statement pledging support "to free colored Americans."[27]

Led by both African American and white members of PFASS, the community of abolitionist women forged by the conventions of 1837, 1838, and 1839 maintained a strong, united stand against slavery and racism. They passed numerous resolutions denouncing the enslavement of blacks in the South and pledging cooperation to end the "peculiar institution." Moreover, they consistently focused on the role of racial prejudice and discrimination in perpetuating slavery. At the 1837 convention, for example, Angelina Grimké moved "that this Convention do firmly believe that the existence of an unnatural prejudice against our colored population, is one of the chief pillars of American slavery—therefore, that the more we mingle with our oppressed brethren and sisters, the more deeply are we convinced of the sinfulness of that anti-christian prejudice which is crushing them to the earth in our nominally free states."[28] The pledge ending this resolution expressed a serious commitment to racial equality: "We deem it a solemn duty for every woman to pray to be delivered from such an unholy feeling, and to act out the principles of Christian equality by associating with them [African Americans] as though the color of the skin was of no more consequence than that of the hair, or the eyes."

During the two conventions that followed, a strong stand against slavery and racism was particularly difficult to maintain because of the rising tide of violence against abolitionists and African Americans.[29] Economic instability lingering from the Panic of 1837 exacerbated racial tensions, and in 1837–1838 Pennsylvania was the site of deep conflict over proposed changes in the state constitution providing for the disfranchisement of African

27. *Proceedings of the First Anti-Slavery Convention of American Women . . . 1837* (New York, 1837), p. 3.
28. Ibid., p. 7.
29. Studies examining violence against blacks and abolitionists during this period include Lapsansky, "Since They Got Those Separate Churches"; Lorimar Ratner, *Powder Keg: Northern Opposition to the Antislavery Movement, 1831–1840* (New York, 1968); Leonard Richards, *Gentlemen of Property and Standing: Anti-Abolition Mobs in Jacksonian America* (New York, 1970); Linda K. Kerber, "Abolitionists or Amalgamators: The New York City Race Riots of 1834," *New York History* 48 (1967): 28–39; John Runcie, " 'Hunting the Nigs' in Philadelphia: The Race Riot of August, 1842," *Pennsylvania History* 39 (1972): 187–218; Elizabeth M. Geffen, "Violence in Philadelphia in the 1840s and 1850s," *Pennsylvania History* 36 (1969): 388–410; and John Melvin Warner, "Race Riots in the United States during the Age of Jackson, 1824–1849" (Ph.D. diss., Indiana University, 1972).

Americans.[30] Late in 1837 as the Philadelphia women prepared to host the second antislavery convention of American women, the murder of abolitionist editor Elijah Lovejoy by a proslavery mob gave the antislavery community its first genuine martyr.[31]

The violence against female abolitionists peaked at the 1838 convention, one of the pivotal episodes in the history of women in nineteenth-century America. Newly married Angelina Grimké Weld[32] delivered her last public address (for the next twenty-five years) while the angry crowd outside shouted and stoned the windows. Grimké's talk was followed by the debut speech of a young Massachusetts woman, Abby Kelley, before a "promiscuous" or mixed-sex assembly. In the years that followed Kelley replaced Angelina Grimké as the foremost woman speaker in the abolitionist cause.[33] In the midst of the furor, Lucretia Mott demonstrated her calm and sure leadership, guiding the "amalgamated" procession of abolitionist women, white and black linked arm in arm, past the howling mob. That night the newly constructed Pennsylvania Hall, created as a temple of "virtue, liberty, and independence," was burned.[34]

The destruction of Pennsylvania Hall by an angry antiabolitionist mob became the symbol of the virulent spirit of slavery and racism threatening the nation.[35] Three years earlier, antislavery agent Charles Burleigh had witnessed similar heroism by the Boston women who had faced down an antiabolitionist mob.[36] On that occasion, Maria Weston Chapman had rallied the women with the cry, "If this is the last bulwark of freedom, we may as well die here as anywhere."[37] Burleigh's description of the valor exhib-

---

30. David McBride, "Black Protest Against Racial Politics: Gardner, Hinton, and Their Memorial of 1838," *Pennsylvania History* 46 (1979): 149–62; and Thomas Anthony Sanelli, "The Struggle for Black Suffrage in Pennsylvania, 1838–1870" (Ph.D. diss., Temple University, 1978).

31. See John Gill, *Tide without Turning: Elijah P. Lovejoy and Freedom of the Press* (New York, 1958); and David W. Blight, "The Martyrdom of Elijah P. Lovejoy," *Pennsylvania History* 39 (1972): 239–49.

32. Two days before her speech Angelina Grimké married famous abolitionist lecturer Theodore Dwight Weld. See Lerner, *The Grimké Sisters*, pp. 233–42.

33. The following are comprehensive studies of Abby Kelley: Margaret Hope Bacon, *I Speak for My Slave Sister: The Life of Abby Kelley Foster* (New York, 1972), and Dorothy Sterling, *Ahead of Her Time: Abby Kelley and the Politics of Antislavery* (New York, 1991). See also the essay by Keith Melder, Chapter 12, in this volume.

34. The words, the motto of the state of Pennsylvania, were engraved on the Hall.

35. Ira V. Brown, "Racism and Sexism: The Case of Pennsylvania Hall," *Phylon* 37 (1976): 126–36.

36. Ibid. See also Brown, "Cradle of Feminism."

37. *Right and Wrong in Boston. Report of the Boston Female Antislavery Society . . . 1835* (Boston, 1836).

ited in 1835 by the members of BFASS applies equally well to the heroism of the women at the fiery 1838 convention: they manifested "courage which [could] calmly meet shame, reproach and insult, in the path of duty, offering no violence itself and unawed by the violence of others."[38]

Instead of deterring the women, opposition and violent intimidation only served to strengthen their resolve. In 1839 at the third, and what proved to be the final, antislavery convention of American women, the abolitionist women affirmed their lasting commitment in a resolution declaring that their "principle, in regards to prejudice against color remained unchanged by persecution, therefore [they resolved] to continue to act in accordance with [their] profession that the moral and intellectual character of persons, and not their complexions, should mark the sphere in which they move."[39]

At these conventions feminist abolitionists also publicly announced that they did not intend to allow their sex to restrict the sphere in which they moved. In New York in 1837, Angelina Grimké had moved and Lucretia Mott had seconded a proposal eventually adopted at the convention "which called forth animated and interesting debate respecting the rights and duties of women": "That as certain rights and duties are common to all moral beings, the time has come for women to move in that sphere which Providence has assigned her, and no longer remain satisfied in the circumscribed limits with which corrupt custom and a perverted application of Scripture had encircled her."[40] With these words, written by Angelina Grimké, nineteenth-century American women first asserted the equality of the sexes, defining men and women essentially as moral beings with the same rights and duties.

By the end of the convention, many of the women who had come together to oppose slavery and racism had begun to develop a new awareness of the oppression of their own sex. Boston abolitionist Maria Weston Chapman,[41] who had been unable to attend the proceedings, summed up this feminist awakening in a letter to the convention: "The present state of the world demands of woman the awakening and vigorous exercise of the power which womanhood has allowed to slumber for ages. She has been oppressed, kept in ignorance, degraded:—not in vain if she has thereby

38. *Proceedings of a Convocation Assembled from Various Parts of the State of Pennsylvania at Harrisburg, Dauphin County on Tuesday, 31st of January, 1837* (Philadelphia, 1837), p. 70.

39. *Proceedings of the Third Anti-Slavery Convention of American Women . . . 1839* (Philadelphia, 1839), pp. 7–8.

40. *Proceedings of the First Anti-Slavery Convention of American Women*, p. 9.

41. Jane H. Pease and William H. Pease present a very useful biographical sketch of Maria Chapman in *Bound with Them in Chains*, pp. 28–59.

learned active sympathy for the enslaved—not in vain, if her sufferings contribute to her salvation.[42] Because Boston women had initiated the efforts to organize the conventions,[43] it was appropriate that they first articulated this feminist dimension among the antislavery women. And the leadership of Maria Weston Chapman was pivotal.[44]

Maria Chapman, a member of an old patrician Boston family, had been educated in England. By the time of the emergence of immediatism she had become a Unitarian. Although influenced by the liberal religious views of William Ellery Channing, a friend and her pastor, she was not encouraged to participate in antislavery reform by her religious community. Chapman was more directly influenced by William Lloyd Garrison.

In 1832 Chapman and three of her sisters, Anne, Deborah, and Caroline Weston, were among "a small band of twelve women" who formed the Boston Female Anti-Slavery Society.[45] The purpose of this organization was to serve as an auxiliary to Garrison's all-male New England Anti-Slavery Society. Fundraising, primarily through the use of antislavery fairs, was the chief function of BFASS. Like PFASS, the Boston society became an important propaganda agency by circulating petitions and antislavery newsletters. Maria Chapman was one of the editors of Garrison's paper, the Liberator. The conflict-ridden lecture tour of English abolitionist George Thompson in 1834–1835 propelled Chapman and BFASS into the limelight of the Massachusetts antislavery community.[46] The tour was marked by

42. Ibid., p. 19.
43. The first discussion of a national association of women abolitionists was generated by a suggestion from BFASS that an executive committee be formed from the officers and members of the various female antislavery organizations "throughout the Union." The members of PFASS read and discussed this proposal but postponed any definite action on it in August 1836. However, when the Boston society wrote in February 1837 urging formation of a national convention, the Philadelphia women responded by sending out a letter to other female societies in Pennsylvania proposing participation in the convention. In addition, a PFASS committee was appointed to contact Methodist women active in antislavery reform to inform them of the proposed convention and request delegates (PFASS, Minutes, February 9, 1836, August 16, 1836, and March 2, 1837, Historical Society of Pennsylvania).
44. Jane H. Pease and William H. Pease present an incisive portrait of Maria Weston Chapman in "The Boston Bluestocking: Maria Weston Chapman," in Bound with Them in Chains, pp. 28–59.
45. Right and Wrong in Boston. See also Margaret Munsterberg, "The Weston Sisters and 'The Boston Controversy,'" Boston Public Library Quarterly 10 (1958): 1–26; Blanche Glassman Hersh, The Slavery of Sex: Feminist-Abolitionists in America (Urbana, Ill., 1978), pp. 11–12; and the essay by Debra Gold Hansen, Chapter 3, in this volume.
46. For an account of Thompson's first lecture tour in the United States in the 1830s, see Duncan Rice, "The Anti-Slavery Mission of George Thompson to the United States, 1834–35," Journal of American Studies 2 (1968): 13–51.

verbal abuse and physical attacks. When an angry mob threatened Thompson on the evening of October 21, 1835, Maria Weston Chapman and other members of BFASS protected him. It was on that occasion that Chapman articulated her willingness to die for liberty.

Chapman was also one of the primary architects of the abolitionist social circle labeled by the historian Lawrence Friedman as the Boston Clique.[47] This tight cadre of reformers consisted of prominent male and female antislavery activists. Men in reform groups had early advocated that women be missionaries, for they felt women should give moral testimony within their own sphere. But sophisticated debates about abolition and other reforms, mutually constructed strategies to combat slavery, and the presence of such strong women as the Weston sisters, Abigail Kelley, and Lydia Maria Child, changed perceptions and expectations of men and women regarding the role of women reformers. Chapman and her sister reformers carved out a more active and assertive position for themselves and women generally in the parlors of the Boston Clique. Soon opinions developed in private spilled into the public arena. And when the women of the Boston Clique attempted to assert their new position in the formal organizations of Massachusetts abolitionism, conflict erupted.

Massachusetts thus became the stage for the opening act of the controversy over "the woman question." Soon after the first women's convention ended, the Grimkés' lecture tour of New England sparked debate about the role and status of women in the antislavery movement.[48] First Catharine Beecher, and shortly afterward the congregational clergy of New England, condemned the sisters for overstepping the boundaries of the female sphere and for attempting to usurp the authority of the clergy. Refuting these charges, the Grimké sisters elaborated their argument concerning the moral natures and the rights of women and declared the equality of the sexes in all respects.[49]

47. See Lawrence Friedman's discussion of the community of Boston abolitionists in *Gregarious Saints: Self and Community in American Abolitionism, 1830–1870* (Cambridge, Mass., 1982), pp. 43–67, 129–59.
48. Lerner, *The Grimké Sisters*, pp. 183–204.
49. Catharine Beecher criticized the views Angelina Grimké presented in the treatise Grimké prepared for the women's convention, *An Appeal to the Women of the Nominally Free States* (New York, 1837). Beecher published her critique in *Essay on Slavery and Abolitionism with Reference to the Duty of American Females* (Philadelphia, 1837). The ministers denounced the Grimkés in the "Pastoral Letter: The General Association of the Congregational Churches of Massachusetts under Their Care," *New England Spectator,* July 12, 1837, pp. 106–7. Angelina Grimké answered Beecher in a series of letters eventually collected into one volume as *Letters to Catharine Beecher in Reply to an Essay on Slavery and Abolitionism Addressed to A. E. Grimké* (Boston, 1838). Sarah Grimké responded to the clergy in the second of a series of letters for the

Carolyn Williams

Disagreement about the role of women helped erode the consensus of
female and male abolitionist organizations in Massachusetts. Some member of BFASS objected when in 1838 Maria Weston Chapman, corresponding secretary, demonstrated her agreement with the Grimkés by inserting a
long argument on the equality of the sexes into the society's annual report.
Chapman's opponents, led by the society's president Mary Parker[50] (who
would chair the second women's convention that year), believed that the
"woman question" should be kept separate from abolitionism. When
Chapman and others tested their views by attempting to become members
of previously all-male antislavery groups, such incorporation was perceived
as a manifestation of the "extraneous" issue of women's rights and therefore detrimental to the abolition cause.[51] The controversy over the "woman
question" resulted not only in separations within the male and female abolitionist societies in Massachusetts but ultimately figured prominently in
the division of the national organization, the American Anti-Slavery Society. The explosive debate in Massachusetts prevented Maria Chapman and
BFASS from continuing their lead. It was left to Lucretia Mott and PFASS to
nourish the seed that would a decade later blossom into a full-scale movement for women's rights.

The experience of the Pennsylvania abolitionist community regarding
the inclusion of women was very different. Many of the Pennsylvania
abolitionists were from Hicksite Quaker backgrounds; they had no strong
objections to women working publicly for reform. Indeed, women were
encouraged to participate in the new state, county, and other regional
abolitionist organizations coming into existence late in 1837 and 1838,
while the women's issue was beginning to surface within the antislavery

reform journal, the *Spectator*. (Originally, Mary Parker, president of BFASS, had suggested to
the editor of the *Spectator* that the Grimké sisters write articles on "the Province of Woman."
When these articles were first proposed, Angelina Grimké was already occupied with her re-
buttal to Catharine Beecher. Consequently, Sarah Grimké agreed to write them. She had already written the first article when the pastoral letter was issued. She decided to devote the
subsequent letters, particularly the second one, to a response to the clerical letters.) Eventually
Sarah Grimké's letters were also printed, as *Letters on the Equality of the Sexes and the Condition
of Women Addressed to Mary S. Parker, President of the Boston Female Anti-Slavery Society* (Boston, 1838). For a more complete reconstruction of the developments, see Ceplair, *The Public
Years of Sarah and Angelina Grimké*, pp. 135–323.

50. According to Ceplair, Parker "was a moderate on most issues" and eventually led the
anti-Garrisonian component of BFASS (Ceplair, *The Public Years of Sarah and Angelina Grimké*,
p. 86).

51. Aileen Kraditor presents a fruitful discussion of the controversy over the "woman question" in the abolitionist campaign in *Means and Ends in American Abolitionism: Garrison and
His Critics on Strategy and Tactics, 1834–1850* (New York, 1967), pp. 39–77.

cause.[52] Lucretia Mott and several other PFASS members joined the new state abolitionist organization, a chapter of the American Anti-Slavery Society, with no apparent controversy. At the end of the 1830s, then, PFASS stepped beyond the "female sphere" that until that time had governed the activities of women's antislavery organizations.

Lucretia Mott, who had been instrumental in shaping many PFASS policies, expressed her views on the participation of women in antislavery organizations in a letter to Abby Kelley written in March of 1839, two months before the last women's convention. "The meetings of women imperfect as they are, had their use in bringing our sex forward, exercising their talents, and preparing them for united action with men, as soon as we can convince them that this is both our right and duty." Mott cited the two national "conventions [that] have done something toward bringing woman to a higher estimate of her power."[53]

Ultimately, Mott wrote, she "would be very glad if women generally and men too, could so lose sight of distinctions of sex and to act in public meetings on the enlightened and true ground of Christian equality." Because that was not yet possible, she felt there was "perhaps no better or speedier mode of preparing them for this equality, than for those women whose 'eyes are blessed that they see' to act in accordance with the light they have, and avail themselves of every opportunity offered them to mingle in discussion and take part with their brethren."[54]

Lucretia Mott and other PFASS members "availed" themselves of the opportunity to participate in the Pennsylvania Anti-Slavery Society. Mott and the other women occupied leading positions in this organization in the 1840s; late in 1839, Mott, Sarah Pugh, Mary Grew, and several other PFASS members were among those selected by the Pennsylvania Anti-Slavery Society to represent the state in the World Anti-Slavery Convention scheduled for the spring of 1840 in London.[55]

It must have saddened Lucretia Mott and other feminist-abolitionists that the "woman question" controversy had begun with a feud within BFASS, the organization that first suggested that antislavery women should coordinate their efforts. Although she and other leading PFASS members agreed with Chapman that the abolitionist movement could encompass a

---

52. Numerous references in the minutes of PFASS between 1836 and 1839 are made to individuals and groups in Philadelphia active in creating new antislavery organizations at the local and state levels.

53. Mott to Abby Kelley, March 19, 1839, Friends Historical Library.

54. Ibid.

55. Bacon, *Valiant Friend*, pp. 85, 86.

wide spectrum of opinions and views, Mott attempted to remain neutral regarding the Boston quarrel. She advised Maria Chapman, who had written to her about the Boston society's problems, to stay as close to Parker and the other opponents as possible. But Chapman and many other leading Massachusetts figures did not attend the 1839 women's convention, and 1838 was therefore the last time all the principal women abolitionists came together.[56]

In December of 1839 PFASS, disheartened by the trouble in Massachusetts, sent a resolution expressing "very deep regret [upon witnessing] the unhappy dissensions existing among our Anti-Slavery sisters in Boston, believing that our cause is thereby exposed to reproach and that liberty is wounded in the house of its friends." Consequently, PFASS implored the members of BFASS to put aside their differences and form a united front.[57] Although Mott realized that this organization was hopelessly divided, she continued to advise reconciliation and corresponded with members of both factions. As the breach widened, she commented sadly, "I feel so sorry for them that, all confidence in another is lost and suspicion and jealousy fill their minds."[58]

By early 1840, AASS and male and female societies in Massachusetts had divided into factions. As the various American antislavery organizations prepared for the international convention in England, only Pennsylvania and Massachusetts sent women delegates. Lucretia Mott, along with Boston abolitionists Abby Kelley and Maria Weston Chapman, were appointed to the executive committee of AASS to fill positions vacated by conservatives who had resigned in protest over the "woman question."[59]

Because of the splintering of individual societies and the absence of leaders like Mott, who had sailed for the meeting in England, the annual convention of antislavery women planned for 1840 did not take place. The progress of nineteenth-century feminism was slowed but not stopped by the shattering of consensus within the abolitionist community. The Grimké sisters, whose words first ignited the controversy, had retired. Although BFASS, which had fanned the flame of collective feminism in America, was now hopelessly divided, the Philadelphia society would preserve the embers until an autonomous women's movement rekindled the torch. In the 1840 PFASS annual report, just before the world convention in London, Mary

56. The records of the delegates attending the 1839 convention reveal that Chapman and the other Weston sisters, Child, and Parker were not present (*Proceedings of the Third Anti-Slavery Convention of American Women*, p. 13).
57. PFASS Minutes, December 18, 1839.
58. Ibid.
59. Bacon, *Valiant Friend*, p. 87.

Grew commented on the new dimension to the political activities of antislavery women: "It is a satisfaction to believe that by the concentration of our efforts in this way we do not only advance the cause of emancipation of the slave, but that the fettered mind of woman is fast releasing itself from the thraldom in which long existing custom has bound it, and by the exercise of her talents in the cause of the oppressed her intellectual as well as moral being is rising into new life."[60]

During the national antislavery conventions of 1837–1839 women first envisioned and proclaimed their power to change the world, to better themselves and others. While debating and coordinating tactics to combat slavery and racism, these women constructed, in the words of one historian, an argument "for an aggressive and self-actuated women's movement to carry out whatever activities their conscience might dictate."[61] By 1840 the nucleus of a women's movement existed.

60. PFASS, *Annual Report* (Philadelphia, 1840).
61. Keith Melder, *The Beginnings of Sisterhood: The American Women's Rights Movement, 1800–1850* (New York, 1977), p. 96.

{ 10 }

"Let Your Names Be Enrolled"
Method and Ideology in Women's Antislavery Petitioning

Deborah Bingham Van Broekhoven

*On May 15, 1838, Angelina Grimké spoke at an evening meeting of the Sec-*ond Anti-Slavery Convention of American Women. As rocks crashed through the windows and crowd noises interrupted the speech, Grimké offered her main point: "Especially, let me urge you to petition. Men may settle this and other questions at the ballot box, but you have no such right. It is only through our petitions that you can reach the Legislature. It is, therefore, peculiarly your duty to petition. . . . The South already turns pale at the number sent."[1] In 1838 pale southerners were also angry, and several states were offering rewards for the capture of leading abolitionists. The defection of the Grimké sisters, Charleston natives of respectable slaveholding stock, was particularly shocking, as was their appearance in public meetings with African Americans, male and female. White southerners visiting Philadelphia shared with many local residents the fear of race mixing and economic displacement. By the second night of meetings, these fearful men were angry enough to riot and torch Pennsylvania Hall, the site of the convention.

The controversy and violence evoked by this Philadelphia meeting contrast sharply with earlier incidents of females enrolling in the antislavery cause. No furor arose when in the early 1830s a few women joined men petitioning Congress against slavery. This early quietude was in part due to the small number of petitioners and the unimportance of antislavery issues

1. Mari Jo Buhle and Paul Buhle, eds., *The Concise History of Woman Suffrage: Selections from the Classic Work of Stanton, Anthony, Gage, and Harper* (Urbana, Ill., 1978), p. 76.

to most Americans. More important, antislavery literature from 1831, 1832, and 1833 contains nothing to suggest that the call for women to "let your names be enrolled in the cause of liberty"[2] meant petitioning, and much to suggest that it meant enlisting their quiet influence over family and friends.

Petitioning, however, was not an experience altogether foreign to women in colonial society and the early republic. Petitioning had long been a humble prayer of an inferior—often an orphan, widow, or war veteran—to a superior with power to grant the request. Beginning in the late eighteenth century, the Society of Friends began quietly to petition Congress to act against slavery. Signed only by the clerks of the yearly meeting, these early petitions did not require individual Quakers, male or female, to enroll their names.[3] In 1828, when William Lloyd Garrison began requesting individuals to sign petitions against slavery, both Garrison and local canvassers assumed that those signing would be males.[4] By 1835, however, male organizers openly suggested that women sign and circulate petitions, thereby recognizing the effectiveness of thousands of British women who had petitioned Parliament to end slavery.

The American women who began signing petitions were usually careful to follow the directions of male organizers, who asked women and men to sign separate petitions or columns. These female abolitionists also adhered to the deferential form of earlier petitions from widows or yearly meetings of Friends. Instead of demanding action, women prayed members of Con-

2. A.F.M., "An Address to the Daughters of New-England," *Liberator*, March 3, 1832.

3. This practice continued sporadically into the 1840s, contrasting sharply with the mass petitioning efforts of other abolitionists. See, for example, the "Memorial of the Representatives of the Yearly Meeting of New England Friends, East Greenwich, R.I., May 6, 1846," received December 29, 1846 (HR29A-H1.5), House Record Group 233, National Archives; also "Memorial of the Representatives of the Religious Society of Friends in . . . New York . . . remonstrating against the extension of the area of slavery," received February 15, 1854 (Sen33A-J4, #81), Senate Record Group 46, National Archives. Following Quaker precedent, the first antislavery petition by the New England Anti-Slavery Society was signed by officers only (*Liberator*, February 11, 1832). Unless otherwise noted, all petitions hereafter are from these House and Senate Record Groups, 233 and 46. I am indebted to Linda K. Kerber's analysis of eighteenth-century female petitioners and citizenship in *Women of the Republic: Intellect & Ideology in Revolutionary America* (Chapel Hill, 1980), especially pp. 85–99 and chap. 9.

4. As a newspaper editor, Garrison conducted his 1828 Vermont campaign postage-free through the cooperation of local postmasters to whom he sent petitions. The absence of female signatures on petitions from this campaign suggests that organizers and signers assumed this campaign was directed at the more politically active sex; see, for example, "Petition of George Graves and other inhabitants of Ira, Vermont," received January 1829 (HR20A-G5.1, no. 274) on which the postmaster wrote: "Not one to whom it was presented hesitated to sign it. I presume there is not an individual in this town that would have felt the least reluctance in signing this petition had it been shown them."

gress for a hearing. Addressed to the "Fathers and Rulers of our Country," most petitions began apologetically, "Suffer us, we pray you, with the sympathies which we are constrained to feel as wives, as mothers, and as daughters, to plead with you." In another common text, female signers acknowledged "that scenes of party and political strife are not the field to which a kind and wise Providence has assigned them," adding that if slavery were not a moral issue, they "would not appear thus publicly, in a way which, to some, may seem a departure from their place."[5]

Deferential or not, mass petitioning campaigns by American women were still new in 1837. Before 1837 American antislavery leaders more commonly advised women to influence family members and to pray to God on behalf of the slave.[6] An 1838 account in the *Liberator* suggests how a woman's use of her benign influence might involve her in petitioning. The story concerned a man who received a petition form in the mail but did not understand what to do with it. The man's wife explained, "They want us to get signatures." He responded that in their town this would be difficult. She told him not to worry. If he hitched up the horse, she would collect the signatures. He refused but agreed to think and pray overnight. The next day he drove his wife around town—still assuming she would get at most twenty signatures. Although they covered less than half the town and the wife faced accusations that her behavior was unconstitutional and unbiblical, she nonetheless secured 106 signatures. Antislavery editors used this story to illustrate the importance of female influence,[7] but the account also suggests that even before actual female petitioning campaigns, women's involvement in petitioning was substantial.

Abolitionist editors never dropped their message concerning women's quiet influence. But in 1835 male leaders adopted a bolder course,

5. "Ladies of Massachusetts petition against slavery in the District of Columbia" (HR24A-H1.3, no. 556), n.d.; also "Petition of Ladies Resident in Licking County, Ohio, against Slavery in the District of Columbia," received January 5–7, 1836 (Sen24A-H1). This deferential approach was the most common between 1834 and 1838, with both men and women writing the texts. Gilbert H. Barnes suggests that in 1834 Theodore Weld wrote the "Fathers and Rulers" text used extensively by Ohio women in 1835 and 1836 (*The Anti-Slavery Impulse, 1830–1844* [New York, 1964], chap. 13, n. 7).

6. *Liberator*, March 29, 1834. In their description of British abolitionists, Louis and Rosamund Billington note that women focused on moral and not political purposes, despite their willingness to petition Parliament ("'A Burning Zeal for Righteousness': Women in the British Anti-Slavery Movement, 1820–1860," in Jane Rendall, ed., *Equal or Different: Women's Politics, 1800–1914* [London, 1987], pp. 82–111). Regardless of whether men or women were petitioning, Americans were quick to switch from the British tradition of manuscript petitions to printed petition texts.

7. See the *Liberator* (December 14, 1838) and *Philanthropist* (December 18, 1838), which attributed it to the *Herald of Freedom*.

suggesting that members of the newly formed female auxiliaries conduct their own, separate petitioning. As Angelina Grimké argued in Philadelphia, neither male leaders nor most females viewed petitioning as the first step toward activism. Women initially joined an antislavery society by signing their names to the constitution of the local society. Letting one's "name be enrolled" in the antislavery cause could be a highly orchestrated ritual; in 1835, after a rousing speech at Pine Street (Baptist) Meeting House, Providence, 106 women came forward to sign the constitution of the newly formed Providence Female Anti-Slavery Society.[8] Women who did not enroll at a large public meeting signed or added their names to the constitution in a formal ceremony at the end of each meeting.[9] As the term implies, the experience of enrolling one's name in the antislavery cause was in many cases similar to the experience of the sinner on the anxious bench during a Finneyite revival. There, too, leaders exhorted individuals to let their names be enrolled in a book, although in revivals the frequent presumption was that God had already written names in "the lamb's book of life," and that adding one's name to a church membership roll simply recognized what God had already done.

The passive voice used in the revival phrase, "let your name be enrolled," was particularly appropriate for addressing abolitionist women—and not just those of a Calvinist bent. Most women whose names appear on antislavery society rolls or on an abolitionist petition presented their names primarily as a religious gesture. Because the phrase implied that God was ultimately responsible for one's enrollment, allowing one's name to be associated publicly with the cause merely added another earthly endorsement to the divine purpose. The act of lining up on God's side, however, was not without political implications, since associating one's name with abolitionism was intended to stir political leaders to action. Invoking other images of evangelical revival, Presbyterian Maria Sturges urged, "Let every petition . . . be baptized with prayer, and commended with weeping and supplication to Him in whose hands are the hearts of all men, that he would turn the channel of their sympathies from the oppressor to the oppressed.

8. *Liberator,* April 18, 1835.

9. Minutes of PFASS (Historical Society of Pennsylvania) and the Kent County [R.I.] Female Anti-Slavery Society (R.I. Historical Society) both mention new members adding their names to the constitution at the meeting when the new member made a commitment to the society and its cause. See *Philanthropist,* December 24, 1842, for a report of the Warren County [Ohio] Anti-Slavery Society, which also had new members (male and female) "sign the constitution."

For God is our only hope."[10] In theory abolitionist men also needed to baptize their petitioning efforts with prayer. But in reality male members of antislavery societies skipped this ritual, perhaps because male petitioning was less controversial and because they frequently hired solicitors rather than canvassing themselves.[11]

For women, enrollment soon meant not only joining but also working on the educational, fund raising, and petitioning projects of an antislavery society. When female societies noted the loss of an active member, they were apt, as they did in the death of Mrs. Hannah Taggart of the Cadiz [Ohio] Female Anti-Slavery Society, to eulogize the departed sister as one who "enrolled her name as an advocate for the poor and oppressed." By 1837 enrollment and active membership also meant petitioning, with the grieving women of Cadiz noting their "momentous duty . . . to petition our national Legislators . . . [as it] is the only mode by which females can publicly make known their grievances."[12]

Separate societies of antislavery women were numerous and active enough by 1836 for their members to take over from paid agents the task of canvassing for petition signatures. Initially women helped to finish or extend male canvassing for a particular petition drive. But soon leaders, male and female, began asking women to sign also. In its December 9, 1836, issue, the *Philanthropist* printed a small notice "To the Females of Ohio,"

10. The Kent County Female Anti-Slavery Society noted the receipt of this message, along with a petition, in its minutes for May 11, 1836, and BFASS acknowledged as new and positive the suggestion from another group of Ohioans that eastern women begin petitioning campaigns (Anne W. Weston, corresponding secretary, to Miss Lucy M. Wright, corresponding secretary of the Portage County Female Anti-Slavery Society, August 27, 1836, in the manuscript correspondence book of BFASS, Massachusetts Historical Society). These letters suggest that not all the impetus for organized female petitioning came from the Northeast. See also the partial reprinting of Maria Sturges's June 13, 1836, address to the women of Ohio in Nathaniel Rogers, *Herald of Freedom* (Concord, N.H.), July 30, 1836, pp. 85–86.

11. Throughout the first two years of the (male) Providence Anti-Slavery Society (1833–1843), the group hired canvassers to circulate petitions. After 1835, when the local women organized both a society and a petitioning campaign, the male group focused on other matters. The manuscript records of the male group are held in the Sophia Smith Collection, Smith College. In these first years of organization, paid agents elsewhere circulated petitions, along with their other duties of public speaking, literature sales, and organizing new societies. Barnes, *Anti-Slavery Impulse*, p. 132, records complaints about the deceitfulness of paid solicitors.

12. "Organization Proceedings," *Philanthropist*, December 5, 1837. See also the September 4, 1838, obituary of Charlotte Emeline Codding, described as "a hopeful convert" in Finney's 1830 Rochester revivals, and someone who "labored from house to house . . . , in pleading the cause of the poor down-trodden slave, with the anti-slavery petitions in hand."

requesting their aid in finishing the canvassing begun by the state executive committee. In this case women enrolled both women and men, with the energetic Maria Sturges coordinating the statewide effort.[13] Sturges also sent an antislavery message and petition for circulation to female anti-slavery societies in New England, as did the Boston Female Anti-Slavery Society.[14]

Encouraged by the Ohio women's campaign, male organizers, and the publicity generated by the House gag on antislavery petitions, members of the Providence, Boston, and Philadelphia female antislavery societies orga-nized more petitioning campaigns, soliciting the aid of female canvassers and female signatories in towns large and small. These early canvassers adopted the deferential approach, noting that politics was "not the sphere to which a kind Providence had assigned them." The petition texts simply asked that women's prayers—all they could do to help—be heard as an ex-pression of moral and religious concern for slave wives, mothers, and chil-dren bereft of legal, male protection.[15]

Despite the religious and deferential language, women's organizing and petitioning against slavery quickly became controversial, even before the first convention of antislavery women in 1837 publicized and extended wo-men's canvassing efforts. By going door to door, the women immediately tripled the number of petition names secured previously by paid male agents.[16] Irritated congressmen quickly noticed the glut of antislavery pe-titions, including the increased number of female organizers and signers.

13. Although the *Philanthropist* article does not mention whose signatures are being sought, male or female, extant petitions from that year include separate men's and women's petitions (and texts), but in several cases the order and similarity of surnames on separate petitions from one location suggests the petitions were circulated by one canvasser. Compare, for example, the "Petition of Jane Stewart & 88 Ladies of Fayette County, Ohio for the Abolition of Slavery in the District of Columbia," with the "Petition of Alexander Coy & 133 Citizens of Fayette County, Ohio," both received December 14, 1837 (HR 25A-H1.8), Folder 4 of 38.

14. The Kent County Female Anti-Slavery Society noted the receipt of the Ohio address and petition in its minutes for May 11, 1836. See note 10, above. The PFASS conducted petition campaigns for most of Pennsylvania—leaving the western section to Pittsburgh women.

15. Ibid. Organizer Maria Sturges admitted that petitioning involved a bold kind of public action to which women were unaccustomed, but she urged canvassers to remain humble, keeping "a deep conviction of the weakness of human effort, unaided by the power and wis-dom of our Heavenly Father." For a different perspective, focusing on how self-consciously feminist abolitionists reinterpreted this humble posturing, see Jean Fagan Yellin, *Women and Sisters: The Antislavery Feminists in American Culture* (New Haven, 1989), especially chaps. 1 and 2. For a discussion of how African American slaves framed their requests for freedom in petitions, see Gary B. Nash, *Race and Revolution* (Madison, 1990), p. 2 and especially chap. 3.

16. *Pennsylvania Freeman*, November 22, 1838, "Petitions"; also Barnes, *Anti-Slavery Impulse*, chap. 13.

From Maine to the Carolinas, community leaders affirmed their belief in male political agency by blaming fanatical ministers, not the women themselves. Rather than arguing pragmatically that the sheer quantity of female petitioners made it impossible for House members to hear their requests, most members of the House argued, with Rep. Jesse Bynum of North Carolina, that female petitioners against slavery were acting to influence politics, hence they were outside their proper sphere.[17] Despite this opposition, Angelina Grimké insisted that female abolitionists petition: "merely setting [their] names to a constitution" was insufficient; women must also circulate "numerous petitions."[18]

Female abolitionists were not the only Americans beginning to petition, for during the 1830s mass petitioning by male voters on a wide range of issues had increased dramatically.[19] Legislators were growing accustomed to petitions that were not just humble requests from individuals or even communities, but which, because of the number of male signers, carried an implicit threat that the signatories might change their voting in coming elections. Regardless of their views on slavery, legislators were not ready to consider the mass petitions of females in the same category as those from voters. In this changing context many abolitionists continued to argue that petitioning was a simple request, not a political lobbying effort, while antiabolitionists often interpreted female petitioning as democracy run amok. Some feminist abolitionists did see petitioning and voting rights as the logical development of American democracy, but most female signers were sincere in asking that their petitions be accepted as prayerful requests, not as political demands.

17. For Bynum's sharp criticism, see U.S. Congress, *Register of Debates in Congress Vol. 13* (Washington, D.C., 1838), pp. 1316, 1329–1330. For Wiscassett, Maine, critics, see the 1835 *Lincoln Intelligencer . . . Extra* (undated broadside, American Antiquarian Society), in which community leaders argued that abolitionism tended to "break up families, and disturb the peace of society." For a broader perspective on the threat abolitionists posed to community leaders, see Leonard Richards, *"Gentlemen of Property and Standing": Anti-Abolitionist Mobs in Jacksonian America* (New York, 1970). Barnes, *Anti-Slavery Impulse,* chap. 11, suggests that the sheer volume of antislavery petitions made it difficult for congressmen to handle other business. See also Lori Ginzberg, "Women and the Work of Benevolence: Morality and Politics in the Northeastern United States, 1820–1885" (Ph.D diss., Yale University, 1985), pp. 49, 145, 165–67.
18. *An Appeal to the Women of the Nominally Free States* (New York, 1837), p. 30.
19. For detailed descriptions and analysis of these political developments, see Ronald P. Formisano, *The Transformation of Political Culture: Massachusetts Parties, 1790s–1840s* (New York, 1983). John L. Brooke suggests that in Massachusetts this new pattern of individual (vs. community) petitioning began with Shay's Rebellion and the elections of 1800 and accelerated when organizing men petitioned for new roads, bridges, and textile companies (letter to author of July 12, 1989); see especially chaps. 7 and 9 in Brooke, *The Heart of the Commonwealth: Society and Political Culture in Worcester County, Massachusetts, 1713–1861* (New York, 1989).

Antiabolitionists still viewed women petitioners as the dupes of fanatical males, who, without the support of weak-minded women—"grannies and misses" as Congressman Jesse Bynum dubbed them—would be ignored. The minutes and literature of female antislavery societies indicate little evidence of naiveté on the part of women signers. Organizers like Grimké and Sturges stressed education on slavery issues as a necessary prerequisite for petition canvassing, particularly education about the abuses to which slave mothers, wives, and children were subjected. Although leading abolitionists were often self-conscious feminists, then, their focus on domestic affairs allowed conservative women to continue petitioning as deferential inferiors and not as self-conscious, political activists.

Despite this self-effacing approach, the policy of some abolitionists to canvass only legal voters and of most congressmen to reject petitions because of the dependent status of their signers suggests that both abolitionists and antiabolitionists saw the mass petitioning of Congress as a public, political act akin to voting.[20] The antislavery women thus found it increasingly difficult to construe their petitioning as apolitical. The high volume of public criticism was surely a factor in female reticence, and questions about the nature and limits of female citizenship made it difficult for women to sign antislavery petitions, even with disclaimers about the exceptional and moral nature of their action. Was antislavery petitioning moral or political? Did women, as John Quincy Adams argued, petition as supplicants, daughters, sisters, and wives? Or was there an implied threat in the prayer; were they in fact pressing congressmen to change their minds and votes? Even the most conservative petitioner hoped that God would use her written prayer as a means to help the slave, presumably through a political act of the legislature. Although most female petitioners were not yet arguing explicitly for a more democratic concept of citizenship, by the very act of petitioning they were in fact unconsciously broadening the notion of female citizenship.[21] Because Garrison framed his call for the im-

20. The congressional record of debates during the gag on slavery issues (1836–1844) reveals the later bias; attempts by petitioners to label signatures "l.v." (for legal voter) indicate that more ordinary citizens shared elite concerns about the status of petitioners. For an example, see LC Box 91, NA Box 21, HR24A-H1.3, "Petition of 841 Citizens of RI of the Denomination called Free Will Baptists solemnly protesting . . . [the Nebraska Bill]." For one earlier case of women joining male petitioners for religious reasons, see Raymond C. Bailey, *Popular Influence upon Public Policy: Petitioning in Eighteenth-Century Virginia* (Westport, 1979), p. 44. In the course of his efforts to subvert the Gag Rule, John Quincy Adams was also accused of presenting the petitions of slaves, servants, and "colored" residents.

21. Kerber, *Women of the Republic,* pp. 283–87.

mediate abolition of slavery as a moral rather than a political imperative, female abolitionists could ignore the value of petitioning as a powerful tool in political negotiation. Even self-consciously feminist abolitionists continued to see their antislavery activity as a moral imperative. Thus women often explained their determination to continue petitioning, despite legislators' failure to listen or act, by suggesting that the act of petitioning would at least "clear their skirts" of some responsibility for the evils of slavery and indicate that, like the biblical woman contributing her mite to the poor, "we have done what we could."[22]

Such pious disclaimers, however, could not hide the real political impact of the petitioning campaigns. Critics increasingly characterized women's petitions as political meddling, while petition texts continued to present female intentions as apolitical. The Providence Female Anti-Slavery Society, for example, accepted limits on female activity in an address it circulated with an 1836 petition text. The petition, it argued, expressed the members' moral obligations as Christian women to "Love our neighbor as ourselves," to "Love one another as Christ hath loved us," and in regard to the slaves, to "Do unto others as we would that they should do unto us."[23] By structuring their speech with passages from Scripture, the Providence women could claim that their petitioning was not a political act but only the humble prayer of subordinates to superiors, "peculiarly appropriate to women." Their petition text offers as exemplary the biblical story of the importunate woman who, because she made a pest of herself, was eventually granted her request. Abolitionists solicited Christian women of America to petition Congress until their request, too, was eventually granted.[24]

Thousands of women did sign petitions, but many remained reluctant, some because they sensed that antislavery petitioning was in fact political, disclaimers notwithstanding. In August 1836, Harriet Peck reported that canvassers of her Kent County (R.I.) society had secured "between two and three hundred names," despite "various objections . . . made to signing it, . . . [because] some ladies seemed to consider it a departure from their

22. See "Petition of women of Providence," received September 1837 (HR24A-H1.3).

23. The August 1836 petitioning circular published by the Providence society was not separated from the actual petition text, as the organizers intended, and so is attached to the "Petition of women of Wakefield and North Kingston [R.I.] against slavery in the District of Columbia" (HR24A-H1.3), Box 91, No. 59, n.d. received.

24. Ibid. The story of the importunate woman is from Luke 18:1–8. Another common Scripture reference was to the weak, sinful woman who intruded into a male meeting in order to anoint Jesus. Jesus both defended and praised her actions in the phrase borrowed by abolitionists to describe female petitioning: "She has done what she could" (Mark 14:8). Other texts mention the life-saving petition of Esther as their model (HR24A-H1.3).

proper place, and excused themselves by saying they did not wish their names to appear in Congress."[25] Canvassers from the Fall River (Mass.) society encountered similar objections when they solicited female signatures. A worker reported that one woman called the petitioning efforts "ridiculous," and that another "lady told me with a coldness and dignity of speech, and a glance of the eye which said, 'You are out of your sphere,' that she considered this altogether a political subject, and thought it . . . exceedingly improper for her to interfere with men's business!"[26] Peck countered this objection as groups did elsewhere, by emphasizing the family and moral reasons for petitioning: "But while the wives and mothers—the daughters and sisters of our land, and helpless innocent infants too, are bought and sold and treated like brutes, does female delicacy require us to be silent upon the subject, or to remonstrate against such tyranny only in private? No! While woman is enslaved, degraded, dishonored, woman should never be ashamed to plead for her relief—even with the learned Statesmen who assemble annually in the Legislative halls of the nation. If they refuse to grant our petitions, then the responsibility rests upon them." Peck and her sister organizers were interpreting petitioning as the duty of Christian women, an act of charity toward their sisters in slavery, not their political right. Political action remained the sphere of male legislators. But Peck also voiced a second argument for petitioning: "We have been told repeatedly that the ladies of Great Britain, (by petitioning Parliament) did much towards hastening the cause of Emancipation, in the British West Indies.—And shall we, the republican daughters of Columbia be less zealous in the cause of Freedom than they!"[27]

This second argument suggests that female petitioners were absorbing not just new patriotism, but the political reasoning offered by men when petitioning. Petition texts also reflect these republican concerns. One text printed and circulated by "ladies of Massachusetts" notes that slavery violates both "precepts of the Gospel" and principles in the Declaration of Independence. Many women gladly signed the same generic texts used by men, several of which referred to political issues of jurisdiction and to the republican's obligation to exercise the constitutional right of free

25. *Pawtucket Record and Free Speech Advocate,* September 10, 1836 (front page). This account is from the annual report of the Kent County Female Anti-Slavery Society, as written by corresponding secretary Harriet Peck for the group's first annual meeting, August 11, 1836.

26. These extracts from the Fall River report appeared in the *Liberator,* May 24, 1839, accompanied by a brief note from Elizabeth Buffum Chace, then an officer of the Fall River Female Anti-Slavery Society.

27. See n. 25.

expression.[28] Some women still acknowledged the exceptional nature of their request, but reduced the number of deferential phrases in their petitions. In 1838 women of Fall River simply adopted the text used by local men to demand that the House of Representatives restore the right of petition, "IMMEDIATELY."[29]

One cannot easily categorize petitions or petitioners, with some women clinging to the language of deference while brave advocates of suffrage adopted the language of rights and republican citizenship. Indeed, petition texts often incorporated both the old, deferential and the new, republican language. But female petitioners generally focused most on woman's moral "duty to supplicate for the oppressed" and "the suffering." Deference to legislators and domestic concerns framed women's prayers on behalf of "the slaves of our sex" and "defenseless victims." Stressing the apolitical reasons for their action, petitioners even argued they "would be less than women" if they did not plead on behalf of female slaves.[30]

Although the number of female petitioners was increasing in the 1830s, the special pleading, the criticism of petitioners, the private objections to signing, and the contents of a few private letters all suggest that petitioning was never an easy activity for women—not even when in the latter half of the decade they constituted the majority of abolitionist petitioners. Canvassing for signatures could be both an ordeal and a test of commitment. In 1839 Phebe Jackson inquired of a friend, "How do you succeed in your work of petitioning?" and confessed, "*I do dread* it & did I dare to withold [*sic*] my contribution of labor, I should do it without hesitation." Similarly, Harriet Hale of Providence explained to friends that the annual petition

28. See "Petition of Ladies of Hanover Anti-Slavery Society, Massachusetts," received March 21, 1836, Select Committee on Slavery in the District of Columbia (HR25A-G22.4) and "Petition of Females of Hamilton County, Ohio," received February 6, 1837 (Sen24A-H1). For a broader discussion of how American women interpreted the republican value of citizen participation apolitically, by seeing the teaching of moral values as a domestic and moral responsibility, see Kerber, *Women of the Republic.*

29. "Petition of Sarah Borden and other women of Fall River against the gag rule," received February 16, 1838 (HR 25A-H1.8). An increased use of one-sentence petition texts may also reflect greater national organization and pragmatism: petitions this short were often read into the congressional record as tabled, despite the Gag Rule. State and local petitions more frequently retained deferential language. Male petitioners, however, sometimes rebelled against the humble language of generic texts, as when men crossed out "as humble supplicants" from "Petition of Inhabitants of Barnstable County, Massachusetts against Slavery in District of Columbia," received February 29, 1836 (HR25A-G22.4).

30. "Petition of Women of Providence, RI, in relation to slavery," received March 3, 1849 (Sen 30A-J3); also "Petition of the Ladies of Atwater, Portage County, Ohio, praying for the abolition of slavery in the District of Columbia," received March 12, 1838 (HR25A-H1.7, Folder 6).

drive of her female society continued, but with insufficient canvassers, as "few are found possessing that self-denying spirit requisite to lead them from house to house to obtain signatures to a petition. This of all others is considered the most thankless & difficult field of labor. Oh for the spirit of the early martyrs which would enable us to desire the posts of greatest danger & toil." After one extensive canvass, Kent County women restricted their efforts to fewer villages. They also requested Garrison to come speak in the hope that his presence would attract converts, thereby making their canvassing easier.[31] One senses the degree of importance and anxiety attached to petitioning in a letter from Harriet Peck inquiring from North Carolina how the work was going back home: "I dreamed of circulating the petitions about Coventry & Washington, with what success I cannot tell."[32]

Although the women's conventions were temporarily successful in extending, coordinating, and publicizing the efforts of women petitioners, female petitioning declined during the 1840s. This decline roughly coincided with the rise of the anti-Garrisonian American and Foreign Anti-Slavery Society (1840), the Liberty Party (1844), and the Free Soil Party (1848), all organizations that favored political means to end slavery. Both political parties had excluded the slavery issue from their conventions and platforms before 1844, so women could easily interpret their petitioning against slavery as moral, not political. But when feminist abolitionists began asserting political rights for themselves and Liberty Party leaders advocated legislation limiting slavery, ignoring the political dimensions of antislavery activism became more difficult. Those female abolitionists who were uneasy with the Garrisonians' promotion of women's rights were left without an institutional home.

The sharp decline in women's petitioning during the 1840s signifies that critics had managed to identify female petitioning as a political activity akin to advocating women's suffrage. By 1840 disputes over the role of women had split members of the American Anti-Slavery Society into two organizations, and by 1845 those wanting to use political parties to press for

31. Jackson to Helen Garrison, Providence, September 30, 1839 (Antislavery Collections, Boston Public Library); Hale was secretary of the Providence Ladies Anti-Slavery Society in February 1841 when she wrote this comment to the Philadelphia society (manuscript records of PFASS, available as part of the microfilm collections of Historical Society of Pennsylvania). The records of the Kent County Female Anti-Slavery Society are in the manuscript collection of the Rhode Island Historical Society.

32. Harriet Peck to Perez [& Joanna] Peck, New Garden, September 7, 1837, Peck Collection, Friends Historical Collection, Guilford College, Greensboro, N.C.

antislavery legislation had begun to form the new Liberty Party. These changes made it more difficult for women to remain visible in antislavery organizations, first because leaders of the American and Foreign Anti-Slavery Society condemned most public activity by females as irreligious, and second because the Liberty Party's adoption of antislavery goals asserted the political nature of antislavery agitation. Particularly harmful to women's activism was the Liberty Party's proposal that slavery, however much a moral issue, could be ended through political and legislative means. This argument undermined the claim of female petitioners that their activity was simply religious or moral. Despite the attempt by antiabolitionists to label all female abolitionists as feminists, many antislavery women who remained active into the 1840s and 1850s stayed clear of women's political conventions and continued to believe women's proper sphere was the home and that their antislavery work was moral, not political.[33]

Even before "the woman question" became a major issue, some abolitionists preferred male petitioning. Although in 1838 James Birney printed pleas for female help in his antislavery newspaper, the future Liberty Party candidate also discounted female petitioning by underscoring the greater influence of male petitioners on congressmen: "Not woman, now *the people* pray / Hear us—or *from* us ye will hear! / Beware! a desperate game ye play! / Tis men that thicken in your rear."[34] Perhaps, like Charles G. Finney, Birney had pleaded for female help only because he saw women's aid as a new measure necessary when male laborers were lacking.

Both direct criticism and the continued preference for petitions from legal voters devalued women's petitioning. Only within Garrison's old organization did women continue to hold official responsibilities for education, fund-raising, and petitioning. Female abolitionists endured criticism, continuing to petition against both race-based slavery and what some

---

33. James B. Stewart, *Holy Warriors: The Abolitionists and American Slavery* (New York, 1976), chaps. 4 and 5, provides a clear overview of political options available to abolitionists, including those who preferred "moral suasion." With the exception of Nancy Hewitt, recent scholars of female abolitionism have followed nineteenth-century antiabolitionists in assuming that most women who opposed slavery were also advocates of women's rights. This friendly sharing of anxiety over their antislavery petitioning may have been an important factor in the continued activism of stalwarts. For further discussion of this issue, see my book, *Abolitionists Were Female: Rhode Island Women in the Antislavery Network* (University of Illinois Press, forthcoming), esp. chap. 5.

34. *Philanthropist*, January 2, 1838. For one of the most popular forms of the argument against female abolitionism (including petitioning), see Catharine Beecher, "An Essay on Slavery and Abolitionism" (1837), reprinted in Jeanne Boydston, Mary Kelley, and Anne Margolis, *The Limits of Sisterhood: The Beecher Sisters on Women's Rights and Woman's Sphere* (Chapel Hill, 1988), pp. 125–29.

construed as "the slavery of sex."[35] But even though their membership in antislavery organizations was shrinking, female petitioners outnumbered the women participating in either women's rights or antislavery meetings. For after 1845 neither Garrisonian women nor women representing newer antislavery groups constituted the majority of female petitioners.

What happened to the activist women who never recognized "the slavery of sex"? During the 1840s and 1850s, many women focused their petitioning efforts strictly on local issues; the women of Ohio and Rhode Island, for example, petitioned their state legislatures to end laws restricting educational opportunities for blacks. Many Friends abandoned both new and old organizations of abolitionists, boycotted slave-grown produce, and promoted the use of free-grown cotton and sugar. After the Gag Rule was lifted in 1842, some Garrisonian abolitionists neglected petitioning as no longer effective. The American and Foreign Anti-Slavery Society tried to enroll women as canvassers but dampened female support by specifying that only legal voters should sign the petitions.[36]

35. Barnes first suggested that female petitioning "opened a way toward citizenship" (*Anti-Slavery Impulse*, p. 143). More recent historians have expanded this thesis considerably: see Blanche Glassman Hersh, *The Slavery of Sex: Feminist-Abolitionism in America* (Chicago, 1978); Keith Melder, *The Beginnings of Sisterhood: The Women's Rights Movement in the United States, 1800–1850* (New York, 1977); Nancy A. Hewitt, *Women's Activism and Social Change: Rochester, New York, 1822–1872* (Ithaca, 1984); Gerda Lerner, "The Political Activities of Antislavery Women," in her book *The Majority Finds Its Past: Placing Women in History* (New York, 1979), pp. 112–18; Lori Ginzberg, " 'Moral Suasion is Moral Balderdash': Women, Politics, and Social Activism in the 1850s," *Journal of American History* 73 (December 1986): 601–22; and Yellin, *Women and Sisters*.

Dividing reformers into several groups, Hewitt notes the persistence of moderate reform efforts by less radical abolitionist women. The best long-term study of female petitioning is Judith Wellman's "Women and Radical Reform in Antebellum Upstate New York: A Profile of Grassroots Female Abolitionists," in Mabel E. Deutrick & Virginia C. Purdy, eds., *Clio Was a Woman: Studies in the History of Women* (Washington, D.C., 1980), pp. 112–31. Another quantitative study of male and female petitioners is Edward Magdol, *The Antislavery Rank and File: A Social Profile of the Abolitionists' Constituency* (Westport, Conn., 1986).

36. For examples of petitioning directions and texts, see *Philanthropist*, November 3, 1841, and *North Star*, February 22, 1850. In both cases all the petition texts begin: "The undersigned, citizens and electors of the State of. . . ." James B. Stewart, *Holy Warriors: The Abolitionists and American Slavery* (New York, 1976), notes the Garrisonian decline of interest in petitioning as one result of the 1840 old vs. new organization split (see especially pp. 92–94). The *Philanthropist*, August 28, 1844, reported attempts by abolitionists, through the Ohio Ladies Education Society, to repeal the state's discriminatory "Black Codes." Examples of women petitioning the Rhode Island House of Representatives include "Memorial from Citizens respecting persons of color," received January 17, 1844; also "Petition of E Thurber & others respecting slavery," received February 7, 1844 (R.I. State Archives).

With so little national leadership, it is surprising to find that after 1845 some women were still petitioning. Here the petitions themselves provide clues. Some words of deference to male political authority survive, but elaborate references to "Fathers and Rulers" are rare. More women signed petitions jointly with men, rather than produce their own. In female petitions deference is no longer the most prominent theme; instead, they emphasize the responsibilities of female citizens. This shift in focus suggests that many women continued as petitioners after 1845 not because they had joined Garrisonians in abandoning traditional religion and deference to male leaders—most had not made this conscious decision—but because they had developed a new political consciousness of their responsibilities as female citizens of the American republic. As religious women, they were concerned with the vulnerability of unprotected female slaves, and as female citizens they also felt responsible for the nation's moral state.[37]

Although they were not self-conscious radicals in the same way that contemporary advocates of women's rights were, female petitioners were in fact broadening and complicating notions of female citizenship. Harriet Peck's explanation of her petitioning efforts, for example, gives a republican rationale for her efforts, but instead of asserting her own rights, she expresses concern for female slaves who lacked brother, father, or husband to protect them. And though Peck left her family to pursue missionary work in North Carolina, her letters emphasize family ties and paternal support much more frequently than independent action.[38] Peck valued her own father's advice and care, and her concern for female slaves "lacking the protection of a father" is not merely a rhetorical device.

37. Both Nancy Cott, *The Bonds of Womanhood: "Women's Sphere" in New England, 1780–1835* (New Haven, 1977) and especially Kerber, *Women of the Republic* (see p. 285) note the coexistence of female deference and active citizenship. Similarly, in 1849 women petitioned against slavery by citing moral concerns for the female slaves "who are afforded no legal protection for the heart's dearest ties, or Woman's 'sacred honor'" and by expressing concern that slavery prevented the United States, "this 'Model Republic,'" from implementing fully "the great principles of Liberty" (from a "Petition of Women of Providence, R.I., in relation to Slavery," received March 3, 1849 [Sen 30A-J3]). This popular "women of America" text was commonly used by female petitioners into the 1850s.

38. The dreams she recorded during her stay in North Carolina concern just these two subjects, the life of her family at home and canvassing for signatures on antislavery petitions (see note 32). Other family letters, several of which recount dreams of home, are held by Peck descendent Kenneth White, Cumberland, R.I. In real life Harriet's father escorted her from her Rhode Island home to a missionary teaching position in North Carolina and upon her return two years later gave her minute instructions about packing and travel.

The Massachusetts Female Emancipation Society was more explicit in asserting the propriety of female involvement in antislavery politics. Arguing that antislavery concerns were proper, albeit political, concerns for women, society members not only petitioned but sewed a "liberty banner" for the town in their congressional district that cast the most votes for the Liberty Party candidate. Although they were wary of "the woman question" or any discussion of female equality, leaders of this group urged women to petition not simply for moral reasons but because women had "direct influence" on Congress: "for let every woman remember that the representation in our country is according to the number of the population, without regard to sex."[39] This "direct influence," however, was direct only in the sense that women might influence the antislavery views of male voters. Organizers in all camps assumed that women would exert this influence through nonpolitical, moral channels.[40] Few noted that petitioning might involve more than familial duties.

If petition texts, directions, and occasional comments suggest that female leaders gained a new sense of political influence, what of the consciousness of ordinary signers? Their signatures provide one clue. Petitioners who signed their names as females expressed a consciousness of political responsibilities as women. When signing with men, female petitioners generally used the generic terms "inhabitant" or "resident," and only rarely "citizen." The printed texts occasionally reflected this general acceptance of a separate, private, women's sphere. Females in Abington, Massachusetts, altered a generic petition beginning "The petition of the undersigned, citizens" to read "petition of the undersigned, women." This alteration highlights the general confusion over what to call female petitioners. Petitions printed specifically for females to use designated the prayer as one from "ladies" or "women." The more general terms "inhabitants" or "residents" were commonly used for male or mixed-gender petitions. Although one might interpret "citizen" as a generic term applicable to both male and female, most petitions from "citizens" were signed by men only. Even female organizers, who presumably had a stronger than average sense of their citizenship, sometimes hesitated to sign such petitions, leading Nantucket

---

39. "Address of the Massachusetts Female Emancipation Society, to the Women of New England," appendix to *First Annual Report of the Massachusetts Emancipation Society* (Boston, 1841), pp. 16–18. This new organization of antifeminist, anti-Garrisonian abolitionists was more short-lived than the Liberty Party.

40. Ibid., p. 18. The address closes by asking women to "remember the woes... of the wretched slave mother as she drags her weary, lacerated limbs to the field after a sleepless night, with her sick and dying babe." And how might northern women help the poor slave mother and child? "Circulate a petition."

organizers to prefix the adjectives "male and female" to the term citizen on a petition.[41]

The mistakes of petitioners also provide clues to women's self-perception. Most female and mixed gender petitions fail in some measure to follow the directions provided by national or regional organizers.[42] Most petitioners assumed that male and female signatories should or would be evaluated separately by legislators; consequently, the least common mistake was to mix male and female names.[43] The most common mistake was in the actual signing, for despite explicit directions, female petitioners more often than men used pencil rather than ink and even more frequently allowed someone else to sign for them. Lists of names in one hand appear only occasionally on men's petitions, but they are usual in women's petitions.[44]

41. This altered petition came from women of Abington, Massachusetts, n.d. (HR27A-H1.7). The mixed-gender Nantucket petition was received December 11, 1845 (HR29A-H1.1).

42. The signed petitions used in this study include all the surviving Rhode Island petitions in the National Archives (about 140), plus a sampling from other Northeastern states, Ohio, Michigan, and North Carolina. I also looked at several mixed-gender petitions (clustered in 1845) in the Rhode Island State Archives file of "Petitions to the General Assembly, Failed."

43. Interestingly, the most blatant deviation from the format that stipulated separate columns for men and women occurred among the African American community in Providence. For a petition by "women of America" men's signatures were included among the "colored" women who presumably circulated their section of the petition without regard to gender. See the "Petition of Women of Rhode Island against slavery," received February 6, 1837 (HR24B). Of the ninety petitions signed by men only, fewer than 20 percent included obvious errors. Of the sixty-two female petitions, forty-three or 70 percent included obvious errors. Although fewer in number, the female petitions in this sample included many more signatures than the greater number of male petitions.

44. Petitions from four Rhode Island communities suggest that regardless of period, women were many times more apt than men to allow another woman to sign their names. Perhaps because of their greater political experience, male petitioners erred much less frequently. Petition directions were complex, written in long articles accompanying petitions printed in newspapers or appended to separately printed petitions circulated by state or regional antislavery societies. Only one of twenty-one men's petitions included lists of names in one handwriting, but twenty-four (of twenty-five) women's petitions included copied names. Of the fifteen petitions signed by both men and women, fourteen had copied names and most of these copied lists were female names. On nine of the fifteen petitions signed by men and women, the only copying of names in the same hand occurred in the female columns. In the above figures I am excluding the smaller number of cases in which individuals were illiterate, made their mark, then allowed someone else to inscribe their name next to the mark, although there were more of these instances of illiteracy among female signers. The four communities sampled were Providence, North Providence (which included Pawtucket and Valley Falls), Smithfield, and Kent County (which included parts of Coventry, Warwick, and Phenix village). The majority of these petitions were from the years of heaviest petitioning, 1836–1839. Petitions from other states and years also reflect these differences.

Printed directions often told individuals to sign in their own hand. But since neither Gag Rule proponents nor local organizers criticized the mere listing of names, this irregularity seems to have been a widely accepted form of female deference. Petitioners were clearly not concerned about charges of fraud. It may be, too, that copying names, rather than securing actual signatures, was a shortcut taken by canvassers who assumed the compliance of other known abolitionists. For women accustomed to the revival call, "let your name be enrolled," allowing the listing of one's name, not the actual signing, was the significant act. As Harriet Peck noted, potential signers knew the appearance of their name in the legislative forum was the likely result of such enrollment, regardless of who penned their names.[45]

In sum, after 1845 the increased discussion of slavery by male politicians meant that most women retreated from the earlier practice of circulating separate women's petitions. Although hesitant to cast themselves as individual citizens in the same sense their fathers, brothers, sons, and husbands were, nevertheless these women expressed a heightened sense of community involvement by enrolling their names on petitions along with men in their families and churches. Certainly these women shared with feminist abolitionists growing self-awareness and involvement in politics. But rather than speaking out as individual citizens concerned about specific rights, these women assumed their civic responsibilities by petitioning as part of a family, church, or reform community.

During the Mexican War, women petitioners organized against this loss of life but still did not comment on how the war was linked politically to the issues of slavery and territorial expansion. Unlike most earlier petitioners, these persistent women used titles of "Miss" and "Mrs." to make clear their deferential posture and their relationship to a man of influence.[46]

45. The inclusion of children's names was another way abolitionists expressed their assumption that petitioning was the prayer of a Christian group more than an individual political act. Both men and women sometimes allowed children to sign, despite a specific age restriction mentioned in organizers' directives. Children who signed, however, indicated their deference and minor status by listing their ages and signing next to older family members. There is no hint in the petitions that signers accepted the argument that adults should defer to the antislavery opinion of children; see Henry C. Wright, *The Slave's Friend*, no. 2 (New York, 1837), pp. 87–88. For another interesting example of children participating in what seems to be conceived of as family and community politics, see Elsa Barkley Brown, "To Catch the Vision of Freedom: Reconstructing Southern Black Women's Political History, 1865–1885," Newberry Library Seminar in American Social History (October 15, 1991).

46. "Petition of [137] Women of Providence, Rhode Island, in relation to Slavery," received March 3, 1849 (Sen 30A-J3). At least in Rhode Island, earlier female petitioners rarely used any titles. Gerda Lerner, "The Political Activities of Antislavery Women," suggests that more radical women self-consciously omitted reference to their marital status. For another female pe-

Even women whose expanded political consciousness led them to use more forceful language continued the conservative practice of referring to themselves as "ladies."[47] One group of Vermont petitioners adopted the traditional tone of female deference by emphasizing their status as "humble ladies," but were otherwise aggressive in requesting Congress "to Abolish Slavery, and the Slave Trade in the District of Columbia."[48]

These Vermont women had learned much about practical politics in the decade following the women's antislavery conventions. Responding directly to negative depictions of abolitionist women, they challenged, for example, "a distinguished Senator" who "said in the Senate Feb. 4, 1840, that [they] were 'out of our appropriate arena' and could not 'recognize the right of country-women to interfere with public affairs,' and a New York editor that [they] 'had better be shaking bed-*ticks* rather then poli-*tics*.'" Their stated reasons for action showed political consciousness and purpose: "We believe our Grandmothers assisted in gaining the Independence of our Nation by helping to 'shake the red-coats' and we feel that it cannot be denied us *now* the bare 'right of petition,' especially when we have to be governed by laws which we have *no* voice in making."[49] Exhibiting more awareness of the political debate in Congress and the press than concern for the suffering of female slaves, these petitioners communicated political

tition that also avoids the term "citizen," see the handwritten, original text composed by writer Sophia Little, the single most active abolitionist in Newport throughout the antebellum period; "Petition of inhabitants of Newport, R.I. praying the repeal of the late act of Congress for the delivery of fugitives," received February 25, 1851 (Sen 31A-J7). Little had just completed another attack on the fugitive act in her novel about fugitives, *Thrice through the Furnace* (Pawtucket, R.I., 1852). Another story by Little which emphasized the special helplessness of slave mothers was printed in pamphlet form as *The Branded Hand; A Dramatic Sketch. Commemorative of the Tragedies at the South in the Winter of 1844–5* (Pawtucket, R.I., 1845).

47. A number of antislavery groups changed their name from "ladies" to "female" antislavery society, presumably to include more of the female community. For an example, see the manuscript record book of Kent County Female Anti-Slavery Society, minutes for March 30, 1838 (Rhode Island Historical Society).

48. "Petition of 72 Ladies of Vermont for the Abolition of Slavery and the Slave Trade in the District," received December 17, 1847 (HR30A-G4.1). They illustrated their concerns by relating the story of two female slaves, seized and sold by federal marshals as payment for debts owed by a defaulting master.

49. These women were adapting a common allusion to women supporters of the American Revolution; see the *Herald of Freedom* (September 2, 1837) story, "Female Petitioners," adapted from the *Boston Times*. One 1854 petition against slavery preserves the forms of deference by including three separate columns for names; one for legal voters, one for men not legal voters, and the third for "women of influence"; see "Petition of 841 Citizens of RI of the denomination of Christians called Free Will Baptists solemnly protesting," received May 4, 1854 (HR33A-F24.4.11).

concerns by mentioning "rights," thereby undermining the words of female deference with which they had framed their request. More often, however, women balanced the language of later antislavery petitions by mentioning both moral and political concerns and keeping the tone deferential.

Most of these persistent petitioners avoided discussion of women's rights, but they continued to hone their political skills by advocating temperance, education, and prison reform. When in 1861 the country moved toward disunion, many of these female citizens readied a new "women of America" petition. Led by educator Emma Willard, fourteen-thousand women from fourteen states respectfully prayed that members of Congress seek peace by "not allow[ing] party or sectional prejudices to prevail over a spirit of mutual reconciliation." Deferential in form, this petition begged Congress as "father, protector,—brother, and friend,—not to abandon us."[50] With the war under way, more self-consciously political abolitionists organized fifteen-thousand women from 161 communities and twelve states to petition for an end to slavery.[51] In both cases women chose deferential language to formulate their prayers for political change, although the later group showed more political self-consciousness by framing their request in republican and patriotic language. Not surprisingly, many of these antebellum petitioners resurfaced after the war, when abolitionists Phebe Jackson and Sophia Little organized prayer meetings and enrolled thousands of Rhode Island women in a petition campaign for temperance laws. Jackson herself delivered to the legislature a petition signed by fifteen thousand men and women.[52] By the 1870s these female petitioners seemed comfortable asserting not only moral and familial but also political concerns through petitioning. These persistent petitioners, although they did not lead the feminist crusade for suffrage, illuminate the continuities between antebellum and postbellum reforms. However little or much they drew

50. "Memorial of Emma Willard," received March 1, 1861 (Sen 36A-J3).

51. "Petition of 15,000 women praying for the abolition of slavery," received April 14, 1862 (HR 37A-G17.2, Oversize Box). The petition still incorporates the form of deference, "respectfully and earnestly petition[ing] that you will at an early date adopt such measures as, in your wisdom, you may think proper to accomplish this end," but offers patriotic, republican reasons for advancing "the cause of humanity and virtue" and preventing "future difficulties in the National government."

52. Abolitionist women are omitted from Barbara Leslie Epstein, *The Politics of Domesticity: Women, Evangelism, and Temperance in Nineteenth-Century America* (Middletown, Conn., 1981), see pp. 5–6; for mention of Little and Jackson's postwar temperance petitioning, see the Rev. J[acob] Sam'l Vandersloot, *The True Path; or, Gospel Temperance* (New York, Cincinnati, Chicago, 1878), p. 576, and especially the "Origin" section of *Souvenir W.C.T.U.* pamphlet (Providence, R.I., 1894).

from republican discourse, these women expressed their growing concerns about political issues. Southerner Jesse Bynum was correct: once enrolled in a cause, even American "grannies and misses" who restricted their petitioning to subjects of "domestic" concern proved formidable and disruptive mothers, wives, daughters, sisters, and citizens.

{ II }

Graphic Discord
Abolitionist and
Antiabolitionist Images

Phillip Lapsansky

The conflict in the 1830s between immediatist abolitionists and their opponents was fought with pictures as well as words. In this essay I examine the development and use of illustrations in the propaganda arsenals of abolitionists and antiabolitionists. In them, in graphic discord, there is a significant body of literature on the issues of slavery and antislavery, the role of women in society and social movements, and the place of blacks in nineteenth-century America.[1]

In 1837 "Clarkson," an anonymous contributor to the New Haven *Religious Intelligencer,* admonished the Grimké sisters: "The people of the North want no person to 'undeceive' them on this subject. The wickedness, cruelty and oppression of slavery were perfectly understood in the North forty or fifty years ago . . . the injustice and horrors of slavery were as well described as you can now describe them."[2] As Clarkson points out, the decade of the Grimké sisters and the "modern abolitionists" followed a half century of organized antislavery efforts in the United States, and much of the program and tactics of the immediatists of the 1830s amplified those of their predecessors. Like these modern abolitionists, the earlier antislavery societies produced literature exposing the cruelty and injustice of slavery.

1. All of the items illustrated in this essay are from the collection of the Library Company of Philadelphia except figures 2, 3, 16, 17, and 18, from the Historical Society of Pennsylvania; and figures 4 and 5, from the Friends Historical Library, Swarthmore College. My thanks to these three institutions for permission to reproduce materials from their collections.

2. Gilbert H. Barnes and Dwight L. Dumond, eds., *Letters of Theodore Dwight Weld, Angelina Grimké Weld and Sarah Grimké, 1822–1844,* 2 vols. (1934; rept. Gloucester, 1955), 1:365.

They petitioned local and national government against slavery. They helped support black schools and assisted with chartering black churches. And they fought against racism by providing legal aid to fugitives and fighting against the kidnapping of free blacks into slavery. Further, like the American Anti-Slavery Society, the earlier organizations attempted to pull their local groups into a national movement—the American Convention for Promoting the Abolition of Slavery, active from 1794 into the 1830s.

What was new to the movement of the 1830s? First, antislavery societies now spread rapidly, driven by the militance and evangelical moral fervor of the immediatist message. Second, blacks became increasingly involved in abolition groups. Third, and of particular importance, women became publicly involved for the first time. Many women consciously practiced racial integration in their budding organizations, and in their fight for their right to equal participation in the antislavery struggle they first raised in an organized fashion the fundamental issues of women's rights.

Amplifying this antislavery message, newly introduced steam-powered presses in major urban centers drove publishing capacity up and costs down. By 1835 these presses could produce fifty-five thousand impressions an hour, a more than tenfold increase over 1833. And, in 1835, AASS published over a million pieces of literature, a ninefold increase over previous years "at only about five times the expense." This flood of antislavery publications made the movement seem larger and more threatening to its opponents than its actual numbers would suggest.[3]

Rolling off the presses primarily in New York, Boston, and Philadelphia were illustrated books and tracts, lithographed prints, and broadsheets with woodcuts; monthly periodicals such as the *Anti-Slavery Reporter,* the *Anti-Slavery Record,* and the *Slave's Friend;* annual almanacs; and a wide variety of printed ephemera, including candy wrappers, envelope stickers, song sheets, and stationery. In addition there were the newspapers; best known are the *Emancipator,* the *Anti-Slavery Standard,* the *Friend of Man,* the *Anti-Slavery Bugle,* the *Pennsylvania Freeman,* and William Lloyd Garrison's paper, the *Liberator.* In addition to its own printed productions, the American antislavery movement imported and reprinted the latest works from the British movement, as it had since the 1780s.

The skillful use of graphic propaganda by modern abolitionists of the 1830s was another legacy of their predecessors, who had developed a basic iconographic vocabulary which the immediatists expanded. The

---

3. Leonard L. Richards, *"Gentlemen of Property and Standing": Anti-Abolition Mobs in the Jacksonian Era* (New York, 1970), pp. 71–73; American Anti-Slavery Society, *Third Annual Report* (New York, 1836), p. 7.

eighteenth-century abolitionists understood and appreciated the heightened impact graphics brought to the antislavery argument. In 1787 Benjamin Franklin, then president of the Pennsylvania Society for Promoting the Abolition of Slavery, wrote Josiah Wedgwood on the impact of Wedgwood's kneeling slave cameo, recently distributed in America: "I have seen in their [viewers'] countenances such Mark of being affected by contemplating the Figure of the Suppliant . . . that I am persuaded it may have an Effect equal to that of the best written Pamphlet in procuring favour to those oppressed People." And a half-century later, at the first women's antislavery convention, Sarah Grimké resolved "that we regard anti-slavery prints as powerful auxiliaries in the cause of emancipation, and recommend that these 'pictorial representations' be multiplied a hundred fold; so that the speechless agony of the fettered slave may unceasingly appeal to the heart of the patriotic, the philanthropic, and the christian."[4]

From the late eighteenth-century movement came three sets of images that greatly influenced the illustrated propaganda of the abolitionists of the 1830s. The famous 1789 representation of the cross section of a slave ship packed with chained black bodies lying in every available inch of the vessel was reprinted countless times throughout the age of American slavery. The 1790s produced a series of pictures, reprinted in clusters of seven to a dozen, depicting whippings and other punishments of slaves, slave auctions, separation of slave families, and other atrocities. Most famous of all, from 1787, was the image of the chained, kneeling slave asking, "Am I Not a Man and a Brother?"

The first two series of images were journalistic. The view of the slave ship came from the actual investigation of the conditions of the slave trade by the British Society for Promoting the Abolition of the Slave Trade. Similarly, the illustrations of atrocities emerged from descriptions supplied to Parliament by abolition supporters in 1790 and 1791. This second series frequently accompanied reprints, in whole or part, of an important antislavery text, *An Abstract of the Evidence Delivered Before a Select Committee of the House of Commons . . . On the Part of the Petitioners for the Abolition of the Slave Trade*. Figures 1 and 2 are early American examples of the slave ship and cuts illustrating the text of the *Abstract*. In 1789 Philadelphia printer Mathew Carey issued about twenty-five hundred copies of the slave ship engraving for the Pennsylvania Society for Promoting the Abolition of Slavery. The traveling medicine dealer Tobias Hirte published the unique

4. Franklin letter reproduced in Sidney Kaplan, *The Black Presence in the Era of the American Revolution 1770–1800* (Washington, D.C., 1973), p. 236; *Proceedings of the Anti-Slavery Convention of American Women . . . 1837* (New York, 1837), p. 14.

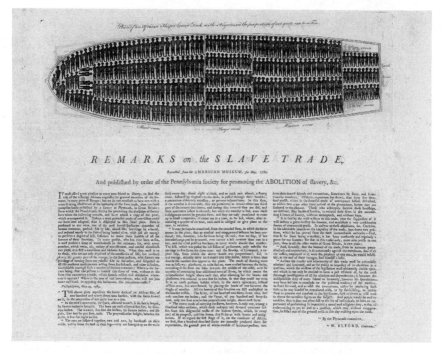

Fig. 1. *Remarks on the Slave Trade* (Philadelphia: Mathew Carey, 1789). Broadside, engraving with letterpress. Courtesy Library Company of Philadelphia

German-language broadside, with cuts by James Poupard, in Philadelphia in 1794. Many of the images produced by the abolitionists of the 1830s follow the tradition of directly illustrating a text that presents actual, documented reports of events or conditions of slavery and racism.[5]

The figure of the kneeling slave was purely allegorical, appealing directly to the heart. The supplicant slave struck a profound and familiar iconographic chord—imagine him bearded, kneeling under the weight of a large wooden cross. This self-conscious image spoke not to slavery but to the

5. *An Abstract of the Evidence Delivered Before a Select Committee of the House of Commons in the Years, 1790 and 1791; On the Part of the Petitioners for the Abolition of the Slave Trade* (London, 1791); and *Abridgement of the Minutes of the Evidence: Taken Before a Committee of the Whole House, to Whom It Was Referred to Consider of the Slave Trade*, 4 vols. (London, 1789–1791). Other early appearances of the slave ship diagram in the United States include the May 1789 issue of Carey's magazine the *American Museum;* Charles Crawford's expanded new edition of his 1784 pamphlet *Observations upon Negro Slavery* (Philadelphia, 1790); Thomas Branagan's *The Penitential Tyrant* (New York, 1807); both the Philadelphia and London 1808 editions of Thomas Clarkson's *History of the Rise, Progress and Accomplishment of the Abolition of the Slave Trade*, and subsequent abridgments; and at least three editions of New York publisher Samuel Wood's pamphlet *Mirror of Misery* (New York, 1807, 1811, and 1814). The above works by Branagan and Wood also include illustrations from the text of the *Abstract.*

204

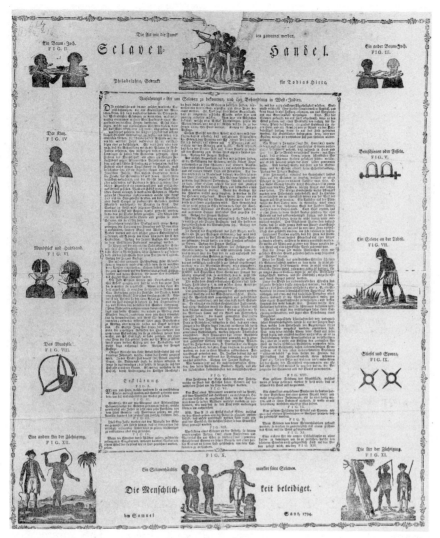

Fig. 2. Tobias Hirte, *Sclaven-Handel* (Philadelphia: Samuel Saur, 1794). Broadside, woodcuts with letterpress. Courtesy Historical Society of Pennsylvania

movement against slavery, uniting those who answered "Yes" to the supplicant's plea. By 1828 British abolitionists contrived a female counterpart, "Am I Not a Woman and a Sister?" Thus antislavery women introduced a powerful sexual element into the argument, depicting female innocence threatened by the unchecked power of the slave master. The picture first appeared in America in the May 1830 issue of Benjamin Lundy's abolition periodical, *The Genius of Universal Emancipation,* in the "Ladies'

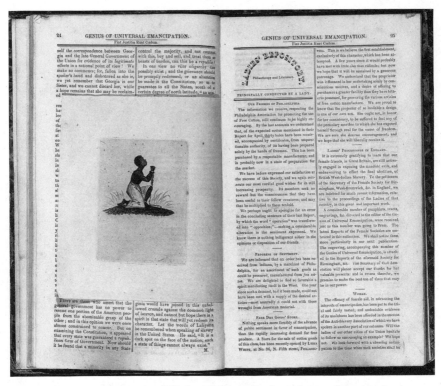

Fig. 3. Engraving, in *Genius of Universal Emancipation*, 3d ser. 1 (May 1830). Courtesy Historical Society of Pennsylvania

Repository" section, written and edited by the pioneer female abolitionist Elizabeth Margaret Chandler (figure 3). In 1832 William Lloyd Garrison adopted the symbol with its motto as a running head for the "Ladies Department" of the *Liberator*. Beneath the female supplicant appeared the writings of many early female activists, including African Americans Maria Stewart, Sarah Mapps Douglass, and Sarah Forten. The supplicants adorned countless abolitionist books, pamphlets, newspapers, periodicals, broadsides, letterheads, and printed ephemera. They were also replicated on handicraft goods and even manufactured items such as chinaware, tokens, linen, and silk goods sold by the antislavery women at their annual fund-raising fairs (figures 4 and 5).

The supplicant slave was the first antislavery movement allegory, but not the last. Images of slaves and slavery were soon interwoven with national symbols. Later, whites appear in these scenes, representing abolitionists pleading the slave's cause (figure 6). The actual and the allegorical joined in

Fig. 4. Pin cushion, board with stencil illustration on fabric, ca. 1835. Courtesy Friends Historical Library of Swarthmore College

scenes of enslavement juxtaposed to American national symbols such as the flag or the Capitol, highlighting the contradiction between American slavery and American freedom.

Through the 1830s the immediatists of AASS bombarded their opponents with "incendiary" graphics. Illustrations of instances of cruelty and abuse of slaves were important tools in the effort to create antislavery sentiment throughout the North. One example, figure 7, returns to the threatened virtue of the female supplicant. It depicts the whipping of black women and accompanies a text reporting instances of brutality toward slave women.

Fig. 5. Antislavery token, copper, New Jersey, 1838. Courtesy Friends Historical Library of Swarthmore College

Many abolitionist graphics also portray scenes of violence and prejudice against northern free blacks, reflecting the influence of black members and supporters on the movement during the 1830s and the movement's stated opposition to race prejudice. Figure 8 shows the mob assault in 1834 on Prudence Crandall's school for black girls in Canterbury, Connecticut, emphasizing the cowardly brutality of a mob of white men attacking black girls. The official opposition of AASS to the American Colonization Society was a significant political victory for blacks, who had agitated against the ACS program since its inception in 1817. Figure 9, captioned with several quotes documenting the forced emigration of blacks, attacks the program and supporters of ACS.

Irony, an important element in antislavery rhetoric, was also used in graphics, as in figure 10, a response to the denunciations of antislavery "incendiary" illustrations. The editor of the *Anti-Slavery Record* notes that this month's "incendiary picture" was one commonly used in Southern newspapers. "The cast from which it was taken was manufactured in this city, for the southern trade, by a firm of stereotypers, who, on account of the same southern trade, refused to stereotype the Record, *because* it contained just such pictures! Now, how does it come to pass, that this said picture when

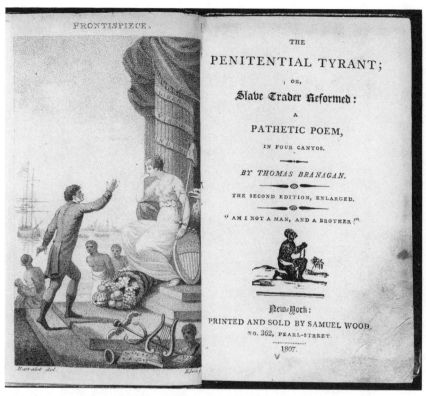

Fig. 6. Thomas Branagan, *The Penitential Tyrant; or, Slave Trader Reformed . . . the Second Edition, Enlarged* (New York: Samuel Wood, 1807). Courtesy Library Company of Philadelphia

printed in a southern newspaper is perfectly harmless, but when printed in the Anti-Slavery Record is perfectly incendiary?"[6]

The efforts of antiabolitionists to stifle antislavery petitioning campaigns in Congress, the mob assaults on abolitionist meetings and presses, and the attempts to ban distribution of antislavery literature through the mail were used by the abolitionists to link the antislavery cause to First Amendment freedoms. Figure 11 is an 1836 broadside supporting the petitioning campaign against slavery in the District of Columbia. Here scenes of slavery and of the slave trade accompany a text exposing official complicity in slavery in the capital, including the unjust arrest and enslavement of free blacks. Added below are the names of the 163 congressmen who voted for the Gag Rule against receiving antislavery petitions.

6. *Anti-Slavery Record* 2 (July 1836): 12.

Fig. 7. "How Slavery Improves the Condition of Women." Woodcut in *The American Anti-Slavery Almanac, for 1840* (New York: American Anti-Slavery Society, [1839]). Courtesy Library Company of Philadelphia

COLORED SCHOOLS BROKEN UP, IN THE FREE STATES.

When schools have been established for colored scholars, the law-makers and the mob have combined to destroy them;—as at Canterbury, Ct., at Canaan, N. H., Aug. 10, 1835, at Zanesville and Brown Co., Ohio, in 1836.

Fig. 8. "Colored Schools Broken up, in the Free States." Woodcut in *The American Anti-Slavery Almanac, for 1840* (New York: American Anti-Slavery Society, [1839]). Courtesy Library Company of Philadelphia

Figure 12 is a two-panel lithograph depicting two attacks on the anti-slavery movement. The top panel shows a diabolical King Cotton figure directing a lynch mob against an abolitionist, a reference to Amos Dresser, a traveling book peddler seized and whipped by a Nashville mob when antislavery literature was found in his possession. The bottom panel illustrates the mob attack in July 1835 on the Charleston, South Carolina, post office, where antislavery literature was removed and burned in the street. Later that year, President Andrew Jackson, in his message to Congress, urged "passing such a law as will prohibit, under severe penalties, the circulation in the Southern States, through the mail, of incendiary publications."[7]

Abolitionists also projected images of black freedom and emancipation, emphasizing peaceful, hard-working, grateful freedmen assisted by benevolent whites. Figure 13, showing free blacks working and celebrating under the banner of "Emancipation," was incorporated into the *Liberator* masthead following the 1838 emancipation in the British colonies. The illustration of black children clustered around their white teacher (figure 14) was the running title page cut for the children's magazine the *Slave's Friend*.

7. *Message of the President of the United States to the Two Houses of Congress . . . December 8, 1835* (Washington, D.C., 1835), p. 28.

" NUISANCES " GOING AS " MISSIONARIES," " WITH THEIR OWN CONSENT."

Having driven colored people from school, we next DRIVE them to Liberia. " They sent out two shiploads of vagabonds that were COERCED away as truly as if it had been done with the cartwhip."—*R. J. Breckenridge,* 1834. " I am acquainted with several, who nformed me that they received SEVERAL HUNDRED LASHES to make them WILLING to go."—*Thomas C. Brown, from Liberia,* 1834 " When emancipated, the s es should be colonized in Africa, *or somewhere else,* WHETHER THEY BE WILLING OR NOT."—*Rev. T. Spicer, of the Troy* (*Meth.*) *Conference, Letter to Z. Watchman, Jan.* 20, 1836. In 1836, when an agent of the society was attempting to colonize 65 emigrants from Ky. and Tenn. 22 of them escaped,(at Pittsburgh, and at N. Y.) not having been made " WILLING " to go.

Fig. 9. " 'Nuisances' Going As 'Missionaries,' 'With Their Own Consent.' "
Woodcut in *The American Anti-Slavery Almanac, for 1839* (New York: American Anti-Slavery Society, [1838]). Courtesy Library Company of Philadelphia

The allegorical engraving "The Truth Shall Make You Free" (figure 15), showing white women assisting the elevation of blacks, was commissioned from the black engraver Patrick Henry Reason by the Boston Female Anti-Slavery Society as the frontispiece to its first literary annual, the *Liberty Bell.*

The patronizing attitude evident in these images does speak in part to the limits of racial egalitarianism in the movement. In spite of the society's stated principles, sections of AASS were not free from racism. Many abolitionists also took a paternalistic view of blacks as fit objects for white benevolence and tutelage, and probably found it ennobling to be part of a movement that gave voice to what Sarah Grimké called "the speechless agony of the fettered slave." There is undeniably a smug, self-congratulatory quality to these images—not too surprising from a movement that regarded slavery a sin and opposition to it righteousness. Northern blacks, individually and through their organizations, frequently criticized these aspects of the antislavery movement and also often faulted northern abolitionists for slighting such concerns as black education, employment

Who bids?
"INCENDIARY PICTURES."

Owing to the absence of the Editor no "incendiary picture" was prepared for this number of the Record. We have, however, procured and placed above a little one—"inflammatory, incendiary, and insurrectionary in the highest degree"—which is in common use at the South. The cast from which it was taken was manufactured in this city, for the southern trade, by a firm of stereotypers, who, on account of the same southern trade, refused to stereotype the Record, *because* it contained just such pictures! Now, how does it come to pass, that this said picture when printed in a southern newspaper is perfectly harmless, but when printed in the Anti-Slavery Record is perfectly incendiary? We have nothing further to say about it till this question is answered.

Fig. 10. "Who Bids? 'Incendiary Pictures.'" Woodcut in *The Anti-Slavery Record* 2 (July 1836). Courtesy Library Company of Philadelphia

opportunities, and political rights. But African American activists of the 1830s generally recognized that the antislavery movement included the only organized antiracist forces operating in the larger American society.[8]

More important, the benign scenes of industrious freedmen were attempts to promote emancipation as safe, to counter the fears of slave violence raised by their opponents. Antiabolitionists never let anyone forget that the decade of the 1830s began with the bloody Nat Turner insurrection, often attributed to the fiery pamphlet of black Bostonian David Walker.[9]

8. For information on black activists in the antislavery movement, see Benjamin Quarles, *Black Abolitionists* (New York, 1969).

9. David Walker, *Walker's Appeal, in Four Articles, Together with a Preamble to the Colored Citizens of the World, But in Particular, and Very Expressly to Those of the United States of America* (Boston, 1829). Walker's pamphlet appeared in three editions between 1829 and 1831. For a brief discussion of southern "Walkerphobia," see Clement Eaton, "A Dangerous Pamphlet in the Old South," *Journal of Southern History* 2 (1936): 323–44. A fuller study of Walker and his activities is Herbert Aptheker, *One Continuous Cry* (New York, 1965).

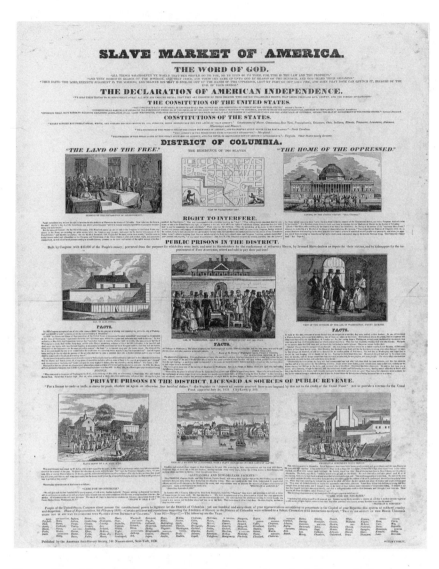

Fig. 11. *Slave Market of America* (New York: American Anti-Slavery Society, 1836). Broadside, wood engravings with letterpress. Courtesy Library Company of Philadelphia

Also, they regularly recalled "the horrors of St. Domingo" in their rhetoric. Their most frequently stated motive for stifling abolitionist discussion was that such discussion could encourage slave revolts. As part of their effort to defuse fears of violence, the antislavery movement did not produce representations of black violence, self-assertion, or control.

SOUTHERN IDEAS OF LIBERTY.

Sentence *passed upon one for supporting that clause of our Declaration viz. All men are born free & equal.* " *Strip him to the skin! give him a coat of Tar & Feathers!! Hang him by the neck, between the Heavens and the Earth.!!! as a beacon to warn the* Northern Fanatics *of their danger!!!!* "

NEW METHOD OF ASSORTING THE MAIL, AS PRACTISED BY SOUTHERN SLAVE-HOLDERS, OR

ATTACK ON THE POST OFFICE, CHARLESTON, S.C.

Fig. 12. *Southern Ideas of Liberty* and *New Method of Assorting the Mail, As Practised by Southern Slave-Holders. Or Attack on the Post Office, Charleston, S.C.* [Boston? 1835]. Double panel lithograph. Courtesy Library Company of Philadelphia

Fig. 13. Detail, masthead illustration for the *Liberator,* March 2, 1838, and thereafter. Courtesy Library Company of Philadelphia

If the images of the abolitionists of the 1830s flow from a fifty-year-old tradition, the same cannot be said of their antiabolitionist counterparts. The illustrations supporting a decade of antiabolitionist and antiblack violence and suppression built on a burgeoning strain of antiblack caricature. These graphics targeted urban, northern free blacks—not slaves, but those blacks who shared the same space with northern whites and sought the same things—jobs, housing, opportunity. Reflecting the growing racism of northern whites, and particularly white workers, these early caricatures depicted free blacks as apish inferior imitators of whites, sometimes ridiculously comic, often threatening.

Where did all this begin? Throughout the eighteenth century, crude cuts of blacks appeared in newspapers accompanying advertisements for slave sales or runaways, and black figures appeared in advertisements for a variety of products such as lamp and boot blacking and ink. There were also the occasional shop signs, such as that of Joseph Prichard, a Philadelphia merchant who in 1735 relocated to Market Street at "the sign of the Black Boy."[10] But to see the origins of consistent and coherent antiblack caricature we should look to early nineteenth-century Boston.

Beginning in 1808 Boston's black community celebrated the closing of the Atlantic slave trade on July 14 with parades, church services, public meetings, and banquets. Perhaps as early as 1815 a satirical broadside was published which ridiculed the black celebration. These broadsides, usually illustrated, were published annually until at least 1830. Figure 16 is an example from 1822. We do not yet know how far these images spread, but the text of an 1819 version appears in a Charleston, South Carolina, almanac from 1820.[11] These cartoons, which may well present the earliest consistent

10. *American Weekly Mercury,* December 4, 1735, p. 3.
11. Joshua Sharp, *Country Almanack, for 1820* (Charleston, 1819), p. 23.

216

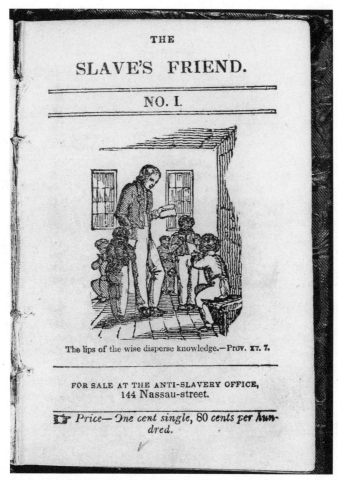

THE

SLAVE'S FRIEND.

NO. I.

The lips of the wise disperse knowledge.—Prov. xv. 7.

FOR SALE AT THE ANTI-SLAVERY OFFICE,
144 Nassau-street.

☞ Price— One cent single, 80 cents per hundred.

Fig. 14. Woodcut wrapper illustration for the *Slave's Friend* (1836–1839). Courtesy Library Company of Philadelphia

pattern of American racist caricature, are prototypical of the enormous volume of such material that followed. With a derisive graphic depiction of blacks and a comic text featuring malapropic orations, toasts, jokes, and songs, these broadsides presage the minstrel show.

By 1819 Philadelphia artists James Thackera, David Claypoole Johnston, and Edward W. Clay had produced satirical etchings denigrating blacks. Thackera's 1819 etching (figure 17) is accompanied by his explanation: "The Black gentry aping their masters, dress quite as extravagantly, and frequently wear their clothes, long before they are cast off. They not only ape

Fig. 15. "Truth Shall Make You Free." Engraving by Patrick Henry Reason in the *Liberty Bell. By the Friends of Freedom* (Boston: For the Massachusetts Anti-Slavery Fair, 1839). Courtesy Library Company of Philadelphia

the dress of their masters, but also their cant terms, being well versed in the fashionable vocabulary."[12]

Later, in 1828, Edward W. Clay's series of etchings, *Life in Philadelphia,* gave an American refinement to the popular caricature of middle class nouveau riche pretension. His cartoon series targets Philadelphia's black middle-class community and shows them in ridiculous and pompous posturings and poses, and subtly or blatantly as a threat. Figure 18, for example, offers an irresponsible-looking black barber who with a mixture of glee and menace holds a straight razor to an apprehensive white patron. Philadelphia historian John Fanning Watson described his African American neighbors of this period as "dressy blacks and dandy colour'd beaux and belles" noted for "their aspirings and little vanities" and their "overweening

12. Manuscript note by Thackera accompanying the etching in his sketchbook, in the collection of the Historical Society of Pennsylvania.

Fig. 16. Detail, *Grand and Splendid Bobalition of Slavery* (Boston, 1822). Broadside, woodcut with letterpress. Courtesy Historical Society of Pennsylvania

fondness for display and vainglory."[13] One of Clay's cartoons from this series (figure 19) illustrates Watson's sentiments in its caricature and dialogue: "How you find yourself dis hot wedder Miss Chloe?" "Pretty well I tank you Mr. Ceasar only I aspire too much."

13. John Fanning Watson, *Annals of Philadelphia* (Philadelphia, 1830), p. 479.

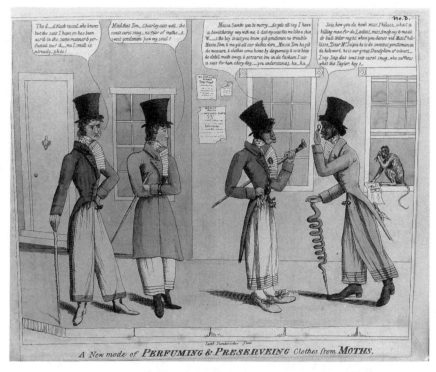

Fig. 17. *A New mode of Perfuming & Preserveing Clothes from Moths. Saml. Slandersides Fecit.* Etching with color by James Thackera (Philadelphia, 1819). Courtesy Historical Society of Pennsylvania

Clay's series went through at least three editions by 1830. Published—and republished—in England as well as America, Clay's series of caricatures made Philadelphia's black middle class the butt of an international joke and was widely influential. In Boston, David Claypoole Johnston, formerly a Philadelphian, may have been influenced by Clay's work to return to black Philadelphia as a setting for his etching "The African Mawworm," an 1830 caricature of a black church service at "Lmbd. St. Philada." (figure 20). Several black churches were located in the vicinity of Philadelphia's Lombard Street.

Among northern white workers, fear of job competition with blacks was an enduring source of antiblack feeling and sometimes of mob action. Cartoons such as "The Results of Abolitionism!" (figure 21) reflected and fueled this discontent, with its dramatic depiction of role reversal on the job, showing blacks as bricklayers lording it over white laborers. And mob action, defended as a manifestation of overwhelming public

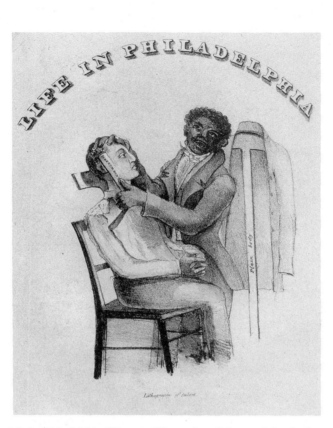

Fig. 18. *Life in Philadelphia*. Wrapper illustration, lithograph by Anthony Imbert [New York, ca. 1829–1830]. Courtesy Historical Society of Pennsylvania

opinion, was also celebrated, as in "The Abolition Garrison in Danger, & the Narrow Escape of the Scotch Ambassador," an anonymous lithographed cartoon celebrating the attack by "gentlemen of property and standing" on William Lloyd Garrison in Boston in 1835 (figure 22). By including the retreating figure of Scottish abolitionist George Thompson, disguised as a woman, this cartoon also depicts the antislavery movement as a foreign conspiracy. The Boston mob's original target was a meeting of the Boston Female Anti-Slavery Society, where it was rumored Thompson would speak. In the cartoon a cowardly Garrison pleads, "Help children of Africer—help brothers Oh Oh," while a righteously indignant well-dressed mob shouts "Down with the incendiary Abolitionists"; "Lynch the rascal"; and "Give him a coat of Tar and feathers." The retreating Thompson mutters "de'il hae me if I'll be a Martyr in sie a black cause."

Fig. 19. *Life in Philadelphia Plate 4.* Etching with color by Edward W. Clay (Philadelphia: S. Hart, [1829]). Courtesy Library Company of Philadelphia

The active role of women in the antislavery movement, on the lecture platform, as organizers of their own meetings and societies, and as petitioners to Congress intensified the antiabolitionist attack. Future president John Tyler denounced the women petitioners as "the instrument of destroying our political paradise . . . the presiding genius over the councils of insurrection and discord . . . a fiend to rejoice over the conflagration of our dwellings and the murder of our people."[14] The female petitioners, raged Senator Benjamin W. Leigh of Virginia, had "unsexed themselves." The Massachusetts Congregationalist Hubbard Winslow charged the activist women with "the alienation of the sexes, the subversions of the distinguishing excellence and benign influence of women in society, the destruction of the domestic constitution, the prostration of all decency and order, the reign of wild anarchy and shameless vice."[15]

14. Lyon G. Tyler, *Letters and Times of the Tylers,* 2 vols. (Richmond, 1884–85), 1:577.
15. *Congressional Globe,* January 19, 1836; Hubbard Winslow, *"The Appropriate Sphere of Woman": A Discourse Delivered in the Bowdoin Street Church, July 9, 1837* (Boston, 1837), p. 16.

Fig. 20. "The African Mawworm Lombd. St Philada." Etching in David Claypoole Johnston, *Scraps for the Year 1830. Designed Etched and Published by D. C. Johnston* (Boston, [1830]). Courtesy Library Company of Philadelphia

Clearly, the activities of the abolitionist women touched raw nerves enough to elicit a violent response from the large antiabolitionist and antiblack public. Early activists such as the emigré radical reformer Frances Wright, the Quaker leader Lucretia Mott, and the Boston African American political writer Maria Stewart had, in the late 1820s and early 1830s, violated "the appropriate sphere of women" by taking their ideas to the public lecture platform. Their examples helped inspire the formation of the female antislavery societies and led others such as Angelina and Sarah Grimké, Maria Weston Chapman, and Abby Kelley to fight the enormous tide of public opinion for the right of women to engage in social activism. Nor was the example of early reformers such as Frances Wright lost on those who opposed women venturing beyond their appropriate, proper sphere. "A Downwright Gabbler, or a goose that deserves to be hissed" is a caricature of Wright, done about the time of her July 1829 lecture in Philadelphia (figure 23). Wright's name entered the vocabulary as well. When Hubbard Winslow, denouncing the female abolitionists in 1837,

Fig. 21. *The Results of Abolitionism!* (n.p., ca. 1835). Wood engraving with letterpress. Courtesy Library Company of Philadelphia

declared "The world has had enough of Fanny Wrights," he was confident his listeners understood the reference.[16]

Many of the activist women's groups, as well as the antislavery conventions of American women, were deliberately interracial—a denunciation in deed of racism—and they firmly voiced an antiracist position: "Resolved, that this Convention do firmly believe that the existence of an unnatural

16. Winslow, *The Appropriate Sphere*, p. 15.

THE ABOLITION GARRISON IN DANGER, & THE NARROW ESCAPE *of the* SCOTCH AMBASSADOR.

Fig. 22. *The Abolition Garrison in Danger, & the Narrow Escape of the Scotch Ambassador* (Boston, October 21, 1835). Colored lithograph. Courtesy Library Company of Philadelphia

prejudice against our colored population, is one of the chief pillars of American slavery—therefore, that the more we mingle with our oppressed brethren and sisters, the more deeply we are convinced of the sinfulness of that anti-Christian prejudice."[17] The women's bold venture into the political arena, combined with their unapologetic association with their black co-workers, incited the most powerful response from their critics, the linking of the antislavery movement to "amalgamation," or interracial association, and miscegenation.

The fulminating antiabolitionist rhetoric joining antislavery and amalgamation was accompanied by lacerating graphics. Figure 24 is one of a series on "Practical Amalgamation" showing such scenes of interracial love and courtship. This cartoon illustrates—and promotes—the antiabolitionists' deepest racial and sexual fears, showing a vigorous black man being fondled by a lovely and willing white woman; and, to underscore the

17. *Proceedings of the Anti-Slavery Convention*, p. 13. The language here is a precise political statement, directed against the colonizationists and other antiabolitionists who constantly referred to a "natural" prejudice to justify slavery and the subordination or removal of blacks.

A DOWNRIGHT GABBLER,
or a goose that deserves to be hissed—

Fig. 23. *A Downright Gabbler, or a goose that deserves to be hissed* (Philadelphia: J. Akin, ca. 1829). Etching. Courtesy Library Company of Philadelphia

revulsion of this misalliance, an effete, unappealing white man courts a grotesquely caricatured black woman.

A further attack on antislavery women is "Abolition Hall," an anonymous lithograph showing the scene at Pennsylvania Hall in Philadelphia in May 1838, at the time of the second Anti-Slavery Convention of American Women (figure 25). This interracial gathering, one of several large antislavery meetings at the newly opened hall that week, particularly incited antiabolitionist sentiment, and on May 17 Pennsylvania Hall was attacked and burned by a mob, following a session of the women's convention. In this depiction the hall appears as an amalgamation brothel, with white and black couples lolling in the windows and embracing on the streets. At the lower left, a black boy embraces a white girl. The sign in the foreground reading "Abolition by Brown David Paul" refers to the antislavery lawyer David Paul Brown, a featured speaker at the hall's opening ceremonies. City authorities, whose deliberate inaction encouraged the mob, quickly blamed

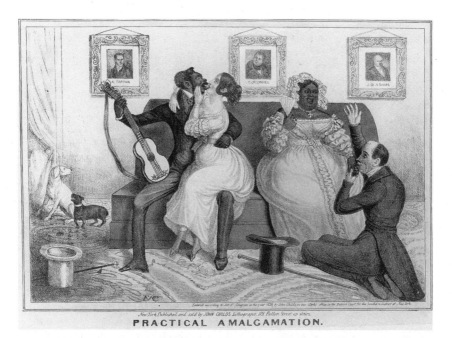

PRACTICAL AMALGAMATION.

Fig. 24. *Practical Amalgamation*. Colored lithograph by Edward W. Clay (New York: John Childs, 1839). Courtesy Library Company of Philadelphia

the violence on its victims, charging that abolitionists were guilty of "openly promulgating and advocating doctrines repulsive to the moral sense of a large majority of our community."[18]

Like "Abolition Hall," "The Black and White Abolition Coach" and "Johnny Q. Introducing the Haytien Ambassador to the Ladies of Lynn, Mass." (figures 26 and 27) directly attack the women's antislavery organizations. The first was inspired by Clarissa Lawrence, a black Salem, Massachusetts, delegate to the third women's convention. On her return, Lawrence desegregated the overnight packet from New York when a white companion urged her to share a cabin. The following morning, other passengers learned a forbidden black had occupied a cabin and voted seventy-five to twenty-four against allowing such a breach of decorum and custom. The episode enjoyed considerable attention in the press, where outraged editors used it to prove the amalgamating tendencies of the abolitionists.[19]

18. [Samuel Webb], *History of Pennsylvania Hall Which Was Destroyed by a Mob on the 17th of May, 1838* (Philadelphia, 1838), p. 180.
19. *Liberator,* May 24 and 31, 1839, discusses the incident and the reaction to it.

Fig. 25. *Abolition Hall. The evening before the conflagration at the time more than 50,000 persons were glorifying in its destruction at Philadelphia May—1838. Drawn on stone by Zip Coon.* Salt print photo of unrecorded lithograph, ca. 1850. Courtesy Library Company of Philadelphia

Fig. 26. "The Black and White Abolition Coach." Woodcut in *The United States Comic Almanac, for the Year 1840.* [Boston, 1839]. Courtesy Library Company of Philadelphia

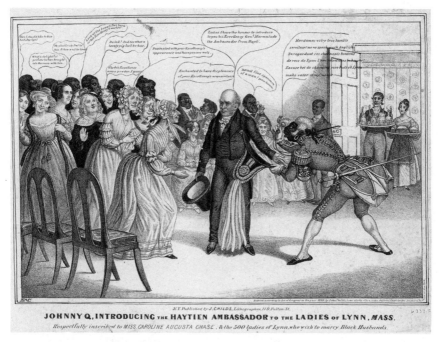

Fig. 27. *Johnny Q, Introducing The Haytien Ambassadore To The Ladies Of Lynn, Mass. Respectfully inscribed to Miss Caroline Augusta Chase & the 500 ladies of Lynn who wish to marry Black Husbands.* Lithograph by Edward W. Clay (New York: J. Childs, 1839). Courtesy Library Company of Philadelphia

In the second cartoon, the women of the Lynn Female Anti-Slavery Society, surrounded by black suitors, gaze lasciviously at the supposed Haitian ambassador, a thick-lipped, powder-wigged black grotesquery in military uniform. The women are remarking, "What a delightful purfume he has brought into the room with him," "How I should like to kiss his balmy lips!" Meanwhile the ambassador, General Marmalade, accompanied by John Quincy Adams, addresses the ladies in fractured French that degenerates into caricatured black dialect:"Excuse but de charming rose buds ob Lynn make vater in my mouse."

This cartoon, as the title tells us, is "respectfully inscribed to Miss Caroline Augusta Chase & the 500 ladies of Lynn who wish to marry Black Husbands." It is a response to the activities of the Lynn Female Anti-Slavery Society—Abby Kelley's old group—headed in 1839 by Aroline (not Caroline) Chase. The Lynn society and other Massachusetts women's antislavery groups petitioned the state legislature to rescind race-proscriptive laws, including an old ban on interracial marriage. The five hundred Lynn petitioners, joined by several thousand signatories from other groups, were ultimately successful.

For the rest of the century the conflicting graphic patterns of the 1830s influenced the depiction of slavery, of blacks, and of reformist women. Even as new antislavery books and pamphlets flowed from commercial publishers beyond the organized movements, their illustrations recalled the antislavery images of the 1830s. Similarly, the antiblack and antiabolitionist library of images spawned countless imitators, creating clichéd dandified, malapropic blacks, grotesque black women, and white reforming harridans. And although abolition's opponents certainly carried the day with the voluminous racist caricature of the rest of the century, abolitionist graphics, in their principled consistency and abundance, comprise a significant literature on human rights.

{ 12 }

Abby Kelley and
the Process
of Liberation

Keith Melder

Shortly after attending the second Anti-Slavery Convention of American Women
in 1838, Abby Kelley wrote to a sister about abolitionists and other reformers: "Those who go in the fore-front of this as well as in all other reforms
must bear all manner of censure, scorn, contempt, reproach, and still se-
verer persecution." But opposition should embolden, not retard protest:
"The more persecution a good cause meets, the stronger of course is the
evidence that there is the greater cause for its prosecution."[1] With these
words, Kelley recorded her own progress toward self-liberation. Her words
also testified to the importance of the women's convention she had recently
attended and anticipated her life's work for the next three decades.

Two themes dominated Abigail Kelley's early years as a reformer: the
process of personal liberation she experienced and the impact of the wom-
en's national antislavery meetings on her career between 1837 and 1839. Although today less well known than Angelina and Sarah Grimké, Lucretia
Mott, and Susan B. Anthony, in her own time Abby Kelley was famous as
a pioneer feminist abolitionist.[2] Kelley liberated herself consciously and deliberately from the restraints custom and religion placed on her conduct.

An early version of this essay was presented to the National Museum of American History
colloquium, February 16, 1988. The opportunity to participate in the colloquium was instrumental in my development of the basic arguments made here.

1. Abby Kelley to Olive and Newbury Darling, July 22, 1838, Worcester Historical Society
(hereafter cited as WHS).

2. Blanche Glassman Hersh discusses feminist abolitionist women in *The Slavery of Sex:
Feminist-Abolitionists in America* (Urbana, 1978), especially pp. 4–7.

The circumstances of her liberation, as well as the results, are worthy of attention. Crucial to Kelley's liberation were three factors: encouraging conditions in her surrounding environment, immediate personal experiences, and institutional structures that influenced her decisions. She later became one of the first activists to articulate the issue of women's rights purely as a raw confrontation between man and woman.

Abby Kelley was profoundly influenced by the three antislavery conventions of American women of 1837, 1838, and 1839. She participated in two of them, and if we can judge from her own life, these important occasions in the history of American social agitation deserve more serious attention than they have received from students of reform and from historians of American women. The conventions created a sense of common purpose for antislavery feminists like Kelley and sparked a consciousness of power and sisterhood among those in attendance which soon spread to women they influenced.

Like several leading women antislavery advocates, Abigail Kelley, born in 1810, was a Quaker. One of eight daughters in a farm family with nine children, she grew up primarily in rural sections of central Massachusetts in and around Worcester. Although she attended the Providence Friends' School in the late 1820s, she was not wealthy. In the 1830s, when Kelley was in her early twenties, she began teaching in Friends' schools and was lucky to find a position in the one at Lynn, Massachusetts, where a prosperous community of Quakers flourished.[3]

A lively environment surrounded Kelley in Lynn. During the 1830s many people in the town experienced changing conditions in their lives, for some a loosening of old limits but for others a tightening of constraints and the imposition of new burdens. A "revolution in choices" is one historian's term for the unusual range of industrial, social, religious, and political alternatives suddenly available.[4] Lynn was in the midst of important industrial changes as shoemaking, the town's dominant business, moved from small ten-footer artisan shops into factories where bosses,

3. Among the studies of Abby Kelley (Foster) are Jane H. Pease, "The Freshness of Fanaticism: Abby Kelley Foster, An Essay in Reform" (Ph.D. diss., Univ. of Rochester, 1969); Margaret Hope Bacon, *I Speak for My Slave Sister: The Life of Abby Kelley Foster* (New York, 1974); Nancy H. Burkett, *Abby Kelley Foster and Stephen S. Foster* (Worcester, 1976); and Joel Bernard, "Authority, Autonomy, and Radical Commitment: Stephen and Abby Kelley Foster," *Proceedings of the American Antiquarian Society* 90 (1981): 347–86. The latest, most thorough biography is Dorothy Sterling, *Ahead of Her Time: Abby Kelley and the Politics of Antislavery* (New York, 1991).

4. On the idea of a "Revolution in Choices," see Robert H. Wiebe, *The Opening of American Society: From the Adoption of the Constitution to the Eve of Disunion* (New York, 1984), chap. 8.

not journeymen, controlled production. Although not yet mechanized, the skilled work of shoe manufacturing was subdivided, and management passed into the hands of a relatively few factory owners. Many owners were also Quakers.[5]

Industrial changes brought social tension to the community, stimulating resistance from organized workers and artisans. In 1833, about the time of Kelley's arrival, women shoe binders gathered at the Friends' Meeting House to found the Female Society of Lynn and Vicinity for the Protection and Promotion of Female Industry. The women protested employers' efforts to reduce prices paid for their work and urged their co-workers to unite and assert their rights to set prices for labor. "Let us become a band of sisters, each considering the welfare of the society as her own peculiar interest." But in the face of opposition and defections from its ranks, the society failed to achieve its aims. Abby Kelley surely knew of this effort among the shoe binders, many of whom were about her own age.[6]

Kelley read a reform-minded local newspaper, the *Lynn Record*, that chronicled and advocated a variety of social movements, including the anti-Masonic crusade, temperance, and organized labor. Although not exactly a mouthpiece for ordinary workers, this paper praised campaigns such as the moral reform battle against prostitution. The *Record* also lauded the anti-slavery cause and professed shock at the widespread riots against the abolitionists. As a young teacher new in town, Abby Kelley formed close ties with other young people, especially women, and involved herself in their flourishing social movements.[7]

The Lynn Friends Meeting, which engaged Kelley to teach in its school, was unsettled at this time. The "new light" movement of the 1820s had brought turmoil, dissension, and opposition from conservative elders. Although Lynn's Quakers were not severely divided by the Hicksite split in the Society of Friends, as many meetings had been, some members of the Lynn meeting's liberal minority felt encouraged to work for liberation and

5. Paul G. Faler, *Mechanics and Manufacturers in the Early Industrial Revolution: Lynn, Massachusetts, 1789–1860* (Albany, 1981). See also David N. Johnson, *Sketches of Lynn, or the Changes of Fifty Years* (Lynn, Mass., 1880), a reminiscence by an observer.

6. *Lynn Record*, June 18, 1834; see January through June 1834 issues for details about the shoebinders' struggle to organize. See also Keith Melder, "Women in the Shoe Industry: The Evidence from Lynn," *Essex Institute Historical Collections* 115 (October 1979): 270–74.

7. *Lynn Record*, ca. 1834–1837; Anna Breed to Abby Kelley, November 4, 1838, William Bassett to Abby Kelley, November 12, 1838, M. E. Robbins to Abby Kelley, January 21, 1839, Abby and Stephen S. Foster Papers, American Antiquarian Society (hereinafter cited as AAS).

social justice. A majority of the meeting's members were conservative, however, and stayed aloof from protest movements such as antislavery, fearing that agitation would "have a tendency to draw off the minds of our members."[8]

Kelley heard William Lloyd Garrison preach against colonization, probably in 1832, and embraced the radical Garrisonian antislavery movement, becoming ever more involved in abolition work. "At length, my whole soul was so filled with the subject that it would not leave me in school hours." Beginning about 1835, she served as corresponding secretary of the Lynn Female Anti-Slavery Society, one of the growing network of women's antislavery organizations.[9] Her commitment to abolition was the first step in her liberation.

The crusade against slavery had a strong appeal for women, as the Lynn Female Anti-Slavery Society self-consciously declared at its first annual meeting in 1836: "In this sphere it is not denied that woman may operate with propriety and efficiency. It is womans woes that call most loudly for our efforts to free them, and their children from the most cruel oppression from degradation, and outrage in every form—'When woman's heart is bleeding, Shall woman's voice be hushed?' Truth is stronger than error!" Kelley gained local prominence, making articles to sell at the Boston antislavery fair, raising funds, circulating petitions, and corresponding with other women abolitionists. Her conduct reflected a growing impatience with conventional habits and notions of woman's "sphere."[10]

In the spring of 1837 Abby Kelley took another long step toward her liberation. At the urging of antislavery co-workers, she traveled to New York City as a delegate from Lynn to the first Anti-Slavery Convention of American Women. One of the earliest reform gatherings run by and for women, the New York meeting increased Kelley's enthusiasm for the

8. Frederick B. Tolles, "The New Light Quakers of Lynn and New Bedford," *New England Quarterly* 32 (1959): 291–319; Minutes of the Salem Monthly Meeting, July 1837; Epistle from the Yearly Meeting, June 14–19, 1835; Report from the committee to consider slavery, May 1837, Archives of the New England Yearly Meeting of Friends, Rhode Island Historical Society.

9. Abby Kelley Foster, Reminiscences, January 26, 1885, Abby Kelley Foster Papers, WHS.

10. *Record of the Female Anti-Slavery Society of Lynn*, first annual meeting, May 27, 1836, Lynn Historical Society (hereafter cited as LHS); Ann G. Chapman to the Ladies Lynn Anti-Slavery Society, August 31, 1836, Foster Papers, AAS; Abby Kelley to H. G. Chapman, February 1837, Weston Collection, Boston Public Library (hereafter cited as BPL); Lucy W. Foster to Abby Kelley, March 27, 1837, Foster Papers, AAS.

cause. In New York Kelley met several leading women abolitionists—Angelina and Sarah Grimké, Lucretia Mott, Lydia Maria Child—moral leaders and sisters in struggle. In addition to arguments against slavery, she heard "an animated and interesting debate respecting the rights and duties of woman." At the convention, she herself spoke on the need for women to raise antislavery funds, the "imperious duty to make retrenchments from our own personal expenses . . . that we may be the better able to contribute to such funds." Influenced by the New York meeting, when she returned home she urged her local co-workers to speak freely, "to forget ourselves, as much as in us lies, in the absorbing interests of the objects of our association."[11]

In New York she had made the acquaintance of Lucretia Mott. A liberal member and Hicksite preacher of the Society of Friends, Mott became a model of gentle yet relentless female leadership for Kelley and other Quaker women. Mott had attended the first meeting of the American Anti-Slavery Society and was the guiding spirit of the activist Philadelphia Female Anti-Slavery Society. A magnetic and forceful personality, gifted with apparently unlimited energy, she always seemed to have time and resources available to support new causes and to uphold wavering fellow reformers. One of Mott's unique qualities was her spirit of inquiry, leading her on a life-long quest for spiritual liberation. For Abby Kelley, Lucretia Mott was a revelation of liberated Quaker womanhood and an inspiration for her own search for freedom.[12]

During the summer of 1837 Angelina and Sarah Grimké, now conducting a lecture tour of Massachusetts, made a tremendous impression on Abby Kelley. These aristocratic Southern women, both converts to the Society of Friends and firsthand observers and profound critics of slavery, spoke for several days in Lynn and the surrounding area. They appealed especially to women, pointing out women's severe degradation in bondage. Some of their descriptions of female suffering and sexual abuse were explicit and distressing. A Lynn writer described one of their speeches: "Angelina E. Grimké followed in an address of surpassing eloquence and beauty, which it would be mockery in us to describe. The audience

11. *Proceedings of the Anti-Slavery Convention of American Women . . . 1837* (New York, 1837), pp. 9, 14; *Record of the Female Anti-Slavery Society of Lynn*, second annual meeting, June 21, 1837, LHS. See also Ira V. Brown, " 'Am I Not a Woman and a Sister?': The Anti-Slavery Convention of American Women, 1837–39," *Pennsylvania History* 50 (1983): 1–19.

12. On the importance of Lucretia Mott, see Hersh, *The Slavery of Sex,* pp. 14–16, 28–31; Margaret Hope Bacon, *Valiant Friend, The Life of Lucretia Mott* (New York, 1980), pp. 55–85.

seemed astonished at the evidence which their own eyes and ears furnished, having never witnessed such a display of talent in a female. All went out of the meeting full of admiration for the performance and the performer."[13]

The sisters' speeches stirred abolitionists and opponents alike, arousing public sympathies, especially among women, for the sufferings of slaves as family members and producing a strong negative reaction from leaders of the Calvinist clergy. Several ministers preached sermons against the Grimkés' outspoken and outrageous conduct and their speeches to "promiscuous" audiences where men and women assembled together. In Lynn, the Reverend Parsons Cooke of the First Church (Congregational) warned that women's delicacy and moral character were threatened by the sisters' influence.

Abby Kelley is probably the author of a sarcastic review of the Reverend Mr. Cooke's sermon for the *Lynn Record*. Doubting the scriptural basis for his opinions, Kelley scornfully asked how women could know the limits on their duties. "Without such knowledge, our females will be in constant danger of '*shooting*' wildly from their APPROPRIATE SPHERE." Kelley, who favored the course of action taken by the Grimkés as Quakers, women, and opponents of slavery, had already asserted women's duty to speak out in public against slaveholding. Now, noting the vigorous public reactions to the sisters she began a spirited correspondence with the Grimkés. Their example would soon inform her own personal decisions.[14]

Her growing involvement with radical abolition was not, however, the only experience that led Abby Kelley toward personal liberation. During the 1830s her loyalty to the Society of Friends came under increasing strain. Several Quaker beliefs coincided with her sympathies toward activism: the tradition of anticlericalism, of female preaching and speaking in meetings, and of opposition to slavery. Indeed, some Quakers, like Kelley, interpreted the Grimké sisters' lecture tour and their apparent "martyrdom" as powerful living symbols of their faith. But a majority of Quakers evidently feared the divisive impact of the antislavery agitation on the society. Among the

13. *Lynn Record*, June 28, 1837; other accounts of the sisters' lectures are found in the *Record* of July 5 and 26, August 2, 16, and 30, 1837.
14. Parsons Cooke, *Female Preaching, Unlawful and Inexpedient....* (Lynn, Mass., 1837). The review signed "ALPHA" and attributed to Kelley appears in the *Lynn Record,* August 30, 1837. For a detailed interpretation of the Grimké lecture tour see Katharine Du Pré Lumpkin, *The Emancipation of Angelina Grimké* (Chapel Hill, 1974), pp. 108–46. See also Keith E. Melder, "Forerunners of Freedom: The Grimké Sisters in Massachusetts, 1837–38," *Essex Institute Historical Collections* 103 (July 1967): 223–49; Gerda Lerner, *The Grimké Sisters From South Carolina: Rebels against Slavery* (New York, 1967), pp. 168–98.

Lynn Friends, where orthodox members opposed those demanding social activism in the "world," Kelley sided with the activists.[15]

Also in 1837, when she was twenty-six, a more intimate experience challenged Abby Kelley's personal identity: her father died, leaving a profound sense of loss and a feeling of emptiness. Her bereavement was traumatic and disturbed Kelley's sense of self; without the apparent security and strength gained from the support of a male parent, she now confronted her own feelings of inadequate worth and purpose. As she struggled with her grief, she noted: "Father's death taught me the necessity of looking beyond earthly things for a support."[16]

A year later Abby Kelley deepened her commitment to the campaign against slavery. In May 1838 she attended the second Anti-Slavery Convention of American Women in Philadelphia, where she witnessed the dramatic burning of Pennsylvania Hall. In New York the year before, Kelley had spoken several times. Now she spoke again, at least once while the convention was disrupted by a violent mob, and to a meeting of both sexes. It was her first address to a "promiscuous" audience in response to the "still small voice within, which may not be withstood." In Philadelphia she once again called attention to the duty to raise funds by "laboring devotedly in the service of the spoiled, and by contributing with unsparing liberality to the treasury of the slave."[17]

The Philadelphia convention reinforced Kelley's passion for the antislavery cause and her compassion for the victims of slavery and racism. Walking arm-in-arm with black women abolitionists, helping to protect them as the mob howled around Pennsylvania Hall, Kelley gained a new sense of sisterhood with her African American co-workers. She also learned about the dangers of racial oppression through her new friends, the cultivated black members of PFASS—Margaretta, Harriet, and Sarah Forten, and Sarah Mapps Douglass—who confronted prejudice daily. Kelley seems to have struck up a particular friendship with Douglass, a schoolteacher and Quaker who had withstood discrimination from white Quakers. In the aftermath of the antislavery riots, Douglass sent Kelley a small gift, "in token

15. William Bassett to Abby Kelley, November 12, 1838, AAS; see also the *Liberator*, May 1, 8, 15, 1840, pp. 71, 73–74, 80. Disputes within the Society of Friends occasioned by the abolitionists are treated briefly in Margaret Hope Bacon, *Mothers of Feminism: The Story of Quaker Women in America* (New York, 1986), pp. 91–95, 109–12.

16. Abby Kelley to Newbury Darling, December 10, 1837, Abby Kelley Foster Papers, WHS; see also Eliza Earle to Abby Kelley, February 28, 1837, AAS.

17. Samuel Webb, *History of Pennsylvania Hall, Which Was Destroyed by a Mob, On the 17th of May, 1838* (Philadelphia, 1838), p. 126; *Proceedings of the Anti-Slavery Convention of American Women . . . 1838* (Philadelphia, 1838); *Liberator*, July 27, 1838, p. 117.

of my respect and gratitude to you, for having stood forth so nobly in defense of Woman and the Slave. . . . Our hearts have been cheered and animated and strengthened by your presence."[18]

A few weeks later at the New England Anti-Slavery Convention, Abby Kelley became a source of contention between Garrisonian abolitionists and members of the clergy. First was the issue of membership: should women attend the convention on an equal basis to men? Some ministers, asserting their supremacy in moral enterprises, viewed women's membership as an insult. To compound the insult, Kelley was appointed to help prepare a memorial "beseeching [the clergy], in the name of God and humanity, to bear their testimony against the sin of slavery." Outraged, several clerics lodged a formal protest against these unorthodox proceedings.[19]

The women's antislavery conventions and Abby Kelley's other experiences around 1837 and 1838 forced her to question her purpose in life. In doing so, she was attracted to the idea of devoting herself completely to the antislavery cause by emulating the example of the Grimké sisters and becoming an antislavery lecturer. " 'Tis a great joy to see the world grow better in any thing," she wrote. "Indeed I think endeavors to improve mankind is the only object worth living for."[20]

At about this time Kelley and her cohorts were resisting conservative institutions by initiating the "comeouter" movement to renounce organizations, such as the Congregational Church and the federal government, that inhibited freedom of speech and inquiry. To William Lloyd Garrison, Kelley wrote: "My heart was truly rejoiced, to see that persecution's fires still have the same effect on thee as heretofore. . . . I trust the time is now *fully* come when thou wilt take a decided stand for *all truths*." Comeouter, utopian, and "ultraist" ideals inspired many members of New England's intelligentsia, as well as more ordinary social activists—but Garrisonian abolitionists were most pronounced in their opposition to institutionalized restraints.[21]

18. Sarah M. Douglass to Abby Kelley, May 18, 1838, AAS. On the patterns of racial prejudice toward Philadelphia's respectable African Americans see Emma Jones Lapsanksy, " 'Since They Got Those Separate Churches': Afro-Americans and Racism in Jacksonian Philadelphia," *American Quarterly* 32 (Spring 1980): 54–78.

19. *Liberator,* June 8, 1838, pp. 90–91, June 22, 1838, pp. 97–98.

20. Abby Kelley to Newbury Darling, December 10, 1837, WHS.

21. Abby Kelley to William Lloyd Garrison, October 20, 1837, Garrison Papers, BPL. On utopianism and come-outer trends among abolitionists and others, see Lewis Perry, *Radical Abolitionism: Anarchy and the Government of God in Antislavery Thought* (Ithaca, 1973), especially chap. 4; John L. Thomas, "Romantic Reform in America, 1815–1865," *American Quarterly* 17 (1965): 656–81. Nancy Hewitt defines three kinds of women's organizations that

Abby Kelley and the Process of Liberation

In 1838, after gaining prominence in the regional and national meetings of the women's antislavery movement, Abby Kelley abruptly retired from her teaching job and from social activism. Explaining that she needed to care for her widowed and sickly mother, Kelley entered a period of seclusion. "Whether I shall ever enter into the work that I felt so deeply on, . . . I cannot now tell. I hope to do my duty," she wrote at the time. Her correspondence in the years 1838–1839 shows that she sought advice and help from the Grimkés, Lucretia Mott, and other leading abolitionists. Years later, she recalled studying biblical texts and reformist tracts for guidance.[22]

The idea of liberation from oppression was familiar to Americans of Kelley's generation. On one level, such liberation could resemble religious conversion. In order to overcome the religious inhibitions that seemed to limit her freedom of action, Kelley studied, prayed, and meditated, just as thousands of evangelicals did during religious awakenings. She later remembered gaining strength from her mother's approval, although other family members tried to dissuade her from undertaking a career in public agitation. About a disapproving sister she wrote, "She little understands my feelings, if she thinks contempt and persecution . . . would turn me from what I conceive to be my duty."[23]

Kelley's self-analysis did not, however, fit the stereotypes of religious meditation. Letters she received during her seclusion indicate that although she sought divine guidance and inspiration, her aim was to throw off religious authority, not surrender to it. Reassuring Kelley about the value of her nontraditional struggle, Angelina Grimké Weld discussed her own earlier dilemmas. "So strong was my attachment to the Society of Friends . . . that I did not know how to engage in anything which I knew would alienate them from me. . . . Deep was the conflict on my soul for many weeks." Lucretia Mott characteristically urged Kelley to take the most radical course of action. "I should be very glad if women generally and men too, could so lose sight of distinctions of sex as to act in public meetings, on the enlightened and true ground of Christian equality." Women, Mott believed, had benefitted from their experience in gender-

---

developed in one city from the 1820s onward: benevolent societies, evangelical perfectionist groups, and ultraists who worked for radical social changes; see Nancy A. Hewitt, *Women's Activism and Social Change: Rochester, New York, 1822–1872* (Ithaca, 1984), especially p. 225.

22. Sarah M. Grimké to Abby Kelley, June 15, 1838, AAS; Sarah M. Grimké to Anne W. Weston, July 17, 1838, Weston Collection, BPL; Abby Kelley to Newbury and Olive Darling, July 22, 1838, Abby Kelley Foster, Reminiscences, January 26, 1885, WHS.

23. Abby Kelley to Newbury and Olive Darling, July 22, 1838, WHS.

segregated meetings, but the time had come for them "to act in accordance with the light they have, and avail themselves of every opportunity offered them to mingle in discussions and take part with their brethren."[24]

One day in the winter of 1839, after reading Scripture, Abby Kelley saw the light. The text she remembered was: "Not many wise men, after the flesh, not many weighty, not many noble, are called: But God hath chosen the foolish things of the world to confound the wise, and God hath chosen the weak things of the world, to confound the things which are mighty, and base things of the world, and things which are despised, and things which are not, to bring to naught things that are, that no flesh should glory in his presence."[25] As a Quaker, she interpreted this revelation as an inspiration of the "inner light" directing her to go out among the people to explain their responsibilities for denouncing sin and for aiding the helpless.

At this stage of her liberation, Kelley perceived a partial weakening of the barriers limiting her self-expression. Her passion for the cause of the slave seemed unbounded. "I rejoice to be fully identified with the despised people of color. If they are despised, so ought we their advocates to be." Yet she was still unsure of herself, for she needed to practice her new vocation and gain confidence. Although exhilarated by the sense of possibilities before her, she seemed afraid of the outcome.[26]

Her decision to follow a "call to lecture" marked another stage of liberation, and in the spring of 1839 Kelley experienced trial by violent ordeal. She began by speaking in rural northern Connecticut, where she had earlier held a few meetings and could depend on an initial audience and support network of Quaker families. She could also feel comfortable there, for she stayed with a sister. Her message, unlike that of the prominent and urbane Garrisonians from Boston, would be aimed toward simple country folk who shared her rural attitudes. "My mission has been back among the people, amid the little sources of public sentiment; among the hills and hamlets—among the opposed but the comparatively unsophisticated; and I have no weapon but the gospel of truth in its simplicity."[27]

24. Angelina Grimké Weld to Abby Kelley, January 24, 1839, WHS; Lucretia Mott to Abby Kelley, March 18, 1839, AAS; see also Henry C. Wright to Abby Kelley, February 25, 1839, AAS.

25. 1 Corinthians 1:26–29.

26. Abby Kelley Foster, Reminiscences.

27. New York *National Anti-Slavery Standard*, November 19, 1840, p. 93. On Kelley's early lectures in Connecticut see Abby Kelley to Anne W. Weston, May 29, 1839, Weston Collection, BPL; Hannah H. Smith to Abby Kelley, July 25, 1839, AAS; Olive Darling to Abby Kelley, September 18, 1839, AAS.

In Connecticut, a conservative state known as a "land of steady habits," strong resistance to Kelley's lecture tour was exhibited almost at once. The novelty of a woman speaking in public attracted curious listeners, made her notorious, and awakened the ferocity of her opponents. She gained confidence as she attempted in the summer of 1839 to organize women's meetings at Hartford, but she soon found the clergy united in opposition to the meetings. She persisted nonetheless. When a Hartford minister was heard to remark, "She had better be at home washing dishes," Kelley commented furiously, "Either the New Testament is fiction, or else we live in a land of heathenism."[28] The pattern of persecution continued as she traveled into western Connecticut, but she refused to be intimidated. One observer wrote: "Slanders . . . increase her faith and animate her zeal." She was an indefatigable agitator, speaking day after day, receiving support from small clusters of sympathetic farmers and rural folk but seldom from people of influence.

At the same time that Kelley was pointing the way toward a new independence for women, cultural historian Ann Douglas has argued, New England clergymen like Hartford's Horace Bushnell were concluding an informal pact with their female parishioners. The women accepted a clerical definition of their "sphere" as passive, domestic, meekly sentimental, and Christian and in exchange gained religious and social prestige and an illusion of power, or "influence" as *Godey's Ladies Book* put it. Perhaps this interdependence of the clergy and their middle-class women supporters explains to some extent the fierce opposition to Kelley's lectures in Connecticut. Kelley and other antislavery feminists, unwilling to accept limits set by evangelical ministers, actively challenged the tacit pact described by Ann Douglas.[29] Indeed, the clash between the single upstart woman and the clergy grew more intense through the year, until Kelley found herself in a direct confrontation with powerful men who felt compelled to protect their cultural authority.[30]

The next year, 1840, saw this confrontation intensify. The battle briefly entered the religious press when Kelley wrote an article defending women's preaching for the Congregational *Connecticut Observer.* Her claim echoed the Quaker defense of human equality earlier articulated by the Grimké sisters. "Whatever ways and means are right for men to adopt in reforming the world, are right also for women to adopt in pursuing the same

28. *Liberator,* September 13, 20, 1839, pp. 148, 150.
29. Ann Douglas, *The Feminization of American Culture* (New York, 1978), especially pp. 27–70.
30. *Liberator,* September 6, 1839, p. 142, and especially letter dated Washington, Conn., September 13, signed "Vindex," September 27, 1839, p. 154.

object." "The human mind in its natural structure, in its constitution, is the same, wherever found—whether enveloped in a black or white, a male or a female exterior." But the editor stifled further discussion by rejecting additional articles.[31]

A representative of Connecticut's establishment expressed the general opinion of his class when he almost pleaded for Kelley to leave the state. "We have waited patiently . . . the *person* who alone has troubled Israel [to] leave this land of strangers and return to her native State." As her notoriety spread, in far-off Ohio an Oberlin College faculty member feared "that young ladies accustomed to read compositions before considerable classes of young men were on the high road to Abby Kelleyism."[32]

Anger overflowed at a meeting of the male-dominated Connecticut Anti-Slavery Society in 1840. When the minister in charge denied her the right to speak because of her sex, Kelley objected and talked back to the outraged cleric who, in a tantrum, denounced the woman intruder and her power. He shouted out his prejudices and fears. "No woman shall speak or vote where I am moderator. I will not countenance such an outrage on decency. I will not consent to have women lord it over men in public assemblies. It is enough for women to rule at home." He feared the results of women dominating men. "Where woman's enticing eloquence is heard, men are incapable of right and efficient action. She beguiles and blinds men by her smiles. . . . I had enough of woman's control in the nursery. Now I am a man, I will not submit to it." On he went, screaming about petticoat government and similar offenses to good order. When he had finished, the antislavery society finally voted to silence the woman.[33]

Abby Kelley suffered her worst ordeals in western Connecticut. In the town of Washington she spoke several times, then discovered on her return that the minister had preached that she sought to destroy the harmony of the church. His text was from Revelation. "I have a few things against thee, because thou sufferest that woman, Jezabel, which calleth herself a prophetess, to teach and to seduce my servants to commit fornication." The minister described her as "travelling over the country, day and night, with she knows not whom, but always with *men,* husbands leaving their wives to

---

31. Hartford *Connecticut Observer and New-York Congregationalist,* March 7, 1840, p. 38; Kelley's article was entitled "The Woman Question." See ibid., March 28, 1840, p. 50, for the journal's denial of further publication of Kelley's views.

32. *Liberator,* June 19, 1840, p. 97; J. P. Cowles to Amos A. Phelps, December 9, 1839, Phelps Papers, BPL.

33. *Liberator,* May 29, 1840, p. 86.

become her knights errant, calling all men brothers. . . . I blush for the sex!"
After this episode the townspeople shunned Kelley.[34]

In another village a clergyman slandered Kelley and her Quaker religious
faith, calling her "a very bad woman." Her meetings there were increasingly disrupted, and finally a meeting for women was mobbed. Another
town snubbed Kelley, refusing her a meeting place. She remembered a conversation with a "man of gentlemanly dress". " 'I hear you want to hold a
meeting in this town.' I replied in the affirmative. He replied. 'You cannot
do it; if you attempt it, it will be at your peril,' shaking his fist in my face
as he uttered these words. Rising, I replied, 'Then I shall shake the dust off
my feet as a testimony against you.' His rage was terrible, and with half-
smothered-threats he left the house." Silenced and humiliated, Kelley fled
the place.[35]

These collisions between Abby Kelley and orthodox Protestantism were
part of a larger power struggle among reformers and religious leaders during the 1830s and 1840s. Garrison's wing of the antislavery movement was
locked in a bitter contest with other branches of abolitionism over money
and leadership. Connecticut's clergymen apparently feared not only a sav-
age, uncontrollable woman but the disorganizing tendencies of the whole
abolitionist crusade. In Kelley's opinion, "It is not the woman question
that is at the bottom of the difficulty," but the "tottering pro-slavery
church—the church must be sustained, right or wrong."[36]

The year ended, orthodoxy temporarily triumphant in the land of steady
habits. For Abby Kelley, however, it marked another crucial stage in
her self-liberation. Leaving Connecticut, she could look back on intense
struggles and proud achievements. She had faced severe opposition and
demonstrated a capacity to surmount physical and psychological odds.
She was free. But what did freedom mean? Experience suggested that to
be responsible for herself, a woman had to act without restraint from man
and mankind.

At about the time of her Connecticut ordeal, Abby Kelley was again
thrust into the forefront of a battle among men and women for control of

34. Revelation 2:20; Abby Kelley Foster, Reminiscences; *National Anti-Slavery Standard*,
October 8, 1840, p. 71.

35. *National Anti-Slavery Standard*, October 8, 1840, p. 70; Abby Kelley Foster, Reminiscences.

36. Abby Kelley to Newbury Darling, June 12, 1840, AAS. The power struggle within the
antislavery movement has been examined from several perspectives. One of these is well expressed in Aileen Kraditor, *Means and Ends in American Abolitionism: Garrison and His Critics
on Strategy and Tactics, 1834–1850* (New York, 1967).

the national antislavery movement. At the 1840 American Anti-Slavery Society annual meeting, supporters of William Lloyd Garrison, who favored women's freedom of speech, confronted opponents of women's right to act freely. Nominated to the society's business committee, Kelley personified the issue that split the organization into two factions. An observer described the vote. "All went on swimmingly till it came to A. Kelly—then there was, first an immense *yes* and when the contrary . . . was called for a superbe *no*." After a close vote the Garrisonians won control. Numerous clergymen and orthodox laymen then withdrew, later forming a new national antislavery society.[37]

In a final symbolic statement of liberation, in March 1841 Kelley resigned from the Uxbridge (Mass.) Monthly Meeting of the Society of Friends, on the grounds that the society tolerated slavery and the spirit of slavery. As she put it, she "disowned" the society.[38] She exulted in a sense of relief and freedom. "We have good cause to be grateful to the Slave for the benefit we have received to *ourselves,* in working for *him.* In striving to strike *his* irons off, we found, most surely, that *we* were manacled *ourselves:* not by *one* chain only, but by many: in every struggle we have made for him, we find we have been also struggling for ourselves—We . . . acknowledge, that, altho' much shall have been secured to the slave, yet *more* will have been secured to those who have labored for him."[39]

Clearly, Kelley's trials between 1836 and 1841 changed her life in fundamental ways. We can generally identify five stages in her metamorphosis. During her time of receptivity, before 1836, Kelley questioned her allegiance to Quaker orthodoxy and joined in social agitation. In 1837–1838 she became deeply engaged in the antislavery movement and troubled about her goals in life. An interval of seclusion and study in 1838–1839 gave Kelley the opportunity to explore antislavery arguments and make a tentative commitment to the cause. For more than a year after her provisional dedication to abolition, she traveled in Connecticut trying out her gifts as an agitator and testing her nerve against opponents. By the end of 1840 she had proven herself and emerged a fully liberated person.

The sequence of Abby Kelley's liberation parallels two other kinds of traumatic personal confrontations: the nineteenth-century religious con-

37. Anne W. Weston to Maria W. Chapman, May 30, 1840, Weston Collection, BPL; see also Keith E. Melder, *Beginnings of Sisterhood: The American Woman's Rights Movement, 1800–1850* (New York, 1977), pp. 108–12.

38. Abby Kelley to William Lloyd Garrison, September 30, 1841, Garrison Papers, BPL.

39. Abby Kelley in "An Anti-Slavery Album, or Contributions from Friends of Freedom," p. 100, Western Anti-Slavery Society Collection, Library of Congress.

version experience, and the twentieth-century identity crisis. Conversion, "the awakening of the sinner to the true nature of his or her depraved state and the final regeneration of the soul through a process of self-abasement and unconditional surrender to the will of a gracious God," had much in common with Kelley's anguished quest for freedom. Religious conversions involving profound emotional crises, radical changes in convictions, and deep commitments of faith were common throughout the nineteenth century, especially during revivals. Kelley's liberation exhibited some elements of conversion, including her adoption of an unorthodox and highly personal religious stance.[40]

And like religious conversions, Kelley's course also bears striking similarities to the identity crisis as described by Erik H. Erikson in his book *Young Man Luther*. For some young people like Luther, Erikson argues, maturation involves a dramatic process of discarding old identities and acquiring a new sense of self, an ideology, and a mission in life. Erikson calls this process an identity crisis or "second birth."[41] Adopting Erikson's schema, we can argue that between the years 1837 and 1841 Abby Kelley underwent a series of wrenching breaks in her personal life. Responding to a receptive environment, challenging personal experiences, and demanding yet sympathetic institutional structures, Kelley was encouraged to redefine herself.

Did other antislavery feminists undergo such crises and redefinitions, and make dramatic life choices? In all probability, many did. Angelina Grimké, one of Abby Kelley's role models, certainly had a conversion and liberation experience when she was in her twenties. Lacerated by convictions of sin and inadequacy, and deeply opposed to slavery, Grimké left the Episcopal Church for the Presbyterian, then joined the Society of Friends. Still unsatisfied and seeking a meaning for her life, Grimké suddenly found freedom and a vocation in radical abolition after a long period of soul-searching, much as Kelley later did. As biographer Katharine Du Pré Lumpkin narrates the story, after her initial liberation was frustrated, Grimké passed through stages of anxiety, preparation, decision, explosive activity, and testing, similar to those experienced by Kelley.[42]

Blanche Glassman Hersh, studying fifty-one women she calls feminist abolitionists, finds that most were strongly influenced by irresistible

40. Susan Juster, "'In a Different Voice': Male and Female Narratives of Religious Conversion in Post-Revolutionary America," *American Quarterly* 41 (March 1989): 34–62, quotation on p. 34.
41. Erik H. Erikson, *Young Man Luther: A Study in Psychoanalysis and History* (New York, 1962), especially pp. 41, 14.
42. Lumpkin, *Emancipation of Angelina Grimké*, especially pp. 70–146.

religious impulses. "Ironically, reform became the main religion for most of them, replacing formal church-going as a means of expressing their faith." These women, Hersh suggests, "subjected traditional Protestant beliefs to intense scrutiny and repeated re-examination," achieving "liberation from orthodox doctrine." Although she stops short of tracing each woman's liberation experience, Hersh writes that "all felt 'called' to a special vocation, usually at an early age."[43]

Comparisons among the feminist abolitionists suggest that many reformers of Abby Kelley's generation shared her sense of liberation. For Quakers, however, this liberation may have been easier to achieve than it was for more orthodox Protestants. In a study of agrarian Quaker women, Nancy Hewitt argues that the sect "proclaimed women's equality before God and in the religious 'meeting' " making conversion to feminism not an offense against religious order, but a "gradual unfolding of the Divine presence." Believing in general equality, Quaker women could shift to feminism more directly than could members of other sects.[44] Individual freedom for women of all sects resulted from a complex series of experiences, circumstances, and choices.

Abby Kelley's liberation and adoption of an agitator's mission suggest useful ways for reinterpreting the antislavery conventions of American women. For Kelley, as for many other women, the conventions were formative and possibly crucial elements in a larger framework of moral choice. When she attended the first convention, Kelley was already involved in the antislavery cause; afterwards she became even more energetic in her activities. The Philadelphia meeting in 1838 found her near the point of full commitment. Gaining strength from other women leaders and observing firsthand the city's intense racism and opposition to the female antislavery enterprise, Kelley could no longer remain silent.

The implications and consequences of these conventions merit closer study. In unprecedented ways, the antislavery conventions of American women established women's agenda for reform. As the women themselves proclaimed:

43. Hersh, *The Slavery of Sex*, pp. 136–38, 129–56. Another example of a comparative study is Jane H. and William H. Pease, "The Role of Women in the Antislavery Movement," in J. Atherton, John P. Heisler, and Fernand Ouelley, eds., *The Canadian Historical Association, Historical Papers Presented at the Annual Meeting . . . 1967*, pp. 167–83. Joel Bernard, "Authority, Autonomy, and Radical Commitment," offers several suggestions concerning Abby Kelley's personality and commitment to reform.

44. Nancy Hewitt, "Feminist Friends: Agrarian Quakers and the Emergence of Woman's Rights in America," *Feminist Studies* 12 (Spring 1986): 27–49, quotation on p. 29.

Abby Kelley and the Process of Liberation

We are told that it is not within the 'province of woman,' to discuss
the subject of slavery; that it is a 'political question,' and we are
'stepping out of our sphere,' when we take part in its discussion. It
is not true that it is *merely* a political question,—it is likewise a question of justice, of humanity, or morality, or religion; a question which,
while it involves considerations of immense importance to the welfare
and prosperity of our country, enters deeply into the home-concerns,
the every-day feelings of millions of our fellow beings.[45]

Abby Kelley, an outstanding spokesperson for this agenda, lived according to its principles for the remaining thirty years of her active career. After
enduring her baptism of fire in Connecticut, where she taunted the
(mostly) male authorities who opposed her, Kelley began an astonishing
personal crusade. She became one of the most energetic and influential of
all Garrisonian abolitionists, and for more than a decade the leading
woman in the field. Again and again she answered calls for her aid, such as
this one from Pennsylvania in 1844: "Will Abby Kelley come[?] The fact is
she *must*. We are in a critical situation & we must have help."[46] During
ceaseless lecture tours through New England, Pennsylvania, New York, and
the Old Northwest during the 1840s and 1850s, Kelley carried the message
of immediate abolition and "no union with slaveholders" across the land.
Her marriage to fellow abolitionist Stephen S. Foster in 1845 only increased
her devotion to the cause. She energized Garrison's followers especially in
Ohio, founding and giving financial sustenance to a Garrisonian newspaper, the *Anti-Slavery Bugle,* as the movement's western organ. Her visits to
Oberlin College in 1846 electrified and scandalized that campus, impress-
ing Lucy Stone and several other women students there. She was a tireless
fundraiser for and promoter of the *Liberator* and other publications sponsored by her co-workers. Laboring past endurance, she literally wore herself out, inspired by the vision she achieved during her time of liberation.[47]
But did Abby Kelley actually achieve self-liberation? In order to assess
Kelley's personal struggle and her later accomplishments, we need a serious

45. Anti-Slavery Convention of American Women, *Address to Anti-Slavery Societies* (Philadelphia, 1838).
46. E. M. Davis to Maria W. Chapman, September 10, December 16, 1844, Weston Collection, BPL; J. M. McKim to Abby Kelley, October 26, 1844, AAS.
47. Abby Kelley Foster's two-decade career as an antislavery lecturer and agent is treated in
Sterling, *Ahead of Her Time,* chaps. 9–15; for the incidents at Oberlin College see Robert S.
Fletcher, *A History of Oberlin College: From Its Foundation through the Civil War,* 2 vols. (Oberlin, Ohio, 1943), 1:267–69.

review of the entire women's antislavery movement, a thorough new interpretation of women's roles in the abolition of slavery. Gerda Lerner offered
a preliminary assessment in 1976 and called for additional study. Arguing
that "the petitioning activities of antislavery women in the 1830s and 40s
were of far greater significance . . . than has been previously recognized,"
Lerner challenged scholars to conduct "a re-evaluation of antislavery history, which would give women a less marginal place and see their work as
an integral aspect of the antislavery movement."[48] More recently, Jean
Fagan Yellin has completed a reexamination of the symbolism and achievements of antislavery women that should help move us toward the needed
new interpretion of women's antislavery culture, not only among the core
group of leaders but also among their thousands of accomplices and sisters,
white and black, for they constituted a mass movement.[49]

In any reassessment of the antislavery women, Abby Kelley is certain to
stand out as one of the leading Americans who identified with the slaves as
"bound with them in chains," indefatigably pursuing a solution to America's most serious moral problem. Kelley matured and grew old in the battle for equality, beginning with her liberation ordeal in the late 1830s. In the
battle, which still rages today, Kelley's example and contribution have inspired countless others. At her funeral in 1887 a co-worker in reform eulo-
gized: "She had no peer, and she leaves no successor."[50]

48. Gerda Lerner, "The Political Activities of Antislavery Women," in *The Majority Finds Its Past: Placing Women in History* (New York, 1979), pp. 112–28, quotation on p. 128.

49. Jean Fagan Yellin, *Women and Sisters: The Antislavery Feminists in American Culture* (New Haven, 1989).

50. Lucy Stone quoted in Sterling, *Ahead of Her Time*, p. 387.

{ 13 }

"A Good Work among the People"
The Political Culture of the Boston Antislavery Fair

Lee Chambers-Schiller

The annual Boston antislavery fair had been under way for several days when, at two o'clock in the afternoon of Saturday, December 28, 1843, sales were suspended for five hours while the "friends of West Roxbury" brought in Boston's first "Christkindleinbaum": "a young pine-tree of the exact height of the Hall . . . hung with gilded apples, glittering strings of nuts and almonds, tissue paper purses of the gayest dyes, filled with glittering egg-baskets and crystals of many colored sugar—with every possible needlebook, pincushion, bag, basket, cornucopia, pen-wiper, book-mark, box and doll, that could be afforded for ninepence, with a number affixed to each." Long before the scheduled commencement of the evening's fes-tivities, spectators jammed the stairs and filled the lobby. According to a visitor from Lowell, people "needed little exertion to go forward, when the crowd above was moving, the pressure was so strong in the rear—but, as the children and parents stopped to purchase their tickets, it was only at intervals that we could advance. Some pushed, and others braced back-wards, and 'such a getting up stairs I never did see.'" There was a great deal of laughing as everyone craned to see the tree and to buy the tickets that would entitle them to pick gifts from its branches. So great was the crush that fair managers were forced to delay the exchange until Monday morn-ing when the packages could be removed from the tree and arranged on

My thanks to the University of Colorado Committee on Research and Creative Writing for a Faculty Fellowship which enabled me to begin my research on the antislavery work of Maria Weston Chapman and her sisters.

tables for quick access. As a marketing technique, the Christmas tree was a brilliant stroke.[1]

The Boston Christmas fair was the most successful of all abolitionist fund-raisers. Known as the Massachusetts Anti-Slavery Society Fair from 1834 through 1844, and as the national bazaar of the American Anti-Slavery Society from 1845 until 1858, the fair was replaced with a direct monetary subscription in 1859. What began as a three-hundred-dollar "sale of useful articles" held in a private home and attracting a small circle of progressive individuals, crystallized as a desideratum of Boston's social season and a lucrative moneymaker that raised up to five thousand dollars a year for the abolitionist cause.[2] The 1843 Christmas tree was but one of many innovations in advertising, salesmanship, and social planning that augmented sales, maintained public awareness, and spread the message of abolition.

The fair was scheduled to coincide with the end-of-year gift-giving season and advertised accordingly.[3] Lists of items were published to whet the appetite and bring in a spending crowd.[4] Goods were promoted as being in the latest mode, rare, or unavailable at Boston stores, and included fine sta-

1. "Sketches of the Fair—No. II. The Christmas Tree," *Liberator,* January 23, 1843.

2. There are competing views as to whose was the first fair. Jane and William Pease place it in the Chapman home in 1835. Chapman herself deferred to the 1834 fair sponsored by Lydia Maria Child and Louisa Loring featuring contributions from antislavery societies in Portland, Maine; Concord, New Hampshire; and Newburyport, Amesbury, and Reading, Massachusetts. See Jane H. Pease and William H. Pease, *Bound with Them in Chains: A Biographical History of the Antislavery Movement* (Westport, Conn., 1971), p. 44; *Liberator,* January 25, 1856; *Liberator,* November 22, 1834. It is also unclear how much money was raised by these two fairs. Chapman's history records $300 as the proceeds of the Child fair and $600 for that held in her home in 1835; William Lloyd Garrison, reviewing the history of the fair for *Liberator* (January 23, 1846) recorded the total from the Chapman fair as $300. Fair receipts were variously recorded as gross and net, making comparison difficult; however, receipts moved in thousand-dollar increments approximately as follows: $1,100 in 1838; $2,000 in 1841; $3,754 in 1845; $4,525 in 1846; and $5,011 in 1854.

3. The only exception was 1839, the year in which BFASS split and two fairs were held by different factions of Boston's abolitionist women. The Chapman circle held their fair in October but returned in 1840 to late December after the "new organization" women had left BFASS to found the Massachusetts Female Emancipation Society. For examples of advertising, see printed pamphlets such as the Ninth Massachusetts Anti-Slavery Fair Address, 1842, and newspaper advertisements as in *Liberator,* December 5, 1856: "All that the Ladies-Managers resident in France, Switzerland and Italy could do, as well as those at home, conjointly with their friends in Great Britain, has been already successfully done, to make the Bazaar an unequalled occasion for the purchase of Christmas and New Year's Presents."

4. Anne W. Weston to Amy Post, December 19, 1848, Antislavery Papers, Antislavery Collection, Boston Public Library. All correspondence cited in the following notes is in the Antislavery Collection.

tionery and fancy paper goods; statuary, paintings and drawings; silver, crystal, and fine china; jewelry; embroidery and embroidered goods; woodwork; and perfume. Occasionally, the fair's proceeds were directed to a particular end, identified in the announcement, as another means of spurring attendance.[5] Art works and historic documents were exhibited to spark interest.[6] The organizers attended carefully to matters of style and presentation: the hall was gaily decorated; refreshments were offered; and saleswomen took pains with their dress and deportment.[7] With success, however, came conflict, and, increasingly, social and economic considerations clashed with the primary purpose of the fair, to be a "light unto the world" doing "a good work among the people."[8]

Although the Boston fair drew support from a coalition of abolitionists, the "moral suasionists" set the tone. Their distinctive political culture valued consciousness-raising over fund-raising. Over time, their dominance was challenged, first by evangelical and "political suasionist" women, then by men, and last by their own financial and social success. Partly as a result of marketing decisions made to promote the fair, the bazaar assumed a form and nurtured activities that undermined the synchronism of means and ends which made this fair so unique: the fair itself transformed the attitudes of individuals whose participation provided funds needed to persuade still others. Ironically, the shift from sales to subscription, intended

5. For example, see the announcement for 1839 in which proceeds were devoted to the salary of the Rev. John A. Collins, General Agent of the Massachusetts Society, or the 1853 announcement that proceeds would support the *National Anti-Slavery Standard* and the *Liberator.*

6. A likeness of Prudence Crandall in 1834; flower bouquets in silver vases "associated" with the "struggle for religious liberty in Massachusetts in 1785"; in 1839, a newly minted medal struck for the occasion by the American Anti-Slavery Society; in 1841, a "picture gallery" containing "several old masters, of attraction sufficient to induce and repay a long journey only to look upon them"; in 1842, a miniature village fair wrought in bread dough by Englishwomen (exhibited for a fee in 1850 and sold the following year); a bronze statue by Cumerworth, "The African Woman at the Fountain," in 1852; a letter from the women of England to the women of America with 576,000 signatures in 1853; European autographs authenticated by Adam Black of the *Edinburgh Review* in 1855; and the display of a bust of John B. Estlin in 1857. See *Liberator,* December 20, 1834; November 1, 1839; December 18, 1840; December 16, 1842; January 25, 1850; January 28, 1853; November 25, 1853; December 21, 1855; January 30, 1857.

7. Caroline to Maria W. Chapman, December 1843; Anne W. Weston to Deborah Weston, December 21, 1836, Weston Papers. The hall itself held significance. When Faneuil Hall was acquired for use by the fair in 1845, it was seen as a great coup: "Faneuil Hall belongs to the country" trumpeted the *Liberator.* That year, "Freedom's Bazaar" was first called a national fair (*Liberator,* October 3 and 31, 1845).

8. Anne W. Weston to John B. Estlin, October 27, 1850, Estlin Papers.

to restore moral suasion's primacy of place instead facilitated the cultural victory of political suasion's more conservative view of women's social and political role.

In her study of Rochester, New York, Nancy Hewitt identifies two separate political cultures among abolitionist women: those of the political and moral suasionists. These women differed in their views on the political role of the church, their valuation of electoral politics as a means to end slavery, and their attitude toward the role of women in the cause. The moral suasionists criticized what they saw as the churches' collaboration with slaveholders, advocated individual conversion as the primary means of social change, and supported the full and equal participation of women in the abolitionist movement. They defined their role and that of their fair as bringing the antislavery word to a broader audience. Political suasionists saw themselves and their fair primarily as fund-raisers for the movement. Unable to vote, yet valuing electoral politics, these women served as adjuncts in male-dominated associations focused on garnering greater influence in the expanding arena of democratic politics.[9]

In Rochester, the fairs of various antislavery women's organizations expressed their different political cultures. The moral suasionists were democratically organized, reaching out for potential antislavery converts by including rural women on fair committees, sponsoring fairs in villages surrounding Rochester, and soliciting the participation of both sexes, various ages, and diverse occupations. They sold both "useful" and "ornamental" articles. Political suasionist women, by contrast, worked through an exclusively female association that was hierarchically organized and appealed primarily to an urban audience. Their fair goods tended toward the ornamental and the European import.[10]

In style and organization, the Boston fair displayed elements of both forms and had its own political culture. The fair's managers drew in both women and men from the surrounding countryside whose contributions decorated the hall, supplied the refreshment table, and stocked village-sponsored displays. Yet the Boston fair was also well supported by Euro-

9. Nancy Hewitt, "Women's Antislavery Activism in Rochester, New York," in Hewitt, ed., *Women, Families, and Communities, Readings in American History,* 2 vols. (Glenview, Ill., 1990), 1:151–53. According to Hewitt, "moral suasionists" emerged from Quaker agricultural families structured by seasonal cooperation among household members. "Political suasionist" women lived in families and towns where commercial capitalism linked them to the market economy and produced a division between men's work outside the home and women's work in the home. The religious and class makeup of the Boston fair's managers was more disparate.

10. Hewitt, "Women's Antislavery Activism," pp. 149–51. Hewitt reports that the political suasionist fairs made five times as much money as those of the moral suasionists.

pean friends whose contributions of fancy goods increasingly shaped the social tone of the event.[11] Although many contributors to Boston's fair organized themselves democratically in social and sewing circles, fair management was hierarchically organized and directed by Maria Weston Chapman under the auspices of the Boston Female Anti-Slavery Society.[12] Chapman stood for female equality in the mixed-gender regional and national anti-slavery organizations but held fast to the concept of separate female associations as the base of women's influence in the movement.[13]

Chapman constituted the bazaar as a means of moral transformation, consciously developing strategies to win the hearts of New England for abolition. In every call, advertisement, and report, fair managers proclaimed their commitment to spreading the antislavery message: "The ladies have ever regarded the pecuniary benefit derived from these sales as but one of several reasons in their favor. The main object is to keep the subject before

11. Advertisements for the fourth fair already exemplified this emphasis, detailing the "tempting exhibition" of a "great variety of useful and ornamental articles," including those from England (*Liberator*, December 15, 1837). The printed advertisement for the Eighth Massachusetts Anti-Slavery Fair (1841) announced a representative sampling at this point in the fair's development: "Among the rare articles which will make it worthy of attention, will be a valuable collection of scarce Autographs; . . . Fac-similes of the most interesting English State-papers . . . some of these are very valuable, as the plates are broken. Parisian Note Paper stamped with initials; Illuminate Paper, from Milan; Bronzes, from Rome; Embroidered and Perfumed Composition Bags, from Constantinople; Purses, from Florence; Letter Paper, with a great variety of English Scenery on each sheet; Celebrated places in Scotland in Tartan Envelope; Swiss Carved Wood-work, consisting of Models of the Mountain Cottages, Antique Vases, Work-baskets, paper-folders and Bell-pulls, painted with Alpine scenery and costumes; Beautifully wrought Mother-of-Pearl articles; Lava Box set in silver, from Naples; Ladies' Cuffs; Caps and Coiffures, from Paris; Infants' linen cambric and flannel dresses; Old China; Embroidered Souvenirs and Card-cases, from Frankfort; Watch Cases and Bone-work, from the German baths; Embroidered Caps for gentlemen, from St. Petersburgh; Beautiful Netted Hammocks from Santiago; Shells and Coral from Cape Haytien; Medals, Blotting Books, Writing Cases, and all the vast variety of beautiful things which make this annual occasion so attractive" (Weston Papers). This emphasis produced discomfort and reduced support for the fair among some evangelical Christians and Quakers. See Julia A. Tappan to Anne W. Weston, October 11, 1837, Weston Papers.

12. See Maria W. Chapman to Elizabeth Pease Nichol, September 20, 1858, Garrison Papers. The ostensible managers of the fair, as indicated on the fair call, reflected a fairly small and consistent circle of individuals including Louisa Loring, Mary A. W. Johnson, Thankful and Abby Southwick, Henrietta Sargent, Harriet B. Jackson, Mary G. Chapman, Eliza Lee Follen, and Sarah B. Shaw. However, Maria and her sisters Anne, Caroline, and Deborah made most of the decisions and provided the energy and direction behind the event. Maria W. Chapman's personality and managerial style are integral to the story of the Boston fair but are topics for another time and place.

13. Anne Firor Scott, *Natural Allies: Women's Associations in American History* (Chicago, 1991), p. 47.

the public eye, and by every innocent expedient to promote perpetual discussion."[14] For participants, the fair offered a way to deepen their antislavery understanding; for managers, who channeled the proceeds to antislavery agents, newspapers, and tracts, it was also a means toward the larger end of reversing popular indifference to the evils of slavery.

In promoting moral suasion, the managers developed various mechanisms to arouse the political consciousness of New England women. Chapman used her own considerable powers of persuasion to encourage the formation of antislavery sewing circles—not always an easy task. When Frances Drake failed to establish a society in Leominster, she asked Chapman to write a personalized appeal. "I have read again, and again the address by your committee, to the ladies, but they dont seem to feel, it means them," she explained. This strategy worked and the pattern was repeated throughout the region, as Chapman cultivated contacts and mustered inhabitants of small towns and rural areas into Boston's fair work.[15]

Sewing circles were a captive audience for antislavery education, and the moral suasionists who managed the Boston fair used them to expand women's intellectual horizons, augment their knowledge of slavery, and inform their understanding of antislavery doctrine and strategy. Deborah Palmer of Georgetown wrote to Boston wanting "facts, not fiction, dressed up in the form of interesting tales," that could be read aloud to the women while they worked. "I think it would augment our numbers and cause a more punctual attendance; and not only this, the influence may be diffused into all the families where our members reside, and thus the whole community become *Abolitionized*."[16] The fair announcement for 1845 urged sewing circles working for the fair to pass antislavery petitions and circulate

14. *Liberator,* December 10, 1836. The fair was deemed a good instrument because it reached a new audience: "Many an individual, who would never have read an Anti-Slavery publication, or entered a lecture room, has been induced by curiosity, or the demands of the Christmas or New Year's holiday, to visit this annual scene of abolition business; and has left it with a juster appreciation of the motives, and a clearer comprehension of the measures, of [abolitionists]" (*Liberator,* January 12, 1838).
15. For Leominster, see Frances H. Drake to Maria W. Chapman, June 11, 1843; August 6, 1843, Antislavery Papers. See also December 18, 1842; December 15, 1843; June 22, 1844; and Frances H. Drake to Anne W. Weston, December 10, 1850, Weston Papers. For other such efforts, see Elvira Kimball to Maria W. Chapman, August 2, 1843 and November 26, 1845, Weston Papers; Lucy Earle to Maria W. Chapman, April 17, 1838 [or 1839?], Antislavery Papers; Harriet Miller to Maria W. Chapman, September 21, 1840; S. Lincoln to Maria W. Chapman, September 23, 1840; Charlotte M. Lincoln to Maria W. Chapman, October 12, 1840; and Edmund Quincy to Maria W. Chapman, December 16, 1844, Weston Papers.
16. Deborah P. Palmer to Maria W. Chapman, December 1, 1839, Weston Papers.

tracts during their meetings.[17] So effective were these means of political education that when alternative fund-raising activities were discussed, Sarah S. of Portland, Maine, insisted that "the sewing circle or something to bring people together frequently in a social way . . . be continued, as the diffusion of our principles by this means is constantly going forward. The Portland circle . . . is useful mainly in this direction."[18]

Local circles were encouraged to display their contributions to the fair formally in order to advertise the cause and promote abolition in their communities. In Concord, Massachusetts, the women charged admission, believing that "if we have a good many beautiful things we can make a great trumpeting of them, and thus many will come and pay the entrance fee for the sake of seeing them if they do not intend to buy." Mary A. Estlin of Bristol, England, reported upwards of 120 visitors to her drawing room where, she believed, the exhibition served many of the same purposes as the fair itself: "It gives the opportunity of setting people thinking, telling them what the fair is, & what it is for & how it acts. . . . In one case an admirer was excited to add a great packet of stationery from her husband's store, & many are bent upon doing wonders against next time, & many brought in some additions to the stock, & others carried away the Report of last year's Bazaar & other pamphlets, promising to read & think about the subject."[19] Local showings enlarged the numbers of those touched by the fair.

The custom of displaying goods intended for Boston gradually developed into one of holding community fairs that passed on both sales receipts and unsold donations to the national bazaar.[20] Boston fair managers encouraged this development by lending their expertise and accelerating production.[21] Under Chapman's direction, inventory increasingly circulated back

17. *Liberator,* November 14, 1845. See also a discussion of the value of sewing circles as being "among the best means for agitating and keeping alive the question of anti-slavery" for those "who don't get a great deal of anti-slavery at home have an opportunity of hearing it [read] at the circle" (*Liberator,* December 3, 1847).

18. Abigail Kelley Foster to Anne W. Weston, February 11, 1850, Weston Papers.

19. Martha M. Brooks to Maria W. Chapman, June 27, 1843; Mary A. Estlin to Maria W. Chapman, October 28, 1844; Mary A. Estlin to Anne W. Weston, October 4, 1850, Weston Papers.

20. Both the Weymouth and Lynn fairs were held to precede the Boston fair (*Liberator,* January 7, 1842).

21. John Levy to Maria W. Chapman, March 27, 1843, Weston Papers. The fair announcement of 1850 included an appeal for no let down in the production of goods: "We confidently trust that all . . . will continue their efforts, taking no discouragement from the circumstance that all the articles hitherto contributed may not have found a market at the Boston Bazaar. Their sale at various country Fairs has produced an equal amount of good to the Cause. Nor

to these outlying fairs, creating an annual cycle of antislavery activity in the months preceding and following Christmas. Caroline Weston reported to her sister that she was sending "a parcel for you containing articles for the New Bedford fair—I should have sent more—but we were obliged to furnish Lynn—& after our sales at Lowell we sent a box to *Upton,* a box to *Haverhill,* one to the *Juveniles of Providence*—a very pretty assortment to *Philadelphia*—lots to *Lynn* and *Salem* less to the latter however."[22] When Hannah Wilbur of Dover, New Hampshire, reported that the six to eight remaining members of her once active society were poor and willing to sell goods but unable to provide them, a local fair was established using goods from Providence, Fall River, and Boston.[23]

In communities such as Salem and New Bedford, with large black populations and active black abolitionist groups, separate black fairs were held with goods sent from elsewhere. Some white managers required blacks to purchase their leftovers. Socioeconomic differences between fair markets often led to the re-marking of prices as goods moved from urban to rural fairs, but limited resources within the black community seem not to have been considered when prices were set on goods to stock their fairs.[24] This practice indicates both the racism that remained in the abolitionist movement, for few other small fairs paid in advance for one another's largess, and the competitive nature of local fairs, for communities vied for prestige using the income they generated.[25]

---

are we convinced of any thing more fully than that the number of sales at any Bazaar is in exact proportion to the number and variety of articles displayed" (*Liberator,* October 4, 1850). Although in the early 1840s left-over goods were sold in Boston after the fair ended through individual door-to-door solicitations and displays in the antislavery offices, Maria W. Chapman estimated that by the late 1840s close to one quarter of donations remained to be disposed of at "country fairs" (Maria W. Chapman to Mary A. Estlin, January 20, 1847, Estlin Papers; and Deborah Weston to Mary Weston, January 5, 1840, Weston Papers).

22. Caroline Weston to Deborah Weston, December 26, 1839, Weston Papers.

23. Hannah Wilbur to Maria W. Chapman, December 21, 1841, Antislavery Papers. For requests from fair organizers in Concord and Lynn, see Martha M. Brooks to Maria W. Chapman, June 27, 1843, and Eliza Boyce to Maria W. Chapman, December 1, 1839, Weston Papers. For Fall River and Providence, L. G. B. Bordon to Maria W. Chapman, April 2, 1845, Weston Papers, and Lucinda Wilmarth to Maria W. Chapman, December 20, 1842.

24. Deborah to Caroline Weston, December 29, 1839, Weston Papers.

25. There is, as yet, no detailed study of black fairs. According to fair reports, Boston's black community participated in the Boston fair as saleswomen, contributors, and customers. The report of the 1834 fair explicitly mentions black contributions and participation. See *Liberator,* December 20, 1834, for acknowledgment of the goods sent by black women of Salem and a pointed description of the "modest and polite manners of Miss Susan Paul, who sat at one of the tables, and with which the purchasers were much pleased." Paul was a frequent signatory to the Boston fair call. The report of the 1837 fair noted piously "the disregard of the degrading

Local fairs, like sewing circles and fair displays, offered an opportunity for political education. Here, too, the Boston managers' expertise proved invaluable. From Concord, New Hampshire, came a request to Chapman for letters on antislavery topics to be read at their fair Post Office: "We ... write to the sisters in Boston to ask the further favor of letters from them ... as we have few able pens among us. If you, therefore, your sisters, Miss Mary Chapman, the Sargents, Southwicks, or any others ... will favor us with something of this kind, it will be an additional kindness."[26] Community fairs also allowed local workers and their Boston heroines to interact, socialize, and discuss antislavery doctrine and strategy.[27] While in Fairhaven, Connecticut, to organize a fair, Deborah Weston was grilled by the president of the local female antislavery society about ideological conflict within BFASS. Anne Warren Weston reported a solid turnout of abolitionist sympathizers from the Fitchburg area for an 1845 fair. Despite snow drifts and cold weather, she found "all the elite of Worcester County" waiting to discuss the current state of the movement.[28]

Similarly, for the more isolated worker, fair correspondence proved instructional. Mary and Caroline Phillips of Mansfield Center, Connecticut, asked Chapman, "as a hand to the drowning," to write them about movement politics. Eunice Dorman of Kennebunk, Maine, reached out with "an instinct in the soul, which ever desires to find a spirit with which it can commune: and something seems to say, I may find it in you."[29] In reply, fair managers sent antislavery publications and Garrisonian explanations of current issues and events.[30]

prejudice against color, showed by the absence of complexional distinctions" by purchasers (*Liberator,* January 12, 1838). Rhetorical acknowledgments of a black presence characterized many reports (*Liberator,* January 1, 1841).

26. Mary Clark to Maria W. Chapman, May 8, 1840, Weston Papers. Mary A. Estlin found that the annual fair report served this same purpose in Bristol, England. It was displayed with the goods going to the fair and sent around the community with solicitations of goods. "I haven't seen *this* year's yet," she wrote in 1851, "but the two last (especially the one for 1850) have fitted on to my needs of antislavery treatises for people here better than any other documents in our possession" (Mary A. Estlin to Anne W. Weston, February 13, 1851, Weston Papers).

27. S. W. Thomas to Maria W. Chapman, September 18, 1842, Weston Papers.

28. Anne W. Weston to Caroline and Deborah Weston, February 10, 1845, Weston Papers. See also Deborah Weston to Maria W. Chapman, April 28, 1839, Weston Papers.

29. Mary and Caroline Phillips to Maria W. Chapman, December 12, 1842; Eunice Dorman to Maria W. Chapman, December 25, 1842, Weston Papers.

30. See Elizabeth Niles to Maria W. Chapman, October 23, 1839, Weston Papers. Also, Mary P. Henry to Maria W. Chapman, November 30, 1841, Antislavery Papers; Mary B. Snow to Maria W. Chapman, December 23, 1844; Mary Frizell Manter to Maria W. Chapman, 1840; Esther Moore to Maria W. Chapman, February 11, 1843, Weston Papers.

By this mechanism, individual abolitionists could be supported where no antislavery society existed or where the community was hostile to abolition. As Rachel W. Stearns, of Springfield, put it, "We are sometimes ready to faint, the skirmishes with pro-slavery are so severe, and the regular pitched battle which might be decisive, is delayed so long. . . . [W]e keep up a good heart, but a little more acquaintance with the Boston friends would help exceedingly to keep up our spirits."[31] The printed call for the 1841 Massachusetts Anti-Slavery Fair spoke directly to such women:

In many places, one laborer bears alone the heat and burden of the day. To such we would say, be resolute and self-sustained. You do but *seem* to be alone. Within your call are true and faithful hearts

> "—hearts glowing with a flame,
> Kindled like ours for purposes the same,
> To cheer the watch, to daunt a common foe."

Help shall arise by your side soon, and at the eleventh hour the ranks will be full.[32]

Fair work offered participation in the broad community of abolitionists, and correspondence with fair managers reinforced individual identification with the cause. Managers solicited communication, "for the purpose of benefiting us by your suggestions, and receiving the aid of ours."[33]

As part of the effort to inspire contributors, Chapman and her sisters introduced a new form of antislavery literature, the annual gift book, *The Liberty Bell*.[34] Sold to fair visitors and distributed without charge to fair workers, its presentation or purchase was an acknowledgement of one's contribution to the cause and a memento of the occasion.[35] In an effort to

31. Rachel W. Stearns to Maria W. Chapman, December 18, 1842. See also Sarah Steany to Maria W. Chapman, November 10, 1840, Weston Papers.

32. *Call for the Eighth Massachusetts Fair* [Boston, 1841].

33. Ibid.

34. Fifteen volumes were published beginning in 1839; only 1840, 1850, 1855, and 1857 were missed. For discussion of its production and place in antislavery literature, see Ralph Thompson, "*The Liberty Bell* and Other Anti-Slavery Gift-Books," *New England Quarterly* 7 (March 1934): 154–68.

35. See Frances Drake's report of the value placed on copies of the *Bell* and the competition for them that emerged (Frances H. Drake to Maria W. Chapman, January 18, 1846, Weston Papers). For a discussion of its function in solidifying the Boston Clique, see Lee Chambers-Schiller, "The Cab: A Trans-Atlantic Community" (Ph.D. diss., University of Michigan, Ann Arbor, 1976), pp. 205–8.

appeal to genteel, cultivated readers who shied away from the blunt prose of the antislavery newspapers, Chapman solicited distinguished political and literary figures to write poetry, reflective essays, biographical sketches, and short stories. The American public, wrote Chapman, "must be treated like children, to whom a medicine is made as pleasant as it[s] nature admits. A childish mind desires a small measure of truth in gilt edges, when it would reject it in whitty-brown."[36] The magazine acted as further means of moral suasion among those who saw it displayed in homes or meeting places. As Eliza F. Meriam wrote, "I am tempted to put it carefully by with my other valuables; but it has rung so many touching appeals . . . that I think I must circulate it, among the good people of Framingham, peradventure some of its tones may awaken their sympathy and interest, for the poor slave."[37]

While *The Liberty Bell* carried its message beyond the boundaries of the bazaar, the organizers sought to make the fair a "social anti-slavery exchange" and devised ways to strengthen the commitment and hone the understanding of visitors. Beginning in 1840, an evening soirée was held.[38] The fair afforded "an excellent opportunity for the abolitionists, who had long known each other by report to become personally acquainted; and groups were gathered together in conversation, in all parts of the room."[39] Amid the fraternizing, abolitionist women confirmed their politics.[40] The

36. Maria W. Chapman to Mary A. Estlin, January 27, 1846, Estlin Papers. Included were poems by Elizabeth Barret Browning, William and Mary Howett, and Dr. John Bowring, editor of the *Westminster Review*. American poets included James Russell Lowell, Henry Longfellow, and John Quincy Adams. Testimonials were contributed by leaders in French literary, political, and scientific life—historian Jules Michelet, scientist François Arago, author Gustave de Beaumont, and Baron de Staël-Holstein. Essays by Harriet Martineau and William Johnson Fox were published as were short stories by Margaret Fuller and Lydia Maria Child. For different views of how the annual served as forum for the discussion of women's abolitionist and feminist politics, see Jean Fagan Yellin, *Women and Sisters: The Antislavery Feminists in American Culture* (New Haven, 1989), pp. 59–61; and Karen Sanchez-Eppler, "Bodily Bonds: The Intersecting Rhetorics of Feminism and Abolition," *Representations* (Fall 1988): 34–43.

37. Eliza F. Meriam to Caroline Weston, January 16, 1843, Weston Papers. For a discussion of the stories presented in the *Bell* and their compliance with literary conventions governing nineteenth-century domestic fiction, see Sanchez-Eppler, "Bodily Bonds," pp. 34–35.

38. The first commemorated "the two hundred and twentieth anniversary of the Landing of the Fathers." The fair announcement stated, "There could hardly be a more appropriate celebration of it, than this labor to extend the liberty they came to attain." Tickets were sold for one dollar with proceeds to be credited to the fair's total receipts (*Liberator*, December 11, 1840). One wonders if the soirées began in 1840 because evangelical, non-Garrisonian women might have objected previously to their frivolity and "promiscuous" mingling of the sexes.

39. *Liberator*, January 14, 1842.

40. A. L. Haskell to Maria W. Chapman, December 19, 1840, Weston Papers; Harriet D. Mathews to Maria W. Chapman, November 25, 1845, Weston Papers.

fair's managers scheduled evening lectures by William Lloyd Garrison, Wendell Phillips, James F. Clarke, J. G. Palfrey, Henry C. Wright, and George Thompson. Feminists Lucy Stone and Antoinette Brown were the first female speakers, in 1854.[41] The exhibit of antislavery petitions encouraged signatures from those who had no previous opportunity to sign or had held back.[42]

One of the more dramatic ploys developed by the fair's managers to educate and persuade fairgoers was the use of antislavery slogans and mottoes to decorate the walls and grace the sidewalk signs directing people to the fair.[43] Posters and banners offered abolitionist ideology in stirring aphorisms. According to Chapman, mottoes played an effective role in moral suasion by "bring[ing] Truth and Falsehood in continual juxtaposition." Women visitors and sales personnel grew familiar with the form in sewing circles, where they created propaganda by marking clever plays on words on household articles. They labeled quills "Weapons for Abolitionists"; inscribed on pen wipers "Wipe out the blot of Slavery"; stitched on needle books "May the use of our needles prick the consciences of slaveholders"; worked on watch cases "The political economist counts time by years, the suffering slave reckons it by minutes"; wrought on ornamental stands for alumets "LIGHT, whether material or moral, is the best of all Reformers"; and penned on the central star of a patchwork quilt:

> Mother! when around your child
> You clasp your arms in love,
> And when with grateful joy you raise
> Your eyes to God above—

41. *Liberator,* December 26, 1845; November 13, 1846; January 3, 1851; December 29, 1854. Some of these were controversial choices. George Thompson was a member of Parliament at the time of his speaking. Concern about having a foreign politician speak on an American political subject and memories of the violence attending his earlier antislavery lecture tour worried Garrison. The Westons insisted that he made converts whenever he spoke and their faith seems to have been sustained (Anne W. Weston to John B. Estlin, February 9, 1851, Estlin Papers; Mary A. Estlin to Anne W. Weston, February 13, 1851, Weston Papers).

42. *Liberator,* December 19, 1845. So, too, subscriptions for the *North Star* were offered (*Liberator,* January 14, 1848).

43. Many drew upon biblical or patriotic sources: "Inasmuch as ye have done it unto one of the least of these my brethren, ye have done it unto me"; "Proclaim liberty throughout All the land, unto All the inhabitants thereof"; "Remember them that are in bonds, as bound with them"; and "The Truth shall make us free" (*Liberator,* December 20, 1834). Landlords renting halls for the fair were wary of such slogans, fearing riots and property damage. See Caroline Weston to Anne W. Weston, December 9, 1842, Weston Papers.

Think of the negro-mother.
When her child is torn away—
Sold for a little slave—oh, then,
For that poor mother pray![44]

These mottoes worked by intruding on everyday activities, and forcing individuals to see the familiar in a new way by contrasting the situation of slaves with their own.

Even as the managers of the Boston fair promoted their moral suasionist policies, they faced challenges to their values and leadership. The first opposition emerged from evangelical and political suasionist women in the late 1830s and early 1840s. With the dissolution of BFASS in 1839–1840, the "peelers" formed the Massachusetts Female Emancipation Society, an adjunct to the new, non-Garrisonian organization, the Massachusetts Emancipation Society. These women objected to the degree to which the fair's managers worked so publicly and in cooperation with men. By this time, the production of goods for sale to support charitable causes was well established within the appropriate sphere of female benevolent and religious activity, and many who contributed to antislavery fairs understood their work for the slave as being similar to what they did for the poor and dispossessed in their own communities.[45] Indeed, some societies hewed to a traditional division of labor based on gender in which antislavery men furnished money or materials that the women transformed into saleable items.[46] It was one thing to sew in the privacy of a home, however, and quite another to solicit the public for contributions and patronage or sign a public announcement of the fair to be circulated in newspapers and fliers.

Both Mary Ryan and Lori Ginzberg have shown that benevolent women had a distinct public presence during this period. Yet abolitionist activity was not considered in the same light as participating in a civic pageant dressed as Columbia or petitioning the state legislature for the incorpora-

44. *Liberator,* December 10, 1836.
45. See Barbara J. Berg, *The Remembered Gate: Origins of American Feminism. The Woman and the City, 1800–1860* (New York, 1978); Barbara Epstein, *The Politics of Domesticity: Women, Evangelism, and Temperance* (Middletown, Conn., 1981); Suzanne Lebsock, *The Free Women of Petersburg: Status and Culture in a Southern Town, 1784–1860* (New York, 1984); Jane and William Pease, *Ladies, Women, and Wenches: Choice and Constraint in Antebellum Charleston and Boston* (Chapel Hill, 1990); Nancy A. Hewitt, *Women's Activism and Social Change: Rochester, New York, 1822–1872* (Ithaca, 1984); Lori D. Ginzberg, *Women and the Work of Benevolence: Morality, Politics, and Class in the 19th-Century United States* (New Haven, 1990).
46. A. Farnsworth to Anne W. Weston, May 24, 1839, Weston Papers. See also Oliver Johnson to Maria W. Chapman, December 18, 1844, Weston Papers.

tion of a charitable institution.[47] Abolition was not then a fashionable cause, and women whose names appeared in the newspaper or on a handbill suffered the opprobrium of more conservative women and men.[48] Managers of the fair found it difficult to obtain sponsors in the late 1830s and early 1840s when the role of women in the antislavery movement, including fairs, became widely contested. Ellis Gray Loring and Samuel Sewall, staunch abolitionists, were troubled by the appearance of their wives' names on the call, even though both Louisa B. Sewall and Louisa Loring signed. Elizabeth L. Follen reported difficulty obtaining signatures and "concluded that Sarah Atkinson had better not put her name to this address *this* year, her father will be *too* mad." Sarah did not sign.[49] This disapprobation of husbands and fathers, of ministers, of friends and neighbors created a powerful inducement to retreat for some women.

Despite their fear that antislavery sales were too materialistic and frivolous to be consistent with Christian principles, the MFES established its own fair. Although they were devoted to immediate abolition, evangelical women and political suasionists sought primarily to assist fugitive slaves and improve the condition of free blacks, directing their profits to "the ELEVATION OF THE COLORED POPULATION."[50] Before the split, they had briefly carried a BFASS vote to dedicate funds to a black infant school and the Samaritan Asylum for Indigent Colored Children. Moral suasionists privately supported such institutions but opposed using antislavery society funds for any purpose that might contribute to the longevity of slavery by easing some of its most visible social effects in the North.[51] These differences in orientation exacerbated discord and confusion among antislavery women.[52]

Bad feeling produced fierce rivalry over fair contributions. The women of Boylston made a quilt that the orthodox minister's wife wished to donate to the newly organized MES fair. Others were determined that it

47. Mary Ryan, *Women in Public: Between Banners and Ballots, 1825–1880* (Baltimore, 1990); Ginzberg, *Benevolence*.

48. See Ginzberg's discussion of how various women used the ideology and language of female benevolence to distance themselves from the activities of other women by questioning their morality and the propriety of their behavior. Ginzberg, *Benevolence*, pp. 25–35.

49. Anne W. Weston to Caroline and Deborah Weston, February 10, 1845, Weston Papers; Deborah Weston to Caroline Weston, January 2, 1840, Weston Papers. Ginzberg discusses the case of Sarah B. Shaw who struggled for years over the issue of placing her name on the call. Ginzberg, *Benevolence*, pp. 26–27.

50. *Liberator,* November 29, 1839.

51. Ginzberg, *Benevolence*, pp. 45–46; Hewitt, *Women's Activism and Social Change*, pp. 251–52.

52. See, for example, Melanie A. Parker to Maria W. Chapman, April 22, 1839, Weston Papers.

should go to the MASS fair, as usual. They declared that if it did not, "every stitch which they set (& they had set a good many) should come out." As Deborah Weston reported, "Resolution like that generally carries the day, and so we got the bedquilt."[53] The MES fair never successfully competed and soon died as members turned their attention to charitable works.[54]

The conflict between evangelical and Garrisonian, political and moral suasionists which split BFASS was replicated across New England as women found themselves faced with the choice between reaffirming their alliance with the Boston fair, ceasing fair work altogether, or supporting the new fair during its brief existence. Jerusha L. Bird reported that, in Taunton, "Mrs Woodward told me that she did not think she should do any thing this year she did not feel that interest in the cause that she used to, they were divided, she did not know what they did with the money, and among other things she said Mr Emery had not said one word to her on the subject for more than a year, she being a member of his church." Bird feared that when Emery got word she was collecting articles for the fair, the minister would circulate letters from the Ball sisters of the MFES and clerics of the new organization to thwart her.[55] The women of Athol, Massachusetts, and Mansfield Center, Connecticut, found it suddenly more difficult to drum up contributions because some of their constituency worried about "the propriety of Ladies being associated with men in such a cause and others were frightened at the cry of Garrison, Women rights, and Nonresistance, No Governments, and so on."[56]

In the midst of desertion and conflict, managers of the Boston fair worked to invigorate and sustain their flock. The 1841 call spoke directly "to any who, in view of our protracted struggle and unanticipated perplexities, may be preparing to abandon the cause—The numbers of the enslaved, their sufferings and despair, the crime and danger of the slaveholder, the guilt of his northern confederate, are no less than when they first awoke your conscience, and enlisted your sympathy. Remember the declaration of our Saviour, 'No man having put his hand to the plough, and looking back, is fit for the kingdom of God.' "[57] Chapman maintained a continuous bar-

---

53. Deborah Weston to Anne W. Weston, February 29, 1840, Weston Papers.

54. See the description of the 1840 fair by Mary Robbins, who attended it under the mistaken assumption that she was at the Massachusetts Anti-Slavery Society fair, in Caroline Weston to Weston family, December 1–3, 1840, Weston Papers.

55. Jerusha L. Bird to Maria W. Chapman, November 1, 1840, Weston Papers.

56. Mary L. Phillips to Maria W. Chapman, December 19, 1844; A. W. Hoyt to Maria W. Chapman, December 19, 1844, Weston Papers. See also Mary B. Snow to Maria W. Chapman, December 23, 1844, Weston Papers.

57. *Call for the Eighth Massachusetts Fair.*

rage of letters, tracts, and newspaper articles urging women to continue working, where and as they could. "*Work* ever helps work, begin where you will." She responded to her perception of a "shaken faith" in antislavery organizations by saying that "all manner of mistakes and disagreeable things are incident to human life, & ought not to shake our faith in organizations, unless we have previously rated them more highly than they deserve."[58]

She attempted to disassociate the fair from ideological quarrels by repeating in every arena the standard Garrisonian line that the Massachusetts Anti-Slavery Society, under whose auspices funds would be disbursed, was "unconnected with any religious sect, political party, or peculiar opinion."[59] Managers sought to broaden the fair's appeal by attracting men and women from across the spectrum of abolitionist politics. "What though one be the irreverent and contemned 'Come-outer' from Church and State, the other the Reverend pastor from Conformington," wrote Chapman, "and the third and fourth the honorable Senators from Tarrytown and Mental Reserve, where they see it right to sanction and perpetuate a slaveholding government for this presidential term and the next, or at least until their good company and oath of support shall have abolished the Constitutional guarantees?" According to Chapman, all these parties hated slavery and might find a "common center of attraction" at the fair, although one wonders how such a tone could have swayed anyone not predisposed to accept the claim at face value and how much this effort owed to self-justification.[60]

Whether or not all "parties who hated slavery" participated in the fair, significantly more men certainly did by the mid-1840s. As I noted earlier, the Boston fair had become an event in which men and women interacted, an innovation resisted by evangelical and political suasionists whose rhetoric underplayed women's public agency and reinforced the trope of woman's separate sphere. But moral suasionists, working as agents and lobbyists for the cause and serving on business and executive committees of regional and national associations, were faced with the problem of consistency. These women had insisted on a single standard of moral behavior. In ad-

58. Maria W. Chapman to Henry C. Wright, September 12, 1843; Draft of letter from Maria W. Chapman to J. S. Gibbons, May 25, 1843; Caroline Weston to Maria W. Chapman, [May 1839], Weston Papers.

59. For examples of female societies and individual women who accepted her message and agreed to support the bazaar, see Paulina Gerry to Maria W. Chapman, July 6, 1839; Mary P. Henry to Maria W. Chapman, November 30, 1841; Mary F. Gilbert to Maria W. Chapman, December 23, 1844; Elvira E. Kimball to Maria W. Chapman, August 2, 1843; L. Gates to Maria W. Chapman, December 3, 1845, Weston Papers.

60. *Liberator,* January 23, 1846.

hering to this position, they faced the possibility that men, too, might serve the fair in new ways, perhaps by donating goods for use, sale, or decoration; assisting in hall setup and cleanup; or helping to package and distribute reports of the fair and copies of *The Liberty Bell.*

Men had long been encouraged to purchase goods and join in the social and educational events of the fair.[61] In 1840, the fair call suggested that men wait to make major household purchases so that they might order from antislavery craftsmen. Order books were opened in the antislavery offices to match buyers with suppliers. By the mid-forties, men became contributors to the fair, with the addition of a country produce table selling farm goods "at the highest market prices" and manufacturers' donations "of pieces of white yard-wide factory cotton to cover the tables."[62] As Suzanne Lebsock has noted of men's gradual encroachment on female organizations, charitable institutions, and benevolent associations in Peterburg, Virginia, so too Boston's men sought to improve upon the female antislavery fair.[63] Samuel May trumpeted the call:

> If every abolitionist, every friend of the slave, and of his immediate elevation to the dignity and rights of a man, should feel it an imperative and indispensable duty to furnish a contribution to the Fair himself, and make it part of his (or her) anti-slavery duty to solicit contributions from every neighbor and friend who sympathizes with the sorrows and feels for the wrongs of the slave, the articles of the Fair would be vastly increased in extent, number, and variety.[64]

Samuel Dyer, of South Abington, recognized an opportunity to imprint a more "vigorous and systematic course" upon the fair. He advocated appointing "a committee of the most energetic abolitionists in each of the towns where any aid could be expected, to solicit donations of money, manufactured articles, farm produce, &c." Although he believed this committee might "endeavor to form sewing circles, and if possible enlist the sympathy of woman more fully in the cause," it was principally the men—manufacturers and farmers—whose involvement he sought.

Fund-raising, he argued, was a man's job; men had the experience, the contacts, and the economic resources to expand the enterprise. "Manufacturers of boots, shoes, carpet-tacks, hats, caps, cabinet wares, tin wares,

61. For specific invitations, see *Liberator,* December 22, 1843; December 20, 1844.
62. *Liberator,* March 13, 1840; November 21, 1845.
63. Lebsock, *Free Women,* pp. 225–30.
64. *Liberator,* October 5, 1849.

wooden wares, &c &c., might be induced to give some highly finished article of their manufacture, if for no other purpose than to show their skill or advertise their goods," said Dyer. Contributions need not come solely from abolitionists to support the cause; savvy tradesmen might offer goods for commercial reasons. Dyer thought men could improve upon women's organization of the fair by formalizing its regional operations: "Secretaries of County Societies" should recommend individuals to represent the fair in their locales, and these should be appointed "from the proper source" in order to lend formal authority to their actions.[65] After all, women were not generally appreciated for their business acumen in commercial and manufacturing circles. Charitable women avoided precision in revealing the nature of their funding and their ability to distribute their resources and services. Dyer's was a bold effort to wed the fair directly to male economic and professional networks.[66]

The endeavor did not succeed; the women retained their hold on the Boston fair and its business. Just as they had resisted Dyer's efforts to restructure fair organization, they blocked Samuel May's attempts to determine the timing of fair announcements and otherwise to influence the decision-making process.[67] They did, however, find it pragmatic to turn over production of *The Liberty Bell* to Edmund Quincy and to accept other forms of male assistance.[68] They addressed men specifically as co-workers

65. *Liberator,* October 26, 1849.
66. This would have been a dramatic change. As Hewitt has shown, benevolent women utilized their husbands' commercial ties and resources to support their charitable work. Yet, according to Ginzberg, the ideology of benevolence required that it function at a distance from crass commercialization and that women's agency in "the business of benevolence" be hidden (Ginzberg, *Benevolence,* p. 53). Dyer attributed no value to women's mediation and believed that the business of antislavery was more efficiently managed by men.
67. See his assertion that the fair was "my *business*" and his assertion that Anne W. Weston did not seek his aid sufficiently often in carrying out the fair, "i.e. you do not give me my share." Samuel May, Jr., to Anne W. Weston, November 25, 1848; April 12, 1850, Weston Papers.
68. These accommodations resulted in part from the absence of Maria W. Chapman. She left Boston for Paris in 1848 and did not return until 1855, although her correspondence demonstrates an ongoing involvement with even minor details of the fair. Anne W. Weston took on the role of fair organizer. Anne was neither as energetic nor as efficient as Maria. Nor was she as authoritative an executive. She turned over the *Liberty Bell* to Edmund Quincy in 1850, a year during which several other female fair organizers abandoned the enterprise for European travel or gave up their Boston townhomes, thus limiting the geographical base needed for efficient fair management. See Anne W. Weston to Samuel May [n.d., Ms. B.1.6.13.1], May Papers; Anne W. Weston to Caroline Weston, January 1, 1849, Weston Papers; Anne W. Weston to John B. Estlin, September 27, 1850, Estlin Papers. For other comments on male fair workers, see Anne W. Weston to Maria W. Chapman, April 2, 1849, Weston Papers; and Anne W. Weston to John B. Estlin, February 9, 1851, Estlin Papers.

in the enterprise. "Gentlemen friendly to our object" were urged to contribute Lowell cotton, blank cards, notepaper, envelopes, and other goods needed for the smooth operation of the fair, for donated goods cut expenses and raised profits. The fair's managers made clear, however, that their vision of the fair's purpose would remain. "For our own parts, it is to a companionship of toil and renunciation that we feel morally obliged to invite *men*." Moral suasionist antislavery women hoped that men would come to feel those "increased capacities of heart and mind which the incidents and efforts of the Fairs have given us."[69] Men, like women, might develop that empathy that reinforced the bond between abolitionist and slave—the change of heart that begat changes of consciousness and behavior.

Abolitionist men were not alone in challenging the fair's organizers in the late forties. The rise of the Liberty and Free Soil parties added new contributors, purchasers, and participants.[70] The managers faced a new problem: customers and fair volunteers who, by family ties and the social respectability of the cause, were drawn to assist the fair but were not particularly informed about slavery or committed to moral suasion. At the 1849 fair, for example, a Mrs. Taft brought her sister Ellen to help sell. As Anne Warren Weston explained, "One day two slave holders came in & she fell into great intimacy with them, & told them she was nothing of an Abolitionist & talked all sorts of pro slavery. This made a great talk, & I finally went to Mrs Taft & told her I did not wish her sister there as a sales woman, we could have none but Abolitionists. Mrs Taft fell to crying . . . and said they should all feel greatly mortified at her being sent off & promised that she should be silent."[71] This was not an isolated incident, as Abby Kelley testified when finding an unexpected change in the demeanor and attitude of saleswomen:

> I was surprised at your statement that not more than a half dozen, at most, could be found . . . at the tables—who . . . were there earnestly devoting themselves to raising funds by doing as they would if they were laboring merely for their own selfish purposes. But in passing around the hall from time to time, and observing the entire inattention which prevailed on all hands, and the little care to interest and accommodate purchasers and to induce them to purchase convinced

69. *Liberator*, December 5, 1856; January 25, 1856; and January 24, 1845.

70. See Caroline Weston to Rev. Samuel May, December 2, 1848, May Papers; Anne W. Weston to Maria W. Chapman, August 22, 1848, Weston Papers; and G. R. Russel to Anne W. Weston, September 29, 1848, Antislavery Papers.

71. Anne W. Weston to Caroline Weston, December 28, 1849, Weston Papers.

me that your statement was but too true, and that, had any merchant in Washington street so inefficient a set of salesmen he would forthwith expergate his establishment of the whole of them.[72]

The more successful the fair in attracting a wide audience, the more diverse it became and the more profoundly this diversity influenced its culture.

And the fair was increasingly successful. Harriet Beecher Stowe described the Boston bazaar as "decidedly the most fashionable shopping resort of the holidays."[73] Customers so looked to the fair as the source of unusual goods that, in 1849, they protested the delayed arrival of the Parisian boxes. "Lots of people, particularly rich people, kept back their money, saying they hoped the things would arrive." A separate "French Fair" was held to accommodate these "wealthy whigs" once the steamship docked.[74] "It was becoming a thing of course that the abolitionists should furnish the pro-slavery [jumble] with pretty new-years presents, & be snubbed civilly when they were not pretty enough," wrote Chapman, parodying the attitude of such customers: "Because it is a present for cousin Jenny—& she had been abroad—these people that go abroad come home so particular—& with such good taste!—& I am *afraid* there is not any thing *quite recherche* enough; & *perhaps* you will have prettier things next year—indeed I do *hope* you will exert yourselves, for I should have liked to buy here,—the fair has *such* a reputation!—Good morning."[75] Such patrons, being but casually invested in abolition, wanted bargains and expected prices below those of retail shops in the city. Indeed, Boston's "fancy goods dealers" opposed the rental of Faneuil Hall to the bazaar on the grounds that the fair "undersold them and injured their business." There were fears of a shopkeepers' protest.[76]

Trying to uphold fund-raising over bargain-seeking, the fair managers increasingly displayed their adoption of market values. Chapman, a shrewd business woman, sent from Paris crochet bags that she had purchased for twenty dollars with instructions to sell them for one hundred.[77] Other managers tried to impose fiscal accountability upon their salesforce: "Mrs May fought every step about the marking [of prices on goods]. She

72. Abby Kelley to Anne W. Weston, November 27, 1849, Weston Papers.

73. *Report of the Twenty-first National Anti-Slavery Bazaar* (Boston, 1855), p. 32.

74. Anne W. Weston to Deborah Weston, January 28, 1849, Weston Papers; Sarah May to Anne W. Weston, January 24, 1849, Antislavery Papers.

75. Maria W. Chapman to Elizabeth Pease Nichol, September 20, 1858, Garrison Papers.

76. Anne W. Weston to Caroline Weston, November 12, 1848, Weston Papers.

77. Maria W. Chapman to Anne W. Weston et al., November 14, 1848, Weston Papers.

struggled to give away every thing & *would* privately catch up a thing & mark it without saying a word. We resisted & struggled & Mrs Loring did very well, but it is hard to fight over every article." For example, a black satin apron "worth $6," was first marked at two dollars by an inept helper, then hurriedly raised to four by a frazzled and somewhat insecure fair manager, Sarah Shaw Russell. When Marion Shaw snapped it up as "the greatest bargain she ever saw," her sister belatedly wished she had charged more.[78] Poor weather for the fair, economic downturns, and competition for European goods by other charity bazaars and antislavery fairs sparked managers' fears.[79] Anxious to take advantage of their new social and political élan, they focused on profit taking in the 1850s, finding in commercial success its own reward. Each fair sought to set new records in numbers, quality, and innovativeness of goods; in visitors attracted; and in money made.[80] Market values threatened to eclipse moral ones when a raffle was introduced, to the horror of many who saw it as gambling.[81]

Returning to America, Chapman feared that in the conflict between raising funds and converting people, moral influence had been sacrificed to crass profiteering. Once the fair had caused women to identify with the slave as they crafted sales goods and invented mottoes; now few women even bothered to make their own contributions because the best-selling items were the fancy foreign or factory-made goods and wholesale farm

78. Anne W. Weston to Caroline Weston, January 1, 1849, Weston Papers.

79. See fair reports in the *Liberator*, January 14, 1849, and January 17, 1851. Added to these concerns was the fear of declining support from abroad as some European contributors expressed their dismay at Garrison's unorthodox religious opinions. Some sent their contributions to Frederick Douglass and the Rochester fair. Chapman maintained that this threatened the national antislavery society treasury, but many loyal contributors to the Boston fair argued that "simultaneous efforts to help both sections of Abolitionism [were not] subversive of one another." See Maria Webb to Maria W. Chapman, December 2, 1847; Joseph Lupton to Maria W. Chapman, September 21, 1848; Isabell Jennings to Anne W. Weston, November 1848, Weston Papers; Elizabeth Pease to Anne W. Weston, November 7, 1848, Antislavery Papers; Isabel Jennings to Anne W. Weston, November 29, 1849, Weston Papers.

80. See published fair reports for such details and their increasing emphasis. The competition was seen even in the local fairs around Boston. From Millville, for example, came a request for "finer articles than previously" to be donated to their fair so that they might compete with the antislavery fair in Worcester (Deborah Weston to Caroline Weston, February 17, 1850, Weston Papers).

81. Abby Kelley refused to append her name to the fair call in 1851 because she disapproved of raffles (Abby Kelley Foster to Anne W. Weston, June 15, [1850], Weston Papers). An unknown correspondent from Spring Garden, Ohio, wrote to the fair managers: "It *is* gambling the best we can make of it and it seems to me the high toned principle which characterizes the Old Society ought to shun *all sin*" (n.n. to Anne W. Weston, July 28, 1850, Weston Papers).

produce.[82] Furthermore, the fair was so time-consuming that it was "about to take the place of the cause itself."[83] Chapman decided to do away with the fair entirely and to replace it with a monetary subscription.[84]

For public consumption, the change was justified in terms of the greater popularity of abolition:

> At the beginning, before the principles of the Cause were understood, we could not, with the slightest hope of success, ask of the public . . . direct contributions of money. We, therefore, devised an Annual Bazaar for the sale of contributions of articles, and it afforded an opportunity of great usefulness, both financial and social, to the Cause. But the changed state of the public mind now suggests greater directness in the method . . . and we propose, this year, to give our usual sums and take up our accustomed collections by direct cash subscription.[85]

In private, however, the argument was somewhat different. Chapman believed that Americans should give from their purses with no reward or recompense other than their own sense of righteousness.[86] She sought "to excite a revival" through the means of a subscription that would force peo-

82. The transformation can be traced in the fair correspondence, where advice was given as to what sold well and what should, therefore, be contributed the following year, and in the fair reports where table-by-table descriptions of best sellers were sometimes provided. See, for example, Anne W. Weston to Mary A. Estlin, January 14, 1851, Estlin Papers; and the fair report published in the *Liberator* of January 25, 1850.

83. Maria W. Chapman to Elizabeth Pease Nichol, September 20, 1858, Garrison Papers.

84. Subscriptions were not new in the history of American benevolence or in the antislavery movement. The Society for the Relief of Widows and Children, one of the first female relief associations in the United States, was founded in New York City in 1797 and raised funds through male contributions and female annual subscriptions of $3. In the first year alone, they enrolled two hundred annual subscribers and collected over $1,000 in donations. See Kathleen D. McCarthy, "Parallel Power Structures: Women and the Voluntary Sphere," in McCarthy, ed., *Lady Bountiful Revisited: Women, Philanthropy, and Power* (New Brunswick, 1990), pp. 2–3. Among abolitionists, subscriptions had long supported the publication and distribution of antislavery newspapers and various agencies. Annual and life subscriptions sustained the early antislavery societies and constituted their chief financial resource. See Lucia Weston to Deborah Weston, 1834, and Caroline Weston to Mrs. L. R. D. Hammatt, August 1, 1835, in the Weston Papers; and *Right and Wrong in Boston: Report of the Boston Female Anti-Slavery Society . . . 1835* (Boston, 1836), pp. 77–78. Donations of cash by both men and women had regularly contributed to the success of the fair and were acknowledged in the fair reports. To this point, however, there had been no ceremonial or celebratory collecting of subscriptions.

85. *Liberator,* July 2, 1858.

86. Partial letter from Maria W. Chapman to an unidentified European correspondent early in 1858, Estlin Papers.

ple to examine their complacency and assume individual responsibility for the movement and its finances.[87] The subscription was intended to renew the synchronism between means and ends with which the fair had begun. The managers of the Boston fair had seen the politics of moral suasion erode as their successful outreach yielded such large numbers of participants as to swamp all efforts to convert them. In a sense, the popular and commercial success of the fair contributed to the ideological defeat of its organizers, for in addressing these challenges, the fair's managers radically altered the political culture of the Boston fair by transforming its gender symbology in such a way as to align with more conservative views of women's social role.

Mary Ryan has suggested that women at midcentury changed the public calendar to reflect their own values and celebrate events which held meaning for them.[88] In Boston, in 1858, the moral suasionist women of the abolitionist movement created a new "festival" with their "anniversary" salon.[89] Individuals were invited to pledge a cash amount and come to Boston "to receive our subscriptions, our good wishes, and our thanks, and to unite with us on the occasion." The salon located the source of women's authority in her private role and moral character. "One great object of the change from sale to subscription is to ensure the broadest possible home cooperation," wrote the subscription managers. Although intended to contrast American with foreign contributors, the use of the word "home" resonated with multiple connotations. The subscription was to be a family celebration, and its managers "therefore determined to engage the spacious and splendid Music Hall, to transform it into a succession of drawing-rooms ... where, surrounded by their families, they might welcome their co-workers and sympathizing friends ... for conversation and counsel—for cheer, hope and remembrance—for suggestion, enterprise and resolve—for union of means and of heart in the interests of the holiest and loftiest cause that ever saved and glorified a nation."[90] So private was this event in the

87. Maria W. Chapman to Mary A. Estlin, March 8, 1858, Estlin Papers; and Maria W. Chapman to Elizabeth Pease Nichol, September 20, 1858, Weston Papers.

88. Ryan, *Women in Public,* pp. 49–51.

89. There was some disagreement over naming this occasion. The British objected to the term "festival" as being too frivolous. Some Americans disliked "subscription" because it suggested too directly the solicitation of funds. It was therefore called an "anniversary" (Maria W. Chapman to Mary A. Estlin, July 4, 1858, Estlin Papers). Catherine Clinton has suggested that the subscription salon took its inspiration from the salons of literary and political Paris from which Chapman was but recently returned (Catherine Clinton, "Maria Weston Chapman," in Clinton and G. J. Barker-Benfield, eds., *Portraits of American Women from Settlement to the Civil War* [New York, 1991], p. 157).

90. *Liberator,* February 18, 1859.

managers' construction that the conversations to be held there, "conversations . . . of surpassing interest, covering the whole ground of the Cause in all its history, purposes, collateral bearings and tendencies," did not, in their eyes, permit reproduction in the 1860 Fair Report. Instead, subscribers were invited to read a suitably oblique version of the exchanges in the columns of the *National Anti-Slavery Standard*.[91]

In staging the anniversary as a domestic affair, Chapman obscured the essentially commercial transactions with decorum as well as decor. Discreetly passed envelopes of money or pledges replaced the barter and sale of goods. Female salesclerks were transformed into "ladies of influence" whose womanly example, private morality, and social standing were expected to draw the unconverted to the light. Said Chapman:

> One of our advantages is, that, if there be here properly any such thing as social rank & respectability . . . the Boston abolitionists are that thing;—some by wealth, as America counts riches,—some by various antecedents,—some by high intellectual gifts—*all* by the more than ordinary moral worth which is the cause of their *being* the abolitionist . . . Now we have never thought enough of this real advantage to make the use of it. We can now do.[92]

Distinctions mattered to Chapman. As a radical abolitionist she had experienced neither the social respectability of more conservative charitable women nor the attendant access to political power.[93] Now, with abolition no longer a marginal political position, she inverted the old hierarchy of respectability while laying claim to all its benefits—not unlike the New Testament promise that "the last shall be first." She wrapped herself and her supporters in a cloak of superiority wrought of their moral authority as women, their longevity in the movement, and their sacrifices for the cause. Perhaps moral stature had become as much a concern as moral suasion, and restitution as important as conversion.

The subscription salon enabled Chapman to engage in a bit of one-upmanship with political suasionists who had accused her of unladylike behavior over the past years. She offered as public tableau a domestic parlor inhabited by demure, feminine, and "noble" ladies.[94] The "woman ques-

---

91. *Liberator,* February 10, 1860.
92. Maria W. Chapman to Mary A. Estlin, March 8, 1858, Estlin Papers.
93. Ginzberg, *Benevolence,* pp. 63–65.
94. See Ginzberg's discussion of how various groups of benevolent women sought "to claim and conflate the terms of morality and of femininity as their own" and in so doing to legitimate or undercut other women's activities and set boundaries on their behavior (Ginzberg, *Benevolence,* p. 34).

tion," which had so rent the abolitionist movement, was put to rest in the subscription salon. The anniversary gathering privatized a public space and made a public, political event into an appropriate occasion for ladies to gather. The salon subordinated men, who had so recently threatened to take over fund-raising for the movement, casting them as supplicants for female favor in a setting not their own. The subscription managers reasserted female authority by embedding constructs of gender influence in the structure and form of the event itself. The subscription salon identified the appropriate role of women as being consistent with the doctrine of separate spheres, rooted in the diverse characters of men and women and in woman's special nature—all beliefs which the managers of the Boston fair, especially Chapman, had finessed to one degree or another. The political culture of the subscription salon conformed more closely to the values of political suasionists than had Boston's fair culture.

With the anniversary subscription, Chapman sought to realign the ends and means of consciousness-raising and fund-raising that had characterized early fair work. However, by embodying the "ideology of female benevolence" in a private salon, the subscription focused attention upon categories of sexual difference. Actual ideological and strategic differences among abolitionist women were subsumed in the symbolic differences between men and women—a pattern that would dominate women's politics after midcentury.[95]

Indeed, it is difficult to assess Chapman's effort to reignite the fires of individual conscience. The subscription was a financial success—those of 1859 and 1860 each raised some six thousand dollars—but its impact upon the participants is more difficult to measure.[96] Such a sedate and muted exercise would seem to offer little to spark women's political consciousness or to enlighten their education. Within five years, the American Anti-Slavery Society disbanded. Some moral suasionist antislavery women pursued the broader goals of transforming the racial and sexual structures of American society through the American Equal Rights Association.[97]

95. Ryan, *Women in Public;* Paula Baker, "The Domestication of Politics: Women and American Political Society, 1780–1920," *American Historical Review* 89 (1984): 620–47; Nancy F. Cott, *The Grounding of Modern Feminism* (New Haven, 1987).

96. The *Liberator* reported that "home friends" committed $3,059.54 and the foreign friends $3,057.48 in 1859. Donations the following year totalled approximately the same amount (*Liberator,* February 18, 1859; February 10, 1860).

97. Later still, having converted to political suasion, several managers of the Boston fair would join and serve as officers in the New England Woman's Suffrage Association, including Sarah S. Russell, Armenia S. White, Lydia Maria Child, Mary E. Sargent, and Sarah H. Southwick.

Chapman, however, retained her faith in moral transformation as the way to change society, refusing to bow to the growing popularity of electoral politics. She retired, "used up in the means."[98] One wonders if she and her circle were not caught by the contradictions of their new view of female influence. The subscription salon, with its explicit symbolism of female moral superiority rooted in woman's character and tied to the private sphere, helped to immobilize women who had previously emphasized the similarities of male and female character and the independent role of women in the movement.

98. A phrase that Chapman used to describe the change from fair to subscription, commenting that the subscription allowed the managers to have sufficient energy left to use the money raised through their efforts (Maria W. Chapman to Richard D. Webb, January 4, 1859, Estlin Papers).

{ 14 }

By Moral Force Alone
The Antislavery Women and Nonresistance

Margaret Hope Bacon

The women who participated in the antislavery conventions of 1837–1839 are justly credited with forging the link between the abolition of slavery and the advocacy of woman's rights which was to blossom in the Seneca Falls Convention of 1848, but they also developed an equally important connection: that of the women's movement with the use of nonresistance—or nonviolence, as it is called today. Although the role of nonresistance in the antebellum struggle against slavery has been well documented, the parallel link between nonresistance and the women's rights movement has been largely ignored in the developing literature on nonviolence. This is an unfortunate omission. Most of the abolitionists gave up nonresistance at the time of the Civil War—what Staughton Lynd describes as "the most striking failure of nonviolence in American history to date"—but the women preserved it in their struggle for suffrage and equal rights in the post–Civil War years and into the twentieth century.[1]

The same faith in practical or applied Christianity which animated the early abolitionists to oppose slavery led them to believe that their fight for justice must rely solely on the weapons of truth and love. Taking literally the injunction of Jesus to resist not evil but turn the other cheek, the reformers called themselves "non-resisters." They did not, however, intend to take a pacific stance but to use the sword of the spirit in an aggressive war

---

1. Carleton Mabee, *Black Freedom: The Nonviolent Abolitionists from 1830 through the Civil War* (New York, 1970); Staughton Lynd, *Nonviolence in America: A Documentary History* (New York, 1966), p. xviii.

against slavery, which they hoped to wage by pointing out the sin of the peculiar institution and its adverse effects on the lives of all people and by calling the nation to repentance and renunciation.

William Lloyd Garrison, the young editor of the *Liberator*, evolved his philosophy of nonresistance in part from his contact with Quakers such as Benjamin Lundy and Lucretia and James Mott as well as from his knowledge of Quaker history. But he went much further than most Quakers of his day, carrying the concept of nonresistance to its ultimate conclusions, which included distrust of a government that enforced slavery by the bayonet.

At the American Anti-Slavery Society Convention, held in Philadelphia on December 4, 1833, Garrison spelled out his views in the declaration. Comparing the war the nonresisters were to wage with that of their revolutionary forefathers, he said:

> *Their* principles led them to wage war against the oppressors, and spill human blood like water, in order to be free. *Ours* forbid the doing of evil that good may come, and lead us to reject, and entreat the oppressed to reject, the use of all carnal weapons for deliverance from bondage; relying solely upon those which are spiritual, and mighty through God to the pulling down of strong holds.
>
> Their measures were physical resistance, the marshalling in arms— the hostile army—the mortal encounter. Ours shall be such only as the opposition of moral purity to moral corruption, the destruction of error by the potency of truth, the overthrow of prejudice by the power of love, and the abolition of slavery by the spirit of repentance.[2]

Closely allied with the concept of nonresistance was the refusal to use the products of slave labor, the cotton goods and sugar and rice and dyes raised by slaves. The Free Produce movement, as it was called, began in the eighteenth century when a few Quakers who opposed slavery, most notably John Woolman (1720–1772), began to refuse to wear cotton or dyed garments. Woolman, a traveling Quaker minister, visited slaveowning Quakers in the South to persuade them to give up their slaves. Whenever he visited a household where slaves were used as servants, he preferred to sleep outside on the ground or to pay for his lodging, much to the discomfiture of his host. His refusal to benefit from slave labor or slave products was based not so much on the idea of exerting economic pressure on his opponent (as

2. *Declaration of the Anti-Slavery Convention Assembled at Philadelphia December 4, 1833* [Philadelphia, 1833].

in the modern concept of a nonviolent boycott) as it was on his desire to remain himself clear and free of complicity in slavery. He wrote of this necessity frequently in his journal: "And the oppression of the slaves which I had seen in several journeys southward on this continent and the report of their treatment in the West Indies hath deeply affected me, and a care to live in the spirit of peace and minister just cause of offense to none of my fellow creatures hath from time to time livingly revived on my mind, and under this exercise I for some years past declined to gratify my palate with those sugars."[3]

Woolman was not the only preacher to travel among slaveowners. Several other Quaker ministers made similar trips, including two prominent women: Sarah Harrison (1736–1812) and Patience Brayton (1733–1794). Both of these women sought to convert slaveowners, and both refused to benefit from slave labor while traveling in the South.[4]

At first, the refusal to use slave products was considered a matter of individual conscience, but in the early 1800s several Quaker ministers began to urge the Society of Friends as a whole to adopt a boycott of slave-grown produce. The first person to speak on this subject in Philadelphia Yearly Women's Meeting was Alice Jackson Lewis of Chester County, Pennsylvania, a feminist abolitionist who in 1806 urged her sisters to use their buying power to discourage the institution of slavery. Soon others joined the campaign to enlist other yearly meetings and eventually other churches in the cause.[5]

An influential Quaker advocate of free produce in this early period was Elias Hicks (1748–1830), also a traveling Quaker minister, whose personal refusal to use slave products had a profound influence on the young Lucretia Coffin when she was a student at Nine Partners school and on her future husband, James Mott, then a teacher. Hicks argued that slavery was principally supported by the purchasers and consumers of the produce of slave labor. To the objection that each person's share in slave produce was too minute to matter, he replied that "though the numbers partaking of a crime may diminish the shame, they cannot diminish the turpitude."[6]

3. John Woolman, *The Journal and Major Essays of John Woolman*, ed. Phillips P. Moulton (New York, 1971), p. 157.

4. *A Short Account of the Life and Religious Labors of Patience Brayton, Late of Swansey, in the State of Massachusetts, Mostly Selected from Her Own Minutes* (New York, 1802), p. 26; "Memoirs of the Life and Travels of Sarah Harrison," in *Friends Miscellany* (Philadelphia, 1843), pp. 97–117.

5. Ruth Nuremberger, *The Free Produce Movement* (Durham, N.C., 1942), p. 6.

6. Elias Hicks, *Letters of Elias Hicks; Including Also Observations on the Slavery of the Africans and Their Descendants, and on the Use of the Produce of Their Labor* (Philadelphia, 1861), pp. 8–20.

In addition to denouncing slavery, Hicks preached his own personal brand of Quakerism which put more emphasis on the "Inner Light" than on the historical Jesus. This focus was upsetting to portions of American Quakerism, which was undergoing an evangelical revival, and led to a schism in Philadelphia Yearly Meeting in 1827. The split later spread throughout Quakerdom, creating Hicksite and Orthodox branches. Most Quakers of both branches preferred to work against slavery within small Quaker antislavery societies, but those few radicals who joined the larger antislavery movement were mostly Hicksite. Along with others, they continued the tradition against the use of slave produce.[7]

By the 1820s there were enough Quaker abolitionists and their friends who wanted to avoid slave products to support—often precariously—a number of free produce stores. Women played a decisive role in this movement. James Mott, with the strong encouragement of his wife, Lucretia Mott, ran such a store for a short time in Philadelphia in 1829, when he switched from being a cotton merchant to a wool merchant in order to be free of slave products. Lydia White and Sydney Ann Lewis, both members of the Philadelphia Female Anti-Slavery Society, also ran free produce stores. Sydney Anne Lewis's store was short-lived, but Lydia White's store lasted a record sixteen years. Altogether fifty-three such stores existed between 1817 and 1862, of which at least five were run by women. Most were in Philadelphia, but there were stores also in Boston, Wilmington, and New York City, as well as scattered in New Jersey, Pennsylvania, Massachusetts, Indiana, Ohio, Iowa, and Maine.[8]

Keeping these free produce stores supplied with cotton, sugar, coffee, and rice not raised by slaves required considerable effort and cooperation and gave rise to the development of free produce societies, which also served as centers for public outreach.

A free produce society was formed in Wilmington, Delaware, in 1826 and another in Philadelphia a few months later. A Female Association for Promoting the Manufacture and Use of Free Cotton, formed in Philadelphia in January of 1829, bought cotton which was manufactured into checked fabric for aprons and into bedticking. The association continued to buy bales of raw cotton well into 1833, when its functions were taken over by other

7. Larry Ingle, *Quakers in Conflict: The Hicksite Reformation* (Knoxville, Tenn., 1986). Many Orthodox male Friends were active in the Pennsylvania Abolition Society, founded in 1775, which was considerably less radical than the Garrisonian movement. Of the members of the Philadelphia Female Anti-Slavery Society 61 percent were Hicksite, according to Jean Soderlund's essay, Chapter 4, in the present volume.

8. Nuremberger, *The Free Produce Movement*, p. 119.

such organizations, and many of its members joined PFASS, a strong advocate of free produce.[9]

For a brief time in Philadelphia there was also a Colored Female Produce Society. Elsewhere, women organized local societies, such as the Free Produce Association of Green Plain, in Clark County, Ohio. Many were spurred on by the poetry of Margaret Chandler (1807–1834), who wrote on antislavery and free produce themes in the *Genius of Universal Emancipation*.[10]

At the height of the movement there were altogether twenty-six free produce societies in various parts of the country. In 1838, at the time of the second annual Anti-Slavery Convention of American Women, held in Philadelphia, a Requited Labor Convention met and established the American Free Produce Association, which became the principal buyer of these products. Lucretia Mott became treasurer of this new group, and five women were named to the executive committee. Lydia White served as the retail agent for some years.[11]

The free produce associations bought cotton from non-slaveowning farmers in the South, principally North Carolina, and had it made up into bolts of cloth for retail sale. They also hunted for sugar that was not slave grown, finding suppliers in Puerto Rico and the British West Indies who were opposed to slavery, or buying sugar from Mexico, Java, Manila, and even China. There was never enough sugar to meet the demand, and maple sugar proved a poor substitute. Various abolitionists attempted to make sugar from potatoes or corn. David Child, husband of the writer and abolitionist Lydia Maria Child, devoted himself to a heartbreaking series of experiments in making sugar out of beets.

Because the products were of inferior quality, members constantly had to urge each other to use free produce. The free produce "sweets" were unappealing to Lucretia Mott's grandchildren; the cotton goods were more expensive and of poorer quality. As a result, the supporters of the movement used every occasion to urge each other to stay in line.

At the 1837 Anti-Slavery Convention of American Women, Lucretia Mott introduced the following resolution:

> That the support of the iniquitous system of slavery at the South is dependent on the co-operation of the North, by commerce and manufactures, as well as by the consumption of its products—therefore that, despising the gain of oppression we recommend to our friends, by a

9. Ibid., pp. 16–17.
10. Ibid., pp. 19, 112.
11. Ibid., pp. 25, 81.

candid and prayerful examination of the subject, to ascertain if it be not a duty to cleanse our hands from this unrighteous participation, by no longer indulging in the luxuries which come through this polluted channel; and in the supply of the necessary articles of food and clothing, &c., that we "provide things honest in the sight of all men," by giving preference to goods which come through requited labor.[12]

The 1837 convention issued as a pamphlet *An Appeal to the Women of the Nominally Free States.* Drafted by Angelina Grimké, it received its final shape from a committee of Lucretia Mott, Lydia Maria Child, Abby Kelley, and Grace Douglass, all advocates of free produce. This pamphlet likened the situation of the abolitionists to that of the mothers and fathers of the American Revolution, who determined to boycott British products until the Stamp Act was repealed. "In a little time, large quantities of common cloths were brought to market, and these, though dearer and of a worse quality, were cheerfully preferred to similar articles from Britain."[13]

At the decisive 1838 Anti-Slavery Convention of American Women held in Philadelphia in May, Thankful Southwick, a Quaker and member of the Boston Female Anti-Slavery Society, introduced a resolution on the use of free produce: "Resolved, That it is the duty of all who call themselves abolitionists to make the *most vigorous efforts* to procure for the use of their families the products of *free labor* so that their hands may be clean, in this particular, when inquisition is made for blood."[14]

Again, at the 1839 convention of the same group held May 1–3 in Philadelphia at the Riding Hall, the women agreed on a resolution presented by Martha V. Ball of Boston: "*Whereas,* The consumers of the produce of slave labor, are offering the strongest incentive to the slaveholder to continue his system of oppression, therefore, *Resolved,* That this Convention recommend to abolitionists to abstain from the use of such products, that we may not be guilty of participation in the sin which we condemn, and that, to the power of solemn precepts, we may add that of a pure example."[15] Lucretia Mott and others supported the resolution. It was pointed out that if women were to regard slave produce as the fruits of the labor of their own

12. *Proceedings of the Anti-Slavery Convention of American Women . . . 1837* (New York, 1837), p. 13.

13. Ibid., p. 28.

14. *Proceedings of the Anti-Slavery Convention of American Women . . . 1838* (Philadelphia, 1838), p. 7.

15. *Proceedings of the Third Anti-Slavery Convention of American Women . . . 1839* (Philadelphia, 1839), p. 7.

children they would be less likely to use it. On a more practical level, activists noted that free produce had become more readily available.[16]

Not all the nonresisters supported free produce. Garrison came to believe that it was almost impossible to identify all slave-grown produce, and Abby Kelley concluded that the conditions under which the workers in England and Ireland made cotton yard goods were almost as bad as slavery itself. Nor did all the free produce advocates go along with Garrisonian nonresistance. From 1840 on, the free produce movement became closely associated with the Society of Friends, many of whose members were critical of what they regarded as Garrisonian extremes.[17]

Most of the women who attended the three conventions, however, were enthusiastic supporters not only of the free produce movement but of the whole Garrisonian concept of nonresistance. A strong and lifelong advocate of nonresistance, Abby Kelley, wrote to Maria Chapman in 1837 about her feelings for peace:

> The subject of Peace has of late claimed much of my attention on account of the present aspect of the Abolition-cause getting into the hands of politicians—Will they not prosecute it by the sword, unless peace principles are instilled in the heart of this nation? I know not thy sentiments on this subject, but presume they are in unison with mine—Is Slavery the greatest sin of this nation? Is not something more required of us than what we are now doing?—Please give my love to thy sisters, and ask them if they will write me on the subject alluded to. I would have no one abandon the Anti-slavery enterprise— I would only have them engage in another enterprise, which would establish abolition on an immutable basis . . . Are not some of *you,* who have passed unscathed through *one* furnace ready to enter *another* seven times hotter?[18]

Lydia Maria Child was also at first an advocate of nonresistance, although she sometimes questioned whether it should be demanded of the slave. Writing in the *Liberator* in 1836, she stated that anyone who was not a nonresister, any one who supported defensive war, should agree that the slave had a right to resist: "It has long appeared to me that bloodshed and vio-

16. Ibid.

17. Aileen Kraditor, *Means and Ends in American Abolitionism* (New York, 1967), pp. 218–19; Nuremberger, *Free Produce Movement,* p. 30.

18. Abby Kelley to Maria Chapman, December 19, 1837, Antislavery Papers, Antislavery Collection, Boston Public Library.

lence in *any* case are in direct opposition to the spirit of the Gospel, but if resistance were *ever* justifiable, it would be so in the case of the bereaved and persecuted *slave*. Nothing but a unrighteous prejudice against his color could prevent a consistent vindicator even of defensive war from coming to this conclusion."[19]

The commitment to nonresistance was not, however, wholly academic. One by one, the women began to experience the efficacy of nonresistant means in dealing with hostile mobs, increasing their faith in nonviolent resistance. The first serious experience came in the fall of 1835 when BFASS, then about three years old, attempted to hold its regular annual meeting with George Thompson, the British abolitionist, as a speaker. Sentiment against Thompson was already running high in Boston, and local newspapers printed editorials condemning him and the meeting. Throughout the city handbills were distributed offering a purse of one hundred dollars to "reward the individual who first lays violent hands on Thompson."

Fearing violence, the managers of Congress Hall, which the women had reserved for the afternoon of October 14, withdrew their permission, and the society was forced to postpone its meeting until October 21 and to meet in the local antislavery office. Mob sentiment was running so high that Thompson was urged to leave the city, and the women announced he would not be present. To defend their decision to meet despite public attack and the censure of other women, they issued the following statement:

> We must meet together, to strengthen ourselves to discharge our duty
> as the mothers of the next generation—as the wives and sisters of this.
> We cannot descend to bandy words with those who have no just sense
> of their own duty or of ours, who dread lest the delicacies of the table
> should be neglected, who glory in the darning needle, and whose talk
> is of the distaff. This is a crisis which demands of us not only mint,
> and annise and cummin, but also judgement, mercy and faith; and
> God being our helper, none of these shall be required in vain of our
> hands. Our sons shall not blush for those who bore them.[20]

Despite these efforts to calm the public, trouble lay ahead. When some fifteen or twenty members arrived for their meeting at three o'clock on a Wednesday afternoon, a mob quickly surrounded the building. Garrison, who had come to address the meeting in the place of Thompson and was

19. Lydia Maria Child to Dr. William Ellery Channing, *Liberator,* April 4, 1836.
20. *Right and Wrong in Boston. Report of the Boston Female Anti-Slavery Society . . . 1835* (Boston, 1836), pp. 25–26.

the object of the mob's anger, decided to withdraw to the antislavery office with his friend Charles Burleigh and to lock the door. Garrison's own account of what followed appeared in the *Liberator* on November 7:

> Notwithstanding the presence and frantic behaviour of the rioters in the hall, the meeting of the Society was regularly called to order by the President. She then read a select and exceedingly appropriate portion of scripture, and offered up a fervent prayer to God for direction and succor, and the forgiveness of enemies and revilers. It was an awful, sublime, and soul-thrilling scene—enough, one would suppose, to melt adamantine hearts, and make even fiends of darkness stagger and retreat. Indeed, the clear, untremulous voice of that Christian heroine in prayer, occasionally awed the ruffians into silence, and was heard distinctly even in the midst of their hisses, threats and curses.[21]

The mob finally broke into the hall and knocked down the partition to the office where Garrison and Burleigh had been waiting. They were restrained from doing violence to the two men by the fact that the women continued to conduct their business in the hall as though nothing had occurred. Finally the mayor arrived and ordered the abolitionists to leave. The women disputed him, wanting to know why he did nothing to restrain the mob, many of whose leaders were his personal friends. To his plea that it was dangerous to remain, one of their number, probably Maria Chapman, responded, "If this is the last bulwark of freedom, we may as well die here, as any where." Finally the women closed their meeting with dignity and walked down the stairs and into the crowded street. "When we emerged into the open daylight, there went up a roar of rage and contempt, which increased when they saw that we did not intend to separate, but walked in regular procession," Maria Chapman wrote of the event.[22]

Much of the mob anger was directed against the black members of the group. By walking two by two, one black member linking arms with one white member, the white women offered protection to their black sisters, a form of nonviolent resistance which was to be used frequently by the feminist abolitionists. The women out of the way, the ruffians seized Garrison, put a rope about him, and dragged him through the streets of Boston to the mayor's office. He was placed in protective custody in prison overnight, and the next day he was told he ought to leave the city for awhile, a suggestion with which he complied.

21. *Liberator,* November 7, 1835.
22. *Right and Wrong in Boston,* pp. 29–37, quotations on p. 34.

Still determined to hold their annual meeting, the antislavery women again gathered on October 21 at the home of abolitionist Francis Jackson and were finally able to conduct their business in peace. More experience with hostility was to follow, however. After the 1837 convention Angelina and Sarah Grimké began a tour as agents of the New England Anti-Slavery Society, at first speaking only to all-female audiences but soon addressing mixed or "promiscuous" audiences as well. The Congregational ministers, alarmed by this development, sent out a pastoral letter, warning against "females who itinerate" and suggesting that churches close their doors to the pair. As a result, the two had difficulty finding places to speak and on several occasions had to deal with hecklers. In defending their right to speak, they introduced into public debate the "woman question," which was to lead to more mob violence.[23]

The Grimké sisters themselves were strong supporters of nonresistance. In November of 1837 when Elijah Lovejoy, an abolitionist editor in Alton, Illinois, was shot and killed defending his presses from attack by a proslavery mob, abolitionist opinion was divided. Some viewed his action as heroic, whereas others thought his resort to the use of force weakened their moral position. Angelina Grimké was one of the latter. In a letter to the *Liberator* entitled "Resist not Evil" Angelina Grimké deplored Lovejoy's apostasy from nonresistance:

> As a Christian, then, I deeply mourn the melancholy event. If I could view the murdered Lovejoy as a *Christian martyr* then could I rejoice in the midst of my sorrow, believing the blood of such a martyr would indeed be the seed of our Abolitionist Church which would spring up and bear fruit, not thirty, or sixty, or one hundred, but a thousand fold. Some may think I am unjust in not awarding to our fallen brother the appellation of a Christian martyr; but to such I would say, test it for yourselves. Place in the mouth of the dying Lovejoy the last prayer of the expiring Stephen; "Lord, lay not this sin to their charge." How would these heavenly expressions of forgiveness and good have sounded from one, who wore a deadly weapon at his side—and was determined to *resist* his enemies by force of arms.[24]

Angelina Grimké was not alone in this point of view. Even though PFASS decided to hold a public meeting for the support of Lovejoy's widow, for

23. See Gerder Lerner, *The Grimké Sisters from South Carolina: Pioneers for Woman's Rights and Abolition* (New York, 1971).

24. *Liberator,* December 22, 1837.

instance, the society stated that it regretted that he took up arms, not "the proper means" to pursue the antislavery crusade.[25]

As public opinion turned more decisively against the abolitionists, and proslavery riots frightened the timid, it became increasingly difficult for any branch of the antislavery movement to find a place to hold meetings. As a result the Boston abolitionists had to settle for a stable in early 1837. In Philadelphia even the Quaker meetings began to refuse the use of their houses of worship. The reformers therefore decided to raise money to erect Pennsylvania Hall as a place where free speech would be assured. Opened on May 14, 1838, it was burned to the ground by a mob on May 17, giving the participants in the second Anti-Slavery Convention of American Women, meeting during these tumultuous days, an experience of dealing with mob violence which cemented their adherence to nonresistance.[26]

Prejudice against the abolitionists, who were seen as threatening commercial relations with the South as well as encouraging blacks to compete for white jobs, was particularly strong in Philadelphia at the time, so soon after the financial panic of 1837. When the public learned that blacks and whites, men and women, were going to meet together at the hall, public feeling against racial "amalgamation" flared. Angry crowds gathered around Pennsylvania Hall from its opening on May 14, much of their hostility aimed at the black delegates. Each day the crowd grew a little more threatening, and the feminist abolitionists had to learn to walk through it, heads held high, in order to conduct their meetings.

Within, the Anti-Slavery Convention of American Women was deadlocked on the question of whether it would endorse women speaking to "promiscuous" audiences. This issue, which had been raised by the speaking tour of Angelina and Sarah Grimké, was dividing BFASS, where some women Garrisonians, under the leadership of the Weston sisters, were in favor of promiscuous speaking, and others, influenced by the clerical wing of the movement, were opposed. Many of the New York women were close to the clerical wing and therefore also opposed antislavery women speaking to mixed audiences, whereas PFASS, under the leadership of Hicksite Quakers such as Lucretia Mott, supported public speaking for women. It was finally decided that a meeting would be held outside the formal sponsorship of the convention at which those who believed in a woman's duty to speak to a mixed audience might be heard.[27]

25. PFASS Minutes, December 14, 1837, Historical Society of Pennsylvania.
26. See [Samuel Webb], *History of Pennsylvania Hall Which Was Destroyed by a Mob on the 17th of May, 1838* (Philadelphia, 1838).
27. Ibid., p. 117.

On Wednesday night, when the promiscuous meeting of men and women abolitionists was to take place, the mob outside the hall had grown to ten thousand and was in an ugly mood, threatening to break into the proceedings. The few policemen present sided with the crowd and made no effort to restrain it. Following an opening speech by Garrison, the mob surged into the hall, shouting and threatening. Part of the audience rose in confusion and might have left had not Maria Chapman gotten to her feet and with admirable self-possession spoken calmly for some ten minutes. Next came Angelina Grimké Weld, who had just been married in the presence of some black friends. Rumors about this affair of "social amalgamation" had spread through the city, and at the sight of Mrs. Weld the mob began to shout again and to throw brickbats. Their opposition stirred Mrs. Weld to rhetorical heights. She was followed by Abby Kelley, who made an impassioned maiden speech as an antislavery orator. Lucretia Mott closed the meeting, deploring the fact that the session had not been sponsored by the convention: "Let us hope that such false notions of delicacy and propriety will not long obtain in this enlightened country."[28]

During the night of May 16 notices were posted throughout the city urging "all citizens who entertain a proper regard for the right of *property* and the preservation of the constitution of the Union to interfere forcibly if they must" with the convention. The mob that gathered Thursday was huge and ugly. Daniel Neall, the president of Pennsylvania Hall, visited the mayor with a delegation and asked for protection. They were told that the turbulence was the fault of the abolitionists for holding the convention in the first place. Unable to guarantee the safety of the delegates, Daniel Neall suggested to Lucretia Mott that black women stop attending the sessions, since most of the anger of the crowd seemed to be directed against them. Mott agreed to deliver the message Thursday afternoon but told the women she did not agree with it and hoped no one would act upon it, or be upset by a "little *appearance* of danger."[29]

The women completed their regular business in both morning and afternoon sessions. When it was time to adjourn for the day, many of the participants were clearly anxious about leaving the hall and facing the mob. Lucretia Mott arranged for the women to go arm-in-arm, one black woman and one white woman. She herself led the column, and the women simply faced down the angry onlookers, relying on the moral force of their own courage and sense of right to protect them from attack. It worked,

28. Lerner, *The Grimké Sisters*, pp. 245–46; *History of Pennsylvania Hall*, pp. 123–27.

29. [Laura M. Lovell], *Report of a Delegate to the Anti-Slavery Convention of American Women* (Boston, 1838), p. 16.

as it had worked in Boston, and the women passed through the angry mob unharmed.[30]

Several of the out-of-town abolitionists were staying at the Motts' home on Ninth Street, only a few blocks from Pennsylvania Hall, and rumors were already circulating that the mob would next attack the Motts. William Lloyd Garrison considered it prudent to leave the city. Maria Chapman and Anne Weston left too, since Maria Chapman was in ill health and "overpowered" by the strain, according to a letter of James Mott to Anne Weston. It may be that Chapman was wearied by the long months of conflict within BFASS. Local abolitionists, however, gathered at the Motts, who had decided that nonresistance principles demanded that they not flee. Charles Burleigh helped move some furniture and clothes to a neighbor's. The two younger Mott daughters and Lucretia Mott's mother, Anna Coffin, went next door to the home of Edward and Maria Davis. Since Edward Davis was out of town, J. Miller McKim volunteered to sit with the women.[31]

The abolitionists sitting with James and Lucretia Mott tried to converse calmly, while younger members ran in and out to find out what was happening. By nine o'clock they learned that Pennsylvania Hall was on fire. The mayor had locked the door, told the mob that they were his police, and gone home. Members of the mob had promptly burst the doors down, collected all the books and benches, and burned the hall, breaking the gas pipes to increase the conflagration. Fire companies had arrived and were playing their hoses on the adjacent buildings, but nothing was being done to save the building.[32]

As soon as the hall was consumed, a leader of the mob shouted "On to the Motts" and started up Race Street toward the house on Ninth. But a friend of the Motts intervened. He picked up the shout "On to the Motts" but turned the mob south, not north, at the corner of Ninth and Race. Though the Motts were spared, others were not so lucky. The mob ended up at Mother Bethel Church, founded by Richard Allen as one of the first African Methodist Episcopal churches in the country, which they burned before attacking the nearly Shelter for Colored Orphans.[33]

Deploring this brutal act of race violence, the feminist abolitionists met the next morning at the schoolhouse of Sarah Pugh to complete their convention and pledged themselves to "*expand*, not contract their social rela-

---

30. Ibid., p. 135; *Liberator*, May 18, 1838.
31. James Mott to Anne Weston, June 7, 1838, Boston Public Library; Charles Burleigh to Edward M. Davis, May 28, 1838, Davis Papers, Harvard University Library.
32. Burleigh to Davis, May 28, 1838; *History of Pennsylvania Hall*, p. 140.
33. *History of Pennsylvania Hall*, p. 140; Burleigh to Davis, May 28, 1838.

tions with their black friends." Angelina Weld discussed the riot and its meaning: "We have heard, with grief and shame of the burning of Pennsylvania Hall, last evening, but rejoice in fulness of hope that God will overrule evil for good, by causing the flames which consumed that beautiful Hall, dedicated to virtue, liberty, and independence, to light up the fires of freedom on every hilltop and in every valley in the state of Pennsylvania, and our country at large."[34]

Charles Burleigh, who was becoming an outspoken advocate of nonresistance, praised the women for their courage in meeting in the face of the continued riots in Philadelphia: "The women have done nobly today. They have held their convention to finish their business in the midst of the fearful agitation. Their moral daring and heroism are beyond all praise. They are worthy to plead the cause of peace and universal liberty."[35]

Following the burning of Pennsylvania Hall, debate heightened within AASS over the "woman question" and the advocacy of nonresistance. Some abolitionists objected to the coverage of these issues in the *Liberator* and their inclusion in the speeches of Garrisonians. Garrison, Mott, and others argued that they were not trying to convert all abolitionists to their way of thinking but that all should have the right to express their views. This disagreement surfaced at a special peace convention called by Garrison in September of 1838 to discuss nonresistance. Until this time the American Peace Society had dominated the peace issue. Although women were major financial contributors to the society, they were not allowed to play a public role but were adjured to use their women's influence to work for peace. In some instances they formed auxiliary societies or independent "ladies" peace societies.[36]

Garrison, however, invited women to participate as equals in this meeting and stated in his Declaration of Sentiments that "any person without distinction of sex or color, who consents to the principles of this Constitution may become a member and be entitled to speak at its meetings."[37]

Some members of the clerical wing of the AASS and of the American Peace Association attended the meeting, but they walked out when Abby Kelley called one of their number to order. The remnant founded the New England Non-Resistance Society, dedicated to preaching nonresistance as

34. *Proceedings of the Anti-Slavery Convention of American Women . . . 1838*, p. 10.

35. *Liberator*, May 25, 1838 (letter dated May 18).

36. Wendy Chmielewski, "The Role of Gender and the Role of Women in the Antebellum Peace Movement, 1818–1860," paper presented at Celebrating Our Work Conference, Douglass College, Rutgers University, May 1990.

37. "Declaration of Sentiments" adopted by the (American) Peace Convention, held in Boston, September 18–20, 1838, Swarthmore College Peace Collection.

an alternative to violence, whether expressed in war, the death penalty, or individual acts of self-defense. In the declaration of sentiments, the new society pledged itself to struggle for justice through nonresistant means: "But, while we shall adhere to the doctrines of non-resistance and passive submission to enemies, we purpose, in a moral and spiritual sense, to speak and act boldly in the cause of God; to assail iniquity, in high places and in low places; to apply our principles to all existing civil, political, legal and ecclesiastical institutions; and to hasten the time, when the Kingdoms of this world will have become the kingdoms of our Lord and his Christ, and he shall reign forever."[38]

Of the forty-four people who signed this declaration, twenty were women. Among the feminist abolitionists attending this founding meeting were Abby Kelley, Maria Chapman, Anne Weston, Mary Johnson, Sarah Southwick, Hannah Southwick, Thankful Southwick, and Hannah Stickney. Three of their number, Chapman, Weston, and Thankful Southwick, were elected to the executive committee. Maria Chapman later became one of the editors of the publication the *Non-Resistant,* which the new group launched in Boston in January 1839, and she and other women continued to play a major role in the society for several years.[39]

Despite Garrison's efforts to remove the issue of nonresistance from the antislavery societies, the strife within BFASS continued, and the task of preparing for the third Anti-Slavery Convention of American Women, to be held in May 1839, fell once more to PFASS. Frightened by the burning of Pennsylvania Hall, Philadelphians viewed the approaching convention with a jaundiced eye. Lucretia Mott approached all seven downtown Friends meetings with a request to use their space and was turned down by each, including her own Cherry Street Meeting. The churches were equally opposed; only the Universalists offered space, but it was much too small. The convention was finally forced to meet in a stable, the hall of the Pennsylvania Riding School.[40]

In late April, several days before the convention was to begin, Mayor Isaac Roach called on Mott at her home. He wanted to prevent the outrages that had occurred the previous year, he said, and so he had a few questions and suggestions. Was the meeting to be confined only to women? and if so, only to white women? He did not think much of the Riding Hall idea. Why not hold the meetings in Clarkson Hall, the property of the Pennsylvania Abolition Society, which was already guarded by his officers? If the

---

38. Ibid.
39. Chmielewski, "Role of Gender"; *Non-Resistant,* January 1, 1839.
40. James Mott to "My dear children," March 7, 1839, Mott Collection, Friends Historical Library, Swarthmore; *Proceedings of the Third Anti-Slavery Convention of American Women,* p. 6.

women would not meet in the evening, if they would avoid "unnecessary walking with colored people," and close their convention as soon as possible he thought that it would be possible to keep the peace.[41]

Lucretia Mott regarded Mayor Roach's suggestions as demeaning to women and highly disrespectful of black women. She replied forcefully to the mayor, as she later reported to the convention,

> that Clarkson Hall would not, probably, be large enough for us. We did not apprehend danger in meeting at the house proposed; she doubted the necessity of such protection as he contemplated. We should not be likely to have evening meetings; for, to the shame of Philadelphia be it spoken, the only building we could procure of sufficient size, had but a barn roof, was without ceiling, and could not, therefore, easily be lighted for such a meeting;—that we had never made a parade, as charged upon us, of walking with colored people, and should do as we had done before—walk with them as occasion offered;—that she had done so repeatedly within the last month, meeting with no insult on that account; it was a principle with us, which we could not yield, to make no distinction on account of color; that she was expecting delegates from Boston of that complexion, and should, probably, accompany them to the place of meeting.[42]

The convention assembled on May 1 as planned and went about its business. Soon, however, a messenger arrived from the mayor and called Lucretia Mott out of the meeting to inquire what time the convention would close, as he had several officers in waiting whom he would like to discharge. According to her account to the convention of this conversation Mott had replied "that she could not tell when our business would be finished, but that we had not asked, and, she presumed, did not wish his aid." Whether because of the firmness of the women's principles, or because they were unable to meet at night, this convention passed without incident.[43] For Lucretia Mott and other reformers, this experience cemented their belief that turning to the corrupt power of the state in the form of police protection to guard their meetings was inconsistent with the moral nature of their crusade and ineffectual as well, since the police often shared the prejudices of the mob.

41. *Proceedings of the Third Anti-Slavery Convention of American Women*, p. 6.
42. Ibid.
43. Ibid., pp. 5–6.

Antislavery Women and Nonresistance

The women's experience fostered the developing nonresistance movement. Henry C. Wright, agent of the New England Non-Resistance Society, wrote about the 1839 convention in *The Non-Resistant:*

> The Mayor of the city sent to the Convention and proffered the power at his command, to protect them from the violence of those who might be disposed to molest them. But the women, as I am told, gave him to understand that their confidence was in a higher power, that they dared not put themselves under the protection of clubs, swords and guns, and that their quiet and safety would be too dearly purchased by the destruction of those who might wish to disturb them. Half a day was spent in discussing what notice of the Mayor's offered protection should be entered in the minutes of the Convention whether any notice should be taken of it.[44]

Fresh from this nonviolent victory, Lucretia Mott attended the first annual meeting of the New England Non-Resistance Society, held September 25–27, 1839, in Boston. Here she played a leading role in the debate, insisting on respect for the point of view of others, "the right we cannot deny and ought to respect though the opinion may be such as we disapprove." She also chided the clergymen present for taking up too much time and not giving others a chance to speak. And when Henry Wright, though a staunch advocate of nonresistance, argued that with children some corporal penalties were necessary, she objected, defending a controversial resolution calling on members of the society to apply principles of nonresistance to the government of family life:

> My conviction is that penalty is ineffectual, and that there is a readier and better way of securing a willing obedience than by resorting to it. Some little incident in our own family will often illustrate the truth to us, in a way nothing else could do. One of our little girls when told to go to bed, felt disinclined to obey, and some time after she was discovered hid under the table, thinking it a good piece of fun. No notice was taken of it, and she took her own time. We had forgotten the affair, when she came running downstairs with her little bare feet, saying "do mother forgive me!" It was abundantly more efficacious than the theory of penalty called into practice could have been. I would wish this resolution would pass if we are prepared for it.[45]

44. *Non-Resistant*, June 1, 1839.
45. Ibid., November 16, 1839.

In the discussion that followed, Stephen S. Foster suggested that in some extreme cases punishment might be necessary. Lucretia Mott replied: "The extreme cases which may be brought to demand corporal punishment are like the extreme cases brought to nullify so many other arguments. The reason why such extreme cases occur is, I believe because parents are not prepared. They overlook the fact that a child, like all human beings, has inalienable rights. It is the master that is not prepared for emancipation, and it is the parent that is not prepared to give up punishment."

At this meeting, Mott was elected to the business committee along with Lydia Maria Child, and Maria Chapman and Thankful Southwick retained their posts. Abby Kelley, unable to be present, addressed a passionate letter to the assembly, saying that nonresisters must expect bitter persecution from the clergy who opposed them. "With these we shall be obliged to wage a war of extermination, through the world of the spirit and on their part it will be a struggle of desperation."[46]

Kelley had been under particular attack from the New England clergy, which may have inspired the bitter and militant language she used. But many of the nonresisters used military terms in their eagerness to make it clear that their concept of nonresistance was not one of passivity, but one of opposing evil with nonviolent methods. Lucretia Mott made a strong statement to this effect:

> Robert Purvis has said that I was "the most belligerent Non-Resistant he ever saw," I accept the character he gives me; and I glory in it. I have no idea, because I am a Non-Reisistant, of submitting tamely to injustice inflicted either on me or on the slave. I will oppose it with all the moral powers with which I am endowed. I am no advocate of passivity. Quakerism, as I understand it, does not mean quietism. The early Friends were agitators; disturbers of the peace; and were more obnoxious in their days to charges which are now so freely made than we are.[47]

A few months after the NENRS meeting, Lucretia Mott made nonresistance history when traveling in Delaware with Daniel Neall, the chair of Pennsylvania Hall, and his new wife, her mother's cousin, Rebecca Bunker Neall. Word had spread in this border state that these noted abolitionists

46. Ibid.
47. "Remarks delivered at the Twenty-Fourth Annual Meeting of the Pennsylvania Anti-Slavery Society, October 25–26, 1860," as quoted in the *National Anti-Slavery Standard*, November 3, 1860.

were traveling and speaking, and near Smyrna some men gathered to throw stones at their carriage. Ignoring this attack, the Mott party went on to the home of a local Friend sympathetic to their cause. After tea, some rough-looking men came to the door and demanded that Daniel Neall be turned over to them. When the host refused, more men came and forced their way into the house, badly frightening Rebecca Neall, who was new to antislavery action and unused to violence. Lucretia Mott described the incident in a letter to Maria Chapman: "I pled hard with them to take me as I was the offender if offense had been committed and give him up to his wife—but they declining said 'you are a woman and we have nothing to do with you'—to which I answered, 'I ask no courtesy at your hands on acct of my sex.' "[48]

When the men took Daniel Neall away, Mott followed them, continuing to offer herself as victim. The men finally smeared a bit of tar on Neall, attached a few feathers, and shamefacedly turned him over to the pursuing woman. This story, told over and over again in nonresistance circles, was advanced as further proof of the efficacy of moral weapons in the antislavery battle.[49]

The Philadelphia Female Anti-Slavery Society continued to meet regularly and to serve as a support network for antislavery women until 1870. It also continued to advocate nonresistance as the method of advancing the cause of the slave and later of combating racial discrimination. The society adopted this view in 1842: "Resolved that in the work of abolishing slavery we rely not on the efficacy of physical force or political parties, but on moral power, on the use of those weapons which operate on the heart and conscience."[50]

In 1840, Lucretia Mott was one of several women delegates sent to the World Anti-Slavery Convention in London by the Garrisonians. Refused a seat at this meeting, Mott fought for women's rights with such grace and vigor that she became a role model for a young bride, Elizabeth Cady Stanton, attending the convention with her husband. The encounter of these two resulted in the Seneca Falls Convention of 1848 and the birth of the women's rights movement in the United States.[51]

Many feminist abolitionists joined the new movement, bringing with them their commitment to end slavery and to use nonresistance. Indeed,

48. Lucretia Mott to Maria Chapman, May 13, 1840, Antislavery Papers, Boston Public Library.
49. Ibid.
50. PFASS minutes, May 19, 1842.
51. Margaret Hope Bacon, *Valiant Friend: The Life of Lucretia Mott* (New York, 1980); Elizabeth Griffith, *In Her Own Right: The Life of Elizabeth Cady Stanton* (New York, 1984).

when hostile mobs attacked the early women's rights conventions, the women turned to nonresistant methods to protect themselves and their guests. In 1853, for example, a women's rights convention was broken up on September 6 by the action of a Tammany-led mob, orchestrated by a certain Captain Isaiah Rynders. The following day the women reconvened with Lucretia Mott in the chair and managed to get through their day's agenda despite continued heckling. But in the evening, when Sojourner Truth spoke, the Rynders mob broke in, attacked the men, and jostled the women roughly. Deciding to abandon the effort to continue, Mott organized the men and women present to walk out two by two, as usual assigning each black member a white companion. When she herself was left without an escort she chose Captain Rynders to lead her out. Nonplussed by this unexpected act of trust, the rowdy complied.[52]

Whereas the women's rights movement remained committed to nonresistance through the 1850s, the abolitionists debated its usefulness from the passage of the Fugitive Slave Law in 1851 to the outbreak of the Civil War in 1861. Such events as the struggle between proslavery and antislavery elements in Kansas and John Brown's abortive uprising at Harpers Ferry influenced many abolitionists to decide that force was after all necessary to end slavery. By the time the war began the Weston sisters, the Grimké sisters, and Garrison himself had come to this conclusion, and only a few holdouts such as the Motts, Abby Kelley, and her husband Stephen Foster continued to maintain that the struggle could be continued by "moral means." Even after the war, Mott continued to feel that it had been won primarily by nonviolent means: "I regard the abolition of slavery as being much more the result of this moral warfare which was waged against the great crime of our nation: than coming from the battlefield, and I always look upon it as the result of the great moral warfare. It is true the Government had not risen to the high moral point which was required to accomplish this great object and [felt] it must use the weapons it was accustomed to employ."[53]

In 1866 the Universal Peace Union was launched. More radical than the old American Peace Society, the new organization was committed to the theory of nonviolence, although its use of nonviolent strategies was somewhat limited. This society pressed for removal of military training from the

52. Elizabeth Cady Stanton, Susan B. Anthony, and Matilda Joslyn Gage, *History of Woman Suffrage*, 3 vols. (New York, 1881), 3:557–58.

53. "Remarks Delivered at the Pennsylvania Peace Society at Its Second Anniversary Meeting, November 19–20, 1868," in Dana Greene, ed., *Lucretia Mott: Her Complete Speeches and Sermons* (New York, 1980), pp. 311–14.

schools, an end to the death penalty, fair treatment of the American Indians, the end of lynching, and arbitration of international disputes.

Many of the veterans of the antebellum feminist abolitionist struggles became members, including Lucy Stone, Ernestine Rose, Elizabeth Buffum Chace, Josephine Griffing, and Frances Ellen Watkins Harper. In addition, many younger women joined and learned of the traditions of nonresistance from the older members. One notable recruit was Belva Lockwood, a lawyer and an advocate of international arbitration who became the first woman to be admitted to plead before the U.S. Supreme Court and the second to run for the presidency.

The Pennsylvania Peace Society was revived as an affiliated chapter of the Universal Peace Union, and first James Mott, and after his death Lucretia Mott, served as president. Lucretia Mott was also a vice-president of the union and devoted her latter years to the struggle for peace through these two organizations. She argued that it was possible to advocate nonresistance in a world where not everyone was yet converted to the use of moral force. We do not need to wait until everyone is converted to pure nonresistance, she argued, any more than we had to wait until everyone was converted to antislavery principles. It was possible to banish war and oppression without waiting for universal conversion. As she put it, "We are not to wait until there is no disposition to take revenge, but to declare that revenge shall not be acted out in the barbarous ways of the present."[54]

One campaign that the Universal Peace Union supported was the effort of Julia Ward Howe, a vice-president of the American Peace Society, to promote an international Mother's Peace Festival every June. This was a forerunner of twentieth-century actions by women's peace groups, such as Women's International League for Peace and Freedom and Women's Strike for Peace, to use Mother's Day as a time for nonviolent action for peace. The event was celebrated in Boston, New York, Philadelphia, and Washington during the 1870s.[55]

During the long struggle for suffrage which followed the Civil War and did not end until 1918, women used nonviolent tactics to press their demands. In 1868 women in Vineland, New Jersey, attempted to vote in Union Hall with men as originally permitted by the state constitution of 1776. Rejected, they went through an elaborate protest vote procedure at the other end of the hall. Angelina Grimké Weld and Sarah Grimké went through a token vote process in Hyde Park, New York, in 1870. And in 1872

54. Sermon preached at Race Street Meeting House, Philadelphia, March 14, 1869, in Greene, *Complete Speeches and Sermons*, p. 315.
55. See *Voice of Peace* (Philadelphia and Mystic), July 1873, p. 11; July 1874, p. 61; July 1876, p. 49; July 1877, p. 64.

Susan B. Anthony led a group of sixteen women who cast their ballots in the presidential election. Anthony was tried and found guilty for this act of civil disobedience, but she refused to pay her fine.[56]

Another form of nonviolent protest used by the suffragists was the refusal to pay taxes, citing the principle "no taxation without representation." Dr. Harriot K. Hunt of Boston began paying under protest in 1851. Lucy Stone refused to pay property taxes in 1858 and watched her household goods sold at auction as a result. Lydia Maria Child paid hers under protest, and Abby and Julia Smith of Glastonbury, Connecticut, lost their cows because of a similar refusal. In 1873 Abby Kelley and Stephen Foster refused to pay taxes on their farm and actually lost it at auction to a spiteful neighbor. So much pressure was put on this man by the abolitionist network that he eventually relented and returned the deed to the Fosters.[57]

Susan B. Anthony and others staged a dramatic nonviolent protest in 1876 when they interrupted the Centennial celebration ceremonies in Philadelphia to present their declaration of independence for women. That same year the aged Lucretia Mott urged an audience at the Mother's Peace Festival to boycott Philadelphia's Centennial Exposition because the commissioners were refusing to open the gates on Sunday to working-class men and women.[58]

Nonviolent actions were also widely used by those feminists active in the prohibition movement during this period. The dramatic action of these women in entering saloons, though much ridiculed, was in fact a nonviolent effort to call attention to the plight of working-class wives who saw their husbands' weekly paycheck used to buy liquor. In one particularly imaginative early protest, Amanda Way (1828–1914), a temperance leader in Indiana, organized an army of fifty women which raided all the saloons in Winchester, Indiana, and invited their children, whom they had brought along, to help themselves to the free lunch.[59]

Suffragists and temperance workers continued to use nonresistant techniques until the outbreak of the First World War. At that time the leadership of the suffrage movement felt it would be unpatriotic to continue their protest. One branch of the movement, however, under the leadership of Alice Paul launched a nonviolent campaign for the Nineteenth Amendment. Arrested for peacefully picketing the White House on the charge

56. Margaret Hope Bacon, *Mothers of Feminism* (San Francisco, 1986), pp. 130, 131.
57. Ibid.
58. Stanton, Anthony, and Gage, *History of Woman Suffrage*, 3:28–35; *Voice of Peace*, July 1, 1876.
59. Ernest Cherrington, ed., *Standard Encyclopedia of the Alcohol Problem*, 6 vols. (Indianapolis, 1896), 6:2811.

that they were obstructing traffic, they refused to eat while in jail and resisted forced feeding. Their action aroused the compassion of many other women, who flocked to Washington to join the protest. Eventually they were all released and continued their picketing until the amendment was passed.[60]

Meanwhile, other suffragists under the leadership of Jane Addams formed the Women's Peace Party, which helped to sponsor an international conference of women held in The Hague in 1915. At a second meeting, held in 1919, the group renamed itself the Women's International League for Peace and Freedom, dedicated to combining the struggle for the rights of women with that of the struggle for peace.

The WILPF, as it came to be called, did not limit its membership to absolute pacifists but included many women who were devoted to the search for peace without being committed to nonviolent means. A much smaller group, the Women's Peace Society, founded by suffragist Fannie Garrison Villard (1844–1928), the daughter of William Lloyd Garrison, remained staunch supporters of nonresistance, breaking with WILPF over this issue at a national board meeting in 1922.

Thus the marriage of nonresistance to the women's rights movement, achieved during the three Anti-Slavery Conventions of American Women, continued to have an impact on history well into the twentieth century.

60. Amelia Fry, "The Divine Discontent: Alice Paul and Militancy in the Suffrage Campaign," paper delivered to the Fifth Berkshire Conference, Vassar College, June 16–18, 1981.

Coda: Toward 1848

{ 15 }

"Women Who Speak for an Entire Nation"

American and British Women at the World Anti-Slavery Convention, London, 1840

Kathryn Kish Sklar

The London World Anti-Slavery Convention of 1840 occupies an important place in the history of American women because it was there that Lucretia Mott and Elizabeth Cady Stanton first met and conceived the need for a separate women's rights movement. Not herself an abolitionist, Elizabeth Cady rebelled against her more conservative family by marrying Henry Stanton, a leading abolitionist ten years her elder, and the newlyweds attended the London convention for their honeymoon. There Stanton was transformed by her contact with Mott and other American women delegates to the convention.[1] In her memoirs Stanton lovingly named them: "Emily Winslow, Abby Southwick, Elizabeth Neall, Mary Grew, Abby Kimber, Sarah Pugh, and Lucretia Mott."[2] Winslow and Southwick rep-

I am grateful to Bonnie Anderson, Thomas Dublin, Betty Fladeland, Gerda Lerner, Clare Midgley, Clare Taylor, John C. Van Horne, Jean Fagan Yellin, and an anonymous reader for Cornell University Press for their helpful criticisms of earlier drafts of this essay.

1. Elizabeth Cady Stanton, *Eighty Years and More: Reminiscenses, 1815–1897* (New York, 1898), p. 83; and Lois W. Banner, *Elizabeth Cady Stanton: A Radical for Woman's Rights* (Boston, 1980), pp. 16–22. The influence was not all in one direction. Toward the end of the convention Mott noted in her diary, "Elizabeth Stanton gaining daily in our affections" (Frederick B. Tolles, ed., "Slavery and 'The Woman Question': Lucretia Mott's Diary of Her Visit to Great Britain to Attend the World's Anti-Slavery Convention of 1840," *Journal of the Friends Historical Society*, supplement 23 [1952]: 41). Garrison wrote home to his wife: "Mrs. Stanton is a fearless woman, and goes for woman's rights with all her soul" (William Lloyd Garrison to Helen Garrison, June 29, 1840, in Clare Taylor, comp., *British and American Abolitionists: An Episode in Transatlantic Understanding* [Edinburgh, 1974], p. 91).
2. Stanton, *Eighty Years*, p. 78.

resented the Massachusetts Anti-Slavery Society; Neall, Grew, Kimber, Pugh, and Mott the Pennsylvania Anti-Slavery Society.[3] Stanton remembered that after the hosts refused to seat the women delegates, she and Mott "resolved to hold a convention as soon as we returned home, and form a society to advocate the rights of women."[4] That convention occurred eight years later at Seneca Falls, New York, where it launched the woman's rights movement, which, in turn, became one of the most diverse and creative social forces in American life between the end of the Civil War and the outbreak of World War I.

Despite its enduring importance as a turning point in the history of American women, the London World Anti-Slavery Convention of 1840 has received relatively little scholarly attention.[5] The occasion offers an especially rich opportunity to sharpen our understanding of women's political culture by allowing us to compare British and American women abolitionists. By making such a comparison this essay seeks to establish a larger theoretical point about the study of women's political culture: It is not enough simply to look at women's motivations or institutions; we must also investigate how the male-dominated political environment encouraged or discouraged women's participation.[6]

3. *The Liberator,* April 3 and May 22, 1840. For the American women who attended the convention, see appendix to this chapter.
4. Stanton, *Eighty Years,* pp. 82–83. After 1840 Stanton corresponded actively with the women delegates she met in London. Lucretia Mott summarized an 1842 letter from Stanton to Elizabeth Neal: "She has lately made her debut in public in a temperance speech, and was so eloquent in her appeals as to affect not only her audience, but herself to tears. About one hundred men were present. She infused into her speech a homoeopathic dose of Woman's Right, and does the same in many private conversations" (Anna Davis Hallowell, ed., *James and Lucretia Mott: Life and Letters* [Boston, 1884], p. 228). Susan B. Anthony later noted, "The movement for Woman's Suffrage, both in England and America, may be dated from this World's Anti-Slavery Convention." Elizabeth Cady Stanton, Susan B. Anthony, and Matilda Joslyn Gage, *History of Woman Suffrage,* 6 vols. (New York, 1881), 1:62.
5. Exceptions to this are Douglas H. Maynard, "The World's Anti-Slavery Convention of 1840," *Mississippi Valley Historical Review* 47 (1960): 452–71; and Donald R. Kennon's fine introduction to the topic, "'An Apple of Discord': The Woman Question at the World's Anti-Slavery Convention of 1840," *Slavery and Abolition* 5 (1984): 244–66.
6. "Women's political culture" has recently come into use as a category of historical analysis to aid scholars in analyzing the larger context of women's political activism. It allows us to move beyond the dichotomy between women's culture and women's political activism visible in earlier historical debates, as in Ellen Carol DuBois et al., "Politics and Culture in Women's History: A Symposium," *Feminist Studies* 6 (1980): 26–64.
My use of the term here embraces values associated with women's participation in the public domain as well as their actual behavior. There are three levels of women's political culture: group activity that extends beyond family groups; group activity that expresses a female consciousness or awareness of women's actions *as women;* group activity with the explicit goal of

Comparative studies offer an excellent vehicle for testing large questions. Fortunately, recent research on British women abolitionists now makes it possible to compare British and American antislavery women.[7] A comparison of British and American women antislavery activists illuminates the complex issues that produced dissimilar outcomes on the "woman question" in England and the United States. The American story is a familiar one. Challenges to the equality of women within the antislavery movement and dissatisfaction with William Lloyd Garrison's leadership of the American Anti-Slavery Society led to the formation of the American and Foreign Anti-Slavery Society. The "New Organization," as the Garrisonians called it, excluded women from membership and limited their participation to female auxiliaries.

The English side of the story is less familiar to us today, but it was well known to Lucretia Mott's contemporaries. In England the "woman question" did not disrupt the antislavery movement; women remained effectively sequestered in their own organizations. Even when provoked by the example of American women in 1840, English women antislavery activists did not challenge male leadership. Only men could serve as officers and committee members in the British and Foreign Anti-Slavery Society, and the exclusion of women from leadership positions was already too far advanced to offer a parallel opportunity for British women to mobilize around. When some American women left the 1840 conference determined to work for their own rights, they returned to a fertile environment for doing so. Although a few British women drew feminist conclusions from the 1840 convention, the British antislavery movement did not become a vibrant vehicle for the expression of their discontent.[8] How can we explain

---

advancing the rights or interests of women. Here I speak of the third level of activity by one particular cultural group—white antislavery activists. I do no mean to imply that all women partook of the same political culture. As this comparison with England illustrates, we need to speak plurally of women's political cultures when we speak of more than one polity.

7. See Louis Billington and Rosamund Billington, " 'A Burning Zeal for Righteousness': Women in the British Anti-Slavery Movement, 1820–1860," in Jane Rendall, ed., *Equal or Different: Women's Politics, 1800–1914* (Oxford, 1987), pp. 82–111; Alex Tyrrell, " 'Woman's Mission' and Pressure Group Politics in Britain (1825–1860)," *Bulletin of the John Rylands Library* 63 (1980–81): 194–230; Karen I. Halbersleben, *Women's Participation in the British Antislavery Movement, 1824–1865* (Lewiston, N.Y., 1993); and Clare Midgley, *Women against Slavery: The British Campaigns, 1780–1870* (London, 1992). These authors disagree. Tyrrell and Midgley argue that feminism emerged from British abolitionism; Billington and Billington argue that it did not. Halbersleben falls in between.

8. I certainly agree with Midgley (p. 177) that women's participation in the British antislavery movement was "central to the development of an extra-Parliamentary but public female political culture." The extent to which that political culture lent itself to collective action

these differences between women's political cultures in the United States
and England? British abolitionist women had mobilized several years earlier than American women, and in the 1820s a British woman formulated
the transatlantic movement's most important goal—immediate abolition.[9]
Why, when the Americans had learned so much from their British sisters,

---

on behalf of women was another matter, however. Anne Knight made the strongest statement
of the preconditions for such action in a letter to Maria Weston Chapman (Boston Public
Library A.9.2., v. 13, p. 49): "There were many I believe ashamed at the part they took I believe they can no longer deny the equality of talent as well as worth of their wives sisters
daughters. These ideas discussed often among us are helping the cause. . . . We tell them we
are no longer the same beings as fifty years ago no longer 'sit by the fire and spin' or distill
rosemary and lavender for poor neighbors. . . . thus having been driven into the forefront of
the battle having in the labour of collecting and going from house to house for signatures to
petitions had to fight with beasts of Ephesus who can any longer in this blaze of our superior
experience . . . dare to omit our names from the muster-roll for the counsel-board? we have a
far superior claim to the men." I am grateful to Bonnie Anderson for drawing my attention to
this letter. Eileen Kraditor's *Means and Ends in American Abolitionism: Garrison and His Critics
on Strategy and Tactics* (New York, 1967) remains the most complete survey of the American case. See also Dorothy Bass, "The Best Hopes of the Sexes: The Woman Question in
Garrisonian Abolitionism" (Ph.D. diss., Brown University, 1980). For the British side of the
story, Billington and Billington, "A Burning Zeal for Righteousness." For a good overview of
1840 as a turning point in Anglo-American antislavery cooperation, see David Turley, *The
Culture of English Antislavery, 1780–1860* (London, 1991). In contrast to Billington and Billington, Midgley and Taylor emphasize the continuities between abolitionists and the later British
women's rights movement, though they do not go so far as Tyrrell, "Women's Mission." The
lives of some individuals do offer continuity between antislavery and women's rights, especially Elizabeth Pease [Nichol], Harriet Martineau, Anne Knight, Barbara Leigh Smith
Bodichon, Josephine Butler, and Marion Kirkland Reid. For brief studies of all but Reid, see
Olive Banks, *The Biographical Dictionary of British Feminists,* Vol. 1: *1800–1930* (New York, 1985).
For Reid and for more on Anne Knight, see Susan Groag Bell and Karen M. Offen, *Women,
the Family, and Freedom: The Debate in Documents* (Stanford, Calif., 1983), pp. 192–93, 195–99,
233–38, 242, 248–51; and Gail Malmgreen, "Anne Knight and the Radical Subculture," *Quaker
History* 71 (1982): 100–113. See also Barbara Leigh Smith Bodichon, *An American Diary, 1857–
58,* ed. Joseph W. Reed, Jr. (London, 1972), especially p. 63; Ida Beatrice O'Malley, *Women
in Subjection: A Study of the Lives of Englishwomen before 1832* (London 1933), pp. 305–52; and
Diane M. Worzala, "The Langham Place Circle: The Beginnings of the Organized Women's
Movement in England, 1854–70" (Ph.D. diss., University of Wisconsin, 1982). In keeping
with the greater importance of class distinctions in England, Anne Knight first introduced
woman suffrage in England in 1851 in conjunction with Chartist women, not abolitionists.
See Barbara Taylor, *Eve and the New Jerusalem: Socialism and Feminism in the Nineteenth Cen-
tury* (New York, 1983), p. 282; and Jutta Schwarzkopf, *Women in the Chartist Movement* (New
York, 1991).

9. [Elizabeth Heyrick], *Immediate, Not Gradual Abolition of Slavery; Or an Inquiry into the
Shortest, Safest, and Most Effectual Means of Getting Rid of West Indian Slavery* (London, 1824).
The first edition of the pamphlet did not carry the author's name.

did they become their teachers on women's rights? Why did women's antislavery political culture develop so fast and go so far in the American political context of the 1830s and 1840s? What aspects of American society and politics fueled women's antislavery activism?

Answers to these questions elucidate the history of women's involvement in the American antislavery movement and show us that a complete analysis of women's political culture must extend beyond a study of women's political activism per se to embrace features of the larger cultural and social polity that invited or deterred women's political activism. Cross-national comparisons can help us see that just as we cannot explain women's social status by looking to "natural" differences between the sexes, so we cannot explain women's political culture by asserting that "natural" tendencies lead women to express themselves within social movements. Let us first determine what happened in London in 1840 and then place those events within the sociopolitical context of each society.[10]

The World Anti-Slavery Convention was called by the British and Foreign Anti-Slavery Society for June 12, 1840, in Freemason's Hall on Great Queen Street, London. Founded in 1839 to celebrate the emancipation of slaves in British colonies six years earlier and the abolition of an "apprentice" system of semislavery that year, the British society now turned the attention of local English antislavery organizations to "universal abolition," with particular attention to slavery in the United States. Conference organizers invited "the friends of the slave of every nation and every clime. . . . to deliberate on the best means of promoting the interests of the slave, of obtaining his immediate and unconditional freedom; and by every pacific measure to hasten the utter extinction of the slave trade.[11] Despite this inclusive rhetoric, when seven American women representing Massachusetts and Pennsylvania antislavery societies presented themselves as delegates to the conference arrangements committee, the committee refused to seat them, saying that their presence constituted "an innovation on [British] customs and usages" that would subject the convention to ridicule.[12]

Charles Stuart, who more than any other single individual inhabited both the American and British antislavery worlds, had warned the organizing committee that some American delegates were "of the most troublesome description, particularly on the points of intruding women into

10. For the historiography of women in the American antislavery movement, see the Bibliographical Notes to this volume, pp. 335–40.
11. Hallowell, *James and Lucretia Mott*, p. 138.
12. Ibid., p. 196.

public life, and of denying the rightfulness of human governments."[13] The committee subsequently resolved at a meeting on May 15 to accept male delegates only. They also appointed a subcommittee of Joseph Sturge, John Scoble, and William Bevan to welcome the delegates and inform any women of this resolution.[14] The American women delegates could not have been too surprised at this turn of events, which in many ways revisited the dispute that had fractured the American movement a year earlier. Because the conference hosts sided with the "New Organization" in its disapproval of Garrison's leadership, and because the women delegates represented Garrisonian groups, the deck was stacked against women delegates from the outset.[15] But the women were excluded as women, not as Garrisonians. No male Garrisonian delegate was refused a seat; much as the conference organizers might have disagreed with their tactics, they did not exclude James Mott, Isaac Winslow, or Garrison himself. Indeed, Wendell Phillips, a prominent Garrisonian, was appointed one of the convention secretaries.

More than an abstract principle was contested here. Both sides of the divided American movement were struggling to gain the extremely influential moral and financial support of the British movement.[16] Garrisonians had committed themselves to the full incorporation of women within their ranks. Now they had to defend that choice before a jury of their British peers.

Our best source for studying the 1840 convention from the perspective of the American women delegates is the diary of Lucretia Mott, Quaker minister, charismatic speaker, and acknowledged leader of the women dele-

13. Anthony J. Barker, *Captain Charles Stuart: Anglo-American Abolitionist* (Baton Rouge, La., 1986), p. 189. Stuart's anti-woman views were particularly egregious when seen in the context of his very close personal friendship with Theodore Weld, Angelina Grimké's husband. For the Weld-Stuart friendship see Angelina Grimké Weld to Elizabeth Pease, August 14, 1839, in Taylor, *British and American Abolitionists*, p. 81: "As the best beloved friend of my Theodore, and as a truly Christian philanthropist, I have greatly desired to see him under our roof." Angelina and Theodore named their star-crossed son, Charles, after Stuart.

14. Barker, *Captain Charles Stuart*, p. 189.

15. Garrison's letters immediately prior to the convention show that he anticipated a struggle over women's rights there. Knowing that he would arrive after the convention opened, Garrison wrote George Bradburn, Attleboro, Massachusetts, Unitarian minister, "I beseech you, *fail not to have women recognized as equal beings.*" Noting to another correspondent that seating women at a conference "was never heard or thought of in any part of Europe," he thought it "quite probable, that we shall be foiled in our purpose" (William Lloyd Garrison to George Bradburn, April 24, 1840; Garrison to Helen E. Garrison, May 19, 1840, in Louis Ruchames, ed., *The Letters of William Lloyd Garrison*, 2 vols. [Cambridge, Mass., 1971], 2:587, 616).

16. See, for example, Kennon, "Apple of Discord," p. 249.

gates. She arrived in London on June 5, a week before the conference opened. Mott's leadership of the American women delegates flowed from her experience presiding at the 1837 Anti-Slavery Convention of American Women—an event that had no parallel in England.[17] She quickly noticed the influence of "New Organization" men in the exclusion of women delegates. When one of the subcommittee tried "to reconcile us to our fate," Mott "endeavored to show him the inconsistency of excluding women delegates, but we soon found he had prejudged, and made up his mind to act with our New Organization, therefore all reasoning was lost upon him and our appeals made in vain."[18] At a party on June 6, when she heard the "official information that Women were to be rejected," she taunted her tormentors by asking two of her most prominent American opponents "if they had heard that similar course was to be pursued toward the new organization." "Alarmed them," she laconically noted.[19] She and the other female delegates had not spent a month crossing the Atlantic and years defending their rights within the American movement to give up without a fight.

Yet the dispute touched deeper political realities than the "New Organization." One of those realities was the greater integration of women within the American antislavery movement. The American women delegates simultaneously represented separate women's antislavery societies as well as societies that included men and women. Mary Grew, Abby Kimber, Lucretia Mott, Elizabeth Neall, and Sarah Pugh were members of both the Philadelphia Female Anti-Slavery Society and the Pennsylvania Anti-Slavery Society. Similarly, Abby Southwick belonged to both the Boston Female Anti-Slavery Society and the Massachusetts Anti-Slavery Societies.[20] Although the Boston society splintered in 1838 on the question of women's inclusion, weakening BFASS to the point of dissolution, most

17. Tolles, "Lucretia Mott's Diary," pp. 1–85. Much of Mott's diary was reprinted in Hallowell, *James and Lucretia Mott*. Two other national conventions of antislavery women were held in the United States in 1838 and 1839. In her influential essay, "The Martyr Age of the United States," *Westminster Review* 32 (1839): 1–59, Harriet Martineau characterized the 1837 convention as "a great event in history—from the nature of the fact itself." She also noted Mott's role presiding over the convention ("The Martyr Age," p. 36). See *Turning the World Upside Down: The Anti-Slavery Convention of American Women: Held in New York City, May 9–12, 1837* (New York, 1987). After 1840 Mott's leadership became even more prominent. See Dana Greene, ed., *Lucretia Mott: Her Complete Speeches and Sermons* (New York, 1980). For the absence of trans-local British women's conventions, see Billington and Billington, " 'A Burning Zeal for Righteousness,' " passim.
18. Hallowell, *James and Lucretia Mott*, p. 150.
19. Tolles, "Lucretia Mott's Diary," p. 27.
20. *Memorial of Sarah Pugh: A Tribute of Respect from Her Cousins* (Philadelphia, 1888), p. 23. For the Southwick family, see Debra Gold Hansen, *Strained Sisterhood: Gender and Class in the Boston Female Anti-Slavery Society* (Amherst, 1993).

local antislavery societies in the United States before 1840 included both men and women. Conversely, all contemporary British antislavery societies were segregated by sex.[21] The remarkable integration of men and women in the American antislavery movement made it all the more difficult for the American women delegates to accept their exclusion. Indeed, they rejected the organizing committee's decision and planned to carry the struggle to the convention floor.[22]

In London as so often in the United States, arguments about women's status rested on analogies with the status of black people. On the evening of June 11, Mott received a group "sent to us to persuade us not to offer ourselves to the Convention." They told her the convention's title "was a mere Poetical license," and that "all power would rest with the London Committee of Arrangements." When a black delegate from Jamaica "thought it would lower the dignity of the Convention and bring ridicule on the whole thing if ladies were admitted," Mott replied that "similar reasons were urged in Pennsylvania for the exclusion of colored people from our meetings—but had we yielded on such flimsy arguments, we might as well have abandoned our enterprise."[23] The analogy between race and gender was a potent one, even in London, where slaves and free blacks alike were exotic outsiders rather than the familiar and widespread presence they constituted in the United States.

When, on the convention's opening day, some 350 participants heatedly debated the seating of women delegates, only men's voices were heard.[24] According to a British woman friendly to the American women delegates, convention organizers believed that "women thus sent by an entire na-

21. See, for example, "Proceedings of the Meeting of the Pennsylvania State Anti-Slavery Society for the Eastern District . . . 1839," Pennsylvania Anti-Slavery Society Papers, Historical Society of Pennsylvania, which names members of affiliated local societies. For the strict sex-segregation of British societies, even Garrisonian ones, see Billington and Billington, "A Burning Zeal for Righteousness," p. 100.
22. Tolles, "Lucretia Mott's Diary," p. 28. On the last day of the convention Wendell Phillips read a protest against the exclusion of the women delegates signed by him and six other men. Pugh, *Memorial*, p. 26; and *Liberator*, July 31, 1840.
23. Tolles, "Lucretia Mott's Diary," p. 29.
24. Taylor, *British and American Abolitionists*, pp. 95–96. The admission of women was debated through a resolution introduced by Wendell Phillips: "That a Committee of five be appointed to prepare a correct list of the members of this Convention, with instructions to include in such list, all persons bearing credentials from any Anti-Slavery body" (Mari Jo and Paul Buhle, *The Concise History of Woman Suffrage: Selections from the Classic Work of Stanton, Anthony, Gage and Harper* [Urbana, Ill., 1978], p. 79). For the number of delegates, see the *Liberator*, July 24, 1840.

tion are out of their place."[25] This was indeed the issue—whether women could serve in a public capacity that acknowledged their importance in the nation's polity. During the debate the women delegates sat "among the other women that came to see and hear." They were not without defenders, Maria Waring said, for "their men stood up grandly and valiantly for them."[26]

Although not all Americans supported the women, and not all the British opposed them, most of their proponents were compatriots. Mott thought that the defense of the women's admission was "well introduced by Wendell Phillips" of Boston. In a remark that later gained wide renown, Ann Phillips said to her husband as he rose to speak, "Wendell, don't shilly-shally."[27] He then forcefully declared:

> Massachusetts has for several years acted on the principle of admitting women to an equal seat with men in the deliberate bodies of Anti-Slavery societies. . . . We stand here in consequence of your invitation, and knowing our custom, as it must be presumed you did, we had a right to interpret "friends of the slave," to include women as well as men. In such circumstances, we do not think it just or equitable to that State, nor to America in general, that, after the trouble, the sacrifice, the self-devotion of a part of those who leave their families and kindred and occupations in their own land, to come three thousand miles to attend this World's Convention, they should be refused a place in its deliberations.[28]

When asked later to withdraw his motion, he said:

> I would merely ask whether any man can suppose that the delegates from Massachusetts and Pennsylvania can take upon their shoulders the responsibility of withdrawing that list of delegates from your table, which their constituents told them to place there, and whom they sanctioned as their fit representatives, because this convention tells us

25. Margaret Howitt to her sister, [June 1840] quoted in Margaret Howitt, ed., *Mary Howitt, an Autobiography*, 2 vols. (London, 1889), 1:291–92. Opposition to women antislavery speakers in mixed groups persisted in England in the late 1850s. See Ruth Bogin, "Sarah Parker Remond: Black Abolitionist from Salem," *Essex Institute Historical Collections* 110(1974): 137.

26. Maria Waring in Taylor, *British and American Abolitionists*, p. 95. Maria Waring was the sister of Hannah Webb and the sister-in-law of Richard Webb.

27. Carlos Martyn, *Wendell Phillips: The Agitator* (New York, 1890), p. 132.

28. Ibid., p. 131; Buhle and Buhle, *Concise History*, p. 80.

that it is not ready to meet the ridicule of the morning newspapers, and to stand up against the customs of England? In America we listen to no such arguments. If we had done so, we had never been here as Abolitionists. . . . We could not go back to America and ask for any aid from the women of Massachusetts if we had deserted them.[29]

The vast majority of British Quakers at the convention opposed the women delegates; British supporters consisted of a few notorious freethinkers. Dr. John Bowring of Exeter, a linguist, literary critic, anthologist, and world traveller, was the most effective of these. A reformer of the British Exchequer, opponent of the Corn Laws, and a close friend of Jeremy Bentham, he had served as an executor of Bentham's estate. His remarks addressed questions of custom rather than questions of principle. "The custom of excluding females is more honoured in its breach than in its observance," he said, Great Britain being ruled by a woman and the Society of Friends having "given to their women a great, honorable, and religious prominence." He characterized the women delegates as "one of the most interesting, the most encouraging, and the most delightful symptoms of the times."[30] Bowring's faint praise may not have damaged the women's case, but it could not have changed many minds.

George Thompson was the biggest disappointment. A leading figure in the movement that led to the abolition of slavery in the British West Indies in 1833, Thompson was a familiar figure to the American women due to the tremendous success of his speaking tour of the United States in 1834–1835, which was funded by British women's antislavery groups. Thompson had converted many American listeners, including Angelina Grimké and Sarah Pugh, to the goal of immediate emancipation.[31] But on June 12, 1840, he revealed the limits of his support for women in the antislavery movement. After speaking at length in favor of the Garrisonian branch of the American movement, he astonished the women delegates by urging a withdrawal of the motion to seat them. "I have deprecated most sincerely the introduction of the abstract question into this Convention," he said, and asked the women delegates to "promote the peace of the Convention."[32] Garrison

29. Martyn, *Wendell Phillips*, pp. 132–33.

30. *Proceedings of the General Anti-Slavery Convention, Called by the Committee of the British and Foreign Anti-Slavery Society and Held in London from Friday, June 12th, to Tuesday, June 23rd, 1840* (London, 1841), p. 25.

31. Gerda Lerner, *The Grimké Sisters from South Carolina: Pioneers for Woman's Rights and Abolition* (Boston, 1967), p. 120. See also C. Duncan Rice, "The Anti-Slavery Mission of George Thompson to the United States, 1834–1835," *Journal of American Studies* 2 (1968): 13–31.

32. *Proceedings of the General Anti-Slavery Convention*, pp. 32, 35.

later called Thompson's 1840 speech "unfortunate and incoherent." Thompson felt "ashamed," Garrison thought, but had done his best "under peculiar circumstances and without reflection."[33]

Untutored on the "woman question," even sympathetic British men offered only awkward support. The normally charismatic speaker, Daniel O'Connell, leader of the Catholic Emancipation movement, whose appearance at the convention was greeted with "deafening" applause, wrote that "this Convention ought to have warned the American Anti-Slavery Societies to confine their choice to males," but that since "the American ladies have persevered in our holy cause, amidst difficulties and dangers, with the zeal of confessors, and the firmness of martyrs . . . they should not be disparaged or discouraged by any slight or contumely offered to their rights."[34] These ill-matched rationalizations expressed O'Connell's confusion when confronted with a phenomenon unknown in his own culture.

American supporters seemed to feel more comfortable with the topic. George Bradburn, a Unitarian minister and a member of the Massachusetts legislature, endorsed the women with a "voice of thunder":

> We are now told, that it would be outraging the tastes, habits customs and prejudices of the English people, to allow women to sit in this Convention. . . . I ask, gentlemen, if it be right to set up the customs and habits, not to say prejudices, of Englishmen, as a standard, for the

33. William Lloyd Garrison to Henry Clarke Wright, August 1840, in Taylor, *British and American Abolitionists,* p. 110. Thompson's attitude toward the women delegates was particularly disappointing given his reliance during the previous decade on the assistance of Elizabeth Pease. The previous July, Ann and Wendell Phillips had written to Maria Chapman about the upcoming London convention: "Elizabeth Pease . . . longs to see you all, hopes you will come. Miss Pease I like much. Thompson told us she was his right hand man, his amanuensis, his counsellor everything." Ann and Wendell Phillips to Maria Weston Chapman, July 30, 1839, in Taylor, *British and American Abolitionists,* p. 77. In a letter to his wife, Garrison expressed his impatience with the British: "Our country is a century in advance of England on the score of reform." William Lloyd Garrison to Helen Garrison, June 29, 1840, in Taylor, *British and American Abolitionists,* p. 91.

34. Hallowell, *James and Lucretia Mott,* pp. 470–73, and Tolles, "Lucretia Mott's Diary," p. 34. O'Connell's views of the American women were probably based on Harriet Martineau's essay, "The Martyr Age," in which she highlighted the heroism of American women in the face of physical violence. For example, Martineau wrote: "The primary abolitionists of the United States have encountered with steady purpose such opposition as might here [in Britain] await assailants of the whole set of aristocratic institutions at once, from the throne to pauper apprenticeship" (Martineau, *The Martyr Age of the United States of America* [Newcastle-upon-Tyne, 1840], p. 2). Martineau's close relationship with Maria Weston Chapman is evident in Maria Weston Chapman, ed., *Harriet Martineau's Autobiography,* 2 vols. (Boston, 1877).

government, on this occasion. . . . If, in the legislature of [Massachu-
setts] I have been able to do anything in furtherance of this cause . . . it
was mainly owing to the valuable assistance I derived from the
women. . . . My friend George Thompson, yonder, can testify to the
faithful services rendered to this cause by those same women. He can
tell you that when "gentlemen of property and standing," in broad day
and broad cloth, undertook to drive him from Boston, putting his life
in peril, it was our women who made their own persons a bulwark of
protection around him. And shall such women be refused seats here?[35]

Attorney Jonathan Miller of Montpelier, Vermont, former member of the
Vermont legislature and antislavery lecturer, said that women were among
the "primeval abolitionists" in Vermont. "They took it into their heads to
establish a standard of liberty, and were seconded by their husbands."[36]

American opponents of the women delegates referred to the continuing
organization struggles in which women played so large a part. James
Birney relayed a report from Lewis Tappan that Tappan and others who
opposed the membership of women were considering seceding from the
American Anti-Slavery Society.[37] The Reverend Henry Grew was caught in
the middle of this debate, for he opposed women's rights, justifying his position on biblical grounds, yet wanted to defend his daughter's seat in the
assembly. Mott noted, "H. Grew betrayed some inconsistency."[38]

The convention's overwhelmingly negative vote on June 12 was
cheered—"unworthily," Mott thought.[39] The women's key defender,
William Lloyd Garrison, arrived at the convention six days later. "Had he
arrived a few days before the opening of the Convention, we could have

---

35. *Proceedings of the General Anti-Slavery Convention*, pp. 29–30. For more about the Boston
riot to which Bradburn referred, see *Right and Wrong in Boston. Report of the Boston Female
Anti-Slavery Society* (Boston, 1836). Maria Waring wrote about Bradburn: "Bradburn, Phillips
and Garrison are women's rights' men, and one feels themselves more in their presence on that
account. . . . They are some of the moral aristocracy. They regard women not as dolls but as
human beings" (Anti-Slavery Letters to Garrison, No. 6, The Webb Mss., Taylor, *British and
American Abolitionists*, p. 98).

36. *Proceedings of the General Anti-Slavery Convention*, p. 31. For women's leadership in antislavery families see Lawrence Friedman, *Gregarious Saints: Self and Community in American
Abolitionism, 1830–1870* (New York, 1982).

37. *Proceedings of the General Anti-Slavery Convention*, p. 41. See also Bertram Wyatt-Brown,
Lewis Tappan and the Evangelical War against Slavery (Cleveland, 1969); and Annie Heloise
Abel and Frank J. Klingberg, eds., *A Side-Light on Anglo-American Relations, 1839–1858, Fur-
nished by the Correspondence of Lewis Tappan and Others with the British and Foreign Anti-Slavery
Society* (Washington, D.C., 1927).

38. Tolles, "Lucretia Mott's Diary," p. 31.

39. Ibid.

carried our point triumphantly," he insisted in a letter to his wife, but nothing in the evidence supports his optimism, for the exclusion of women delegates involved more than the war between Garrisonians and anti-Garrisonians.[40] Like Mott on an earlier occasion, Garrison protested by withholding his talents. He and three other male delegates from Massachusetts (one, Charles Remond, was a black delegate sent by BFASS), refused to add their names to the official list of delegates and sat with the women. Lucretia Mott tried unsuccessfully to dissuade them from this action—"reasoned with them on the subject—found them fixed," she wrote in her diary.[41] Garrison thought the contest was not in vain. "The "woman question" has been fairly started, and will be canvassed" throughout England, he believed.[42]

Where were the voices of British women during this contest? However inept or eloquent, the debate among men on the convention floor probably meant less to delegates and onlookers than the behind-the-scenes maneuvering between British and American women that climaxed on June 19. For it was one thing for men to oppose the women delegates but quite another for women activists to do the same. Complicating our notion of women's political cultures, representatives of British women's antislavery organizations conveyed their disapproval of the American women by refusing to meet with them. In his published account of the convention, *Three Months in Great Britain,* James Mott said, "I am not alone in believing that this had some influence in the decision of the Convention." The subject of admitting women as delegates "was much talked of in social circles," he said, and the evident coolness of the British women spoke volumes.[43]

---

40. William Lloyd Garrison to Helen E. Garrison, June 29, 1840, in Ruchames, ed., *The Letters of William Lloyd Garrison,* 2:654–55.

41. Tolles, "Lucretia Mott's Diary," p. 36. Garrison wrote to his wife: "This created much uneasiness on the part of that body, and no pains were spared to seduce us from our position; but we remained inflexible to the end—looking on, as silent spectators, from the galleries, from day to day" (Ruchames, ed., *Letters of Garrison,* 2:654).

42. Ibid., p. 655.

43. Hallowell, *James and Lucretia Mott,* p. 199. Elizabeth Pease, the daughter of a textile-factory-owing family in Darlington, who had organized a Women's Abolition Society there in 1836, and Anne Knight, who was to become England's first activist for woman suffrage, were notable exceptions to this coolness among British women. Elizabeth Pease opposed the silencing of the American women. She wrote a friend: "Every obstacle was thrown in the way & no public opportunity was ever afforded them for a free interchange of sentiment with their English sisters. I regretted it deeply and several of us mourned over our utter inability to help it—had we been at our homes, we might have exerted an influence, but here we felt ourselves to be powerless" (Elizabeth Pease to "Dear Friend," July 17, 1840, in Taylor, *British and American Abolitionists,* p. 102). Harriet Martineau also deplored the treatment of the American

On June 17 the American women confronted this reserve directly. "The female delegation... requested they might have an opportunity to confer with their sisters in England on the subject of slavery, by having a meeting with them alone."[44] Revealingly, this request was made through Joseph Sturge, a member of the welcoming subcommittee and the single most powerful member of the British and Foreign Anti-Slavery Society, rather than directly to "their sisters" themselves. With Sturge as go-between, Lucretia Mott must have been expecting the worst from the meeting; if so, her anticipations were confirmed. Her consultation that day with "some Female members of the Several Societies" was a "rather slim affair." British men set the agenda. Although the American women had requested a public meeting, Josiah Forester "asked if a social party of Ladies would answer our purposes," and appointed a committee to arrange it.[45] On June 19, however, Joseph Sturge reported that he "doubted whether the ladies would have a meeting—they feared other subjects would be introduced and he partook of the fear." Mott responded by inviting them "to meet us at our lodgings," and confided to her diary, "much disappointed to find so little independent action on the part of women."[46]

---

women, later writing to Mott: "I cannot but grieve for you, in the heart-sickness which you must have experienced.... We must trust that the spirit of Christ will in time enlarge the hearts of those who claim his name—that the whites, as well as the blacks, will in time be free" (quoted in Douglas Charles Stange, *British Unitarians against American Slavery, 1833–65* [Rutherford, N.J., 1984], p. 58). The example of the American women affected some English women positively, Sarah Pugh thought: "The women there [at the convention] with few exceptions, were not prepared to take our position, though they thanked us most heartily for coming; they would not have been admitted even as visitors had we not come,—now, they say, this privilege will not again be withheld, and they consider it a step gained" (quoted in *Memorial of Sarah Pugh*, p. 27).

44. Hallowell, *James and Lucretia Mott*, p. 199.
45. Ibid., 36.
46. Tolles, "Lucretia Mott's Diary," p. 49; Hallowell, *James and Lucretia Mott*, p. 156. Significantly, William Wilberforce believed that petitions or other activities that drew women outside their homes were not proper for women. For connections between British and American women abolitionists, see Betty Fladeland, *Men and Brothers: Anglo-American Antislavery Cooperation* (Urbana, Ill., 1972), pp. 179, 227–30. For comments on the impact of American women's rights abolitionists on British women abolitionists and hence on British women reformers generally, see Barbara Taylor, *Eve and the New Jerusalem: Socialism and Feminism in the Nineteenth Century* (New York, 1983), p. 277; and Jane Rendall, *The Origins of Modern Feminism: Women in Britain, France and the United States, 1780–1860* (London, 1985), pp. 245–48. In France an autonomous women's movement emerged within the Saint-Simonian movement in the 1830s. Although the movement left a legacy for women in France, England, and the United States, it did not swell into a widespread woman suffrage movement in France. See Claire G. Moses, "Saint-Simonian Men/Saint Simonian Women: The Transformation of Feminist Thought in 1830s France," *Journal of Modern History* 54 (1982): 240–67.

The British women did not act on Mott's invitation until June 27, four days after the convention ended. She described the meeting: "Company of Anti-Slavery Ladies at our lodgings—stiff—poor affair—found little confidence in women's actions either separately or con-jointly with men, except as drudges—some sectarian zeal manifested."[47] Sarah Pugh agreed, recording in her diary: "Alas for our meeting on 7th day evening! Some 20 or 30 women assembled. But they had little to tell us—and had but little desire to hear anything we had to say—seemed very sensitive—fearing they might get 'out of their sphere' should they speak aloud even in a social circle—yet seemed quite pleased with themselves to think they had granted us a meeting!!! Peace be with them! Excuse that last sentence. I am sorry it is written—it is not kind to wish them rest and peace in a false position."[48] Both experienced organizers, Mott and Pugh recognized a hopeless cause when they saw it. Thenceforth they met with individual women sympathizers but abandoned any effort to speak with representatives of women's antislavery organizations. The experience forged strong bonds among the American women. Two years later Lucretia Mott noted, "There is a strong, binding tie of affection with all our band of 'rejected delegates.'"[49]

What differences existed in the larger political setting of the two nations that can help us analyze the different opportunities of British and American women antislavery activists? And how, in turn, can these dissimilar opportunities aid our understanding of women's political cultures in the two societies? Lucretia Mott offered a set of explanations to account for the exclusion of the American women delegates: "English Usage, [the] American New Organization, & sectarian proscription."[50] Although Mott did not elaborate on this terse list, her reasons point us in fruitful directions.

47. Tolles, "Lucretia Mott's Diary," p. 49. Mott later expanded on her view of British women abolitionists in a letter to Maria Chapman, Dublin: "Of course we would not 'thrust ourselves forward' into *such* a meeting, but having come so far to see what could be done for the slave, & being thus prevented doing anything ourselves, we were willing to be mere lookers on & listeners from without, as by so doing we should be the means of many more women having an invitation to sit as spectators—which we found was accounted a very high privilege in this land—by their women who had hitherto most submissively gone forth into all the streets, lanes, highways & byepaths to get signers to petitions, & had been lauded—long & loud for this drudgery, but who had not been *permitted* even to *sit* with their brethren, not indeed much by themselves in public meetings—having transacted their business, as we were informed, by committees" (Lucretia Mott to Maria Chapman, July 29, 1840, in Taylor, *British and American Abolitionists*, p. 104).

48. Sarah Pugh to Richard and Hannah Webb, July 2, 1840, Ms. A.1.2., v.9, p. 66, Boston Public Library. I have not been able to locate any account of this meeting by a British participant.

49. Lucretia Mott to Richard and Hannah Webb, February 25, 1842, quoted in Hallowell, *James and Lucretia Mott*, p. 232.

50. Tolles, "Lucretia Mott's Diary," p. 58.

By "sectarian proscription" Lucretia Mott referred to the strife between Hicksite and Orthodox groups within transatlantic Quakerism. Six of the seven American women delegates to the London convention were Quakers.[51] Elizabeth Neall was fêted in London as the granddaughter of Warner Mifflin, a Quaker raised on a Virginia plantation who freed his slaves in 1775 after paying them for their services since the age of twenty-one.[52] Although BFASS had very few Quaker members—all from the Southwick family—one of them, Abby Southwick, attended the London convention.[53] Emily Winslow, daughter of a Quaker merchant from Portland, Maine, represented MASS.[54] The American delegation might have expected a warmer welcome from British abolitionist women, who tended to be coreligionists. Beginning in 1825 with the Birmingham Ladies' Society for the Relief of Negro Slaves, founded a year before Birmingham's male antislavery society, Quaker women had formed the backbone of most British women's antislavery societies. Many of the founding members came from prominent Quaker families, like the Lloyds and Sturges. Quaker women also stood in the forefront of the British free produce movement.[55] Their shared religious faith meant that British and American women antislavery activists shared friendship and kinship networks. Lucretia Mott exemplified those networks, when, six days before the convention opened, she wrote in her diary, "E[lizabeth] Pease called.... Elizabeth's step-mother—an Irish Friend Sarah Bradshaw—granddaughter of Samuel Hoare—remembered my aunt Elizabeth Barker."[56]

51. Mary Grew, the only non-Quaker, was the daughter of a Baptist minister. The historical literature on Quaker leadership within antislavery movements in England and the United States is vast. See especially Jean R. Soderlund, *Quakers and Slavery: A Divided Spirit* (Princeton, 1985); and David Brion Davis, *The Problem of Slavery in the Age of Revolution, 1770–1823* (Ithaca, 1975). For more on Mary Grew, see Ira V. Brown, *Mary Grew: Abolitionist and Feminist, 1813–1896* (Selinsgrove, Pa., 1991).

52. Tolles, "Lucretia Mott's Diary," p. 33.

53. Hansen, *Strained Sisterhood*, p. 81. The American women delegates were acting within Quaker traditions that supported the notion of women traveling overseas to minister. See Margaret Hope Bacon, "Quaker Women in Overseas Ministry," *Quaker History* 77 (1988): 93–109. Generally, historians have underappreciated the religious impulses informing the early women's rights movement. An exception is Nancy Gale Isenberg, " 'Coequality of the Sexes': The Feminist Discourse of the Antebellum Women's Rights Movement in America" (Ph.D. diss., University of Wisconsin, 1990).

54. Tolles, "Lucretia Mott's Diary," p. 13, n. 1.

55. Billington and Billington, "Women in the British Anti-Slavery Movement," pp. 85, 103.

56. Tolles, "Lucretia Mott's Diary," p. 23. Through Quaker networks and the speaking tours of George Thompson in the United States and William Lloyd Garrison in England, British and American women activists kept abreast of one another's activities. Elizabeth Pease, for example, had been corresponding with Angelina and Sarah Grimké since 1836, when Thomp-

But in England and the United States the larger society offered Quaker women very different opportunities for political expression. That difference was symbolized by the Hicksite-Orthodox schism that rent American Quakerism in the 1820s and 1830s. The Hicksite movement was a response by some (mostly rural) Quakers to departures from traditional Quaker beliefs in the primacy of individual conscience and in an itinerant, voluntarist ministry. Changes promoted by the London Yearly Meeting had "evangelicized" most of British Quakerism and, through an active missionary movement in the United States, converted many urban American Quakers to adopt a settled ministry and to place articles of faith, such as belief in the divinity of Jesus and the doctrine of atonement, before individual conscience. Historians of British Quakerism attribute these innovations to the economic success large numbers of Quakers enjoyed in the eighteenth and early nineteenth centuries, for while prosperity brought social prominence, it did not overcome the disfranchisement of Quaker men, who, along with Catholics and other non-Anglicans, were barred from the suffrage and from political office. Thus Quaker adoption of Anglican-like religious practices was part of a larger effort by Quaker men to make themselves more culturally acceptable, thereby obtaining the franchise and access to political office.[57]

son advised Pease to contact the Grimkés about her plan to form a women's antislavery society in Darlington (Gilbert H. Barnes and Dwight L. Dumond, eds., *Letters of Theodore Dwight Weld, Angelina Grimké Weld and Sarah Grimké, 1822–1844*, 2 vols. [New York, 1934], 1:350). After Thompson lent Pease a copy of Angelina Grimké's *Appeal to the Christian Women of the South*, Pease and her aunt, Sarah Beaumont, arranged for the publication of a British edition in 1837. There readers learned that American women modeled themselves after the activism of British women: "Who wrote that pamphlet which moved the heart of Wilberforce? . . . It was *a woman*, Elizabeth Heyrick. Who labored assiduously to keep the sufferings of the slave continually before the British public? They were women. And how did they do it? . . . By speaking the truth, and petitioning Parliament for the abolition of slavery. And what was the effect of their labors? Read it in the Emancipation bill of Great Britain. Read it, in the impulse which has been given to the cause of freedom, in the United States of America. Have English women then done so much for the negro and shall American women do nothing? Oh no! Already are there sixty female Anti-Slavery Societies in operation. These are doing just what the English women did" (Angelina Emily Grimké, *Appeal to the Christian Women of the South* [1836; New York, 1969], p. 23). Garrison to Pease, November 6, 1837, in Taylor, *British and American Abolitionists*, p. 61, refers to the Grimké–Pease correspondence. Pease's esteem for Grimké doubtless was boosted by Garrison's reference to her in this letter as his "beloved and invaluable coadjutor." Thus relations between British and American women seemed extremely promising in 1837.

57. Not surprisingly, British Garrisonians were concentrated "in areas where the sense of alienation from national institutions was deepest"—i.e., in Scotland and Ireland. C. Duncan Rice, *The Scots Abolitionists, 1833–1861* (Baton Rouge, La., 1981), p. 88. Garrison wrote to Elizabeth Pease in June 1841, "My bitterest opponents in England are found in the Society of

In the United States the "disestablishment" of American churches around 1800 attenuated the ties between church and state, greatly empowering the laity. In the 1830s, although political rights were limited by race, condition of servitude, and sex, they were not constrained by religion. British religious innovations, therefore, were less compelling within the American Quaker community.[58] Indeed they were strongly resisted, especially in rural areas, where Elias Hicks, a Long Island farmer and minister, led the movement against them. Wealthier urban Quakers found the changes more congenial, however. In the schism of 1827 they retained control of the meeting houses in the most important center of Quakerism, Philadelphia, claimed the title "Orthodox" even though they were the innovators, and dubbed their opponents "Hicksites" to ridicule their backward ways.[59]

All religious denominations were more embroiled in the slavery question in the United States than in Britain. By 1830 the great majority of British clergy and churches had roundly denounced slavery as un-Christian. But in the United States religious groups and ministerial opinion, reflecting the economic ties to slave labor among northern parishioners, just as overwhelmingly failed to condemn slavery. Thus American antislavery activists often came to embrace anticlerical views. When Hicksite Quakers joined this larger trend, they became even less acceptable to English Quakers.[60]

The drive toward political assimilation in the British Quaker community prompted that group to shun James and Lucretia Mott as notorious Hicksites. On their second night in London, James Mott was told that "we must not expect to receive much attention from Friends, particularly from such

Friends" (Taylor, *British and American Abolitionists*, p. 152). In this connection future research might explore the extent to which British Quaker meetings developed less liberal attitudes toward female preachers in this era.

58. John D. Cushing, "Notes on Disestablishment in Massachusetts, 1780–1833," *William and Mary Quarterly*, 3 ser. 26 (1969): 169–90; William G. McLaughlin, *New England Dissent, 1630–1833: The Baptists and the Separation of Church and State* (Cambridge, Mass., 1971); and Chilton Williamson, *American Suffrage from Property to Democracy, 1760–1860* (Princeton, 1960).

59. A good summary treatment of this topic is Thomas D. Hamm, *The Transformation of American Quakerism: Orthodox Friends, 1800–1907* (Bloomington, Ind., 1988), pp. 15–20. For the rural-urban argument see Robert W. Doherty, *The Hicksite Separation: A Sociological Analysis of Religious Schism in Early Nineteenth-Century America* (New Brunswick, N.J., 1967). The argument works best in Pennsylvania; among rural New England Quakers the Hicksite movement made no headway.

60. See John R. McKivigan, *The War against Proslavery Religion: Abolitionism and the Northern Churches, 1830–1865* (Ithaca, 1984); and Seymour Drescher, "Two Variants of Anti-Slavery: Religious Organization and Social Mobilization in Britain and France, 1780–1870," in Christine Bolt and Seymour Drescher, eds., *Anti-Slavery, Religion and Reform: Essays in Memory of Roger Anstey* (Hamden, Conn., 1980), pp. 43–63.

as had young people about them, fearing the dangerous tendency of our doctrines." This first "open exhibition of prejudice and bigotry" saddened the Motts, but "[they] soon saw so much of it" that their "sadness was turned to pity."[61] By extension all of the American women delegates were tarred with the brush of Hicksite radicalism. Sarah Pugh, for example, retained her affiliation with Orthodox Quakerism, but by claiming a seat for herself at the convention she became a Hicksite in the eyes of the British. For their part the Motts thought English Quakerism was "in danger of being swallowed up with the unintelligible dogmas of Church and State theology."[62] As Lucretia Mott put it in a letter to Richard and Hannah Webb: "How sorry I am that you—I mean Friends in England, Scotland and Ireland—have engrafted so much of this creed-religion on your simple Quaker stock." She hoped that there would be "some among you with sufficient moral courage to make a stand against the 'church and state' influence . . . [that is] crushing the minds of so many in your midst."[63] Buried in the Hicksite issue, then, was a crucial social question of church-state relations that differentiated the American and British polities on the "woman question."

That distinction was indirectly expressed during Lucretia Mott's first conversations in London with the two women who were to become her strongest British supporters—Elizabeth Pease and Anne Knight. Both discussions centered on theological questions. On her first walk with Pease, Mott said that they "talked orthodoxy." Three days later she met Anne Knight, who "enlarged on the importance of belief in the Atonement."[64]

61. Hallowell, *James and Lucretia Mott*, p. 197.

62. Ibid., p. 200.

63. Lucretia Mott to Richard and Hannah Webb, October 12, 1840, in Hallowell, *James and Lucretia Mott*, p. 194. Nancy Hewitt has convincingly argued that American women were empowered on both sides of the Quaker schism to enter new realms of public debate and power in order to defend their groups' convictions. Hewitt, "The Fragmentation of Friends: The Consequences for Quaker Women in Antebellum America," in Elisabeth Potts Brown and Susan Mosher Stuard, eds., *Witnesses for Change: Quaker Women over Three Centuries* (New Brunswick, N.J., 1989), p. 104.

64. Tolles, "Lucretia Mott's Diary," p. 23, 26. Mott thought that the British religious climate inhibited the initiative of women Friends. She had this to say in her diary about a Liverpool meeting before arriving in London: "The gallery small, designed only for 5 or 6, to the exclusion of women. Some Friends in England also of the opinion that Women would not be called to that office if Men were faithful to their vocation. And these claim to be the legitimate descendants of George Fox & his noble and worthy contemporaries!" ("Lucretia Mott's Diary," p. 17). In 1839 Knight wrote Chapman (without the benefit of punctuation) on the relationship between feminism and religious orthodoxy: "I feel your women to be far above us in the attitude of Christian action and endurance but I fear my beloved friend for those women who . . . have not enough kept in view the total nothingness of human effort without

Pease and Knight overcame their theological differences with Mott and be-friended her, but many other British Quaker women did not.[65] Questions of orthodoxy and atonement carried important social significance in this era when British Quakers sought social acceptance as a step toward full civil and political rights for Quaker men.

Differences in class relations in Britain and the United States also affected the place of women in their respective polities. In the United States, universal white male suffrage undercut class distinctions in political culture while heightening divisions of race and gender. In England, however, the exclusion of working-class and small-property-holding men from the suffrage and from public office dramatized the class components of political culture.[66] As Elizabeth Pease explained to Maria Weston Chapman: "I find very few people who are aware that with you all *white men* are on a legal equality & that consequently our class restrictions, religious disabilities, landed propertied monopolies etc. etc. all the host of oppressions under which we groan resolve themselves with you into distinctions of *sex* or of color. If the English public had this key to the enigma they would be a little more merciful to the transatlantic Amazons as they suppose all the advo-

---

reliance & faith in the only source of all good the Divine Savior of men they have not enough acknowledged 'Him their greater' & so they have been permitted to fall may they repent & seek forgiveness of this their turpitude." To Richard and Hannah Webb, Mott wrote in 1842: "I want to tell you how Anne Knight, in a letter to Margaretta Forten, deplores my 'heresy.' She says, 'Her forbearance of the wrongs encountered in the Fatherland would merit the term Christian, had she not so utterly disowned and insulted her Lord and Savior.... Awfully as I regard this state of deep and hardened revolt, yet I do love Lucretia Mott for her work's sake. It was a joy to me to have the opportunity of offering those attentions which others ne-glected" (Hallowell, *James and Lucretia Mott,* p. 227). Mott and Knight were close in age, both being in their late forties. For more on Knight, see Malmgreen, "Anne Knight and the Radical Subculture."

65. Despite the fact that large numbers of women, many presumably Quakers, attended the evening social occasions at the British and Foreign Anti-Slavery Society rooms, Mott's diary mentions only Pease and Knight. Although "it had not been usual for women to be invited," the presence of the American women opened the way for British women to join the festivities. On the first night Elizabeth Pease was the only British woman present. Perhaps Mott's tribute to Elizabeth Heyrick that evening helped create a congenial environment for the British women, since on the second night "a number more attended; and on the third, nearly as many as of the other sex." Yet, Quakers or not, the interaction of these women with Lucretia Mott was not sufficiently notable to gain entry in her diary. Such was the gulf between her and them (Hallowell, *James and Lucretia Mott,* pp. 24, 196). At an evening party three days before the convention's opening where Mott first learned the "official information that Women were to be rejected," she listed those in attendance as "G. Thompson, A. Knight, E. Pease &c" (Tolles, "Diary of Lucretia Mott," p. 27).

66. For British suffrage laws, see Neville Kirk, *The Growth of Working Class Reformism in Mid-Victorian England* (Urbana, Ill., 1985), pp. 25, 62, passim.

cates of woman's rights to be."[67] Other facts of British political life intruded more forcefully into Pease's life than did those of gender. The 1832 Reform Bill had only recently granted political rights to wealthy Nonconformist men, and Pease was preoccupied with her efforts to aid the campaigns of male relatives for political office. Thus universal white male suffrage opened doors for American women and women's rights advocates that remained closed to British women.[68]

Yet the alienation between British and American women abolitionists cannot be attributed solely to the struggle by British Quakers to achieve respectability within British society, or to differences in class relations in the British and American polities. Differences in the social, political, and economic significance of slavery within each society also widened the gap. In the United States slavery and the racism that sustained it defined the culture and affected the livelihood of a substantial part of the population. In England—beyond the large profits generated for sugar investors—the effects of slavery and of racism were more indirect, especially after 1833.[69] In the United States, then, antislavery activity constituted a far greater challenge to the social, political, and economic status quo.

67. Elizabeth Pease to Maria Weston Chapman, January 10, 1853, Ms.A.9.2.p.4, Boston Public Library. For more on Maria Weston Chapman, see Jane H. Pease and William H. Pease, "The Boston Bluestocking: Maria Weston Chapman," in their book *Bound with Them in Chains: A Biographical History of the Antislavery Movement* (Westport, Conn., 1972), pp. 28–59. One of the most knowledgeable observers of the American and British antislavery movements, Samuel May, Jr. (1810–1899), a Unitarian from Leicester, Massachusetts, explained the differences in the two movements as due to class-based differences in the two polities: "I know that 'heresy' and 'radicalism' are even worse hated in England than with us—being regarded, for the most part, as rather low & vulgar, beside criminal. I know that 'Society' with you is much more sharply divided—classes & ranks more strictly defined, than with us. I suppose that you have not a well-educated and thinking *labouring, farming, mechanic* class to anything like the extent that we have in the Northern States. You yourself suggest that, with you, reform must commence with the higher classes, at least that it is of primary importance to get those classes right. With us, it is exactly the opposite" (Samuel May to J. B. Estlin, February 28, 1853, in Taylor, *British and American Abolitionists*, p. 393).

68. A cousin of Elizabeth Pease was the first Quaker Member of Parliament.

69. This is not to say that slavery had no impact on British life; the strength of the antislavery movement alone demonstrates slavery's influence. The effects can be seen in the triangular trade, in the correlation of "free" labor with slave labor in the Chartist movement, in missionary movements and the new forms of British colonialism after 1850, and in British racism. Nevertheless, slavery's consequences in England were mild in comparison with those in the United States. The best brief summary of recent scholarship on British antislavery historiography is Thomas C. Holt, "Review Essay: Explaining Abolition," *Journal of Social History* 24 (Winter 1990): 371–78, which emphasizes the demise of British slavery when it moved from a peripheral phenomenon to one that tried in the late eighteenth century to obtain protection from the metropolitan polity.

This challenge was obvious in the pervasive violence American abolitionists encountered. The terrorist tactics of proslavery groups—murdering abolitionist publishers, burning meeting buildings to the ground, dragging abolitionist leaders at the end of a hanging noose, tarring and feathering—were unknown in England.[70] Consequently, a sizable segment of American abolitionists adopted more radical action than any of their English counterparts.[71] And consequently the Americans welcomed help from any quarter, even from women.

The goal of immediate rather than gradual emancipation appealed strongly to women on both sides of the Atlantic because it cast the slavery question in moral and religious rather than political or economic terms. In both countries women stood in the forefront of the movements that substituted immediate for gradual emancipation. Yet "immediatism" presented very different opportunities to women abolitionists in England and the United States.

The goal of immediate emancipation was justified on moral grounds and denied owners' rights to compensation. Within a decade of its original proposal in Elizabeth Heyrick's 1824 pamphlet, *Immediate, Not Gradual Abolition of Slavery*, immediatism had swept away older gradualist and colonizationist approaches of the Anglo-American antislavery movement.[72] Leader of the Leicester Ladies Anti-Slavery Association, Heyrick urged that a "holy war" and a "Christian crusade" replace the political calculations that dominated antislavery activism. Emphasizing these moral qualities and consumer boycotts of slave products, her pamphlet appealed particularly to women. British women's antislavery societies began to endorse consumer boycotts and immediate abolition in 1825, four years before male leaders such as Joseph Sturge steered men's groups in that direction, and they proudly distinguished themselves from men.[73] Heyrick's ideas

70. Antiabolitionist violence is studied in Leonard L. Richards, *"Gentlemen of Property and Standing": Anti-Abolitionist Mobs in Jacksonian America* (New York, 1970); Theodore M. Hammett, "Two Mobs of Jacksonian Boston: Ideology and Interest," *Journal of American History* 62 (1976): 845–68; and Margaret Munsterberg, "The Weston Sisters and the Boston Mob," *Boston Public Library Quarterly* 9 (1958): 183–94.

71. As Eric Foner has remarked, "It will not do to defang the abolitionist crusade: it was indeed a radical impulse, challenging fundamental aspects of American life and none so deeply embedded as racism" (Foner, *Politics and Ideology in the American Civil War* [New York, 1980], p. 63).

72. Heyrick, *Immediate, Not Gradual Abolition of Slavery*.

73. Martha Gundry, *Letters to a Friend* (1825), quoted in Elizabeth Heyrick, *Letters on the Necessity of a Prompt Extinction of British Colonial Slavery* (London, 1826), quoted in Kenneth Corfield, "Elizabeth Heyrick: Radical Quaker," in Gail Malmgreen, ed., *Religion in the Lives of English Women, 1760–1930* (London, 1986), pp. 44–46. By 1831 there were at least forty-seven

spread first among women in Great Britain, then to men and women in the United States, before finally being adopted by male abolitionists in England.

News of the embrace of immediatism by women abolitionists in Great Britain was carried to the United States by Elizabeth Margaret Chandler, a Philadelphia Quaker who in 1826 at the age of nineteen began editing the "Ladies' Repository" pages of Benjamin Lundy's *Genius of Universal Emancipation*.[74] Chandler paid special attention to "the English Ladies' Anti-Slavery Societies," printed many extracts from Elizabeth Heyrick's "Letters on the Prompt Extinction of British Colonial Slavery," and exhorted American women to imitate their English sisters.[75] Lundy reprinted Heyrick's *Immediate, Not Gradual Abolition* serially in 1825.[76] In the United States, men's and women's immediatist societies were established in quick succession after William Lloyd Garrison in 1831 started the *Liberator,* the nation's first immediatist newspaper.[77]

The circumstances of the founding of the American Anti-Slavery Society in 1833 suggest the greater risks immediatism entailed in the United States, for the policy not only challenged slavery but also attacked racial hierarchies. Voluntary societies throughout the South (many of them female) could safely organize for gradual emancipation or emancipation linked with

women's antislavery societies in England. See also David Brion Davis, "The Emergence of Immediatism in British and American Antislavery Thought," *Mississippi Valley Historical Review* 49 (1962): 209–30.

74. Merton L. Dillon, "Elizabeth Chandler and the Spread of Antislavery Sentiment to Michigan," *Michigan History* 39 (1955): 481–94. It is not clear when Lucretia Mott first became committed to the cause of immediate emancipation. In 1826 James Mott established a free produce store in Philadelphia, so the Motts were doubtlessly in contact with the free produce aspect of British women's antislavery activism at an early date. For more on the Anglo-American antislavery connection, see Turley, *The Culture of English Antislavery*, pp. 196–226.

75. Wendell Phillips Garrison and Francis Jackson Garrison, eds., *William Lloyd Garrison 1805–1879: The Story of His Life, Told by His Children*, 4 vols. (New York, 1885–1889), 1:146; Benjamin Lundy, ed., *Poetical Works of Elizabeth Margaret Chandler with a Memoir by Benjamin Lundy* (Philadelphia, 1836); and Benjamin Lundy, ed., *Essays Philanthropic and Moral* (Philadelphia, 1836).

76. Heyrick's essay appeared in the *Genius of Universal Emancipation and Baltimore Courier* 1, no. 14 (November 26, 1825) through no. 18 (December 31, 1825). One of Chandler's British correspondents might have been Mary S. Lloyd, who also wrote Lucretia Mott, urging her to nurture the founding of women's antislavery societies in the United States. In London Mott was disappointed that Lloyd was not at the convention (Tolles, "Lucretia Mott's Diary," p. 18).

77. John L. Thomas, *The Liberator: William Lloyd Garrison: A Biography* (Boston, 1963), pp. 114–27. In 1832 the New England Anti-Slavery Society (later called the Massachusetts Anti-Slavery Society) and the Boston Female Anti-Slavery Society were formed; in 1833 they were followed by the Pennsylvania Anti-Slavery Society, the Philadelphia Female Anti-Slavery Society, and the American Anti-Slavery Society.

emigration.[78] Similarly, it was relatively safe to insist, as abolitionists in England did, upon immediate emancipation in distant colonies. Far more threatening than either of these stands was the call for immediate uncompensated emancipation in the United States, for immediatism actively sought the destruction of an entrenched, indigenous system of labor and racist social relations.

In the North, the immediatists' vision of moral and social racial equality disrupted set patterns of race discrimination.[79] Contact among black and white women and black and white men occurred frequently in the American antislavery movement, especially in Philadelphia. For example, Lucretia Mott noted that in the early days of the Philadelphia Female Anti-Slavery Society she "had attended only one convention—a convention of colored people." There for the first time in her life she "heard a vote taken," until then knowing only the Quaker method of group consensus. A short time later when she and others formed PFASS, "there was not a woman capable of taking the chair . . . and we had to call on James McCrummel, a colored man, to give us aid in the work."[80] This interaction fostered challenges to racism on the part of some white as well as black antislavery women immediatists in the United States. The presence of African Americans in Quaker meeting houses and in many female antislavery societies prompted Angelina Grimké to condemn "the existence of an unnatural prejudice against our colored population" as "one of the chief pillars of American slavery."[81] British women immediatists, whose daily life did not include contact with black people, did not take it upon themselves to challenge racist attitudes.

The threat of immediatism to the American social order was compounded by its appeal to a large, restive slave population. The specter of slave uprisings had risen dramatically with the 1829 publication of David Walker's *Appeal . . . to the Colored Citizens of the World, But in Particular and Very Expressly to Those of the United States,* which forcefully called for violent

78. For example, *Genius of Universal Emancipation* carried a notice of a meeting in August 1825 of the Female Manumission Society of Jamestown, North Carolina, which encouraged "the manumission and emigration of slaves."

79. See, for example, the view of immediatism presented in Archibald H. Grimké, *William Lloyd Garrison, the Abolitionist* (New York, 1891), pp. 70–73.

80. Hallowell, *James and Lucretia Mott,* p. 121.

81. Resolution passed by the 1837 Anti-Slavery Convention of American Women, *Proceedings of the Anti-Slavery Convention of American Women* (New York, 1837), p. 13. For more on Angelina Grimké's campaigns against northern racism, see Gerda Lerner, "The Grimké Sisters and the Struggle against Race Prejudice," *Journal of Negro History* 48 (1963): 277–91; and Carolyn Williams, "Religion, Race, and Gender in Antebellum American Radicalism: The Philadelphia Female Anti-Slavery Society, 1833–1870" ((Ph.D. diss., UCLA, 1991), chap. 5.

revolt. Fear of slave uprisings rose after 1831, when Nat Turner led a revolt of some seventy slaves in southeast Virginia, killing fifty-seven men, women, and children.[82] Meanwhile, southern repression prompted free blacks to migrate North, where the growth of free black communities amplified northern race prejudices. For these and other reasons, policies urging immediate emancipation carried a much heavier burden of social consequences in the United States than in Great Britain. In this context men and women abolitionists were pushed into more radical tactics than those that characterized the English movement; accepting women as equals was one of those tactics.

William Lloyd Garrison, the first white American antislavery leader to champion immediacy, accepted help from Lucretia Mott from the beginning. In 1830, having left Benjamin Lundy's *Genius of Universal Emancipation* and seeking support for his own paper, Garrison accepted the Motts' aid in locating a hall where he might speak in Philadelphia. When his talk was criticized as "uninviting and defective," Lucretia Mott gave him some sympathetic Hicksite advice: "William, if thee expects to set forth thy cause by word of mouth thee must lay aside thy paper and trust in the leading of the Spirit."[83] He took her words to heart and became "the orator *par excellence* of the Abolition movement in America."[84]

Garrison's debts to Lucretia Mott increased during the founding meeting of AASS in Philadelphia. For safety's sake the meeting was not openly publicized. The sixty-odd delegates represented gradualist organizations that were keenly aware of the risks involved in endorsing immediatism. When two leading philanthropists declined an invitation to preside at the convention their skeptical statements about immediatism made a "sensible impression" on the gathering. At that moment Garrison must have been intensely grateful for the presence of Lucretia Mott among the convention's four women "visitors," for she reminded delegates that "right principles are stronger than great names. If our principles are right, why should we be

82. For a good overview of slave rebellions, see Eric Foner, ed., Introduction, *Nat Turner* (Englewood Cliffs, N.J., 1971).

83. Garrison and Garrison, *William Lloyd Garrison*, 1:203; Bacon, *Valiant Friend*, p. 54. Of the Motts Garrison afterwards wrote: "If my mind has since become liberalized in any degree (and I think it has burst every sectarian trammel,)—if theological dogmas which I once regarded as essential to Christianity, I now repudiate as absurd and pernicious,—I am large indebted to them for the change" (Garrison and Garrison, *William Lloyd Garrison*, 1:204).

84. Martyn, *Wendell Phillips*, p. 135. Garrison's debt to the Grimké sisters, who were able to represent slavery from the South Carolinian perspective, was also weighty. He wrote Elizabeth Pease in 1837: "Our gifted friends, the Grimkés, are exerting an almost angelic influence wherever they go. Their public lectures are thronged by both sexes, and their triumph over prejudice and error has been most signal" (Taylor, *British and American Abolitionists*, p. 62).

cowards? Why should we wait for those who never had the courage to maintain the inalienable rights of the slave?" Amid cries of "go on," Mott took her seat, her remarks having buttressed the group's resolution at a critical juncture.[85] Though not an official delegate, she spoke frequently. Mott later remembered that "every courtesy was shown to us, every encouragement given to speak or to make suggestions or alteration." She sharpened the convention's rhetoric as well as its resolve. For example, she suggested the omission of the last two words in the phrase, "We may be personally defeated, but our principles never can be." She later summarized her experience there in glowing terms: "It was with difficulty, I acknowledge, that I ventured to express what had been near to my heart for many years, for I knew we were there by sufferance; but when I rose, such was the readiness with which the freedom to speak was granted, that it inspired me with a little more boldness to speak on other subjects."[86] Immediatism empowered women in different ways in the United States and Great Britain. In Britain the concept inspired the independent organization of women's antislavery associations. In the United States it sustained women's separate organizations while also opening significant opportunities for women within male-dominated associations.

Sarah Pugh's service as treasurer of the Pennsylvania Anti-Slavery Society every year between 1843 and 1860 exemplified those opportunities. In England as well as in the United States, much of the power of women's associations arose from their ability to raise money for the antislavery cause, but only in the United States did this ability translate into positions of authority within male-dominated organizations. As early as 1839 the business and finance committees of PASS consisted of four men and three women. In 1841 women began to serve on the Executive Committee of PASS and by 1850 five out of twelve members of the Executive Committee were women.[87] Women could be outvoted on these committees, but they could not be ignored.

Although women's organizations absorbed most of the antislavery energies of the vast majority of American women activists (including leaders like Mott, Pugh, Grew, and Kimber), larger, male-dominated organizations—especially in the critically important states of Pennsylvania and Massachusetts—invited women's participation by offering equal membership rights. Some American women shunned the female societies alto-

85. Tolles, "Lucretia Mott's Diary," p. 116.
86. Hallowell, *James and Lucretia Mott*, p. 115.
87. "Proceedings of the Meeting of the Pennsylvania State Anti-Slavery Society, May 1839, and October 1850," Pennsylvania Anti-Slavery Society Papers, Historical Society of Pennsylvania.

gether. The antislavery work of Lydia Maria Child was done almost entirely outside of female associations. Child wrote Mott in 1839:

> I have never very earnestly entered into the plan of female conventions and societies. They always seemed to me like half a pair of scissors. . . . You will remind me of the great good done by that society. I admit it most cordially. I am thankful there *were* those who could work heartily in that way. To pay my annual subscription, and occasionally make articles for sale, was all I ever could do freely and earnestly. . . . For the freedom of women, they have probably done something; but in every other point of view, I think their influence has been very slight.[88]

In 1840 Child became a member of the Executive Committee of the American Anti-Slavery Society and in 1841 began editing its weekly, the *National Anti-Slavery Standard*.[89] No woman leader of equal stature functioned independently of women's organizations in England.

Although the greater opportunities for women within the American antislavery movement meant that some women worked independently of women's societies, others carried those societies to a national level of organization. In 1837, 1838, and 1839 the growing power of women's political culture within the antislavery movement generated national conventions of abolitionist women, events that had no parallel in England.

At the first such convention delegates threatened the social status quo by assaulting racial prejudice against free blacks in the north.[90] And in Philadelphia in May 1838, partly as a result of the mingling of black and white delegates at the second national convention of antislavery women, an immense angry mob drove delegates out of their meeting hall and burned the building to the ground.[91] The women's endorsements of racial cooperation alarmed otherwise sympathetic community leaders. "Our proceedings, though not yet published, have greatly roused our pseudo-abolitionists," Mott wrote her son-in-law in 1838.

88. Hallowell, *James and Lucretia Mott*, p. 136; Milton Meltzer and Patricia Holland, *Lydia Maria Child: Selected Letters, 1817–1880* (Amherst, 1982), pp. 106–7.

89. See Deborah Pickman Clifford, *Crusade for Freedom: A Life of Lydia Maria Child* (Boston, 1992), and Louis Filler, "Lydia Maria Child," in Edward T. James et al., eds., *Notable American Women, 1607–1950: A Biographical Dictionary* (Cambridge, Mass., 1971).

90. *Proceedings of the Anti-Slavery Convention of American Women*, p. 13. About one tenth of the total number of delegates were black women, according to Sarah Pugh, *Memorial*, p. 18.

91. Pugh, *Memorial*, p. 21. About three thousand delegates were present in Pennsylvania Hall when it was attacked (*History of Pennsylvania Hall, Which was Destroyed by a Mob on the 17th of May, 1838* [Philadelphia, 1838], p. 137). See also Ira V. Brown, "Racism and Sexism: The Case of Pennsylvania Hall," *Phylon* 37 (1976):126–36.

Our good Dr. [Joseph] Parrish . . . has left no means untried to induce us to expunge from our minutes a resolution relating to social intercourse with our colored brethren. . . . And when he failed in this effort, he called some of the respectable portion of the colored people together at Robert Douglas', and advised them not to accept such intercourse as was proffered them, and to issue a disclaimer of any such wish. This they have not yet done; but it has caused not a little excitement among us.[92]

British antislavery women never faced this sort of violence, nor were they called on to witness against racism in this way. In keeping with their milder antislavery climate, Elizabeth Pease wrote to her constituency in 1838: "Be not afraid. We ask you not to do anything, to incite in anything unbecoming to your sex. Ours is not the tented field."[93] British women understood that men represented "the more public movement," whereas they undertook "the humble laborious part of the work."[94]

In the United States, antislavery activism required a greater commitment to recast social norms, such as the prohibition against women speaking to mixed assemblies of men and women. British abolitionist women did not violate this prohibition; American women did.[95] As a result, American women abolitionists became adept at defending their actions. Delegates to the 1837 Anti-Slavery Convention of American Women resolved that

the time has come for woman to move in that sphere which Providence has assigned to her, and no longer remain satisfied in the circumscribed limits with which corrupt custom and a perverted application of Scripture have encircled her; therefore that it is the duty of woman, and the province of woman, to plead the cause of the oppressed in our land, and to do all that she can by her voice, and her pen, and her purse, and the influence of her example, to overthrow the horrible system of American slavery.

This resolution was too radical for twelve of the seventy-one delegates. These twelve voted against it and asked to have their names recorded in the minutes as "disapproving."[96] Their opposition highlights the extent to

92. Hallowell, *James and Lucretia Mott*, p. 130; Dillwyn Parrish, *The Parrish Family* (Philadelphia, 1925), pp. 154–55.

93. Anna M. Stoddart, *Elizabeth Pease Nichol* (London, 1899), p. 64.

94. Quoted in Tyrrell, "Woman's Mission," p. 226.

95. Billington and Billington, "Women in the British Anti-Slavery Movement," p. 95.

96. *Proceedings of the Anti-Slavery Convention of American Women*, p. 9.

which antislavery activity in the United States carried women into new forms of political expression.

Women's petition campaigns in both countries furnish another example of how larger political systems produced different outcomes for British and American women, even though they engaged in very similar activity. Both political systems recognized the right to petition—a right peculiarly relevant to women, who could not vote. In England the development of women's antislavery associations in the 1820s led to petition campaigns in the early 1830s asking Parliament for the immediate emancipation of slaves in British colonies. William Wilberforce opposed women "stirring up petitions" as unsuitable for the female character "as delineated in scripture," but women ignored him, and on one 1833 petition they obtained 187,000 signatures.[97] These petitions contributed substantially to Parliament's decision that year to end slavery in the British West Indies.[98]

Petitioning activity by American women also followed quickly upon their formation of local women's societies but produced a different outcome.[99] In the United States, where the political system was far less capable of dealing with the slavery issue, the petition campaign stopped the functioning of the U.S. House of Representatives in 1837 when John Quincy Adams read petitions name by name. Revealing the inability of American political institutions to solve the slavery dispute, the petitions precipitated Gag Rules to block Adams's tactic.[100] For American women the petition campaign ultimately exposed the inadequacy of governmental

97. Billington and Billington, "Women in the British Anti-Slavery Movement," p. 91.

98. Fladeland, *Men and Brothers,* pp. 206–7.

99. In a letter to Elizabeth Pease in 1837, William Lloyd Garrison compared the American women's petition movement with that of British women. "As in England, so in this country—the women have done and are doing more for the extirpation of slavery than the other sex. In their petitions to Congress, they outnumber us at least three, perhaps five to one" (William Lloyd Garrison to Elizabeth Pease, November 6, 1837, in Taylor, *British and American Abolitionism,* p. 62).

Gerda Lerner's analysis of the petitions confirms Garrison's estimates. During the 1837–1839 campaign twice as many female signatures were collected as male signatures. From Massachusetts, Connecticut, and Pennsylvania, female signatures outnumbered males 42,031 to 12,055. In March 1838 Angelina Grimké formally addressed a committee of the Massachusetts legislature, presenting them with a women's petition with twenty thousand signatures (Lerner, "The Political Activities of Anti-Slavery Women," pp. 117, 120). Also see Deborah Van Broekhoven's essay, Chapter 10, in the present volume.

100. James Brewer Stewart, *Holy Warriors: The Abolitionists and American Slavery* (New York, 1976), pp. 83–85. For Parliament's response to petitions, see Seymour Drescher, "Public Opinion and the Destruction of British Colonial Slavery," in James Walvin, ed., *Slavery and British Society, 1776–1846* (London, 1982), pp. 22–48. Drescher noted that there was never "even the hint of an appeal to civil discord" in the British movement (p. 47).

institutions and led to a conviction that government could not solve the slavery problem.[101] The petition campaign of British women who argued for the extension of British privileges to slaves held in British colonies reinforced their respect for government. Urging a significantly different goal, American women petitioned for an end to government's support of slavery. This helps us understand why "the woman question" and the "no government" plank became so closely identified within Garrisonian abolitionism and why they so alienated the British women.

Different social and political circumstances for women in England and the United States produced different consequences even in such parallel and seemingly innocuous events as fund-raising fairs. On both sides of the Atlantic between 1837 and 1860 women's fund-raising activities sustained not only their own female societies but the male mainstream of the antislavery movement. Before 1837 women's subscriptions and donations were crucial to the movement's growth. As early as 1826 four British women's societies contributed four hundred pounds of a total income for the Anti-Slavery Society of fifteen hundred pounds, or more than 25 percent. The next year the national society was indebted to women for more than half its total donations.[102] In the 1840s British women expanded their financial clout through a fund-raising technique developed by evangelical women's societies—the bazaar, where women's handicrafts were donated and sold. American women adopted the same strategy even earlier. Lydia Maria Child organized the first antislavery fair in the United States in Boston in 1834. It received handicrafts from several women's antislavery societies in New England and netted three hundred dollars.[103] The next year Sarah Pugh began to coordinate fund-raising fairs annually in Philadelphia at Christmastime in conjunction with the meeting of the Pennsylvania Anti-Slavery Society.[104]

In the 1850s, when the American fairs reached their peak, we discover a revealing distinction between fund-raising efforts by American and British women—some fairs in the United States needed police protection against antiabolitionist violence. After John Brown's effort to provoke a slave up-

101. The "no government" perspective of American women abolitionists has been analyzed by Lori D. Ginzberg, *Women and the Work of Benevolence: Morality, Politics, and Class in the Nineteenth-Century United States* (New Haven, 1990). See also Lewis Perry, *Radical Abolitionism: Anarchy and the Government of God in Antislavery Thought* (Ithaca, 1973).

102. Billington and Billington, "Women in the British Anti-Slavery Movement," pp. 84, 86.

103. Benjamin Quarles, "Sources of Abolitionist Income," *Mississippi Valley Historical Review* 32 (1945): 63–76; and Lee Chambers-Schiller's essay, Chapter 13, in this volume.

104. Pugh, *Memorial*, p. 86. See also Orwin Rush, "Lucretia Mott and the Pennsylvania Antislavery Fairs," *Bulletin of Friends Historical Associations* 36 (1946): 69–75.

rising by attacking the military arsenal at Harpers Ferry early in 1859, Lucretia Mott and other antislavery women sheltered Brown's wife in Philadelphia.[105] Brown was executed just before the Philadelphia Female Anti-Slavery Society's annual fair opened in December 1859. Believing the fair an incitement to riot in the violence-plagued city, the sheriff "took possession of the hall, locked its doors, and thus closed the business of the fair." As on many previous occasions, this challenge presented American women's antislavery political culture with an opportunity for growth. Sarah Pugh described the occasion to a British friend. Those deciding how to respond to the sheriff were "all ladies, surrounded by gentleman, who looked with wonder on the 'irrepressible women,' amazed to see them so 'plucky,' and declaring they would vote for them for the Legislature. Such were the comments that we afterwards heard had been made, while we were engaged in grave debate as to the best thing to be done under the circumstances. One spectator longed for the power of making a picture that would be historical."[106]

Antislavery movements in England and the United States relied heavily on women's fund-raising activities, but American women had more power to be an historical force in their own right because slavery was more central to the nation's destiny. If power can be defined as the ability to control the distribution of social resources, women antislavery activists in England and the United States both exercised power. But the escalating violence in American society presented American women with more choices than British women faced. Their opportunities were greater, and so, therefore, was their growth as political agents.

Women's political cultures were not made by women alone. In 1841, Richard Webb, one of few British Garrisonians, explained to Maria Chapman why British abolitionists—men and women—had shifted their loyalty from Garrison to the "New Organization." "The glory of the Glasgow antislavery [society] melted away at the breath of their priests and New Organization.... I suppose they whispered 'Infidel! Unitarian! Women becoming lords of the creation.... Non-resistance—bloodshed and anarchy.' They need have said no more when presto! all their hearers grew pale, and banished the American Society from their purses and their prayers forever." Webb's comment epitomized the different social contexts of American and British women's activism. "People here," he continued, "have never

105. Pugh, *Memorial*, pp. 93–94.

106. Ibid., pp. 95–96. Another interpretation of this quotation can be found in Lori D. Ginzberg, "Moral Suasion is Moral Balderdash: Women, Politics, and Social Activism in the 1850s," *Journal of American History* 73 (1986): 601–22.

been placed in the same circumstances. . . . Touch Church or touch party in your antislavery efforts and all their zeal for the slaves would be scattered in the twinkling of an eye."[107]

A full appreciation of antislavery women requires us to take a complex view of women's political cultures and locate women within the society and polity of which they were a part. This comparison of British and American antislavery women has looked beyond women's motivations and institutions to explore how the larger political environment encouraged or discouraged women's participation. The women's rights movement was nourished within American abolitionism by some of the most fundamental features of American political life. No mere sport of circumstance or projection of the personalities of the Grimké sisters, nor an inevitable outcome of abolition in any political circumstance, women's rights flourished as an expression of qualities basic to American society in the 1840s. Some of those qualities made political institutions more democratically accessible, such as the disestablishment of religion and universal white male suffrage. Other qualities drastically limited the effectiveness of political institutions, such as the entrenchment of slavery and racism in American social, economic, and political life and the apparent inability of government to solve the growing conflict between free labor and slave labor systems. This combination of factors opened new and remarkable opportunities for women. More profoundly challenged to alter the sociopolitical status quo and less deeply rooted in class and other social distinctions than their English counterparts, American women abolitionists followed their own unique trajectory.

Appendix

The following women delegates were named as representing Massachusetts: Maria Chapman, Eliza S. Philbrick, Emily A. Winslow, Eliza Barney, Lydia Maria Child, Abby Kelley, Harriet Martineau. Lucretia Mott, Mary Grew, Sarah Pugh, Elizabeth Neall and Abby Kimber were listed for Pennsylvania. All of the Pennsylvania delegates attended the conference; all the Massachusetts delegates except Emily Winslow were unable to attend. Although Winslow and her father represented Massachusetts, they lived in Portland, Maine. Like many other New Englanders, they affiliated with the Massachusetts society, which until 1835 was named the New England Anti-Slavery Society. See Roman Zorn, "The New England Anti-Slavery Soci-

107. R. D. Webb to Maria Weston Chapman, November 20, 1841, in Taylor, *British and American Abolitionists*, p. 157.

ety: Pioneer Abolitionist Organization," *Journal of Negro History* 52 (1957): 157–76; and see the list of members attached to *Eighth Annual Report of the Board of Managers of the Mass. Anti-Slavery Society, Presented January 22, 1840* (Boston, 1840). Harriet Martineau stayed home due to illness. Otherwise, as a British citizen and an American delegate, she might have brought new issues into the seating debate. See Betty Fladeland, "Harriet Martineau," in Fladeland, *Abolitionists and Working-Class Problems in the Age of Industrialization* (Baton Rouge, La., 1984), pp. 74–92.

Several sources confirm the number of women delegates as seven. (See, for example, Maria Waring's account in Clare Taylor, comp., *British and American Abolitionists: An Episode in Transatlantic Understanding* [Edinburgh, 1974], p. 95.) But sources differ in their identification of the second Massachusetts female delegate. Some name Ann Phillips, some Abby Southwick. Donald R. Kennon, "'An Apple of Discord': The Woman Question at the World's Anti-Slavery Convention of 1840," *Slavery and Abolition* 5 (1984): 248, listed Phillips rather than Southwick. Ann Green Phillips was traveling in Europe with her husband, Wendell, at the time, so she may not have obtained official papers from the Massachusetts society. This, combined with her disabilities as an invalid, may account for her exclusion from Stanton's account and from the *Liberator* list. A niece of Maria Weston Chapman and a cousin of Mary Grew, Ann Phillips was raised in the Chapman household. See Carlos Martyn, *Wendell Phillips: The Agitator* (New York, 1890), pp. 128, 138; James Brewer Stewart, *Wendell Phillips: Liberty's Hero* (Baton Rouge, 1986), p. 77; and Irving H. Bartlett, *Wendell and Ann Phillips: The Community of Reform, 1840–1880* (New York, 1979), p. 36. Abby Southwick, who with other members of her family were the only Quaker members of the Boston Female Anti-Slavery Society, seems to have been added later to the Massachusetts roster. For Southwick's Quaker affiliation, see Debra Gold Hansen, *Strained Sisterhood: Gender and Class in the Boston Female Anti-Slavery Society* (Amherst, 1993), p. 81.

Mott and Phillips were accompanied by their husbands, James and Wendell; Winslow and Grew by their fathers, Isaac and Henry. Pugh, Kimber, Neall and Southwick were unattended by husbands or fathers. My decision to treat Southwick as a delegate arises from her unaccompanied status, her Quaker background, the fact that she was the only woman delegate from Boston, and her inclusion in Stanton's list. The most concise source for brief biographies of Americans at the London convention is Frederick B. Tolles's editorial notes in "Slavery and 'The Woman Question': Lucretia Mott's Diary of Her Visit to Great Britain to Attend the World's Anti-Slavery Convention of 1840," *Journal of the Friends Historical Society*, supplement 23 (1952).

Bibliographical Notes

The authors of the foregoing essays have provided full documentation for those essays in the footnotes. Two authors—Jean Fagan Yellin and Kathryn Kish Sklar—have written more extensive bibliographical notes that provide background and context for all of the essays in this volume. The editors have chosen to print those notes here.

Jean Fagan Yellin

A standard history of nineteenth-century American women remains Eleanor Flexner, *Century of Struggle: The Woman's Rights Movement in the United States* (Cambridge, 1959). The pioneering studies are Gerda Lerner, *The Grimké Sisters from South Carolina: Pioneers for Woman's Rights and Abolition* (New York, 1967); Jane H. Pease and William H. Pease, "The Role of Women in the Antislavery Movement," in John P. H. Atherton and Fernand Ouellet, eds., *Canadian Historical Association, Historical Papers Presented at the Annual Meeting . . . 1967*, pp. 167–83; Aileen Kraditor, *Means and Ends in American Abolitionism: Garrison and His Critics on Strategy and Tactics, 1834–1850* (New York, 1967), chap. 3; and Alma Lutz, *Crusade for Freedom: Women of the Antislavery Movement* (Boston, 1968). For other important studies written in the first years of the modern feminist movement, see William Taylor and Christopher Lasch, "Two 'Kindred Spirits': Sorority and Family in New England, 1839–1846," *New England Quarterly* 36 (1963): 25–41; Carroll Smith-Rosenberg, *Religion and the Rise of the American City: The New York City Mission Movement, 1812–1870* (Ithaca, 1971); Smith-Rosenberg, "Beauty, the Beast, and the Militant Woman: A Case

Study in Sex Roles and Social Stress in Jacksonian America," *American Quarterly* 23 (October 1971): 562–84; Jane H. Pease and William H. Pease, *Bound with Them in Chains: A Biographical History of the Antislavery Movement* (Westport, Conn., 1972); Smith-Rosenberg, "The Female World of Love and Ritual: Relations between Women in Nineteenth-Century America," *Signs* 1 (1975): 1–29; Kathryn Kish Sklar, *Catharine Beecher: A Study in American Domesticity* (New Haven, 1973); Keith E. Melder, *Beginnings of Sisterhood: The American Woman's Rights Movement, 1800–1850* (New York, 1977); and Nancy Cott, *The Bonds of Womanhood: "Woman's Sphere" in New England, 1780–1835* (New Haven, 1977).

A landmark examination of American antislavery women is Blanche Glassman Hersh, *The Slavery of Sex: Feminist-Abolitionists in America* (Urbana, 1978). The newest full-length study is Jean Fagan Yellin, *Women and Sisters: The Antislavery Feminists in American Culture* (New Haven, 1989).

Recent discussions of the organized activities of women include Barbara J. Berg, *The Remembered Gate: Origins of American Feminism. The Woman and the City, 1800–1860* (New York, 1978); Barbara Leslie Epstein, *The Politics of Domesticity: Women, Evangelism, and Temperance in Nineteenth-Century America* (Middletown, Conn., 1981); Estelle Freedman, *Their Sisters' Keepers: Women's Prison Reform in America, 1830–1930* (Ann Arbor, 1981); Mary P. Ryan, *Cradle of the Middle Class: The Family in Oneida County, New York, 1790–1865* (New York, 1981); Nancy Hewitt, *Women's Activism and Social Change: Rochester, New York, 1822–1872* (Ithaca, 1984); Anne M. Boylan, "Women in Groups: An Analysis of Women's Benevolent Organizations in New York and Boston, 1797–1840," *Journal of American History* 71 (1984): 497–523; Lori D. Ginzberg, *Women and the Work of Benevolence: Morality, Politics, and Class in the Nineteenth-Century United States* (New Haven, 1990); Kathleen D. McCarty, ed., *Lady Bountiful Revisited: Women, Philanthropy, and Power* (New Brunswick, 1990); and Anne Firor Scott, *Natural Allies: Women's Associations in American History* (Urbana, Ill., 1991).

For the organizational activities of antebellum African American women, see Dorothy Porter, "The Organized Educational Activities of Negro Literary Societies, 1828–1846," *Journal of Negro Education* 5 (1930): 556–66, 568–69, 574–76; rpt. in August Meier and Elliott Rudwick, eds., *The Making of Black America: Essays in Negro Life and History* (New York, 1969); Gerda Lerner, ed., *Black Women in White America: A Documentary History* (New York, 1972); Rosalyn Terborg-Penn, "Discrimination against Afro-American Women in the Women's Movement, 1830–1920," in Sharon Harley and Rosalyn Terborg-Penn, eds., *The Afro-American Woman: Struggles and Images* (Port Washington, 1978), pp. 17–27; James O. Horton and Lois Horton, *Black Bostonians: Family Life and Community Struggle in the*

Antebellum North (New York, 1979); Paula Giddings, *When and Where I Enter: The Impact of Black Women on Race and Sex in America* (New York, 1984); Dorothy Sterling, ed., *We Are Your Sisters: Black Women in the Nineteenth Century* (New York, 1984), a documentary history; Emma J. Lapsansky, "Friends, Wives, and Strivings: Networks and Community Values Among Nineteenth-Century Philadelphia Afroamerican Elites," *Pennsylvania Magazine of History and Biography* 108 (1984): 3–24; Lois Horton, "Community Organization and Social Activism: Black Boston and the Antislavery Movement," *Sociological Inquiry* 55 (1985): 182–99; Kathleen C. Berkeley, "'Colored Ladies Also Contributed': Black Women's Activities from Benevolence to Social Welfare, 1866–1896," in Walter J. Fraser, Jr., R. Frank Saunders, Jr., and Jon L. Wakelyn, eds., *The Web of Southern Social Relations: Women, Family, and Education* (Athens, Ga., 1985), pp. 181–203; rpt. in Darlene Clark Hine, ed., *Black Women in American History from Colonial Times through the Nineteenth Century*, 4 vols. (New York, 1990), 1:61–83; James O. Horton, "Freedom's Yoke: Gender Conventions among Antebellum Free Blacks," *Feminist Studies* 12 (1986): 51–76; Elsa Barkley Brown, "Womanist Consciousness: Maggie Lena Walker and the Independent Order of St. Luke," *Signs* 14 (1989): 610–33; rpt. in Darlene Clark Hine et al., eds., *Black Women in American History: The Twentieth Century*, 4 vols. (New York, 1990), 1:153–168; Emma J. Lapsansky, "Feminism, Freedom and Community: Charlotte Forten and Women Activists in Nineteenth-Century Philadelphia," *Pennsylvania Magazine of History and Biography* 113 (1989): 3–19; and Anne Firor Scott, "Most Invisible of All: Black Women's Voluntary Associations," *Journal of Southern History* 56 (1990): 3–22.

For the relationships between women's culture and politics, see Ellen Carol DuBois et al., "Politics and Culture in Women's History: A Symposium," *Feminist Studies* 6 (1980): 26–64. The notion of a public political culture of American women in the Revolutionary period is discussed in Mary Beth Norton, *Liberty's Daughters: The Revolutionary Experience of American Women, 1750–1800* (Boston, 1980); and Linda K. Kerber, *Women of the Republic: Intellect and Ideology in Revolutionary America* (Chapel Hill, 1980). For innovative discussions of women's public culture in the nineteenth-century, see Suzanne Lebsock, *The Free Women of Petersburg: Status and Culture in a Southern Town, 1784–1860* (New York, 1984); Sara Evans, *Born for Liberty: A History of Women in America* (New York, 1989) and Mary P. Ryan, *Women in Public: Between Banners and Ballots, 1825–1880* (Baltimore, 1990). For brief, particularly useful discussions of nineteenth-century women's political culture, see Mary P. Ryan, "The Power of Women's Networks: A Case Study of Female Moral Reform in Antebellum America," *Feminist Studies* 5 (1979): 66–85; Nancy Hewitt, "The Social Origins of Women's Antislavery Politics in Western New York," in Alan M. Kraut, ed., *Crusaders and Compromisers: Essays on the Relationship of the Antislavery Struggle to the Antebellum Party System* (Westport, Conn., 1983), pp. 205–33; Paula Baker, "The Domestication of Politics: Women and American Political Society, 1780–1920," *American Historical Review* 89 (1984): 620–47; and Anne M. Boylan, "Women and Politics in the Era before Seneca Falls," *Journal of the Early Republic* 10 (1990): 363–82.

Kathryn Kish Sklar

Recent historiography on women in the American antislavery movement begins with Aileen S. Kraditor's essay "The Woman Question" in her *Means and Ends in American Abolitionism: Garrison and His Critics on Strategy and Tactics, 1834–1850* (New York, 1967), and Gerda Lerner, *The Grimké Sisters from South Carolina: Pioneers for Woman's Rights and Abolition* (Boston, 1967). See also Alma Lutz, *Crusade for Freedom: Women of the Anti-Slavery Movement* (Boston, 1968); Katharine Du Pre Lumpkin, *The Emancipation of Angelina Grimké* (Chapel Hill, 1974); Milton Meltzer, *Tongue of Flame: The Life of Lydia Maria Child* (New York, 1965); Jane H. Pease and William H. Pease, *Bound with Them in Chains: A Biographical History of the Antislavery Movement* (Westport, Conn., 1972); Dorothy Sterling, *Ahead of Her Time: Abby Kelley and the Politics of Antislavery* (New York, 1991); Blanche Glassman Hersh, *The Slavery of Sex: Feminist-Abolitionists in America* (Urbana, 1978); Robert Abzug, *Passionate Liberator: Theodore Dwight Weld and the Dilemma of Reform* (New York, 1980); Margaret Hope Bacon, *Valiant Friend: The Life of Lucretia Mott* (New York, 1980); Lee Virginia Chambers-Schiller, *Liberty, A Better Husband—Single Women in America: The Generations of 1780–1840* (New Haven, 1984); Jean Fagan Yellin, *Women and Sisters: The Antislavery Feminists in American Culture* (New Haven, 1989); Lori D. Ginzberg, *Women and the Work of Benevolence: Morality, Politics, and Class in the Nineteenth-Century United States* (New Haven, 1990); Wendy Hamand Venet, *Neither Ballots Nor Bullets: Women Abolitionists and Emancipation during the Civil War* (Charlottesville, 1991); and Deborah Bingham Van Broekhoven, "The Fabric of Antislavery Networks," in *Abolitionists Were Female: Rhode Island Women in the Antislavery Network* (Urbana, Ill., forthcoming).

Published primary sources include Milton Meltzer and Patricia Holland, eds., *Lydia Maria Child: Selected Letters, 1817–1880* (Amherst, 1982); Bert James Loewenberg and Ruth Bogin, eds., *Black Women in Nineteenth-Century American Life: Their Words, Their Thoughts, Their Feelings* (University Park, Pa., 1976); Larry Ceplair, ed., *The Public Years of Sarah and Angelina*

Grimké: Selected Writings, 1835–1839 (New York, 1989); Peter Ripley, ed., *The Black Abolitionist Papers,* 5 vols. (Chapel Hill, 1985–92); Dorothy Sterling, ed., *We Are Your Sisters: Black Women in the Nineteenth Century* (New York, 1984); Brenda Stevenson, ed., *The Journals of Charlotte Forten Grimké* (New York, 1988); Marilyn Richardson, ed., *Maria W. Stewart: America's First Black Woman Political Writer: Essays and Speeches* (Bloomington, Ind., 1987); and *Turning the World Upside Down: The Anti-Slavery Convention of American Women: Held in New York City, May 9–12, 1837* (New York, 1987).

This book builds on the work of historians who have analyzed structural components of women's political culture in the antislavery movement. That trend began with Gerda Lerner, "The Political Activities of Anti-Slavery Women," in her book *The Majority Finds Its Past* (New York, 1979), pp. 112–28, where Lerner's analysis of women's antislavery petitions discovers links between two levels of women's activism—women's community and family networks, and speaking tours by women antislavery leaders, particularly Angelina and Sarah Grimké. Ellen DuBois discusses how features of women's political activism led to feminism in "Women's Rights and Abolition: The Nature of the Connection," in Lewis Perry and Michael Fellman, eds., *Anti-Slavery Reconsidered: New Perspectives on the Abolitionists* (Baton Rouge, La., 1979), pp. 238–51. Nancy Hewitt uses community structures to compare abolitionist women with other expressions of women's political culture in *Women's Activism and Social Change, Rochester, New York, 1822–1872* (Ithaca, 1984); "The Social Origins of Women's Antislavery Politics in Western New York," in Alan Kraut, ed., *Crusaders and Compromisers: Essays on the Relationship of the Antislavery Struggle to the Antebellum Party System* (Westport, Conn., 1983), pp. 205–33; and "Feminist Friends: Agrarian Quakers and the Emergence of Woman's Rights in America," *Feminist Studies* 12 (1986): 27–49. See also Keith E. Melder, *Beginnings of Sisterhood: The American Woman's Rights Movement, 1800–1850* (New York, 1977); Judith Wellman, "Women and Radical Reform in Antebellum Upstate New York: A Profile of Grassroots Female Abolitionists," in Mabel E. Deutrich and Virginia C. Purdy, eds., *Clio Was a Woman: Studies in the History of American Women* (Washington, D.C., 1980); Anne M. Boylan, "Timid Girls, Venerable Widows, and Dignified Matrons: Life Cycle Patterns among Organized Women in New York and Boston, 1797–1840," *American Quarterly* 38 (1986): 779–97; and Karen Sanchez-Eppler, "Bodily Bonds: The Intersecting Rhetorics of Feminism and Abolition," in *Representations* (Fall 1988): 34–43.

Analyses of women's antislavery societies include Ira V. Brown's " 'Am I Not a Woman and a Sister?': The Anti-Slavery Convention of American Women, 1837–1839," *Pennsylvania History* 50 (1983): 1–19; Brown, "Cradle of

Feminism: The Philadelphia Female Anti-Slavery Society, 1833–1840,"
Pennsylvania Magazine of History and Biography 102 (1978): 143–66; Debra
Gold Hansen, *Strained Sisterhood: Gender and Class in the Boston Female
Anti-Slavery Society* (Amherst, 1993); Edward Magdol, *The Antislavery Rank
and File: A Social Profile of the Abolitionists' Constituency* (Westport, Conn.,
1986), especially pp. 71, 165; Amy Swerdlow, "Abolition's Conservative Sisters: The Ladies' New York City Anti-Slavery Societies, 1834–1840," Chapter 2 in this volume; and Carolyn Williams, "Religion, Race, and Gender in
Antebellum American Radicalism: The Philadelphia Female Anti-Slavery
Society, 1833–1870" (Ph.D. diss., University of California, Los Angeles,
1991).

Black women abolitionists have been studied in Louis Ruchames, "Race,
Marriage and Abolition in Massachusetts," *Journal of Negro History* 40
(1955): 250–73; Benjamin Quarles, *Black Abolitionists* (New York, 1969);
Ruth Bogin, "Sarah Parker Remond: Black Abolitionist from Salem," *Essex
Institute Historical Collections,* 110 (1974): 120–50; Ira Brown, "Racism and
Sexism: The Case of Pennsylvania Hall," *Phylon* 37 (1976): 126–36; Paula
Giddings, *When and Where I Enter: The Impact of Black Women on Race and
Sex in America* (New York, 1984); James O. Horton, "Generations of Pro-
test: Black Families and Social Reform in Ante-Bellum Boston," *New En-
gland Quarterly* 49 (1976): 242–56; George A. Levesque, "Black Boston:
Negro Life in Garrison's Boston, 1800–1860" (Ph.D. diss., State University
of New York, Binghamton, 1976); Rosalyn Terborg-Penn, "Discrimination
against Afro-American Women in the Women's Movement, 1830–1920," in
Sharon Harley and Rosalyn Terborg-Penn, eds., *The Afro-American
Woman* (Port Washington, N.Y., 1978), pp. 17–27; Janice Sumler-Lewis,
"The Forten-Purvis Women of Philadelphia and the American Anti-Slavery
Crusade," *Journal of Negro History* 66 (1981–1982): 281–88; R. J. M. Blackett,
*Building an Antislavery Wall: Black Americans in the Atlantic Abolitionist
Movement, 1830–1860* (Baton Rouge, La., 1983); Lois Horton, "Community
Organization and Social Activism: Black Boston and the Antislavery Move-
ment," *Sociological Inquiry* 55 (1985): 182–99; Emma J. Lapsansky, "Femi-
nism, Freedom and Community: Charlotte Forten and Women Activists in
Nineteenth-Century Philadelphia," *Pennsylvania Magazine of History and
Biography* 113 (1989): 3–19; Nell Irvin Painter, "Sojourner Truth in Life and
Memory: Writing the Biography of an American Exotic," *Gender and History* 2 (1990):3–16; Shirley J. Yee, *Black Women Abolitionists: A Study in Activism, 1828–1860* (Knoxville, Tenn., 1992); Carleton Mabee with Susan
Mabee Newhouse, *Sojourner Truth: Slave, Prophet, Legend* (New York,
1993); and Bettye Collier-Thomas, *Frances Ellen Watkins Harper: Abolitionist and Feminist Reformer* (Chapel Hill, forthcoming).

Notes on Contributors

Margaret Hope Bacon is a Philadelphia author and lecturer who has written frequently on historical subjects. Her articles have appeared in numerous periodicals, including *Quaker History* and the *Journal of Social Work*. She has written biographies of Abby Kelley Foster and Lucretia Mott and is the author of *Mothers of Feminism: The Story of Quaker Women in America* (1986), as well as many other books and articles. Bacon graduated from Antioch College with honors in 1943.

Ruth Bogin has been Adjunct Professor of History at Pace University since 1979. Coeditor of *Black Women in Nineteenth-Century American Life: Their Words, Their Thoughts, Their Feelings* (1976), she has written articles and presented papers on antislavery literature, abolitionism, nineteenth-century women, black women leaders, and the quest for equality during the American Revolutionary era. She received her Ph.D. from Union Graduate School in 1978.

Anne M. Boylan is Associate Professor of History at the University of Delaware. She received her Ph.D. from the University of Wisconsin–Madison in 1973 and is the author of *Sunday School: The Formation of an American Institution, 1790–1880* (1988) and of articles in the *Journal of American History, American Quarterly, Feminist Studies,* and the *Journal of the Early Republic.*

Notes on Contributors

LEE CHAMBERS-SCHILLER is Associate Professor of History and chair of the department at the University of Colorado at Boulder. She is the author of *Liberty, A Better Husband: Single Women in America, The Generations 1780–1840* (1984), and is writing a biography of Maria Weston Chapman. Some of her work has appeared in *New Research on Women* and *FRONTIERS: A Journal of Women Studies*. She received her Ph.D. in 1977 from the University of Michigan.

DEBRA GOLD HANSEN received her Ph.D. from the University of California, Irvine, in 1988 and is Assistant Professor of Library and Information Science at San Jose State University (Fullerton campus). She is the author, with Mary P. Ryan, of the essay "Public Ceremony in a Private Culture: Orange County Celebrates the Fourth of July," in Rob Kling, Spencer Olin, and Mark Poster, eds., *Postsuburban California: The Transformation of Orange County Since World War II* (1991), and of *Strained Sisterhood: Gender and Class in the Boston Female Anti-Slavery Society* (1993).

NANCY A. HEWITT, Professor of History at Duke University, received her Ph.D. from the University of Pennsylvania in 1981. Her work has appeared in *Feminist Studies* and *Women's Studies Quarterly*, and she is a founding editor of *Gender and History*. She is the author of *Women's Activism and Social Change: Rochester, New York, 1822–1872* (1984) and the editor of *Women, Families, and Communities: Readings in American History* (1990), and *Visible Women: New Essays on American Activism* (1993).

EMMA JONES LAPSANSKY is Curator of the Quaker Collection at Haverford College. Her work on African American history, particularly the development of the nineteenth-century Philadelphia African American community, has appeared in the *Pennsylvania Magazine of History and Biography* and the *American Quarterly*. A Ph.D. in American Civilization from the University of Pennsylvania (1975), she is the author of *Neighborhoods in Transition: William Penn's Dream and Urban Reality* (1994).

PHILLIP LAPSANSKY, Research Librarian at the Library Company of Philadelphia, is a graduate of Temple University's American History Honors Program. His twenty years of work with the Library Company's Afro-American Collection has included curating numerous exhibitions and compiling *Afro-American 1553–1906: Author Catalog of The Library Company of Philadelphia and The Historical Society of Pennsylvania* (1973).

KEITH E. MELDER, Curator in the Division of Political History at the Smithsonian Institution, received his Ph.D. in American Studies from Yale

University in 1964. He contributed four biographical articles to *Notable American Women 1607–1950: A Biographical Dictionary* (1971) and has published articles on a variety of topics, including nineteenth-century women's benevolence, Josephine Griffing, and the Grimké sisters. Melder is also the author of *Beginnings of Sisterhood: The American Woman's Rights Movement, 1800–1850* (1977).

NELL IRVIN PAINTER is the author of three books, the latest of which is *Standing at Armageddon: The United States, 1877–1919* (1987). She received her Ph.D. in American History from Harvard University in 1974 and is currently Edwards Professor of American History at Princeton University. Painter is working on a biography of Sojourner Truth and a book on sexuality in the United States South.

KATHRYN KISH SKLAR is Distinguished Professor of History at the State University of New York, Binghamton. She is the author of *Catharine Beecher* (1973), one of six books she has published on women's history. She is the author of numerous scholarly articles and has contributed chapters to many books, including Seth Koven and Sonya Michel, eds., *Mothers of a New World: Maternalist Politics and the Origins of Welfare States* (1993). Sklar received her Ph.D. from the University of Michigan in 1969.

JEAN R. SODERLUND, Professor of History at Lehigh University, received her Ph.D. from Temple University in 1982. She has been an associate editor of *The Papers of William Penn* and is the author of *Quakers and Slavery: A Divided Spirit* (1985) as well as numerous articles and papers on women's history and African American history. Soderlund is the co-author, with Gary Nash, of *Freedom by Degrees: Emancipation in Pennsylvania and Its Aftermath* (1991).

AMY SWERDLOW, Professor of History and Director, Graduate Program in Women's History, Sarah Lawrence College, is editor of and contributor to *Household and Kin*, co-editor of *Class, Race, and Sex: The Dynamics of Control* (1983), contributor to *Rocking the Ship of State* (1989) and *Sights on the Sixties* (1992), and author of *Women Strike for Peace: Traditional Motherhood and Radical Politics in the 1960s* (1993).

DEBORAH BINGHAM VAN BROEKHOVEN, Assistant Professor of American History at Ohio Wesleyan University, received her Ph.D. from Bowling Green State University in 1976. She is the author of *Abolitionists Were Female: Rhode Island Women in the Antislavery Network* (Urbana, Ill., forthcoming). Some of her articles have appeared in *Rhode Island History* and *Psychohistory Review*.

JOHN C. VAN HORNE is Librarian of the Library Company of Philadelphia and Editor of *The Papers of Benjamin Henry Latrobe*. He received his Ph.D. from the University of Virginia in 1979. Among his other publications is *Religious Philanthropy and Colonial Slavery: The American Correspondence of the Associates of Dr. Bray, 1717–1777* (1985).

CAROLYN WILLIAMS received her Ph.D. from the University of California, Los Angeles in 1991. She is Assistant Professor of History at the University of North Florida. She has presented papers at several conferences including the Organization of American Historians and the Southeastern Women's Studies Association. Currently she is writing an entry on Charlotte Forten for the projected *American National Biography*.

JULIE WINCH, author of *Philadelphia's Black Elite: Activism, Accommodation, and the Struggle for Autonomy, 1787–1848* (1988), received her Ph.D. in History from Bryn Mawr College in 1982. She is Associate Professor of Black Studies and History at the University of Massachusetts, Boston. Her numerous papers and articles explore such topics as the kidnapping of free blacks and the links between American free blacks and Haitians.

JEAN FAGAN YELLIN, who received her Ph.D. from the University of Illinois in 1969, is Distinguished Professor of English at Pace University. The author of numerous writings on 19th-century American literature and culture, her scholarship emphasizes women, blacks, and radicals. She is the editor of Harriet Jacobs's *Incidents in the Life of a Slave Girl. Written by Herself* (1987), and co-compiler of *The Pen Is Ours: A Listing of Writings by and about African-American Women before 1910* (1991). Her most recent book is *Women and Sisters: The Anti-Slavery Feminists in American Culture* (1989).

Index

Index

Index

American Convention for Promoting the Abolition of Slavery, 202
American Equal Rights Association, 273
American Free Produce Association, 279
American Moral Reform Society, 110
American Peace Society, 288, 294–95
American Woman Suffrage Association, 29–30
Andrews, Charles C., 123–24
"Anna Elizabeth," 103–4
Anthony, Susan B., 29–30, 86, 157, 296, 302n
Anti-Slavery Appeal (Walters), 23
Anti-Slavery Bugle, 151, 151n, 202, 247
Anti-Slavery Convention of American Women
    1837, 5, 10–16, 34, 40–41, 43n, 116–17, 172n, 234–35, 246–47, 307, 307n; African American women at, 11–12, 40, 47, 57n, 116, 120, 134–35, 168–69, 327n; and Boston Female Anti-Slavery Society, 51–52, 57n, 64, 135, 160, 172n; and free produce, 279–80; and petitioning, 78, 184–85; and public speaking, 328–29; and racial integration, 224–25, 225n; and racism, 169, 327; and women's rights, 160, 171–72, 177, 235, 275
    1838, 16–17, 34, 117, 120, 129, 169–71, 176, 231, 246–47, 284–87, 307n; African American women at, 117, 117n, 120, 286; and Boston Female Anti-Slavery Society, 64, 160; and free produce, 279–80; and nonresistance, 286–88; and petitioning, 17; proceedings of, 34–35n, 160; and promiscuous audiences, 285–86; and racial integration, 224–26, 327; and racism, 169; and women's rights, 160, 177, 275. *See also* Pennsylvania Hall
    1839, 16, 117, 160, 176, 176n, 246–47, 289–91, 307n; African American women at, 117, 117n, 120, 227, 290; and Boston Female Anti-Slavery Society, 160; and free produce, 280–81; and nonresistance, 291; and petitioning, 17; proceedings of, 34n; and racial integration, 224–25, 290; and racism, 169; and women's rights, 177, 275
    1840 (proposed), 46, 176

Anti-Slavery Record, 202, 208–9, 213, fig. 10
Anti-Slavery Reporter, 202
Anti-Slavery Standard. See National Anti-Slavery Standard
Appeal in Favor of That Class of Americans Called Africans (Child), 7–9, 14n, 48
"Appeal of Clerical Abolitionists on Anti-Slavery Measures," 53–54
Appeal to the Christian Women of the South (A. Grimké), 149, 317n
Appeal . . . to the Colored Citizens of the World (Walker), 324
Appeal to the Women of the Nominally Free States, 34n, 116, 134, 173n, 280
"Appeal to Woman" (S. Forten), 116–17, 117n
Arago, François, 259n
Armory Hall (Boston), 2
Association for the Benefit of Colored Orphans (New York), 134, 136
Atkinson, Elizabeth, 26
Atkinson, Sarah, 262
Atlantic Monthly, 152
Atlantic slave trade, 216–17
Atlee, Dr. Edwin, 69

Ball, Joseph, 57n
Ball, Lucy, 45, 56–57, 56–57n, 61, 64n, 263
Ball, Martha, 45, 56–57n, 60–61, 63–64n, 64, 263, 280
Banneker Institute (Philadelphia), 94–97
Barbadoes, C., 58n, 59
Barker, Elizabeth, 316
Barney, Eliza, 332
"Beatrice" (pseud.), 107
Beaumont, Gustave de, 259n
Beaumont, Sarah, 317n
Beecher, Catharine, 15, 173; *Essay on Slavery and Abolitionism,* 173n
Belknap Street Baptist Church (Boston), 136
Beman, Mrs. Jehiel C., 58–59, 58–59n, 65n
Beman, Rev. Jehiel C., 65n
Benedict, Mary F., 43n
Benedict, S. W., 43n
Benevolent societies, 1–2, 10, 12, 19, 63, 86
    African American women's, 119–37; and abolition, 125; and gender conventions, 123–24, 133–34; male sponsorship of,

Index

Benevolent societies (*cont.*)
    123–24; membership of, 130–31, 132;
    and mutual assistance, 122–23, 127–28,
    130; organizational names of, 125–27;
    and promiscuous audiences, 124–25;
    and public behavior, 131–33; and public
    speaking, 133; and racism, 132–34
    white women's, 26, 34, 123–27, 130–31,
    135, 136
Benson, George, 147
Bentham, Jeremy, 310
"Bera" (pseud.), 104, 109, 116
Beriah Baptist Church (New York), 39
Bethel African Methodist Episcopal
    Church (Philadelphia), 102n
Bethel Presbyterian Church (Rochester),
    26–27
Bethune, Mary McLeod, 158
Bevan, William, 306
Bias, Eliza Ann, 116, 116n
Bias, James J. G., 116n
Bird, Jerusha L., 263
Birmingham (Eng.) Ladies' Society for the
    Relief of Negro Slaves, 316
Birney, James, 191, 312
Black, Adam, 251n
"Black and White Abolition Coach," 227–
    28, fig. 26
Black bourgeoisie, 99
"Black/White Fight against Slavery and for
    Women's Rights" (Katz), 23
Blanchard, Elisha, 57n
Bodichon, Barbara Leigh Smith, 304n
Bogle, Amelia M., 71, 97n, 117n
Bogle, Robert, 117n
Boston Antislavery Fair, 59, 62–63, 249–
    74, 250–51n, 253, 253n, 266n, 269n, 330;
    African American participation in,
    256–57n; and community fairs, 255–58,
    255–56n; and evangelical women, 261–
    64; at Faneuil Hall, 268; and Free Soil
    Party, 267; gender roles within, 261–
    62, 265–66; goods sold at, 49, 234,
    249–53, 256n, 262–63, 265–69; lectures
    at, 260, 260n; and *The Liberty Bell*,
    258–59, 265–66; and Liberty Party,
    267; male participation at, 264–67,
    266n; and moral suasionists, 251–55,
    259–64, 267, 269–71; petitioning at,

260; political education at, 257–61;
    and political suasionists, 251–52, 261–
    64; proceeds of, 49, 250n, 251, 251n;
    replaced with monetary subscription,
    251–52, 269n, 270–71, 274n; as social
    exchange, 259
Boston Baptist Sewing and Social
    Circle, 63
"Boston Clique," 173
"Boston Controversy." *See* Boston Female
    Anti-Slavery Society
Boston Female Anti-Slavery Society, 2, 8,
    12–13, 36, 39, 43, 45–65, 129, 137, 172;
    African American members of, 46–47,
    56–59, 57–58n, 65, 65n, 134; and "Bos-
    ton Controversy," 54–65, 62n, 64–65n,
    176, 257, 263, 285, 287, 289, 307; disso-
    lution of, 45, 58–61, 65, 176, 250n, 261,
    307; education of African Americans,
    47, 262; factionalism within, 46, 54–
    65, 62n, 64n, 65n; fairs of, 2, 48–49,
    57, 57n, 59, 62–63, 65n, 172, 268; found-
    ing of, 6, 46, 172, 323n; fundraising of,
    46–47, 49, 172; membership of, 26, 36,
    46–47, 49, 61–62, 61n, 316, 333; mob
    violence against, 1, 38, 49–50, 120,
    170–73, 221, 282–83; petitioning of,
    12–13, 38, 51, 62, 172, 184; and public
    role of women, 37, 46, 79, 174–76;
    racial integration within, 47, 57n; and
    women's rights, 43, 159–60; at World
    Anti-Slavery Convention, 307, 313, 316.
    See also Anti-Slavery Convention of
    American Women (1837/38/39); Boston
    Antislavery Fair; Garrisonian aboli-
    tionists; *Liberty Bell;* Thompson,
    George
Boston Female Moral Reform Society, 63n
Bowers, Elizabeth, 97
Bowers, John C., 110, 110n
Bowers, Margaret, 110n, 116
Bowers, Mary, 110n
Bowring, Dr. John, 259n, 310
Boycotting, 161, 192, 277, 280
Bradburn, Rev. George, 306n, 311–12, 312n
Bradshaw, Sarah, 316
Branagan, Thomas, 206, 209
Brayton, Patience, 277
Brazil, 7

Index

Index

Index

Index

Index

Index

Index

Index

Index

Racism, 7, 165–69, 246, 324; against African American women, 10–11, 19, 120, 133, 135, 165–66, 237–38; within antislavery movement, 11–12, 40, 40n, 56n, 60, 134–35, 160, 166–69, 212, 256, 327; against free blacks, 166, 208; and mob violence, 68, 283, 285–87, 290; among Quakers, 111n, 167. *See also* Abolitionists: African American women; Benevolent societies: African American women

Radical abolitionism, 2, 26–28, 54, 93–94, 236, 272, 278. *See also* Garrisonian abolitionists

Ray, Charles B., 129n

Ray, Henrietta Green Regulus, 129, 129n

Rayner, Mrs., 61n

Reading Room Society (Philadelphia), 102

Reason, Patrick Henry, 212, 218, fig. 15

Reform, 3, 16n, 63, 96, 106, 124–25; African American women and, 121–22, 127, 129, 132–34, 137, 140; white women and, 130n, 131–32

Reformed Presbyterian Church, 28

Regulus, Laurent (Lawrence), 129n

Reid, Marion Kirkland, 304n

Religious conversion, 244–45

Religious Intelligencer (New Haven), 201

Religious revivals, 33, 144

Remarks on the Slave Trade, 203–4, fig. 1

Remond, Charles, 313

Remond, Sarah Parker, 156–57

Republican Motherhood, 4, 39

Requited Labor Convention (1838), 279

"Resist not Evil" (A. Grimké), 284

Results of Abolitionism!, 220, 224, fig. 21

Reynolds, F., 124

Rhode Island, organizations in: Kent County, 182–84n, 187–88, 190; Providence, 182, 183n, 187, 187n, 190n

Richardson, Marilyn, 156

Richardson, Rev. J. D., 124

Riley, Elizabeth, 122

Rising Daughters of Abyssinia (New York), 40, 125, 126n, 136

Roach, Isaac, 289–90

Robinson, Marius, 150–52, 151n

Rochester (N.Y.) Female Anti-Slavery Society, 26–28

Rochester (N.Y.) Female Moral Reform Society, 27

Rochester (N.Y.) Ladies' Anti-Slavery Society, 28–30

Rose, Ernestine, 86, 223, 295

Rush, Christopher, 126

Russell, Sarah Shaw, 269, 273n

Russwurm, John, 132

Rynders, Capt. Isaiah, 294

Saint Matthew's (Episcopal) Free Church (New York), 128n

Saint-Simonian movement, 314n

Saint Thomas's African Episcopal Church (Philadelphia), 70, 102n, 110n

Salem, Philis, 58n

Salem (Mass.) Female Anti-Slavery Society, 61

Samaritan Asylum for Indigent Colored Children (Boston), 47, 57, 63, 134, 137, 262

Sargent, Catherine, 62

Sargent, Henrietta, 51, 62, 64, 253n

Sargent, Mary E., 273n

Sargent family, women of, 50, 257

Scarlett, Adeline Saunders, 58n

Scarlett, John E., 130n

Scarlett, Margaret, 129, 130n, 133

Sclaven-Handel, 203–5, fig. 2

Scoble, John, 306

Scott, Orange, 35n

Scott, Patricia Bell, 157–58

Sea Islands, 94

Seaman's Aid Society (Boston), 59

Sears, Susan, 61n

Second African Presbyterian Church (Philadelphia), 102n

Second Great Awakening, 144

Second Women's Rights Convention (Rochester), 28

Separate spheres, 4, 6, 19, 25, 159, 185, 194; woman's sphere, 27, 40, 44, 53, 108–10, 171, 173, 188, 191, 223, 225, 234, 236, 241, 247, 264. *See also* Public role of women; Public speaking by women

"Separation" (S. Forten), 115

Sewall, Louisa, 50–51, 262

Sewall, Samuel Edmund, 50–51, 262

Sewing circles, 9, 59, 63, 83, 254–55

Index

Index